Understanding Korean Law

Understanding Korean Law

First edition published by Seoul National University Press in 2024

Seoul National University Press
1 Gwanak-ro, Gwanak-gu, Seoul 08826, Republic of Korea
Tel: +82-2-880-5252
Fax: +82-2-889-0785
Homepage: http://www.snupress.com
Facebook: @snupress1947
Instagram: @snupress
E-mail: snubook@snu.ac.kr

ISBN 978-89-521-3241-3 (93360)

This book was written under the editing of the Seoul National University Asia-Pacific Law Institute, supported by the Seoul National University Law School Foundation.

Understanding Korean Law

Edited by SNU Asia-Pacific Law Institute

SNUPRESS
Seoul National University Press

Table of Contents

Preface

The burgeoning interest in Korea and Korean culture prompted a corresponding interest in Korean law and legal system. Growing number of law students as well as seasoned legal scholars and practitioners across diverse jurisdictions are seeking credible resources on Korean law and legal studies. However, this thirst for knowledge often encounters a scarcity of reliable English-language sources. While a handful of English books on Korean law do exist, they tend to focus narrowly on specific legal domains rather than offering a comprehensive overview. Thus, there exists a compelling need, both within Korea and beyond its borders, for an introductory text on Korean law presented in English.

Responding to this demand, the Seoul National University Asia-Pacific Law Institute and School of Law have collaborated to publish *Understanding Korean Law* — an introductory treatise written in English. Comprising 13 meticulously crafted chapters, this book provides a panoramic view of Korea's legal landscape, spanning from foundational principles enshrined in the constitution to contemporary challenges posed by AI, from the intricacies of criminal justice to the complexities of international jurisdictions and dispute resolutions.

In compiling this volume, we adhered to a set of guiding principles. Firstly, we aimed to strike a balance between depth and readability in each chapter. To achieve this, we adopted a less formal scholarly tone and minimized excessive footnoting, ensuring accessibility for readers of varying levels of expertise. Secondly, we recognized the importance of presenting a broad overview of each legal domain. Rather than delving into individual issues, we opted to provide a comprehensive bird's-eye view, acknowledging the inherent trade-off with depth. Thirdly, while maintaining this panoramic perspective, we actively addressed contemporary challenges within each area of law. By integrating analytical perspectives on pressing issues, we tried to furnish readers with insights into the dynamic landscape of Korean law and jurisprudence.

This book is not without its limitations. The selection of thirteen distinct areas of law, each corresponding to a separate chapter, is not exhaustive. Should there be further editions, buoyed by the support of our readers, we are committed to expanding the coverage to encompass additional legal domains. Additionally, a central challenge in this project has been navigating the delicate balance between providing a broad, accessible overview and delving into the intricacies of each legal topic. In future revisions, we aim to address this trade-off more effectively by actively incorporating feedback from our readers.

We owe a debt of gratitude to the dedicated authors whose scholarly contributions have shaped this volume. While all thirteen authors were faculty members of Seoul National University School of Law when we commenced this project in 2020, two of them have since transitioned – Prof. Kwang Hyun Suk, who wrote the chapter on private international law, honorably retired from the faculty, and Prof. Youngjoon Kwon, who wrote the chapter on contract law, was appointed as a Justice of the Supreme Court of Korea. The academic rigor and expertise of all thirteen authors form the bedrock of this comprehensive exploration.

We extend our appreciation to the former and current deans of Seoul National University School of Law, Prof. Ki Jeong Han and Prof. JongBo Kim, whose support has been instrumental in realizing this ambitious project. Prof. Kyung-Hoon Chun and Prof. Jong-ik Chon, the former and current associate deans for academic affairs, played crucial roles from the planning through the editing process. We also acknowledge the invaluable contributions of the staff members of the Seoul National University Asia-Pacific Law Institute and School of Law, including Jinhyung Lee and Yejin Kim, who adeptly managed the collection and editing of manuscripts. Finally, we deeply appreciate the professional efforts of the diligent team at Seoul National University Press in bringing this book to fruition.

As *Understanding Korean Law* takes its place among scholarly resources, we hope it will serve as a reliable source for legal scholars, practitioners, and students, fostering a deeper comprehension and research of Korean law and its evolving role in the global community.

March of 2024
Seoul National University Asia-Pacific Law Institute
Director Seongwook Heo

Chapter 1

Constitutional Law and Adjudication*

Woo-Young Rhee**

1. Introduction: Constitutional Development in Korea, 1948-Present

Korea had a long history of monarchical dynasties, whose governments and legal systems reflected Korea's unique language and culture, until the Japanese colonial rule of Korea from 1910 to 1945. After World War II, Korea regained independence but was soon divided into the political entities of South Korea and North Korea. After the US military government in Korea (USAMGIK) administered governance in the southern part of Korea from 1945 to 1948, a general election was held in May 1948 in the southern part of the peninsula to form the first National Assembly of the Republic of Korea. In July 1948, the National Assembly promulgated the nation's initial constitution, i.e., the Constitution of the First Republic of Korea, and elected Syngman Rhee as the nation's president. The Republic of Korea (also referred to as Korea or South Korea) was formally established in August 1948. Then Korea soon suffered Korean War (1950-1953). The constitutional law of the Republic of Korea has undergone substantial changes since 1948.

* This chapter is based on the author's contribution of the book chapter to the online publication of Oxford Handbook of Constitutional Law in Asia (David S. Law, Holning Lau and Alex Schwartz (eds.), published by Oxford University Press in December 2023).

** Professor, Seoul National University School of Law.

As of 2023, Korea has revised its constitution nine times, most recently in 1987, when it adopted the Constitution of the Sixth Republic of Korea, which came into effect in February 1988. Further revision continues to be a topic of active discussion. The Constitutional Court of Korea (KCC), introduced by the 1987 constitutional revision, has brought crucial changes to Korea's constitutional law, in both theory and practice, through its jurisprudence. Over the years, the Korean constitutional system has become more democratic and protective of fundamental rights. The system has also weathered major challenges such as the impeachment of two presidents, Roh Moo-hyun in 2004 (overruled by the KCC) and Park Geun-hye in 2016-2017 (sustained by the KCC). This chapter on Korean constitutional law contains three parts. First, it provides an overview of constitutional developments from the adoption of the current constitution to the present day. Second, it examines the KCC's major decisions. Third, the chapter explores some of the challenges and ongoing debates concerning Korea's constitutional law and system.

(1) Historical Account of Constitutional Law in Korea, 1948-Present

Korea's current constitution was adopted in 1987 through a constitutional revision process in the National Assembly that was endorsed in a national referendum; it came into force in 1988.[1] It embodies critical reforms pertaining to democracy, the protection of fundamental rights, and constitutional adjudication. Prior to these reforms, authoritarianism with wide powers exercised by the president defined several aspects of Korea's constitutional law and system. Governmental powers were heavily concentrated in the presidency, which often usurped powers from the National Assembly in areas like lawmaking and oversight. During this period, particularly under Presidents Park Chung-hee (1963-1979) and Chun Doo-hwan (1980-1988)—both of whom came to power through military coups d'état—, the protections of fundamental rights were lacking in law and its implementation.[2]

1 Korea's current constitution is interchangeably referred to as the '1987 Constitution' based on the year it was revised and the '1988 Constitution' based on the year it went into effect.

2 The constitutional revision did not result in immediate improvement in the

Under authoritarian rule, a mixture of social and political dynamics fomented popular demands for political and legal reform. Korea experienced government-led rapid economic growth and advancements in technology and information science. This growth produced a highly educated citizenry that became increasingly critical of government policies and laws and the country's lack of democratic institutions. As Korea assumed an increasingly larger role in the global community, its citizens became exposed to international standards of human rights and justice that were higher than those at home. The vibrancy of the private sector contrasted starkly with the rigid authoritarianism of the government. Citizen discontent led to demands for increased democratization, the rule of law, and justice. These calls for change culminated in the June 1987 citizen movement, which ultimately produced the constitutional revision of 1987.

That revision made changes in four main areas: (1) democratization, (2) normalization of the relationship between the president and the legislature, (3) protection of fundamental rights, and (4) constitutional adjudication. First, with respect to democratization, the 1987 constitutional revision reintroduced direct election of the president (Constitution Article 67(1))[3] and limited the presidency to a single five-year term (Constitution Articles 70 and 128(2)). The constitutional revision also increased citizen participation in other areas of governance. For example, it incorporated public hearings and legislative consent into the government appointment processes (Constitution Article 86(1))[4] and moved governance closer to local constituencies by restoring the autonomy and lawmaking powers of local governments and assemblies (Constitution Articles 117 and 118) and enabling a voter

protection of fundamental rights, which has improved incrementally in subsequent years through revisions of the relevant statutes and the decisions of the judicial courts and the KCC, which in turn have brought about changes in practice. Korea's civil society and journalism have contributed much to this process through, for example, legislative campaign and petitions, proactively seeking decisions from judicial courts and the KCC, and vigilant monitoring of government activities.

3 Korea had previously provided for direct presidential elections, but it underwent a 15-year period of indirect presidential elections. Prior to the 1987 constitutional revision, the "indirect electoral college process was generally regarded as no more than a rubber-stamp" for the presidential choice made by the incumbent power groups. James M. West and Edward J. Baker, *The 1987 Constitutional Reforms in South Korea: Electoral Processes and Judicial Independence*, 1 HARVARD HUMAN RIGHTS YEARBOOK 135 (1988).

4 See also National Assembly Act (Act No. 19538, revised July 11, 2023 effective July 11, 2023), Articles 64, 65, and 65-2.

initiative system for local ordinances and citizen-led recall mechanisms for local public officials (Constitution Articles 117 and 118).[5] Overall, the 1987 constitutional revision fostered a culture of public participation in government decision-making and increased transparency in government administration. This same spirit also formed the backdrop to Korea's 2007 adoption of the jury system in criminal proceedings, which began to be implemented in 2008, in terms of citizen participation and transparency in judicial decision-making.

The 1987 constitutional revision's second set of reforms reset the balance of power between the executive and legislative branches of government. The current constitution clearly grants the National Assembly the authority to enact statutes while allowing the government[6] to submit legislative bills and the president to veto laws passed by the National Assembly plenary session in the process of enacting the statute (Constitution Articles 40 and 53(4)). Whereas government bills had previously accounted for the considerable bulk of Korean legislation in both volume and substance, since 1988 the National Assembly has gradually assumed the essential role in enacting statutes. The current constitution forbids the president from dissolving the National Assembly and makes it more difficult for the president to declare a state of emergency or to exercise emergency powers (Constitution Articles 76 and 77). It also subjects the executive branch to monitoring and annual auditing by the National Assembly (Constitution Article 61).

The third transformation introduced by the 1987 constitutional revision involved the protection of fundamental rights. The revision expanded the list of rights explicitly protected in the constitutional text. For example, a guaranteed minimum wage was introduced as one of a number of labor and social rights (Constitution Article 32(1)). The spirit of the 1987 constitutional revision has also inspired the legislative protection of rights, such as statutory reforms to further protect freedom of expression and political neutrality in election processes.

Fourth, the 1987 constitutional revision introduced constitutional

5 See also Local Autonomy Act (Act No. 19241, revised March 21, 2023 effective September 22, 2023), Articles 19 and 25.

6 In the language of Korea's current constitution, the "government" in this context refers to the executive branch of government.

adjudication by the KCC as an independent institution and the fourth branch of the government. Constitutional adjudication by the KCC has had widely resonating ramifications for the nation's separation of powers structure and the protection of fundamental rights, which have contributed to further democratization of the political process and overall governance and protection of human rights. This aspect is discussed in further detail in the paragraphs below.

(2) Constitutional Adjudication in Korea, 1988-Present

Fundamental constitutional rights in Korea have gained more substantial protection due to the fourth major reform embodied in the 1987 constitutional revision: the establishment of the KCC (Constitution Articles 111 to 113). The KCC has jurisdiction over determining the constitutionality of statutes upon request of the courts or in response to constitutional complaints filed by citizens (Constitution Article 111). The KCC also rules on constitutional challenges brought by citizens against government actions or inactions that infringe fundamental rights (Constitution Article 111).[7] In addition, the KCC has jurisdiction over the distribution of powers between government bodies, the dissolution of political parties at the request of the government, and impeachment petitions brought by the National Assembly against high-ranking officials, including the president (Constitution Article 111). Under Korea's previous constitutional regimes, various tribunals and committees had *de jure* power of constitutionality review but virtually no *de facto* power. For example, the Constitutional Council that existed during the Yushin constitutional period (1972-1980) was vested with the power to review the constitutionality of statutes but failed to exercise that power.[8] By contrast, the KCC has been proactive in shaping constitutional law through adjudication. In just over three decades from September 1988 to December 2022, the KCC decided 47,271 cases; it held government action to be unconstitutional in 1,062 instances, including 831 in which the KCC

7 The KCC has only limited jurisdiction to review the constitutionality of administrative actions. The Supreme Court of Korea serves as the court of last resort for most challenges to administrative actions. See KCC, *Thirty Years of the Constitutional Court of Korea* 150-151 (2018).

8 Tom Ginsburg, *Constitutional Courts in East Asia: Understanding Variation*, 3 JOURNAL OF COMPARATIVE LAW 80, 85 (2008).

invalidated a statute.[9]

The KCC has also played an important role in the pursuit of transitional justice. In 1996, it decided a case that permitted the prosecution of two former presidents whose power stemmed from the 1979 military coup.[10] The KCC has also adjudicated two impeachment cases against the then-incumbent presidents. Whereas the KCC decided against impeaching then-incumbent president Roh Moo-hyun in May 2004,[11] it upheld the impeachment of then-incumbent president Park Geun-hye in March 2017,[12] leading to an early presidential election in May of that year. President Park's impeachment was the result of several constitutional forces, including Korea's constitutional culture of participatory democracy.[13] The contribution of the KCC to increased protection of fundamental constitutional rights and to further democratization in Korea is analyzed in the next section, using core issues of constitutional law and major KCC decisions.

The essence of constitutionalism lies in that legislation on rights and obligations is bound by a nation's constitution and that the powers of the government, including legislative, executive and judicial powers, are governed by the provisions of the constitution. Since the establishment of popular sovereignty and constitutionalism, the Korean constitution has gradually become directly applicable in and through adjudication. As

9 KCC, General Statistics at https://english.ccourt.go.kr/site/eng/jurisdiction/caseLoadStatic.do.

10 Constitutional Court Decision 96Hun-Ga2, February 16, 1996 (*Constitutionality of the Special Act on the May 18 Democratization Movement, etc.*, 8-1 KCCR 51).

11 Constitutional Court Decision 2004Hun-Na1, May 14, 2004 (*Impeachment of President Roh Moo-hyun*, 16-1 KCCR 609).

12 Constitutional Court Decision 2016Hun-Na1, March 10, 2017 (*Impeachment of President Park Geun-hye*, 29-1 KCCR 1). Both impeachment cases in notes 12 and 13 are discussed in greater detail below in section II-A.

13 Korea's constitutional culture of participatory democracy fostered the public's demand for impeachment, as epitomized by protests known as the candlelight vigil in 2016 and 2017. That popular mobilization bolstered the National Assembly's petition for impeachment, which led to the KCC decision in favor of impeachment in 2017. In addition to having an enormous impact inside Korea, the KCC has taken a leadership role in fostering communication among constitutional jurists from different jurisdictions. For a discussion of the KCC's work and achievement on this front, see Akiko Ejima, *The Influence of International Law on Constitutional Law* and Maartje de Visser, *Regional Judicial Cooperation and Dialogue in Asia*, a paper presented and published at ICON-S Conference in July 2021 at www.icon-society.org/conference_paper/regional-judicial-cooperation-and-dialogue-in-asia/.

in many nations, under the current constitution of Korea, the legislative function of the nation is exercised primarily in the form of enactment of statutes and subsequent revisions thereof by the National Assembly as the designated legislative body, which is constituted through public elections held every four years, along with such lawmaking by the executive branch as executive orders and rulings by the judicial branch including the Supreme Court. On the other hand, under the separation of powers design of the current constitution, the KCC checks and controls the legislative function exercised primarily by the legislative branch as a means to protect the constitution itself and to keep both the process and substance of all legislation in compliance with the constitution as the founding document. Checks on the legislative process are effectively exercised by adjudication over disputes between governmental institutions, as in a case brought by, for example, an individual member of the National Assembly against the Speaker of the National Assembly. Checks on the substance of legislative outcomes in terms of its compliance with constitutional mandates are primarily conducted by way of the review over the constitutionality of a specific statute or its provision(s).

The system under the Korean constitution through which a separate and independent institution reviews the constitutionality of statutes enacted by the National Assembly is grounded primarily in the supremacy of the constitution and constitutional law, combined with the concept of the presumption of constitutionality of the statute and the theories of separation of powers and limited government. In particular, the growing influence of political parties has led to an ever-increasing need to check strategic legislation passed by the legislature to safeguard its constitutionality. The review of the constitutionality of a statute, which helps ensure that the nation's overall political process, including legislation, remains within constitutional bounds, has greater pertinence to both the normative and structural integrity of the nation's legal system as a whole. Indeed, in most modern constitutional democracies, adjudication of constitutionality by an appropriate institution is an essential element of the state, together with the guarantee of fundamental rights, the adoption of representative democracy, the establishment of the constitution, and the implementation of the rule of law, which consists of the separation of powers, the superiority of statutes enacted by the legislature over administrative rulemaking, administration by and under the law, an independent judiciary, and the provision of legal remedies for any governmental infringement of the rights of citizens.

As a part of a complex and multifaceted system that is intended to operate in an integrated, interrelated, and coordinated fashion, constitutional adjudication is ultimately designed to ensure that a wide range of governmental functions are implemented in compliance with the nation's constitution. Specifically, constitutional adjudication limits the powers of government and ensures the constitutionality of legislative acts by the National Assembly, the administrative function of the executive branch, and the judgments rendered by the judicial branch, all while confirming the allocation of powers between national and local governments and the different branches of the government. In doing so, constitutional adjudication both includes direct review of constitutionality and serves adjudicative, political and legislative functions.

Here, issues regarding the legislative nature or function of constitutional adjudication become pertinent, irrespective of the specific form of such adjudication, as long as the constitutionality of a statute is reviewed through that process. Pursuant to the premise of Korea's representative democracy, when a statute or a provision thereof is in violation of the constitution, the National Assembly is to assume the legislative function by repealing or revising that statute or provision. Under the system of constitutionality review of statutes adopted in Korea, constitutional adjudication may be triggered to invalidate a statute or to halt the application thereof, upon the KCC's holding that a statute or its provision(s) violate the nation's highest law. This function of the KCC is equivalent, on the normative plane, to the enactment, revision, and repealing of a statute or a part thereof, which are more conventionally conducted by the National Assembly. Thus, the adjudication by the KCC of the constitutionality of a statute may be perceived as normatively equivalent to legislation by the National Assembly.

Although the KCC's powers to review constitutionality under the constitution of Korea and the Constitutional Court Act are primarily an adjudicative means to protect against the enactment of an unconstitutional statute by the National Assembly and its enforcement by the executive branch, the legislative function assumed by the KCC's adjudication of the constitutionality of a statute has significant additional constitutional ramifications. In a nation governed by the principle of popular sovereignty, the legislative function of the people is assumed by a legislative body that is based on firm democratic legitimacy; thus, any other governmental branch or constitutional institution that exercises normatively equivalent legislative functions should also enjoy democratic legitimacy on a par with that of the legislature.

As a result, the normatively legislative function assumed by the KCC in assessing the constitutionality of a statute demands that the KCC and its decisions enjoy both democratic and constitutional legitimacy. The core issue concerning the democratic legitimacy of the constitutionality review of statutes lies in whether the justices of the KCC who are not elected as representatives by the sovereign populace may justifiably decide the effect of a statute enacted by the National Assembly which is constituted through democratic elections and whose allegiance is deemed to be to the nation rather than to specific constituencies, in light of the principles of democracy and separation of powers. It should be noted that a legislature consisting of democratically elected representatives could still enact a law deemed to be in violation of the constitution. In such a case, should the constitutionality of such a law be decided with binding force by an institution that is independent of the legislative body, this will serve the purpose of checks and balances under the principle of the separation of powers. This is the core legitimizing factor, particularly from the perspective of protection of minorities, of the KCC reviewing the constitutionality of a statute enacted by the National Assembly.

The democratic legitimacy of the constitutionality review of a statute by an independent government institution through adjudication that essentially follows judicial decision-making mechanisms and procedures is based on the following grounds: (a) the principle of substantive democracy that guarantees the liberty and rights of sovereign constituents; (b) the greater norm that majority rule does not suffice to determine in a justifiable fashion on any and all occasions the liberty and rights of the sovereign constituents, including particularly those of minorities; (c) the demand from constitutionalism that the nation's constitutional law be implemented with binding force as it provides for and regulates the liberty and rights of the sovereign constituents in its role as the supreme law; (d) the demand of popular sovereignty that the national government's legislative power should also be subjected to the constitution that was ordained and established by the sovereign constituents; (e) the theory of limited power, mandating that acts of the nation may be endowed with authority and legitimacy only when any and all acts of the nation are restricted within the limits of the constitution; (f) the call from natural justice that no national institution may be justifiably permitted to check, control, or correct its own wrong; (g) the doctrine of separation of powers; and (h) the view that any decision regarding the conformity of an act to the constitution should be conducted by an independent and essentially judicial institution with the requisite expertise and due consideration of precedents.

1) The Organization of the Korean Constitutional Court

The KCC has nine justices, including the president of the KCC (Constitution Article 111(2); Constitutional Court Act Articles 3 and 12(1)).[14] All the KCC justices are appointed by or receive their commissions from the president of Korea (Constitution Article 111(2); Constitutional Court Act Article 6(1)). Of the nine justices, three are directly nominated and appointed by the president of Korea, three are elected by the National Assembly and then appointed by the president of Korea, and the last three are designated by the Chief Justice of the Supreme Court and then appointed by the president of Korea (Constitution Articles 111(2) and 111(3); Constitutional Court Act Article 6(1)).[15] The president of the KCC is appointed from among nine justices by the president of Korea, subject to the consent of the National Assembly after an appointment

14 In addition, the KCC has research officers and assistant research officers who conduct research on cases under the supervision of the KCC justices (Constitutional Court Act Articles 19 and 19-2). Some of these individuals are recruited by way of secondment, typically for one or two years, from the judicial courts and the prosecutors' office (Constitutional Court Act Articles 19(4) and 19(9)), while some are career officers who serve in these research capacities for a renewable 10-year term with an age limit of 60 (Constitutional Court Act Article 19(7)). Further, the Constitutional Research Institute was established in January 2011 as part of the KCC to support constitutional adjudication through research projects in areas relevant to constitutional adjudication on a long-term basis (Constitutional Court Act Article 19-4). The KCC is a member of the Venice Commission, an international organization of constitutional courts in various nations, and has actively participated in international or transnational activities, particularly in Asia. The KCC co-hosted the 5th Asian Conference of Constitutional Justices in Seoul in October 2007.

15 Certain qualifications must be met for an individual to be appointed a justice of the KCC. An appointee must be licensed to practice law, be at least 40 years old, and have served for 15 or more years in any of the following positions or offices: (a) judge, prosecutor, or attorney-at-law; (b) a position or office engaged in legal affairs on behalf of a governmental agency, national or public enterprise, government-supported institution, or other corporation; or (c) a position or office of an assistant professor of law or higher at an accredited university or college (Constitution Article 111(2); Constitutional Court Act Article 5(1)).

hearing (Constitution Article 111(4); Constitutional Court Act Articles 6(2) and 12(2)).

Justices serve renewable six-year terms of office (Constitution Article 112(1); Constitutional Court Act Article 7(1)), during which they may not be involuntarily removed other than for the following reasons enumerated in the Constitution and the Constitutional Court Act: impeachment or criminal conviction with a sentence of imprisonment without labor or a more severe sentence (Constitution Article 112(3); Constitutional Court Act Article 8). Age limits (70 for the president of the KCC and 65 for the other justices) also apply (Constitutional Court Act Article 7(2)). Justices are prohibited from having a political party membership or participating in political activities (Constitution Article 112(2); Constitutional Court Act Article 9), for political neutrality.

2) The Jurisdictions of the Korean Constitutional Court

The KCC is vested under the Constitution and the Constitutional Court Act with jurisdiction over the following matters: constitutionality review of a statute or one or more of its provisions, constitutional complaints, competence disputes between government institutions or agencies, impeachment, and the dissolution of a political party (Constitution Article 111(1); Constitutional Court Act Article 2).

❶ Review of the Constitutionality of a Statute

The KCC has jurisdiction over reviews of the constitutionality of a statute (Constitution Article 111(1)(i); Constitutional Court Act Article 2(i)). From the establishment of the KCC in September 1988 through December 2022, judicial courts filed 1,089 cases with the KCC to request its constitutionality review over the relevant statutes, out of 47,271 cases filed with the KCC over that period.[16] When the issue of whether a statute or a specific statutory provision as the applicable law in a case pending in a judicial court is unconstitutional is material to the holding of that case, the original court, either by request of any of the parties or *sua sponte*, may request a review by the KCC of the constitutionality of the relevant statute or statutory provision (Constitutional Court Act Article 41). An individual party's motion

16 Refer to the case statistics of the KCC at https://english.ccourt.go.kr/site/eng/jurisdiction/caseLoadStatic.do.

for a judicial court to request a constitutionality review by the KCC should specify, in addition to the identities of the parties and the case number, the statute or provision thereof that the moving party or parties interpret to be unconstitutional, the grounds for such interpretation, and any other necessary materials as may be requested (Constitutional Court Act Articles 41(2) and 43). A judicial court's decision on a party's motion to request a KCC review of constitutionality is final and not subject to appeal (Constitutional Court Act Article 41(4)).

Any judicial court at any level may request a constitutionality review by the KCC; however, when a judicial court other than the Supreme Court makes such a request, it should go through the Supreme Court of Korea (Constitutional Court Act Article 41(5)). When a judicial court requests the KCC to review the constitutionality of a statute, the proceedings of the original case at that judicial court are suspended or stayed until the KCC rules on the constitutionality of the statute (Constitutional Court Act Article 42(1)). However, should the judicial court deem a matter to be urgent, all proceedings except for rendering the final decision may continue (proviso of the Constitutional Court Act Article 42(1)). The parties to the original case at the judicial court and the Minister of Justice may submit to the KCC an *amicus curiae* brief on the issue of whether the statute or the provision thereof is in fact unconstitutional (Constitutional Court Act Article 44).

The KCC may dismiss a request for constitutionality review on procedural grounds; otherwise, it will adjudicate on the merits and review the constitutionality of the statute or provision(s) at issue. The KCC will decide either that the statute or its provision(s) are unconstitutional or that the presumption of constitutionality remains intact. The KCC is limited to reviewing and deciding on the constitutionality of the challenged provision(s) (Constitutional Court Act Article 45). However, in exceptional cases, even when the constitutionality of only a specific provision or provisions is challenged, if the KCC determines that a statute is unenforceable in its entirety due to the unconstitutionality of such provision(s), it may hold the entire statute to be unconstitutional (proviso of the Constitutional Court Act Article 45).

Any statute or provisions thereof held to be unconstitutional by the KCC shall lose effect as of the day the decision is rendered (Constitutional Court Act Article 47(2)). Should the statute or provisions thereof concern criminal penalties, however, the loss of effect is retroactive (proviso of the Constitutional Court Act Article 47(2)); in this case, the affected parties may file for a retrial of their criminal convictions (Constitutional Court Act Article 47(3)). A decision that a statute or specific provisions thereof are unconstitutional shall bind all judicial courts, other national institutions and agencies, and local governments (Constitutional Court Act Article 47(1)).

Other than determining whether statutes or provisions thereof are unconstitutional or constitutional, although not expressly set forth in and by the language of the Constitutional Court Act, the KCC has also decided to the effect that statutes or provisions thereof are constitutional in part, unconstitutional in part, or nonconforming to the constitution. In the last case, the KCC has rendered such decisions of nonconformity of statute with the constitution often with the recommendation for the National Assembly for statutory revision, more often these days designating a specific date as the time limit for such revision.[17]

❷ Adjudication of Constitutional Complaints

The KCC has the jurisdiction to hear and decide on cases based on a constitutional complaint. Under the constitutional complaint system set forth in Korea's Constitution and Constitutional Court Act, anyone whose constitutionally guaranteed basic rights have been infringed by the government through either action or inaction may file a constitutional complaint with the KCC for redress. In the other four types of cases over which the KCC has jurisdiction—review of the constitutionality of statutes, impeachment, competence disputes, and political party dissolution—the claimant is a government institution, such as a judicial court, the National Assembly, or the executive branch or one of its agencies. However, in constitutional complaint cases, claimants are private parties, as this provision seeks to relieve such persons from the infringement or violation of their

17 This practice has been criticized by judicial courts which have taken the position that a decision of partial or conditional constitutionality or unconstitutionality or nonconformity with the constitution does not bind judicial courts as such a decision indicates no more than a suggested approach to statutory interpretation on the part of the KCC. Relatedly, for an analysis of nonconformity decisions by the KCC, particularly from the perspective of National Assembly legislation, see Woo-Young Rhee, *Decision of the Korean Constitutional Court of Nonconformity of Statute with the Constitution and the Subsequent National Assembly Legislative Process in Korea's Constitutional Democracy*, 20(1) JOURNAL OF KOREAN LAW 1-55 (2021).

basic rights. As such, constitutional complaints comprise the largest number and greatest proportion of all cases that the KCC has entertained since 1988.[18] Also for this reason, in constitutional complaint cases, representation by counsel licensed to practice law is required, which in turn mandates the applicable government- or KCC-appointed counsel system (Constitutional Court Act Articles 25(3) and 70(1)).

There are two different types of constitutional complaints, the causes for which also differ. The two types of constitutional complaints, with the causes or grounds thereof, are set forth in Articles 68(1) and 68(2) of the Constitutional Court Act, respectively. Under Article 68(1) of the Constitutional Court Act, any person who alleges that her or his basic right, as guaranteed by the constitution, has been infringed or violated by the exercise of or by a failure to exercise governmental power may file a constitutional complaint with the KCC, except against the judgment of a judicial court. However, before filing a constitutional complaint, an individual should exhaust any and all possible proceedings that may provide relief; otherwise, the constitutional complaint will be dismissed. Examples of grounds for filing a constitutional complaint under Article 68(1) are the National Assembly's failure to enact a statute that is mandated by the Constitution and the enactment of a statute that directly infringes upon people's basic rights. A constitutional complaint under Article 68(1) of the Constitutional Court Act should be filed within 90 days after the existence of the cause is known or within one year after the cause occurs, provided that, should a constitutional complaint be filed after other relief has unsuccessfully been sought, that complaint should be filed within 30 days after notification of the final decision in that proceeding (Constitutional Court Act Article 69(1)).

Article 68(2) of the Constitutional Court Act provides a proceeding for an individual who has asked a judicial court to request a KCC review of the constitutionality of a statute or provision(s) thereof in her or his own case pending at that judicial court but has had that request denied by the judicial court. At that point, such an individual may file a constitutional complaint directly with the KCC, asking the KCC to review the constitutionality of the statute or its provision(s). A constitutional complaint under Article 68(2) of

18 Refer to the case statistics of the KCC at https://english.ccourt.go.kr/site/eng/jurisdiction/caseLoadStatic.do.

the Constitutional Court Act should be filed within 30 days after the judicial court has denied the request to refer the issue to the KCC.

When a constitutional complaint is filed, a panel consisting of three KCC justices conducts a preliminary review or screening (Constitutional Court Act Article 72(1)). The panel determines whether a constitutional complaint should be heard by the full bench on the merits or should be dismissed for failure to meet any of the following statutory requisites set forth in the Constitutional Court Act: exhaustion of all available relief proceedings provided by other laws, avoiding challenges to the final decision of a judicial court, time limits applicable for filing, or appointment of counsel or a request for the appointment of government- or KCC-appointed counsel (Constitutional Court Act Article 72(3)). Should the panel fail to reach a unanimous decision to dismiss within 30 days, the case is transferred to the full bench (Constitutional Court Act Article 72(4)).

It should be noted that, although a constitutional complaint may not be filed against the final decision or judgment of a judicial court, relief may be sought by filing a constitutional complaint against the decision of a judicial court when that judicial court has applied a statute or statutory provisions that the KCC has previously held to be unconstitutional. Government agencies or public organizations that have an interest in the adjudication of a constitutional complaint and the Minister of Justice may submit *amicus curiae* briefs pertaining to such adjudication (Constitutional Court Act Article 74(1)).

After reviewing a constitutional complaint case on its merits, the KCC either rejects or upholds the complaint. A decision upholding a complaint shall bind all judicial courts and all other government institutions and agencies at both the national and local government levels (Constitutional Court Act Article 75(1)). In the final decision upholding a constitutional complaint under Article 68(1) of the Constitutional Court Act, the KCC is to specify (a) the right infringed or violated and (b) the exercise of or failure to exercise governmental power that was the cause thereof (Constitutional Court Act Article 75(2)). In this case, the KCC may reverse the government action previously taken or hold the failure to exercise a particular government power to be unconstitutional (Constitutional Court Act Article 75(3)). In addition, should the KCC find that the cause of the infringement of rights was statutory, the KCC may hold the relevant statute(s) or statutory provision(s) to be unconstitutional (Constitutional Court Act Article 75(5)).

Should the KCC uphold a constitutional complaint of failure to exercise governmental power, the respondent is required to take action in accordance with the KCC's decision (Constitutional Court Act Article 75(4)).

If a KCC decision upholding a constitutional complaint under Article 68(2) of the Constitutional Court Act holds a statute or statutory provisions unconstitutional, such statute or statutory provisions shall lose legal effect from the day on which the decision is rendered. There is an exception: when a statute or statutory provision(s) setting forth criminal penalties are held to be unconstitutional, they shall lose legal effect retrospectively (Constitutional Court Act Articles 45, 47 and 75(6)). When a constitutional complaint under Article 68(2) of the Constitutional Court Act is upheld, parties previously convicted or with the final decision rendered under the relevant provisions may request a retrial (Constitutional Court Act Article 75(7)).

❸ Adjudication on Impeachment

The KCC has jurisdiction over impeachment proceedings against certain high-ranking public officials, as set forth in the Korean constitution and relevant statutes, should the National Assembly pass a resolution and file a request with the KCC for impeachment (Constitution Article 111(1)(ii); Constitutional Court Act Article 48). The National Assembly may pass a resolution to impeach certain public officials on the ground that they have violated the constitution or a statute in conducting their official duties or responsibilities. These public officials are the president, the prime minister, members of the State Council or ministers of the executive, KCC justices, judges and justices of the judiciary, commissioners of the National Election Commission, the chair and commissioners of the Board of Audit and Inspection, and other public officials as designated by relevant statutes (Constitution Article 65; Constitutional Court Act Article 48). The KCC has heard three impeachment cases in its history, as of December 2022. The first was against President Roh Moo-hyun in 2004; in this case, the KCC decided against impeaching him.[19] The second case involved President Park Geun-hye in 2016 through 2017; in this case the KCC did impeach her.[20] The third

19 Constitutional Court Decision 2004Hun-Na1, May 14, 2004 (*Impeachment of President Roh Moo-hyun*, 16-1 KCCR 609).

20 Constitutional Court Decision 2016Hun-Na1, March 10, 2017 (*Impeachment of President Park Geun-hye*, 29-1 KCCR 1).

impeachment case involved a high-ranking judge of the judiciary in 2021, in which case the KCC dismissed the case as the judge had retired prior to the National Assembly impeachment resolution.[21] In pursuance of the impeachment decision by the KCC against President Park, in March 2017, President Park stepped down, and a presidential election was held in May 2017, in which President Moon Jae-in (2017-2022) was elected.

After a National Assembly resolution to impeach, the chair of National Assembly Legislation and Judiciary Committee files *ex officio* a request for an impeachment proceeding with the KCC by submitting an authentic copy of the written resolution of the National Assembly (Constitutional Court Act Article 49). The public official against whom the impeachment proceeding request is filed with the KCC is suspended from carrying out any official acts until the KCC renders a decision thereupon (Constitutional Court Act Article 50). Should the KCC find that a valid ground for impeachment exists, the KCC renders a decision to remove the public official from office; such official may not hold any public office for five years after the date of the impeachment decision (Constitutional Court Act Articles 53(1) and 54(2)). The decision to impeach a public official by the KCC does not affect the civil or criminal liability of that official (Constitutional Court Act Article 54(1)).

❹ Adjudication on Dissolution of a Political Party

The KCC has the jurisdiction to dissolve a political party upon request by the government (Constitution Article 8(4); Constitutional Court Act Articles 2(iii) and 55). Should the objectives or activities of a political party be contrary to the basic order of democracy, the executive branch of the government may file a request with the KCC to dissolve that party (Constitution Article 8(4); Constitutional Court Act Articles 2(iii) and 55), after a mandatory deliberation of the State Council on the matter (Constitution Article 89; Constitutional Court Act Article 55). When a request for adjudication of the dissolution of a political party is filed with the KCC, the KCC notifies the National Assembly and the National Election Commission of that fact and serves a copy of the request on the political party that is the respondent (Constitutional Court Act Article 58(1)).

If the KCC decides a political party to be dissolved, that party shall be

21 Constitutional Court Decision 2021Hun-Na1, October 28, 2021 (*Impeachment of a Judge*, 33-2 KCCR 321).

dissolved (Constitutional Court Act Article 59).[22] There is no appeal available. The KCC shall serve an authentic copy of the written decision ordering dissolution on the executive branch of the government and a duplicate on the National Assembly and the National Election Commission (Constitutional Court Act Article 58(2)). A decision of the KCC ordering the dissolution of a political party is executed by the National Election Commission, pursuant to the Political Party Act (Constitutional Court Act Article 60). The National Election Commission is to cancel registration of the political party and announce such step to the public. The assets of a dissolved political party revert to the national treasury. It is prohibited to form a substitute party or a party that has the same or similar principles as those of the dissolved political party. No political party is permitted to use the name of the dissolved political party. In 2014, the KCC dissolved the Unified Progressive Party (UPP) and removed its legislators from the National Assembly, which is the only political party dissolution decision rendered by the KCC as of December 2022.[23]

❺ Adjudication on Competence Dispute between Governmental Institutions or Agencies

The KCC has jurisdiction over competence disputes between governmental institutions and agencies at both the national and local levels (Constitution Article 111(1)(iv); Constitutional Court Act Articles 2(iv) and 61(1)). Of the 47,271 cases filed with the KCC as of December 2022, 122 (approximately 0.26%) have involved competence disputes.[24] A governmental institution or agency may file a request for adjudication on competence with the KCC if the respondent's action or inaction, of which the existence or scope of competence is in dispute or controversy, allegedly infringes or is clearly in danger of infringing on the rights or authorities conferred to the claimant by the constitution or relevant statute (Constitutional Court Act Article 61(2)).

22 There has been one such case in the history of Korean constitutional adjudication in which a political party was dissolved by KCC decision. Constitutional Court Decision 2013Hun-Da1, December 19, 2014 (*Dissolution of Political Party*, 26-2 KCCR 1).

23 Constitutional Court Decision 2013Hun-Da1, December 19, 2014 (*Dissolution of Political Party*, 26-2 KCCR 1). See also *infra* notes 39, 40 and 41 and accompanying text.

24 Refer to the case statistics of the KCC at https://english.ccourt.go.kr/site/eng/jurisdiction/caseLoadStatic.do.

A request for adjudication of a competence dispute should be filed with the KCC within 60 days after the existence of the cause becomes known to the claimant or within 180 days after the cause occurs (Constitutional Court Act Article 63(1)).

The decision of the KCC in adjudication on competence disputes concerns the existence or scope of the competence or authority of the parties, which are government institutions or agencies at either the national or local levels (Constitutional Court Act Article 66(1)). The KCC may nullify an action of the respondent or confirm the invalidity of the respondent action that led to the competence dispute (Constitutional Court Act Article 66(2)). When the KCC upholds a claimant's request in a competence dispute case on the ground of inaction of or omission by the respondent, the respondent shall take a disposition in pursuance of the KCC decision (Constitutional Court Act Article 66(2)). The decision of the KCC in a competence dispute adjudication shall bind all state institutions and agencies and local governments (Constitutional Court Act Article 67(1)). However, a KCC decision in a competence dispute case that nullifies an action of a state institution or agency or local government shall not alter the effect that has already been given to a person pursuant to such action (Constitutional Court Act Article 67(2)).

2. Core Constitutional Law Issues in Korea and Major Decisions of the Korean Constitutional Court

The KCC is widely viewed as an active body that has generated a large amount of landmark precedents. While a full survey of the KCC precedents is beyond the scope of this chapter, this section highlights major developments in the different areas of KCC jurisprudence, from the constitutional law perspective.[25]

25 For a public survey covering a larger number of landmark KCC decisions, see *supra* note 7, *Thirty Years of the Constitutional Court of Korea.*

(1) Calibrating Power under the Separation of Powers: Review of Constitutionality, Transitional Justice, and Impeachment

Since its establishment in 1988, the KCC has decided numerous cases that have calibrated the powers of respective branches of government, with significant ramifications for how the separation of powers is structured in Korea and for the protection of fundamental rights. Helping to define the KCC's relationship to the political branches of government, its very first ruling struck down a law that granted immunity to the government against provisional attachment of property in civil cases.[26] The KCC held that it was unconstitutional to give the government special treatment in this regard. In doing so, the KCC demonstrated that it would not shrink from striking down unconstitutional legislation. In fact, the KCC has sometimes been quite bold in expansively interpreting its powers to strike down government actions. For example, President Roh Moo-hyun had pledged during the 2003 election campaign to move the administrative functions of the capital from Seoul to the southern Chungcheong region, and the National Assembly subsequently passed a statute to that effect. In 2004, the KCC invalidated that statute on the ground that it violated Korea's unwritten customary constitution.[27] The notion that the KCC can identify and enforce customary constitutional provisions remains controversial in Korean constitutional jurisprudence. According to the KCC, relocation of the capital involves overriding the customary constitution and thus requires approval through a national referendum, as it would if the written constitution were being revised.

The KCC has not limited itself to blocking unconstitutional acts by the other branches. Over the years, the KCC has ruled that not only governmental action but also governmental inaction can violate the constitution. In 1994, the KCC held for the first time that a legislative omission was unconstitutional, ruling that the National Assembly violated its constitutional duties by failing to enact a statute to compensate parties for private railway properties that had been expropriated by the US military

26 Constitutional Court Decision 88Hun-Ga7, January 25, 1989 (*Prohibition on Injunction against Government in Litigation Claiming Property Right*, 1 KCCR 1).

27 Constitutional Court Decision 2004Hun-Ma554, October 21, 2004 (*Special Act for Relocation of the Capital City*, 16-2 KCCR 1).

government in Korea in 1946.[28] Administrative omissions can also violate the constitution, according to KCC rulings. In 2011, the KCC ruled that the failure of the Minister of Foreign Affairs to take steps to resolve conflicts between Korea and Japan concerning claims for compensation of World War II-era Korean "comfort women" was unconstitutional.[29]

The KCC's jurisdiction and constitutional responsibility for hearing impeachment petitions brought by the National Assembly place the KCC squarely in the middle of inter-branch conflict between the legislative and executive or judicial branches. The first impeachment case heard by the KCC was against President Roh Moo-hyun in 2004; it ultimately decided against impeachment.[30] Although the KCC found *inter alia* that President Roh had indeed breached his obligation to maintain political neutrality in public elections, it concluded that such legal violation was not sufficiently grave to justify impeachment in light of the important obligations and duties of the president under Korea's constitution. By contrast, the KCC concluded in 2017 that President Park Geun-hye's violations of presidential obligations, including her failure to respect and implement the constitutional order and rule of law, were sufficiently grave to warrant her impeachment.[31]

The KCC has also facilitated transitional justice by tackling the legacy of the authoritarian Yushin period (1972-1980). Exercising the power to review the constitutionality of government actions from decades earlier, the KCC ruled that presidential emergency decrees from the 1970s violated constitutionally protected fundamental rights because the decrees were not proportionate means for achieving a legitimate government purpose.[32] In condemning the emergency orders, the KCC contributed to the nation's process of healing from authoritarian rule. The KCC also upheld a special

28 Constitutional Court Decision 89Hun-Ma2, December 29, 1994 (*Failure of Government to Enact Law for Compensation for the Harm Incurred during Japanese Colonial Rule*, 6-2 KCCR 395).

29 Constitutional Court Decision 2006Hun-Ma788, August 30, 2011 (*Failure of Government to Take Administrative Measures for Compensation from Government of Japan*, 23-2 KCCR 366).

30 Constitutional Court Decision, *Impeachment of President Roh Moo-hyun*, see *supra* notes 11 and 19.

31 Constitutional Court Decision, *Impeachment of President Park Geun-hye*, see *supra* notes 12 and 20.

32 Constitutional Court Decision 2010Hun-Ba132, March 21, 2013 (*President's Emergency Measures Criminally Punishing Criticism of the Constitution*, 25-1 KCCR 180).

National Assembly act that permitted the prosecution of two former presidents, Chun Doo-hwan and Roh Tae-woo, and others who had obtained political power through the 1979 military coup, even though the normal statutory limitations period had expired.[33] The KCC came within one vote of finding that the special legislation violated the constitutional ban on *ex post facto* laws.[34] Ultimately, Presidents Chun and Roh were found guilty then subsequently pardoned by President Kim Young-sam at the prompting of President-elect Kim Dae-jung on the grounds of seeking reconciliation and harmony for Korea's future.

(2) Supporting Deliberative Democracy and the System of Representation: Public Elections, Political Parties, and Free Expression

Another major area of KCC precedents concerns deliberative democracy, the political process, and the system of representation. The KCC has decided crucial cases addressing voting, elections, and political parties.[35] In a landmark case from 2000, the KCC struck down a statutory provision that required an excessive monetary deposit from candidates for the National Assembly and set strict limits on recovering those deposits.[36] The KCC held that the excessive nature of these conditions infringed on the right to hold public office, the right to equality, and voters' freedom of choice. The KCC also took issue with a statutory provision that allocated proportional representation seats in the National Assembly among political parties based on the vote share of each party in general elections for electoral district

33 Constitutional Court Decision 96Hun-Ga2, 96Hun-Ba7, 96Hun-Ba13 (consolidated), February 16, 1996 (*Constitutionality of the Special Act on the May 18 Democratization Movement, etc.*, 8-1 KCCR 51).

34 *Id.* In a separate case, the KCC also ruled that a statute confiscating property rewarded for collaboration with Japan during Japanese colonial rule was exceptional; it did not violate the constitution's ban on retroactive legislation because it could be justified. Constitutional Court Decision 2008Hun-Ba141, March 31, 2011 (*Confiscation of Property Awarded for Pro-Japanese Collaboration*, 23-1 KCCR 276).

35 For an analysis of the KCC decisions on public elections and political parties, see Woo-Young Rhee, *Judicial Review of the Public Election Law in the Republic of Korea*, 23(4) NEW ASIA 48-78 (2016).

36 Constitutional Court Decision 2000Hun-Ma91, July 19, 2001 (*'One Person Two Votes' in Public Elections for District and Proportional Representation*, 13-2 KCCR 77).

representatives. The KCC held that this system was unconstitutional insofar as it denied voters an opportunity to directly vote for their preferred political party in determining proportional representation, which might not be the same preference as in their electoral district elections.[37]

In addition to safeguarding fair and free elections, the KCC has promoted deliberative democracy by ruling that the rights of opposition political parties were violated when the Speaker of the National Assembly failed to provide them proper notice about a planned legislative session, thus undermining their participation in legislative deliberation.[38] Not all of the KCC's decisions pertaining to deliberative democracy, however, have come to the defense of opposition parties. Korea's constitution grants the KCC the power to dissolve a political party if the "purposes or activities of a political party are contrary to the fundamental democratic order" (Constitution Article 8(4)).[39] In 2014, the KCC exercised this power for the first and thus far only time.[40] It dissolved the Unified Progressive Party (UPP) and removed its legislators of both proportional and electoral district representatives from the National Assembly. The KCC reasoned that dissolution of a political party is justified if, first, the party poses a concrete danger of causing a substantial threat to the fundamental democratic order and, second, dissolution is a proportionate response to that threat. In concluding that dissolution of the UPP was warranted, the KCC considered, among other things, the fact that the UPP's leaders had plotted to commit treason and sought to bring the socialist governing approaches of North Korea to South Korea.[41]

The KCC has also protected freedom of expression as a foundational

37 *Id.* For another major voting rights case, see Constitutional Court Decision 2009Hun-Ma256, July 24, 2014 (*Restriction on the Voting Right and Right to Referendum of Overseas Electors*, 26-2 KCCR 173), which declared unconstitutional a statute restricting the voting rights of Korean nationals living overseas.

38 Constitutional Court Decision 96Hun-Ra2, July 16, 1997 (*Legislative Railroading against Members of Opposition Party*, 9-2 KCCR 154).

39 Constitution of the Republic of Korea, Article 8(4).

40 Constitutional Court Decision 2013Hun-Da1, December 19, 2014 (*Dissolution of Political Party*, 26-2 KCCR 1). See also *supra* notes 22 and 23 and accompanying text.

41 Some critics have charged that this decision might unduly restrict freedom of assembly and freedom to express dissenting political viewpoints. See Associated Press, "South Korea court orders breakup of 'pro-North' leftwing party" *The Guardian* (December 19, 2014) at https://perma.cc/7PMG-QSD9.

building block for deliberative democracy. It has struck down several statutory provisions that restricted freedom of speech,[42] along with statutory provisions that set strict limits on the time, place, and manner of exercising freedom of assembly.[43] In some cases, however, the KCC has rejected claims that freedom of expression had been violated. For example, in a series of cases, the KCC held that restrictions on certain public servants' ability to participate in labor unions did not excessively restrict their freedom of expression.[44]

(3) Protecting Personal Liberty: Self-Determination, Privacy, Right to Freedom, and Due Process in Criminal Procedure

The KCC has played a crucial role in protecting personal liberties in Korea. It has handed down major decisions on various aspects of personal liberty including self-determination, privacy, and physical freedom especially in criminal proceedings, as well as freedom of expression as indicated in the preceding paragraph. Korea previously had a statute requiring users of

42 For example, in Constitutional Court Decision 2007Hun-Ma1001, December 29, 2011 (*Prohibition on Election Campaign via the Internet*, 23-2 KCCR 739), the KCC struck down a statute that prohibited certain forms of political speech on the internet 180 days prior to public elections. In Constitutional Court Decision 2008Hun-Ba157, issued December 28, 2010 (*Act of Spreading False Information via the Internet*, 22-2 KCCR 684), the KCC declared unconstitutional a statute that punished spreading false information on the internet for the purpose of harming the public good because the notion of harming the public good was too vague. The KCC had previously declared unconstitutional a statute that granted the government broad power to order internet service providers to "refuse, suspend, or restrict" communications that it deemed subversive; Constitutional Court Decision 99Hun-Ma480, June 27, 2002 (*Ban on Subversive Communication on the Internet*, 14-1 KCCR 616). In Constitutional Court Decision 93Hun-Ga13, October 4, 1996 (*Prior Inspection of Motion Pictures*, 8-2 KCCR 212), the KCC held that it was unconstitutional to require all motion pictures to be inspected by the government's Public Performance Ethics Committee before they could be shown to the public.

43 Constitutional Court Decisions 2011Hun-Ga29, April 24, 2014 (*Ban on Nighttime Outdoor Assembly and Demonstration*, 26-1 KCCR 574); 2008Hun-Ga25, September 24, 2009 (*Ban on Nighttime Outdoor Assembly*, 21-2 KCCR 427); Constitutional Court Decision 2013Hun-Ba322, May 31, 2018 (*Ban on Outdoor Assembly within 100 Meters of National Assembly Building*, 30-1 KCCR 88).

44 Constitutional Court Decisions 2003Hun-Ba50, October 27, 2005 (*Prohibition of Labor Union Activity of Public Officials*, 17-2 KCCR 238); 2003Hun-Ba51, August 30, 2007 (*Prohibition of Labor Union Activity of Public Officials*, 19-2 KCCR 213); 90Hun-Ba27, April 28, 1992 (*Prohibition of Labor Union Activity of Public Officials*, 4 KCCR 255).

internet forums or message boards to verify their real identities online, thus foreclosing the possibility of anonymous participation. The KCC held in 2012 that, except for limited time periods in public election contexts, this law violated the individual right of self-determination regarding private information.[45] In 2021, the KCC held unconstitutional the part of the public election law requiring verification of real identities for those expressing themselves on online bulletin boards during the public election campaign period.[46] In another case, the KCC ruled that a statute allowing involuntary hospitalization of mentally ill patients lacked sufficient procedural safeguards and thus violated patients' rights to physical freedom.[47] The KCC has also ruled that the criminal punishment of adultery violated the rights to sexual self-determination, secrecy, and privacy.[48] In April 2019, the KCC reversed its earlier decisions to strike down Korea's criminal prohibition of abortion as violating women's right of self-determination.[49]

Criminal investigation and punishment can be legitimate reasons for restricting an individual's personal liberty, but human rights require that such restrictions be carefully determined. The KCC has developed a considerable body of precedents regarding when such restrictions are unconstitutional. It has deemed a variety of statutory provisions to be violations of criminal defendants' rights, concerning, e.g., the scope of arrest warrants,[50] restrictions on access to assistance of counsel[51] and prosecutorial

45 Constitutional Court Decision 2010Hun-Ma47, August 23, 2012 (*Real-Name Identity Verification System on the Internet*, 24-2 KCCR 590).

46 Constitutional Court Decision 2018Hun-Ma456, 2020Hun-Ma406, 2018Hun-Ga16 (consolidated), January 28, 2021 (*Real-Name Identity Verification for Online Expression during Public Election Campaign Period*, 33-1 KCCR 32).

47 Constitutional Court Decision 2014Hun-Ga9, September 29, 2016 (*Involuntary Hospitalization of Mentally Disabled Patient*, 28-2 KCCR 276).

48 Constitutional Court Decision 2009Hun-Ba17, February 26, 2015 (*Criminal Punishment of Adultery*, 27-1 KCCR 20). For another major KCC decision concerning privacy, see the 2001 case in which the KCC ruled that regulations concerning lavatories at police detention facilities violated individuals' right to privacy because they lacked sufficient covers to shield users from being viewed by others (Constitutional Court Decision 2000Hun-Ma546, July 19, 2001 (*Installation of Lavatories at Police Detention Facilities*, 13-2 KCCR 103)). Relatedly, see also Constitutional Court Decision 89Hun-Ma214, December 24, 1998 (*Restriction on Real Property by Designation of Green Belts*, 10-2 KCCR 927), in which the KCC protected the right of citizens to make decisions concerning private property.

49 Constitutional Court Decision 2017Hun-Ba127, April 11, 2019 (*Criminal Punishment of Abortion*, 31-1 KCCR 404).

50 Constitutional Court Decision 92Hun-Ga8, December 24, 1992 (*Restriction on*

evidence,[52] and authorization of an investigative agency to request location-tracing data from telecommunications companies.[53] The KCC has also ruled that the police violated the rights of crime suspects when the police granted journalists permission to take and release photographs of a handcuffed suspect under interrogation in a police station.[54] It held that granting such permission infringed criminal suspects' right to personality.

The KCC has in recent years been more protective of freedom of conscience. Reversing a decision from seven years earlier, the KCC held in 2018 that the Military Service Act was unconstitutional insofar as it did not offer conscientious objectors a form of service as an alternative to mandatory military service.[55] Without an alternative service option, conscientious objectors were subject to imprisonment for a year and a half and subsequently suffered disadvantages such as restrictions on public employment. The KCC ruled that, although the public interests of national security and fairness in the assignment of military duties were significantly important, the limitation on freedom of conscience was not a proportionate means for promoting those interests.

(4) Implementing Equal Protection and Supporting Diversity amid the Changing Demographics of a Global Community

The KCC has decided cases concerning various forms of discrimination

Acquittal notwithstanding Non-Guilty Judgment at Trial upon Prosecution's Felony Charge, 4 KCCR 853).

51 Constitutional Court Decision 2011Hun-Ma122, August 29, 2013 (*Assistance of Counsel*, 25-2 KCCR 494).

52 Constitutional Court Decision 94Hun-Ma60, November 27, 1997 (*Prosecution's Denial to Defense Counsel of Access to Criminal Investigation Record*, 9-2 KCCR 675).

53 Constitutional Court Decision 2012Hun-Ma191, June 28, 2018 (*Use of Location-Tracing Data by Investigative Agency*, 30-1 KCCR 564).

54 Constitutional Court Decision 2012Hun-Ma652, March 27, 2014 (*Taking and Releasing Photograph of Handcuffed Suspect during Police Interrogation at Police Station*, 26-1 KCCR 534).

55 Constitutional Court Decision 2011Hun-Ba379, June 28, 2018 (*Mandatory Military Service with No Available Alternative Service Option for Conscientious Objectors*, 30-1 KCCR 370). Compare this decision with a preceding KCC decision in which the KCC previously addressed the issue of conscientious objection to military service in Constitutional Court Decision 2008Hun-Ga22, August 30, 2011 (*Conscientious Objection to Mandatory Military Service based on Religious Belief*, 23-2 KCCR 174).

in Korean society. In addition to equality rights, these cases have often implicated other constitutional rights. The KCC has demonstrated that it will subject certain forms of discrimination to a proportionality analysis. For example, the KCC has applied proportionality analysis to gender discrimination.[56] In 1999, it struck down a statute that awarded discharged soldiers extra points in their examinations for civil service positions.[57] While acknowledging that the government has a valid interest in supporting veterans through social policies, it held that the point system's differential treatment was not proportionately related to that goal and thus violated the equality rights of both women and men who could not serve in the military due to disability. Importantly, the KCC found impermissible gender discrimination even though the statute indirectly discriminated against women. The point system had a disproportionate impact on women because women are not subject to mandatory military service and thus much less likely than men to have veteran status. The KCC also held that the point system impermissibly infringed on the fundamental right to hold public office. In another landmark gender discrimination case, the KCC invalidated a statute codifying the traditional head of household (hoju) system of family registration. Under this explicitly patriarchal system, every family was defined by law as having a male head of household, and this position was passed down, with very limited exceptions, to direct male descendants.[58] In declaring that this system did not conform with the constitution, the KCC introduced far-reaching changes to gender dynamics across Korean society.[59]

56 Article 11 of the Constitution of the Republic of Korea prohibits "discrimination in political, economic, social or cultural life on account of sex, religion or social status." In addition, the Constitution contains provisions that prohibit gender discrimination specifically in the contexts of employment (Article 32) and family life (Article 36).

57 Constitutional Court Decision 98Hun-Ma363, December 23, 1999 (*Addition of Extra Points for Discharged Soldiers in Civil Examinations for Public Service*, 11-2 KCCR 770).

58 Constitutional Court Decision 2001Hun-Ga9, February 3, 2005 (*Male House Head ('Hoju') System*, 17-1 KCCR 1).

59 For other major cases in which the KCC declared that family law regulations violated gender equality, see Constitutional Court Decision 95Hun-Ga6, July 16, 1997 (*Ban on Same-Surname-Same-Origin Marriage*, 9-2 KCCR 1), which held that the prohibition of marriage between women and men who share the same surname and patrilineal line violates constitutional protections of gender equality, dignity, and the pursuit of happiness; and Constitutional Court Decision 2003Hun-Ga5, December 22, 2005 (*Compulsory Use of One's Father's Surname and Origin of Surname*, 17-2 KCCR 544), which held that requiring children to use their birth-

Gender is not the only ground of discrimination that prompts KCC proportionality analysis. As noted above, the invalidated policy that favored discharged soldiers discriminated the bases of both disability and gender. Another more straightforward case of disability discrimination involved the government's support of the visually impaired. Several cases have addressed the constitutionality of a statute providing that only the visually impaired can be licensed to work as massage therapists.[60] In 2017, the KCC upheld this restriction against alleged violations of the right to an occupation and right to equality of those who are not visually impaired.[61] The KCC held the statute to be proportionately related to the goal of promoting the welfare of the visually impaired. Age is among the other grounds of discrimination that have prompted the KCC to apply proportionality analysis. In 2008, it carried out such an analysis and held that age restrictions on a particular civil service position violated the rights to equal protection, to pursue a vocation, and to hold public office.[62]

The KCC has not always applied proportionality analysis in discrimination cases. In some instances, it has instead deferred to the legislature by evaluating whether the impugned legislation was arbitrary.[63] For example, the KCC took a deferential approach in upholding an anti-corruption law against complaints that the statute discriminated against journalists and private school teachers by including them within the law's definition of "public officials."[64] The KCC has also applied this lenient test of arbitrariness in repeatedly rejecting claims that the criminalization of same-sex sexual

father's surname violates constitutional protections of dignity and gender equality.

60 Constitutional Court Decisions 2003Hun-Ma715, May 25, 2006 (*Monopoly of Vocation of Massage Therapists by Visually Disabled Persons*, 18-1 KCCR112); 2006Hun-Ma1098, issued October 30, 2008 (20-2 KCCR 1089); 2008Hun-Ma664, July 29, 2010 (22-2 KCCR 427); 2011Hun-Ga39, issued June 27, 2013 (25-1 KCCR 409); 2017Hun-Ga15, December 28, 2017 (29-2 KCCR 264).

61 Constitutional Court Decision 2017Hun-Ga15, December 28, 2017 (*Monopoly of Vocation of Massage Therapists by Visually Disabled Persons*, 29-2 KCCR 264).

62 Constitutional Court Decision 2007Hun-Ma1105, May 29, 2008 (*Age Limit in Civil Service Examination*, 20-1 KCCR 329).

63 The KCC has yet to clearly explain its criteria for determining when claims of discrimination trigger proportionality analysis; see Ilhyung Lee, *Korean Perception(s) of Equality and Equal Protection*, 31 BOSTON COLLEGE INTERNATIONAL & COMPARATIVE LAW REVIEW 53, 57 (2008).

64 Constitutional Court Decision 2015Hun-Ma236, July 28, 2016 (*Constitutionality of Anti-Corruption Law of the Prohibition on Improper Solicitation and Graft Act*, 28-2 KCCR 128).

intimacy between military personnel violates equality rights based on sexual orientation.[65] At the opposite extreme, the KCC has sometimes found unconstitutional discrimination without applying proportionality analysis. For example, it held that a labor law concerning the government's foreign trainee system was unconstitutional because there was no rational basis for its differential treatment of foreign trainees.[66]

3. The Road Ahead: Challenges to the Law and the System of Korea's Constitution

(1) Challenges to Reform Governmental Structures and Institutions

Korea's constitution establishes a presidential system in which the president is elected for a nonrenewable five-year term. There is no office of vice president, but the president nominates and appoints a prime minister with an appointment hearing and the consent of the National Assembly. Such current governmental structure was developed in the wake of the 1987 citizen democratization movement to prevent prolonged authoritarian rule and abuse of presidential powers of the kind previously long experienced in Korea. The nonrenewable presidential term has certainly contributed to peaceful regime changes every five years—if not sooner, as was the case following President Park Geun-hye's impeachment in 2017. The nonrenewable presidential term has also contributed to a more balanced relationship among the various branches of government, most noticeably in the relationship between the president and the National Assembly.

Despite the benefits of the current system, there has been considerable debate over two proposed alternatives. The first is a presidential system with a once-renewable four-year term in place of the current limit of a single nonrenewable term of five years. Proponents of this reform link the potential abuse of presidential powers primarily to the adequacy of checks

65 E.g., Constitutional Court Decision 2012Hun-Ba258, July 28, 2016 (*Military Criminal Act Prescribing Punishment by Imprisonment for "Other Indecent Conduct"*, 28-2 KCCR 1).

66 Constitutional Court Decision 2004Hun-Ma670, August 30, 2007 (*Labor Ministry Regulation Infringing Labor Rights of Foreign Trainees of Industrial Technology*, 19-2 KCCR 297).

on presidential power rather than the duration of the presidency. They argue that a president who cannot run for reelection has diminished incentives to listen to constituents and develop public policies to earn their support. This proposal also has the possible merit of coordinating the presidential term with the four-year term of the National Assembly. Former president Moon Jae-in (2017-2022) submitted during his presidency a constitutional revision bill incorporating this reform to the National Assembly in March 2018, but the bill failed to proceed in the legislature and was accordingly discarded.

The second alternative to the current system involves the adoption of a mixed presidential-parliamentary system, in which the prime minister is not nominated or appointed by the president but is instead either nominated or elected by the National Assembly. Under this proposal, the prime minister, and thus indirectly the National Assembly, would in turn have greater influence over the selection and removal of government ministers. Preference for this alternative is one reason why former president Moon's 2018 constitutional revision proposal failed to garner sufficient support in the National Assembly. There has been very little discussion of moving toward a full parliamentary system due to a lack of popular support. Proponents of the mixed presidential-parliamentary system argue that the only legitimate alternative to the current presidential system in terms of more balanced government powers and ultimately the protection of fundamental rights is one that further shifts powers from the president to the legislature. They argue that such an institutional arrangement would foster cooperation and responsible behavior in the Korean politics. These debates over alternatives to the current presidential system show no signs of waning.

(2) Challenges to the System of Public Election and Representative Democracy

Several interrelated issues feature in the ongoing debate over reform of Korea's legislative structure. First, there has been constant debate over whether the nation should move from a unicameral to a bicameral legislature. Except for a brief period from 1960 to 1961, Korea has always had a single legislative chamber. Unicameralism contributes to expedient lawmaking as proposed legislation needs to be reviewed in only one house.[67] This was particularly important in Korea's early history, when the nation needed to establish or reconstruct virtually every institution of government, industry and society, following the Korean War (1950-1953). Now that Korea has a more mature legal system in a rapidly diversifying society, some commentators have suggested that bicameralism is preferable because it would promote more robust deliberation from more diverse perspectives on legislation.[68] In addition, in contemplating the potential reunification of South Korea with North Korea, a bicameral legislature may be more suitable for a possible federal system of government at least as a provisional system design. The current unicameral system fosters an environment where intense lobbying is targeted at a small number of lawmakers in the standing committees of a single legislative house. Adopting bicameralism might help to address this concentration of power and lobbying in regard to legislation. Some commentators worry, however, that even the unicameral National Assembly has become deadlocked too often and that a bicameral system would heighten the risk of deadlock, particularly in a divided government.[69]

Other commentators support maintaining unicameralism and instead reforming the composition of the legislature to enhance its representativeness, most notably by increasing the amount of proportional representation. Korea's National Assembly currently consists of 253 members elected directly from electoral districts and 47 members elected through a party-list proportional representation system. One proposal is to increase the percentage of proportional representation seats.[70] In 2019,

67 Other aspects of institutional design, combined with practice and data, also contribute to legislative expediency in Korea, with certain side effects. For example, the standing committees of Korea's National Assembly — a unicameral legislature with the concentrated authority and the explicit obligation to review all bills and pass, modify, or reject them — play a critical role in screening and streamlining bills more than intended, at least partly due to the exponentially increased number of bills submitted to the National Assembly. Relatedly, the budgets for all branches of government in Korea are prepared and submitted by the executive branch to the National Assembly for its review and determination.

68 In this regard, to promote deliberation, statutory rules currently render legislative bills referable simultaneously to two standing committees for debate, if deemed necessary, as well as to the committee of the whole; see National Assembly Act (Act No. 19538, revised July 11, 2023 effective July 11, 2023) Articles 63, 63-2.

69 See National Assembly Research Service Report No. 1369 (dated October 24, 2017), available online at https://www.nars.go.kr/eng/report/view.do?page=121&cmsCode=CM0136&categoryId=all&searchType=TITLE&searchKeyword=&brdSeq=21967.

70 See National Assembly Research Service Report No. 1366 (dated October 17, 2017) at https://www.nars.go.kr/eng/report/view.do?page=121&cmsCode=CM0136&cat

the National Assembly revised the Public Official Election Act to change the method of distributing proportional representation seats by adopting a partial mixed-member proportional representation system modeled to some extent on the German system; it was used for the general election held on April 15, 2020,[71] and is currently subject to reform discussions.

Another topic of debate is devolution of power to local governments. During his successful election campaign in 2017, former president Moon Jae-in pledged as a candidate to seek constitutional revisions that would transfer governmental powers from national to local authorities. His administration subsequently announced directives and guidelines for decentralization over a five-year period. Shortly thereafter, the National Assembly formed a special committee to examine a variety of decentralization proposals on matters such as expanding the lawmaking and taxation powers of local governments and redesigning institutions to facilitate local government input on national legislation.[72] Directives and guidelines for devolution have continued in the current administration of President Yoon (2022-2027).

There have also been proposals to revise the constitution to enlarge the role of direct democracy. The constitution currently allows the president to submit important "policies of diplomacy, national defense, unification, and other matters relating to the national destiny" to a national referendum (Constitution Article 72).[73] Revision of the constitution itself must also be approved by national referendum (Constitution Article 130).[74] In recent years, there have been growing calls to expand direct democracy by allowing voter initiation of legislation in statute-making and establishing a voter-initiated recall system for elected public officials including members of the National Assembly. At the local government level, laws already permit voter

egoryId=all&searchType=TITLE&searchKeyword=&brdSeq=21964.

71 Public Official Election Act (Act No. 16864, revised and as effective January 14, 2020; currently Act No. 19234, revised March 14, 2023 effective September 15, 2023).

72 This committee was also tasked with addressing the issue of expanding fundamental rights.

73 The KCC has held that the president should not conduct a national referendum for the purpose of seeking a vote of confidence; Constitutional Court Decision 2004Hun-Na1, issued May 14, 2004 (*Impeachment of President Roh Moo-hyun*, 16-1 KCCR 609).

74 Constitution of the Republic of Korea, Article 130.

initiatives for enacting local ordinances and recalling local officials.[75] While multiple bills have been submitted to the National Assembly in recent years to adopt a voter initiative legislation system in the National Assembly and a recall system for members of that body, these bills have all been rejected on the ground that such systems would violate the constitutional doctrines of exclusive statute-making authority vested in the National Assembly and of nonbinding delegation. Thus, expansion of direct democracy at the national level in Korea would appear to require constitutional revision after further reflection and discussions.

(3) Challenges to Expand the Protection of Fundamental Rights

Recent conversations about constitutional revision in Korea in terms of fundamental rights protection, including those reflected in the constitutional revision bill advanced by former president Moon Jae-in in March 2018, seek to expand and clarify constitutional protections for fundamental rights. The proposed revisions would have made explicit that certain fundamental rights are constitutionally protected for all persons regardless of their nationality or residency status. These inalienable rights included the rights to human dignity, pursuit of happiness, equality, life, general freedom, privacy, conscience, religion, and expression. However, the revisions would continue to limit the applicability of other rights to only Korean nationals. This category of rights included social rights such as the rights to a vocation, property, and education and social welfare, along with rights having to do with national defense and the economy. The 2018 constitutional revision bill also sought to strengthen labor rights, especially those of public officials, and to add explicit rights protections that would apply under special circumstances such as natural disasters or national crises. Although the National Assembly did not pass that particular bill, the

75 See Local Autonomy Act (Act No. 19241, revised March 21, 2023 effective September 22, 2023). Discussions on developing a national recall system in Korea have also been inspired and influenced by the UK's Recall of Members of Parliament Act of 2015 (An Act to Make Provision about the Recall of Members of the House of Commons; and for Connected Purposes; 2015 c. 25). For a historical account of Korea's direct democracy measures as incorporated into its system of local autonomy, see Woo-Young Rhee, *Recently Introduced Measures of Direct and Participatory Democracy and Their Constitutional Ramifications in the Republic of Korea*, 4 NATIONAL TAIWAN UNIVERSITY LAW REVIEW 41 (2009).

relevant proposals and issues continue to be discussed and may resurface in one form or another.

4. Conclusion

The Korean constitutional system has undergone significant changes in the more than seven decades since the Republic of Korea was founded in 1948. The 1987 constitutional revision was a watershed that brought about democratization and increased protection of constitutional rights. Since the KCC was established in 1988 through this 1987 constitutional revision, its decisions have been instrumental in furthering the ideals of democratization and respect for fundamental rights, although that progress has not been linear. As to the future, there is lively ongoing debate over potential constitutional reforms[76] aimed at ensuring that both the structural elements and the rights protections of the Korean constitutional law and system will continue to meet the needs and conditions of a society that has changed profoundly over the last 70 years.

76 For the constitutional reform discussion around the 25th anniversary of the current Constitution of the Republic of Korea, see Woo-Young Rhee, *Constitutionalism and the Discussion of Constitutional Revision in the Republic of Korea in the First Decade of the Twenty-First Century*, 42 HONG KONG LAW JOURNAL 43 (2012).

Chapter 2

Contract Law

Youngjoon Kwon*

1. Introduction

In most jurisdictions where a continental legal tradition prevails, a civil code is the central norm at the core of private law. As the word "civil" suggests, a civil code is closely related to the daily lives of citizens and the private legal matters arising therefrom. Therefore, a civil code shapes the very foundation of a society. Korea is no exception to this. The Korean Civil Code (CivC) was first enacted in 1960. Before then, Japanese Civil Code was in effect while Korea was under Japanese colonial rule (1910-1945). In 1945, with the end of the World War II and Japan defeated, its colonial rule ended. The victorious Allies took over Japan's former colonies, and Korea was soon divided at the 38th parallel of latitude between the Soviet Union in the north and the United States in the south.

The new government of the Republic of Korea (South Korea) was established on August 15, 1948 in the southern part of the Korean peninsula. The creation of a new state generated momentum to rebuild Korea's legal system. To facilitate this process, a Committee of Law Compilation was organized under the newly established government. The committee took responsibility for drafting the CivC, a process that demanded considerable time and effort. The outbreak of the Korean War (1950-1953) made this

* Justice, Supreme Court of Korea (Former Professor in Civil Law, Seoul National University School of Law).

daunting task even more difficult. Despite all the challenges, a draft of the CivC was prepared, deliberated, and finally enacted into law; the CivC was promulgated on February 22, 1958, and came into effect on January 1, 1960. In the course of the drafting process, laws of various civil law jurisdictions like Germany, Switzerland, and France were examined.

The CivC is undoubtedly the product of the continental legal tradition. Patterned after Germany's *Pandekten* system, the CivC is a comprehensive and fundamental body of norms covering the entire area of private law. It consists of five separate books: general provisions (Book 1), the law of rights in *rem* (Book 2), the law of obligations (Book 3), family law (Book 4), and the law of inheritance (Book 5). Reflecting the influence of the Pandekten system, the CivC places the general principles of civil law at the forefront of the code (Book 1) and provides rules on specific areas of law (Books 2 through 5) under those principles. Each book tends to follow the same pattern of providing general principles at the beginning before moving on to detailed contents. Accordingly, the CivC is a highly systematic yet also deeply abstract code. Although this approach might make the CivC a logical and systemic body of norms, it can also render it less accessible and readable for the ordinary citizen.

I have been given the task of providing an overview of contract law in Korea, but what I call contract law in this chapter is not an official title in law. Rather it is an aggregate body of substantive law that combines contract-related provisions scattered throughout the CivC and certain similar provisions in other special statutes. Most of the CivC provisions appear in Book 3, which deals with the law of obligations and has a separate chapter called "Contract." Meanwhile, other parts of the CivC contain provisions that, despite the lack of explicit reference, are applicable to contracts. For example, provisions on a juridical act in general in Book 1 are in practice mostly about contracts, since a contract is the central figure of a juridical act.

Given the diversity of legal doctrines in the vast area of contract law, it would not be feasible to cover every point in this chapter. Rather, I address several fundamental issues that are most important in contract law: namely, contract formation and its validity, contract interpretation, breach of contract and remedies, and discharge of a contract. Unjust enrichment is also addressed as a related topic. Although unjust enrichment *per se* is not necessarily considered part of contract law, it often becomes intertwined with contract law when a contract is invalid or discharged.

2. Contract Formation and Its Validity

Under Korean contract law, a contract is formed when parties voluntarily make an agreement to be legally bound by it.

(1) Agreement

First, a contract is formed only when there is an 'agreement' among the parties. The CivC postulates that a contract is formed by accord between an offer and an acceptance. An offer is a declaration of intention to make a contract in a concrete and definite manner, while an acceptance is a declaration of intention to accept that offer. To a certain extent, the CivC employs the mirror image rule regarding acceptance; a reply to an offer in the form of an acceptance but containing additions, limitations, or other modifications of the initial offer is deemed a rejection of the offer and constitutes a counter-offer (Article 534).[1] An offer becomes effective when it reaches the offeree and cannot be withdrawn unless the withdrawal reaches the offeree before or at the same time as the offer (Article 527). This means that an offer can be binding on an offeror once it reaches the offeree.

A more fundamental and comprehensive justification for the formation of a contract lies in the existence of an agreement in which a meeting of the minds occurs. In practice, it is much more important to determine whether there is an agreement rather than to micro-analyze whether there was an offer and an acceptance, since the essence of a contract is an agreement in which an accord of intents occurs. Consequently, it is quite natural to say that contract interpretation requires an exploration of the intent of the parties, as I explain below in the discussion of contract interpretation.

(2) Voluntary Agreement

Second, a valid contract requires a 'voluntary' agreement among the parties. Freedom of contract is a fundamental principle in contract law, and Korean law recognizes freedom of contract as a constitutional and fundamental right. Forcing a party to reach a certain agreement against his or her will

1 The number of the article in this chapter indicates the article in the CivC, unless otherwise indicated.

infringes this fundamental freedom. Reaching a voluntary agreement does not necessarily mean that all parties must clearly understand every detail of the agreement before the contract is concluded. As is often the case with standard-form contracts, some parties, such as consumers, do not understand or even perceive everything that is stated in lengthy and complicated contracts. An agreement is still deemed to exist when a party agrees to accept all the terms and conditions as they are contained in the contract presented by the other party, regardless of his or her actual knowledge and comprehension of such terms and conditions. This practice may pose a threat to the fairness of a contract. The potential unfairness of a standard-form contract is specifically noted and separately addressed in the Korean legal system. Korea has a special statute to regulate standard-form contracts—the Act on the Regulation of a Standard-Form Contract—which imposes additional duties on business entities to provide information at the time of contract execution and provides additional regulations on the fairness of the contract's terms.

There are some exceptions to the overall principle of voluntariness. These exceptions are often recognized to serve compelling public interests. In the CivC, for example, there is an exception for the purchase of a structure or trees on land subject to superficies. Article 283 of the CivC entitles a person with the right to superficies on a land to request a settlor of the superficies for purchase of the structures (mostly buildings) or trees thereon when the settlor refuses to extend the period of superficies. Upon this request, a contract for the purchase of the structure or trees is formed by the force of law, regardless of the settlor's intent. This provision aims to protect any structures or trees on the land from being destroyed or removed, which might result in the reduction of social utility. Similar provisions exist in the CivC, such as Articles 285, 316, 643-647.

(3) Agreement to Be Legally Bound

Thirdly, a contract purports to be a "legally binding" agreement. Therefore, it is important to distinguish a non-binding agreement from a binding one. A contract is enforceable only when the agreement incorporates the mutual intention of all parties to be legally bound by it. A mere social agreement, such as an agreement to treat somebody in return for his or her hospitality or an agreement to help somebody with homework, cannot constitute a contract, since the parties concerned generally do not intend any legal consequences from that agreement. The intention of the parties to be legally bound to the agreement may be inferred from several factors, including the nature of the agreement, the wording of the contract, and the parties' statements or conducts in the course of making the contract. In practice, there is not always a bright line between a legal and a non-legal agreement. There is no single standard for testing whether the parties intended to create a legal relationship.

Whether a best efforts clause is legally binding often becomes an issue in this regard. It is a clause in which parties express the intent to exert their best or reasonable efforts regarding certain matters. Whether this can become a legal ground for enforcement is an issue of controversy. While there have been a series of Supreme Court decisions denying the legally binding effect of best efforts clauses,[2] whether a specific best efforts clause is legally binding must be determined on a case-by-case basis by identifying the intent of the parties to the contract regarding the clause.[3] In general, the more clearly and specifically the act subject to best efforts is defined, and the more reasonable the trust placed by the other party regarding the realization of said act, the more likely a best efforts clause will be found to be legally binding.

(4) No Consideration and Formality Required

There is no requirement for consideration in Korea. This differs from common law jurisdictions where consideration, which is generally defined as something bargained for and received by a promisee from a promisor is required for enforcement of a contract. In line with this, a gratuitous contract, in which one party gives something to another party but receives nothing in return, is still an enforceable contract under Korean law. What ultimately matters is whether the contracting parties agreed to be legally bound by a voluntary agreement, as described above.

Further, as a general rule, no formality is required to create or enforce

2 Supreme Court Decisions 93Da32668, March. 25, 1994; 96Da16049, October 25, 1996.

3 For example, Supreme Court Decision 2018Da223054, January 14, 2021, acknowledged the legally binding effect of a best efforts clause.

a contract under Korean law. Therefore, a contract can be made either orally or in writing. Signatures of the contracting parties are also not required for the formation or enforcement of a contract, although it is customary for the parties to stamp a seal or sign their names at the end of a contract when it is concluded in writing.

This no-formality rule is theoretically connected with the notion of freedom of contract. According to the Constitutional Court of Korea, freedom of contract includes freedom of formality.[4] Thus, contracting parties can freely choose the form of the contract, and along the same line of thinking, choose a contract that has no form at all. Consequently, the statute of frauds as recognized in common law does not exist in Korea. No matter how large the total amount of a sales contract is, it does not need to be made in writing or signed to be enforced.

However, there are some statutory exceptions to the no-formality rule. For example, Article 11 of the Act on Contracts to Which the State is a Party stipulates that any contract governed by that act is to be in writing. Similar provisions are found in other statutes, including Article 6 of the Installment Transactions Act and Article 8 of the Arbitration Act. The legal effect of non-compliance with these regulations varies. Under the aforementioned acts, non-compliance renders the contract invalid, but non-compliance with other consumer-related laws is generally construed as not affecting the validity of the contract.

(5) Validity

It is one thing to say that a contract has been formed and quite another to say that it is valid. This means that simply forming a contract does not automatically lead to its validity. Further, when there is an inherent factor that may invalidate a contract, that contract may be valid at the time of its formation but may be invalidated by *ex post* factors, such as avoidance of a contract by one of the parties.

Factors that render a contract either void or voidable fall into one of two categories: (i) the contract does not comply with the form or content specifically designated by law, or (ii) the expressions of intent that

4 Constitutional Court Decision 89Hun-Ma204, June 3, 1991.

constitute the contract are defective. Generally, a contract does not require any particular form to gain validity. There are no provisions or statutes comparable to the statute of frauds found in common law. However, there are some exceptions. We have seen above the requirement that a contract to which a government is a party be in wiring (Act on Contracts to which the State is a Party Article 11). In terms of content, a contract is void when its content is in breach of good morals and social order (Article 103) or mandatory law. A contract is also void when one party takes advantage of a weaker party and makes an excessively unfair contract (Article 104). Finally, a contract is also void or voidable when there is a defective expression of intent. A false declaration (Article 107) and a sham transaction (Article 108) are typical grounds for the nullity of a contract. A mistake (Article 109), fraud and duress (Article 110), or lack of the capacity to perform a juridical act (Articles 5, 10, 13) are all grounds for avoidance of the contract. Another party's breach of a contract does not in itself invalidate the contract. In addition, if a party wishes to assert that another factor that invalidates a contract, that party has the onus of proving that claim.

Although a contract is generally rendered null in its entirety, Article 137 of the CivC allows partial nullity if the contract would have been made without the invalid part. The same principle is applied to partial voidance. This is often used by the courts in modifying contracts to ensure fairer outcomes. In cases where excessive attorney fees were at issue, the Supreme Court used this device to render the excessive portion of the fee uncollectable while leaving an appropriate portion valid, based on the assumption that the attorney and client might have made a contract at that fee level.[5] The Supreme Court stretched the doctrine to some extent in order to judicially modify the contents of a contract for the purposes of reaching an equitable conclusion.

3. Contract Interpretation

There is no specific provision in the CivC that stipulates how one should read and interpret a contract. However, the Supreme Court of Korea

5 Supreme Court Decisions 91Da8722, December 13, 1991; 91Da29804, March 31, 1992.

has, in a number of different cases, enunciated various principles of contract interpretation. These principles, as developed through case law, can be categorized as follows: (i) natural interpretation, (ii) normative interpretation, and (iii) supplemental interpretation. Since these are general canons of contract interpretation applicable to both written and oral contracts, I first explain these general rules and then proceed to explain how text functions in a written contract.

(1) Seeking Intent of the Contracting Parties

1) Natural Interpretation

Natural interpretation is the interpretation of a contract based on the actual intent of the parties. Such interpretation is particularly useful when the parties have agreed to a contract, but the plain language of the contract is different from what the parties had intended. For example, party A and party B enter into a contract with the intent to conclude an agreement for the sale of property 1. By mistake, the contract lists property 2 as the subject of the agreement. Based on the principle of natural interpretation, this contract should be interpreted as having been entered into with respect to property 1 rather than property 2, thus reflecting the true intent of the parties. The Supreme Court of Korea has held in a similar case that for "contract interpretation one should, in general, not limit oneself to the text of the contract but should search for the true intent of both parties."[6]

2) Normative Interpretation

Normative interpretation is the interpretation of a contract based on the objective meaning of the contract, as read from the point of view of a reasonable counterparty. If the parties' actual intents are in accord, it is sufficient to interpret the contract based on that mutual intent (i.e., natural interpretation). However, most disputes over contract interpretation arise when one party expresses an intent that is understood differently by another party. The question in such cases is which party's understanding should form the basis for interpreting the contract. Under the principle of normative interpretation, the contract is interpreted based not on the intent

6 Supreme Court Decision 93Da2629, 2636, October 26, 1993.

of the party having expressed it, but as it would have been understood by a reasonable counterparty. In this regard, the Supreme Court held that "the interpretation of a juristic act consists of clearly defining the objective meaning given by the party to the juristic act, without being limited to the plain language employed, but rather with a reasonable interpretation of the objective meaning the party attributed to the juristic act based on the plain language, irrespective of the actual intent of the party."[7]

3) Supplemental Interpretation

When a court is confronted with a situation that has not been contemplated by the contract, the court supplements the contract with the presumed intent that the parties would have had at the time of the contract. This interpretive exercise can be said to constitute an exception to the freedom of contract, as the court supplements the parties' contract by relying on what the parties would have agreed upon, rather than what they actually agreed to. Therefore, supplementary interpretation is applied to augment a contract where there is a lacuna in the contract that cannot be addressed by either natural or normative interpretation. In this regard, the Supreme Court has held as below:

> If both parties to a contract made the same error in respect of matters which form the premise or bases of the contract and omitted to address such matters, the contract may be interpreted by supplementing it on matters which the parties would have agreed upon had it not been for such mistake.[8]

The court further noted that the basis for such supplementation is "not the actual or subjective intent of the parties but an equitable intent which is objectively determined taking into consideration the purpose of the contract, trade practices, applicable laws, principles of good faith, etc."[9]

7 Supreme Court Decision 2008Da90095, 90101, May 14, 2009.
8 Supreme Court Decision 2005Da13288, November 23, 2006.
9 Supreme Court Decision 2005Da13288, November 23, 2006.

4) Commonality in Interpretation Methods: Seeking the Intent of the Parties

Since the principle of party autonomy and freedom of contract constitute the core ideas of contractual law, it is natural to seek to interpret a contract in accordance with the intent of the parties. The foregoing principles of natural, normative, and supplemental interpretation provide different mechanisms for determining such intent. In other words, the ultimate goal of interpretation is to define 'the intent of the parties to the given contract,' in pursuit of which natural interpretation relies on the parties' 'actual intent.' Normative interpretation relies on the parties' 'reasonable intent,' and supplemental interpretation relies on the parties' 'presumed intent.'

(2) Means of Ascertaining Intent: A Written Contract

In order to determine the parties' intent, a court needs to refer to certain means of ascertaining that intent. While it is possible to describe these means in a number of ways, they can be succinctly expressed as comprising the text of the contract on the one hand and the context of the contract on the other. In other words, the interpreter uses the words of the contract and the circumstances surrounding the contract to determine the parties' intent. Of course, if the contract is an oral agreement, there will be no text to interpret. In practice, however, most contracts are in writing (including the agreement at issue), and thus the interpreter may rely both upon the text and context of a contract in the course of interpretation.

1) Text

The wording of the contract is the primary source of contract interpretation. Text is an important medium that the parties use to express their true intent. Therefore, interpretation based on the wording of the contract is not contrary to the principle of natural interpretation, which requires interpretation to be in accordance with the true intent of the parties. Further, text is an objective means for the communication of the parties' mutual intent. Therefore, interpretation of a contract based on its wording is also in accord with the principle of normative interpretation, which requires objective interpretation from the point of view of a reasonable party. In practice, the Korean courts give due importance to the actual wording of the contract in interpreting its meaning. Accordingly, when presented with a contract and any other relevant documents, the starting point of the court's inquiry is the text of the contract. In this regard, the Supreme Court held that for written instruments such as contracts, "the court shall acknowledge the existence and substance of the intent expressed in the text as it is stated in the contractual document unless there is any counter evidence to deny such stated intent."[10] This ruling indicates that the text of a contract has strong evidentiary value.

2) Context

Context is another factor considered in interpreting contracts; if the text always allowed for only one possible interpretation, disputes over contract interpretation would be far less common. However, the wording of a contract is often abstract and ambiguous; reliance on the text is limited to situations where it is specific and clear regarding the intent of the parties, and parties often attribute different meanings to the words in a contract. In such cases, contracts should be interpreted considering the context as well as the text. The context incorporates various elements including the purpose of the contract, negotiation history, and trade usages.[11] The context functions as an additional means of interpreting the intent of the contracting parties.

3) No Parol Evidence Rule

Korean law does not recognize the parol evidence rule that is found in countries with Anglo-American legal systems; it states that written contracts should be interpreted based solely on the wording of the contract, without reference to any extrinsic evidence that might suggest an alternative meaning. In Korea, it is therefore open to courts to rely, along with the plain language of the contract, on extrinsic evidence that establishes the context of the contract as they endeavor to interpret contracts. Accordingly, there are cases where the court reaches interpretations that contradict the plain written language of contracts on the grounds of extrinsic evidence. Along these lines, the holding of the Supreme Court ruling to this effect is helpful in understanding Korean law:

> If the text expressed by the parties does not clearly show the objective

10 Supreme Court Decision 94Da16601, February 10, 1995.

11 Supreme Court Decision 99Da43486, November 26, 1999.

> meaning, the contract should be reasonably interpreted considering, in general, the form and substance of the plain language, the motive and progress of the juristic acts, the purpose and true intent of the parties behind the juristic acts, commercial practices, etc., and then in accordance with logic, equity, common sense and trade practices of the society.[12]

However, the holding of the Supreme Court ruling to the effect that "the court shall acknowledge the existence and substance of the intent expressed in the text as it is stated in the contractual document unless there is any counter evidence to deny such stated intent"[13] needs to be understood in weighing the evidentiary value of the written text of the contract. This means that a written contract enjoys the presumption that it was made with the substance as written. For example, if the written contract stipulates that a certain piece of property is to be transferred to somebody at a specific price, the existence of that contract as written is presumed. Another party who wishes to overturn this presumption must present evidence that the intent of the parties as to the contract was otherwise.

4. Breach of Contract and Remedies

(1) Breach: Non-performance of Contractual Obligations

When a valid contract is made and its substance is confirmed, the parties have contractual duties to perform their obligations thereunder. The performance of an obligation may also be effected by a third party unless the nature of an obligation does not so permit or the parties have declared a contrary intention (Article 469(2)). The time and place of such performance are to be determined by the parties. If not, the CivC provides supplementary default rules. The time for performance, if not agreed upon in the contract, is when the obligee demands the performance of the obligation (Article 387(2)). Regarding the place for performance in the absence of any agreement, delivery of specific goods shall be made at the place where the

12 Supreme Court Decision 99Da43486, November 26, 1999.
13 Supreme Court Decision 94Da16601, February 10, 1995.

goods were situated at the time of the contract; any other performance shall be made at the obligor's present domicile (Article 467). A tender of performance relieves the obligor of liability for non-performance (Article 461).

When performance is not effected as agreed in a contract or provided by law, the issue of non-performance arises. Non-performance refers to the failure to carry out some activity in accordance with an obligation. When non-performance occurs, an aggrieved party is entitled to demand specific performance in accordance with the contract, unless enforcing such performance is impossible or inappropriate by its nature. Specific performance in the case of non-performance does not require intention or fault in non-performance by the breaching party. In fact, it may be understood as enforcing the agreement to which the breaching party has already consented. Unlike some jurisdictions in which specific performance is regarded as a secondary and equitable remedy in relation to damages, demanding or ordering specific performance does not require inadequacy of damages as a remedy. An aggrieved party is entitled to choose between specific performance and damages and may them both as long as doing so does not amount to double remedy.

(2) Damages in General

The most commonly used remedy for non-performance is to claim damages. In this case, either intention or fault in non-performance is required. This requirement of attributability is clearly different from the case of specific performance where such attributability is not required as its prerequisite for the claim. Article 390 of the CivC provides that if "an obligor fails to effect performance in accordance with the tenor and purport of the obligation, the obligee may claim damages: Provided, that this shall not apply to where such non-performance is not due to the obligor's intention or negligence." Under this article, an aggrieved party is entitled to claim damages for a breach of contract if all the following requirements are fulfilled.

First, non-performance of obligation is required. In the context of a contract, a Korean court will accept that there has been non-performance of a contractual obligation if a breach of contract has been established. Non-performance takes diverse forms. Delayed performance, impossibility of performance, and defective performance are typical examples of non-performance, but the generality of the non-performance clause means that non-performance is not restricted to these types. For instance, an anticipatory breach is another type of non-performance. The aggrieved party bears the burden of proof of the existence of non-performance by the breaching party.

Second, intention or negligence is required. A breaching party must have intent of non-performance of an obligation or be negligent in that regard. Under Korean law, intention is the state of being aware of and desiring (or at least accepting) the relevant result of the non-performance, while negligence is the state of failing to recognize and avoid the relevant result by failing to exercise an appropriate duty of care. Although either intention or negligence is a prerequisite to claim damages, the court will presume that this requirement is satisfied in presented proof of the non-performance of a contractual obligation. Therefore, it is the breaching party (rather than an injured party) that bears the burden of proving that the non-performance was not intentional or negligent.[14]

Third, unlawfulness is required. The non-performance of an obligation is presumed to be unlawful unless there are special circumstances that negate unlawfulness. For example, Article 536(1) of the CivC provides for a right to simultaneous performance that allows a party to a contract to refuse to perform its obligation until the other party tenders performance of its obligation. In cases where a contract party duly exercises its right to simultaneous performance, the *prima facie* non-performance of obligation would not be assessed as unlawful and therefore would not give rise to a right to claim damages. In any case, it is the breaching party that bears the burden of proof regarding the existence of circumstances that negate unlawfulness.

Fourth, damage to an aggrieved party in the form of loss is required. Under Korean law, damage is defined as any involuntary loss or disadvantage suffered by an injured party due to an infringement of legally protected interests.[15] An aggrieved party bears the burden of proving the

14 Supreme Court Decision 84Daka1864, March 26, 1985; Yong-Dam Kim et al. eds., COMMENTARIES ON CIVIL LAW: GENERAL PROVISIONS (1) (주석민법: 채권총칙1), Korean Institute of Judicial Administration 758 (2013) (in Korean).

15 Chang-Soo Yang et al. eds., CIVIL LAW I: CONTRACT LAW (민법 I: 계약법), Parkyoungsa 444-445 (2015) (in Korean).

existence of damage,[16] which must be actual and concrete. Mere harm that *may* materialize into actual loss in the future is not deemed damage until such materialization occurs. This frequently becomes an issue when an aggrieved party alleges that it has suffered damage by bearing an obligation to a third party. For instance, if A (the breaching party) supplied a defective good to B (the aggrieved party), and B alleges that it bears compensatory obligation to its purchaser C (the third party), who allegedly suffered loss arising from the defective good, such obligation is deemed B's loss vis-à-vis A only when such obligation is evaluated as an actual and definite loss to B.[17]

Fifth, causation is required. There must be a causal relationship between the non-performance of an obligation and the damage to an aggrieved party. That is, the loss must be attributable to the act or omission of the party from which recovery is sought. The aggrieved party bears the burden of proving causation. The Supreme Court of Korea has held that the test for causation when determining the scope of liability or the extent of damage caused by a breach of contract is based on the legal doctrine of *adequate causation*.[18] The purpose of this test is to normatively restrict natural causality that can be extended without limit. Adequate causation can be established when non-performance is considered a normatively sufficient cause of the damages, even when the breach itself is not the sole cause of the loss. The presence of other contributing causes may be reflected in the final assessment of the amount of damages but does not *per se* negate causation for purposes of establishing the elements of a claim. While the concept of adequacy is not clearly defined under the CivC itself, Korean courts normatively evaluate the existence of causation by considering all relevant factors, such as the gravity and culpability of the cause, the proximity or directness between the cause and the outcome, and the degree of the damage.

16 Yong-Dam Kim et al. eds., COMMENTARIES ON CIVIL LAW: GENERAL PROVISIONS (1) (주석민법: 채권총칙1), Korean Institute of Judicial Administration 757 (2013) (in Korean).

17 Supreme Court Decision 92Da29948, November 27, 1992.

18 Supreme Court Decision 2010Da81315, January 27, 2012.

(3) Scope of Damages

Under the CivC, the general provision setting forth the scope of compensation for damages caused by contractual breach is Article 393(1), which provides that "the scope of compensatory damages for non-performance of an obligation shall not exceed that of ordinary damage"; Article 393(2) provides that "any damage arising under special circumstances shall be compensated only if the obligor had foreseen or could have foreseen such circumstances." The legal principle set forth in Article 393 can be summarized as (i) any ordinary damages are subject to compensation at any time, whereas (ii) any special damages are subject to compensation only when the obligor could have foreseen the damages. Special damages are distinguished from ordinary damages since not all special damages are subject to compensation; whether special damages in a given case are subject to compensation is determined by the foreseeability of the particular circumstances giving rise to the damages.

Ordinary damages are those which, in ordinary trade usage, are deemed to have occurred if a certain obligation is not performed.[19] The Supreme Court defines ordinary damages as those which, in light of ordinary trade usage and empirical rules of the general public, are deemed to have occurred if an obligation of the type at issue is not performed, unless there exist extraordinary circumstances.[20] Meanwhile, special damages are any and all damages other than ordinary damages; when defined actively, special damages are those that occurred due to an individual, specific, or extraordinary circumstance of a contracting party.[21] In other words, any damages generally and objectively foreseeable by the relevant parties to occur upon non-performance of certain obligation are ordinary damages and thus subject to compensation, while any damages not foreseeable to that extent are subject to compensation only when the obligor had foreseen or could have foreseen the circumstances to which the damages are attributable.[22] Thus, the scope of compensation for damages under the CivC

19 Yoon-Jik Kwak et al. eds., CIVIL CODE COMMENTARY: GENERAL PROVISIONS OF CLAIMS Parts 2 (민법주해: 총칙(2)), Parkyoungsa 477 (1995) (in Korean).

20 Supreme Court Decision 2006Da25745, December 24, 2008.

21 Supreme Court Decision 2006Da25745, December 24, 2008.

22 Yoon-Jik Kwak et al. eds., CIVIL CODE COMMENTARY: GENERAL PRO-

is determined based on the standard of foreseeability.

In general, loss of profits expected to be generated directly from the relevant contract falls under ordinary damages, but loss of profits expected to occur from specific circumstances outside the relevant contract falls under special damages. However, what constitutes ordinary or special damages is to be determined on a case-by-case basis, depending on the details and characteristics of a specific case. For instance, the agreed price or (if no agreed price exists) the market value of an object under a sale agreement is a type of ordinary profit that falls under performance profits. In this regard, if it is impossible to deliver the object that is the subject of the sale agreement due to a contractual breach by the purchaser, the seller may seek compensation against the purchaser for ordinary damages equivalent to the agreed price or the market value. That is because it is already expected under the contract that the seller would receive the agreed price or market value by delivering the object of the sale agreement to the purchaser. Meanwhile, the loss of performance profits that may be generated from a resale of the object of sale may be categorized as either ordinary or special damages, depending on the foreseeability of the loss. According to the Commentaries on Civil Code, such damages are special (extraordinary) damages in a sale of real properties between individuals but ordinary damages in a sale of movables between merchants.[23] This means that even the same type of damages—here, the loss of opportunity for resale—may be evaluated differently, based on the facts of a specific case.

(4) Performance Interests and Reliance Interests

Another perspective on the assessment of damages arising from breach of contract concerns the notion of performance interests and reliance interests. Briefly speaking, the principal approach to the assessment of damages in this regard is that performance interests become the criteria for assessing damages. This arises from the principle of difference,[24] according to which

VISIONS OF CLAIMS Parts 2 (민법주해: 총칙(2)) 534 (1995) (in Korean).

23 Yoon-Jik Kwak et al. eds., CIVIL CODE COMMENTARY: GENERAL PROVISIONS OF CLAIMS Parts 2 (민법주해: 총칙(2)) 538 (1995) (in Korean).

24 Yoon-Jik Kwak et al. eds., CIVIL CODE COMMENTARY: GENERAL PROVISIONS OF CLAIMS Parts 2 (민법주해: 총칙(2)) 468 (1995) (in Korean).

damages are the difference between (1) the profits that might have been earned if the cause of damage did not exist, and (2) actual profits. In this view, damages caused by non-performance of any obligation should be compensated by restoring the obligee to his or her original state in which he or she would have been if the obligation had been carried out as agreed. Therefore, the breaching obligor is to compensate the non-breaching party for such economic profits as would have occurred if the contract had been adhered to in full.[25] This is called the principle of compensation of performance interests.

Performance interests may include future profits. In this line of this thinking, the Supreme Court allows compensation for damages for lost profits to be obtained upon completion of performance of a contract to be executed in the future and the completion of the performance of an already executed contract, as long as certain requirements are met. For instance, according to a Supreme Court decision,[26] if a party under a continuous trade relationship fails to perform its obligation to execute an individual contract without any justifiable grounds, the scope of damages can be as much as all the profits that would have been generated if the transaction contract had continued; these are performance interests.

The Supreme Court also allows compensation of profits lost based on reliance interests in lieu of performance interests.[27] Damages regarding reliance interests are those caused by trust that the relevant contract would be fulfilled properly. For instance, costs of entering into a contract, costs to prepare for the performance of a contract, or losses arising from refusal of a more favorable sales offer by a third party while trusting that another party to an existing contract would fulfill the contract all constitute damages based on reliance interests.[28] The reason why reliance interests can be compensated in lieu of performance interests is that it is not always easy to prove the existence of performance interests. Therefore, reliance interests are compensated to supplement the principle of compensation for performance

25 Supreme Court Decision 2006Da25745, December 24, 2009.

26 Supreme Court Decision 99Da7183, June 25, 1999.

27 Supreme Court Decision 91Da29972, April 28, 1992 (this decision mentions performance profits and trust-based profits together); Supreme Court Decision 2002Da2539, June 11, 2002.

28 Yoon-Jik Kwak et al. eds., CIVIL CODE COMMENTARY: GENERAL PROVISIONS OF CLAIMS Parts 2(민법주해: 총칙(2)) 474 (1995) (in Korean).

interests. This avenue does not necessarily mean forsaking the principle of compensation for performance interests.

(5) Liquidated Damages

Liquidated damages are an agreement to determine in advance the amount of damages to be paid to the obligee by the obligor when grounds for compensation, such as breach of contract, occur in the course of the contract. Liquidated damages are themselves a type of contract. However, cases in which liquidated damages are entered into as an independent contract are rare; more often, text on liquidated damages will be included in the main transaction contract.

Liquidated damages mainly perform two functions. First, they simplify the claim for damages. If liquidated damages exist, the person bringing the claim for damages can claim the predetermined liquidated damages amount without proving the facts and amounts of actual damage. Liquidated damages simplify the legal process by regulating the issue of compensation in advance. Through this, the parties gain legal stability and predictability concerning compensation. Second, liquidated damages serve to warn the parties. If liquidated damages exist, parties can expect that if they breach the contract, they will have to compensate any damages based on the predetermined amount of liquidated damages. With such a clause, a contracting party will be reminded of the disadvantages of breaching the contract and be more cautious about causing grounds for breach.

The CivC expressly provides one ground for liquidated damages in Article 398(1), which states that the "parties may determine in advance the amount of damages payable in the event of breach of contract." Of course, under the principle of freedom of contract, the parties are free to enter into a contract on any matter not prohibited by law. Therefore, even without such a provision, the parties are free to enter into a liquidated damages contract. In this sense, Article 398(1) of the CivC is there for the purpose of confirmation. CivC Article 398(2) and CivC Article 398(4) have important practical implications. The former states that when the amount of liquidated damages is unduly excessive, the court may reduce the amount to an appropriate sum, while the latter states that an agreement on the sum payable in case of breach of contract (*wee-yak-keum*) is presumed to be liquidated damages.

5. Discharge of a Contract

(1) Discharge of a Contract in General

Just as a contract is formed, interpreted, and carried out, it can also be ended for a variety of reasons. A contract may be null and void at the time of its formation. In that case, a contract never has any legal effect. A contract may also be voided after being validly executed. For example, a contract may be voided or cancelled when it turns out that it was executed by fraud or under duress. However, a contract may also be brought to an end by *ex post* factors, which take different forms.

One example is a voluntary agreement between the contracting parties to terminate their contractual relationship. Based on freedom of contract, parties can freely terminate a contract by agreement, just as they agreed to establish a contractual relationship. These agreements take different forms. Parties may bilaterally and directly agree on termination of a contract; they may also agree to reserve a unilateral right to rescind or terminate a contract. This agreement does not directly end the contract but rather grants a unilateral right to do so to both or either of the parties when certain grounds stipulated in the contract are satisfied.

Furthermore, Articles 543-546 of the CivC allow a party to discharge a contract when there is breach of contract. In that instance, an aggrieved party can rescind a contract, meaning that parties can unwind a contract as if it had never been executed or can terminate a contract, meaning that parties will cease to have a contractual relationship from the point of termination, with the executed part of the contract left intact. Rescission of a contract refers to a declaration of intention that retroactively (*ex tunc*) extinguishes the effect of a valid contract on the grounds of breach of contract. Similarly, contracts can also be terminated, which refers to a declaration of intention that extinguishes the effect of a valid, continuous contract for the future (*ex nunc*) on the grounds of a breach of contract. Termination, as opposed to rescission, matters in the case of a continuous contract. A lease contract is a typical continuous contract in that it requires the obligations of a contract to be performed for a certain period of time (the lease period). In the case of a lease contract, a breach like the lessee's failure to make rent payments constitutes grounds for termination of the contract. However, it does not unwind the contractual relationship that existed up to the point of termination.

Rescission or termination of a contract should be effected by a declaration of such intention to the other party or parties. If there are two parties to a contract, such declaration should be communicated to the counterparty. If there are three or more parties to a contract, unless otherwise agreed, such declaration should be communicated to all other parties. Rescission or termination of a contract has no influence on claims for damages.

The requirements of rescission or termination are not identical. For instance, if there is a delay in performance by a certain party, the aggrieved party may set a reasonable deadline and give peremptory notice demanding its performance and terminate a contract if proper performance does not occur within that period (Article 544). In case of impossibility of performance that is the responsibility of an obligor, the obligee may also terminate a contract without giving peremptory notice (Article 546). Based on these provisions, it is a generally accepted position that a breach of contract entitles the aggrieved party to terminate the contract as long as the breaching party is held responsible for such breach.

(2) Breach in Discharge of a Contract

A breach should be significant enough to frustrate the purposes of the contract and justify the rescission or termination of the contractual relationship. This is different from claims for damages where the significance of the breach is not brought into consideration, as long as the damage occurred as a result of the breach. What kind of breach, then, rises to a level that justifies the rescission or termination of a contract?

The Supreme Court limits default to a breach of a principal obligation and thus excludes breaches of incidental obligations. In one judgement, the Supreme Court held as below:

> In order to rescind a sales contract on the ground of default, the obligation that was breached must be a principal obligation that is indispensable to the fulfillment of the purpose of the sales contract, and for which, if not fulfilled, the seller would not have entered into the contract because the purpose of the sales contract cannot be achieved. In contrast, a party cannot rescind the entire sales contract

on the ground of the breach if the obligation unfulfilled is merely an incidental obligation.[29]

Although the judgement deals specifically with a sales contract, the same logic can be applied to rescission or termination of contracts in general. The ruling of the Korean Supreme Court reflects the view that unless there is a breach of a principal obligation indispensable to achieving the purpose of the contract, upholding the validity of a contract is preferable to annulling it.

The Supreme Court provides a standard to distinguish principal from incidental obligations by stating that "one must look into, without regard to its independent value, the parties' reasonable intentions that were expressed, or manifestly and objectively recognized, in light of the circumstance at the time of execution of the contract, and also consider the contents and purpose of the contract as well as the consequences of the breach of the contract."[30] In light of the foregoing, the more directly an obligation is connected to the purpose of the contract, or the more significantly the breach of the obligation obstructs the fulfillment of the purpose of the contract, the more likely it will be determined to be a principal obligation.

For example, in the sale of a shopping center, the seller sold lots in the center with a designation that a given type of business would be the only one on a floor so that buyers could operate without the risk of direct nearby competition. The seller also required buyers to promise not to unilaterally change their business type to protect the spirit of the one-per-floor requirement. Under these facts, the Korean Supreme Court ruled that this non-competition obligation was a principal obligation since it was indispensable to the fulfillment of the purpose of the contract; furthermore, without its being respected, the buyers would not have entered into the contract because they could not achieve the purpose of the contract.[31] Therefore, the court allowed the buyer to terminate the contract on the grounds of the seller's breach of the above obligation.

In another case of a video production agreement, the Korean Supreme Court held that where the contractor of a video production agreement

29 Supreme Court Decision 97Ma575, April 7, 1997.
30 Supreme Court Decision 2005Da53705, November 25, 2005.
31 Supreme Court Decision 2004Da67011, July 14, 2005.

failed to provide a preview service on the expected date due to schedule delays caused by internal issues, that default was only a breach of procedural obligations that were incidental to the contract and occurred in the course of performing the principal obligation that was the purpose of the contract; therefore, the customer was not entitled to terminate the agreement on the grounds of default of such incidental obligation.[32]

(3) Discharge of a Contract without Regard to Breach of Contract

1) Change of Circumstances

The main purpose of contract law is to enforce valid agreements, as is expressed in the maxim of *pacta sund servanda* (one should abide by agreements). However, the sanctity of contract is challenged when an *ex post* change of circumstances takes place and puts one party in a drastically disadvantageous position. Imposing an excessively onerous burden on a faultless party who had never considered such a risk at the time of the contract seems unfair. The doctrine of change of circumstances addresses this pathological issue of contract law by allowing for the modification or termination of the contract.

The CivC does not have a provision expressly stipulating the principle of change of circumstances, but it has been recognized by academic commentaries as one of the principles derived from the principle of trust and good faith stipulated in CivC Article 2.[33] The Supreme Court had previously taken a negative or unclear position. A party's argument based on the principle of change of circumstances is rarely accepted by courts in Korea. The strict position of Korean courts against the principle of change of circumstances is found as early as a Supreme Court decision from the 1960s. In a case where the purchaser of forest paid the balance of the purchase price 14 years after the execution date of the sale and purchase agreement and requested to register a transfer of title, the price had soared about 202 times, due to sudden changes in economic conditions arising out of the Korean War and two currency reforms. The Supreme Court (decision No.

32 Supreme Court Decision 96Da14364, July 9, 1996.

33 Yong-Dam Kim et al. eds., COMMENTARIES ON CIVIL LAW: GENERAL PROVISIONS (1) (주석민법: 채권총칙), Korean Institute of Judicial Administration 173-174 (2010).

63Da452, September 12, 1963),[34] ruled that even though the value of the won had declined dramatically between the time when the sale and purchase agreement was executed and the time when the balance of the purchase price was paid, and that acquisition of the forest in return for payment of the originally agreed balance was found to be significantly unfair, the seller was not entitled to the right of rescission on the grounds of a change of circumstances.[35]

However, in 2007, the Supreme Court ruled that termination of contract on grounds of a change of circumstances should be recognized as an exception to the principle that the terms of a contract are to be respected in cases where the following conditions are met: (1) a significant change of circumstance occurs that could not have been anticipated by the parties at the time of execution of the contract; (2) this change occurs due to a cause not attributable to the party seeking the right to terminate; and (3) recognizing the binding force of the original contract would lead to a consequence that violates the principle of trust and good faith.[36] The Supreme Court further ruled that the term "circumstances" in this context means the objective circumstances underlying the contract rather than a party's subjective or personal circumstances. The Supreme Court has rendered similar rulings in connection with the principle of change of circumstances ever since.[37] Still, recognizing an exception to a rule did not mean that the Supreme Court immediately began granting termination due to a change of circumstances. However, the Supreme Court has since handed down several decisions in which termination of a contract was admitted due to a change of circumstances,[38] revealing an expansion in its willingness to apply this doctrine.

2) Continuous Contract

A continuous contract may be terminated without breach if the trust

34 Supreme Court Decision 63Da452, September 12, 1963.

35 Yong-Dam Kim et al. eds., COMMENTARIES ON CIVIL LAW: GENERAL PROVISIONS (1) (주석민법: 채권총칙), Korean Institute of Judicial Administration 177-178 (2010).

36 Supreme Court Decision 2004Da31302, March 29, 2007.

37 Supreme Court Decisions 2008Da44368, June 24, 2011; 2019Da276338, June 30, 2021.

38 Supreme Court Decision 2020Da254846, December 10, 2020; Supreme Court Full Bench Decision 2012Da13637, September 26, 2013.

relationship breaks down such that it would be useless to hold the parties to the contract. A continuous contract is a type of contract whose content and performance is determined and influenced by the passage of a certain amount time. Partnership, lease, and employment contracts are all typical examples. In the context of discharge of a contract, a continuous contract is treated differently from a one-time contract in that it is, in principle, subject to termination with prospective extinguishing effect as opposed to rescission with retrospective extinguishing effect. In the context of the contractual relationship, it is more likely that a continuous contract will be founded on a relationship of trust between or among the contracting parties. In this regard, although the CivC only envisages termination of a contract when there is a breach, it would be meaningless and inefficient to bind parties to a contract when, even absent such a breach, there is no longer a relationship of trust. Along this line of thinking, the Supreme Court has ruled that "a continuous contract is based on a mutual trust relationship between parties, and one of the parties can terminate contract *ex tunc* when there is a grave ground for a breakdown in the relationship of trust upon which the contract is founded, due to, for example, inappropriate acts by the other party during contractual period." Even when such an inappropriate act by the other party does not rise to the level of a breach of contract, the counterparty may invoke this doctrine to resolve a contractual relationship that has become meaningless.

6. Unjust Enrichment

Although unjust enrichment in itself is not necessarily a matter of contract law, it is often associated with contract law. This is because when a contract is null and void or is voided, a performance that has been provided to the other party should be returned to the tendering party. This is addressed under unjust enrichment law but is closely related to contracts since it involves the liquidation of contractual relationship. It is in this regard that I address unjust enrichment law.

Article 741 of the CivC provides that "a person who without any legal grounds derives a benefit from the property or services of another and thereby causes loss to the latter shall be bound to return such benefit." This is the general provision regulating the doctrine of unjust enrichment. To quote the Supreme Court, the unjust enrichment regime "imposes upon a person who enjoys enrichment unsupported by any legal grounds the obligation to return such enrichment based upon the principles of fairness and justice," and "where there is a change in property values between certain parties and, such change, while it appears to be justified from a general and formal perspective, creates conflict with the principle of fairness—an ideal sought after under law—from a relative and practical perspective, the regime seeks to remove such conflict by ordering the return of the value of the property acquired by the person so enriched."[39] In brief, the doctrine of unjust enrichment, grounded in the principle of fairness, provides for measures to finally rectify the distortions made to the order of property which cannot be completely resolved by applying individual legal principles alone.

Unjust enrichment can be divided into (1) performance-based unjust enrichment arising in cases where an obligor–obligee relationship terminates, (2) infringement-based unjust enrichment arising in cases where there is an act that objectively infringes the rights of another, and (3) expense-based unjust enrichment arising in cases where the business of another is managed at one's own expense without an obligation to do so. In addition, compensation-based unjust enrichment that occurs in cases where one discharges another's indebtedness without obligation to do so is often discussed as a fourth type. However, if one interprets expense-based unjust enrichment broadly, compensation-based unjust enrichment can be said to be subsumed thereunder. Performance-based, infringement-based, and expense-based unjust enrichment are interpreted as supplementary norms of contract laws, tort laws, and *negotiorum gestio* (management of business) laws, respectively. It is the first category—performance-based unjust enrichment—that supplements an *ex post* legal relationship when a contract is found to have no legal effect. When a given performance, such as making a payment, was carried out on the basis of a contract that is then found to have no legal effect, the benefit from such performance should be returned to the performer because the benefit is "without any legal grounds," as stipulated in CivC Article 741.

Therefore, it is when a contract is found null and void or is cancelled,

39 Supreme Court Decision 2014Da5531, June 25, 2015.

rescinded, or terminated so that it is found to have no legal effect that the law of unjust enrichment steps in and unwinds the benefits derived from performances based on that invalid contract. It should be noted, however, that there is a special provision on rescission. Article 548(1) of the CivC stipulates that if "one of the parties has rescinded the contract, each party shall be liable to restore the other party to his original position: Provided, that the rights of third persons shall not be prejudiced thereby." That is, the CivC makes clear that the rescission of a contract has a retroactive effect and that an obligation to restore the other party to its pre-contract position arises therefrom. In its legal nature, this is a special form of unjust enrichment specifically tailored to the rescission of a contract. Its legal effect is differentiated from ordinary unjust enrichment in that Article 548(2) states that interest accrues on the monies that are to be returned, regardless of the knowledge or ignorance of the unjustly enriched party about the legally groundless state, while ordinary unjust enrichment holds that an unjustly enriched party who did not know of that state is obliged to return only the amount that he or she still possesses, in accordance with Article 747(1).

7. Conclusion

In this chapter, I have addressed several key aspects of Korean contract law, focusing on contract formation and its validity, contract interpretation, breach of contract and remedies, and discharge of a contract, along with unjust enrichment, an issue that is often connected with the discharge or nullity of a contract. On the whole, legal doctrines in the ambit of Korean contract law have been formulated and developed in tune with international trends, thanks to myriad Supreme Court decisions and scholarly opinions that shed new light on the CivC. However, the CivC itself has remained the same since it came into force in 1960. Given that civil code reform has become a global trend in recent decades—Germany, France, China, and Japan are some examples of countries that have undertaken civil code revision—the next task for Korean contract law is to reform and amend the CivC to keep pace with the modernization of society and the ever-evolving globalization of contract law. In fact, CivC reform on a large scale has been attempted twice by the Ministry of Justice, resulting in a 2004 draft and a

2014 draft. However, neither draft made it through the legislative process, largely due to a lack of consensus for comprehensive change at the National Assembly level. Meanwhile, it remains imperative that the CivC, as the fundamental standard of all of Korean private law, provide an up-to-date normative foundation that reflects the needs of Korean society today and tomorrow. In this regard, civil code reform efforts deserve more attention.

Chapter 3

The Law of Real Rights

Ying-Chieh Wu*

1. Introduction

The Law of Real Rights provides for the rules on real rights. Real rights are rights exigible against anyone in the world. This topic is prescribed in Book II of the Civil Code of the Republic of Korea (CivC).[1] CivC adopts the Pandekten System and is thus divided into five books: (1) Book I: General Principles of Civil Law; (2) Book II: Law of Real Rights (Property); (3) Book III: Law of Personal Rights (Obligations); (4) Book IV: Family Law; and (5) Book V: Succession. This structural configuration was imported from the German Bürgerliches Gesetzbuch. The main structural difference between the two codes is that the orders of Books II and III are switched.

CivC was promulgated in 1958 and took effect in 1960. There have been 29 amendments, but no major revision of Book II has been made over the past 60 years. Thus, the Law of Real Rights remains relatively intact, although some special statutes have been enforced to supplement it.[2] Most

* Associate Professor, Seoul National University School of Law.

1 The Civil Code of the Republic of South Korea (CivC) (Official trans. Ministry of Government Legislation, National Law Information Center, Republic of Korea) at https://www.law.go.kr/engLsSc.do?menuId=1&subMenuId=21&tabMenuId=117&query=civil%20act#.

2 For example, the Provisional Registration Security Act (PRSA) and the Act on Security over Movable Property, Claims, Etc. (SMPC). These special acts deal with security interests and will be touched upon in this chapter.

importantly, its judicial interpretation has burgeoned and filled the gap between the law and reality.

Broadly speaking, the Law of Real Rights is divided into two parts: (1) the General Part (Articles 185 to 191) and (2) various types of real rights (Articles 192 to 372). In this chapter, the provisions contained in the General Part will not be explored separately as they are highly abstract. Instead, they will be explained alongside individual real rights for the sake of convenience and efficiency. Seven main real rights will be covered: ownership, superficies, easement, lump-sum lease, hypothec (plus mortgage), pledge (plus mortgage and charge), and lien. We will first explore some fundamental ideas forming the foundation of this area and then analyze the individual real rights enshrined in Book II of CivC.

2. Classification of Things, Real/Personal Rights, and the Numerus Clausus Rule

(1) Classification of Things

Under Korean civil law, 'things' include only physical things, electricity, and natural forces that can be controlled (CivC Article 98). In other words, objects existing only in a conceptual form (i.e., pure rights, such as debts or intellectual property rights) are outside the ambit of 'things.' Things can be classified into immovables and movables. Immovables pertain to land and things firmly affixed thereto (CivC Article 99(1)). Therefore, buildings are not part of land but are instead regarded as constituting separate immovables. In other words, land and buildings are two different types of immovable things. Trees are part of the land on which they stand, but if a cluster of trees are registered according to the Standing Timber Act[3] or are specifically and clearly indicated,[4] they are treated as distinct immovables. Movables are things other than immovables (CivC Article 99(2)). Chattels are archetypal movables.

3 The Standing Timber Act (Official trans. Ministry of Government Legislation, National Law Information Center, Republic of Korea) at https://www.law.go.kr/engLsSc.do?menuId=1&subMenuId=21&tabMenuId=117&query=standing%20timber%20act#.

4 Supreme Court Decision 98Ma1817, October 28, 1998.

(2) Real/Personal Rights

CivC provides for eight types of real rights: ownership; possession; superficies, easements, and lump-sum lease (usufruct rights); and hypothec, pledge, and lien (security rights). Therefore, the holders of these real rights can assert their rights against anyone in the world. On the other hand, personal rights, generally arising from contracts, unjust enrichment, negotiorum gestio, and torts, are exigible only against some specified persons. In other words, a real-right holder can exclude anyone who interferes with his/her real right while a personal-right holder cannot. Furthermore, a real right is protected in a bankruptcy procedure while a personal right is not. The different treatment in bankruptcy or the possibility of actions for recovery ahead of other creditors is the hallmark of all real rights. This is also where an important dichotomy rests.[5]

The object of a real right is generally a physical thing. For example, both land and chattels can be objects of ownership. However, only land can qualify as the object of superficies, easements, lump-sum lease, and hypothec, while chattels are the typical objects of pledge and lien. That said, it must be noted that pure rights, although not recognized as things, can also be the objects of real rights. As discussed in this chapter, a pure right, such as a debt or intellectual property, can be the object of a pledge (i.e., pledge of rights). Furthermore, a real right itself, such as superficies and lump-sum lease, can be offered as the object of a hypothec. Therefore, land, chattels, and pure rights can all be made into objects according to the relevant type of real right.

The foregoing suggests a theoretical lesson. That is, we must distinguish

5 It must be noted that both real- and personal-right holders can claim for damages on the basis of the tort law (CivC Article 750) against a person who interferes with their rights. Thus, for example, those who (1) interfere with another's land through illegal entry, (2) do not return their chattels, or (3) intentionally infringe upon another's personal right all have the obligation, by operation of law (i.e., tort law), to make good the loss incurred by the right (either real or personal) holder in monetary form. The rationale for this is quite obvious: both real and personal rights deserve protection by virtue of the fact that they are rights; otherwise, they can hardly be called rights. However, whether a right can be protected by tort law via monetary compensation and whether a right can be protected ahead of other creditors by way of an action for recovery must be demarcated. Only real rights have the latter feature; thus, such feature is the main difference between a real right and a personal right, -and the availability of tort claims does not help.

between two questions: What are 'things' in law? What can be the objects of real rights? The answer to the first question is, as we have seen, physical things, controllable electricity, and natural forces. However, the answer to the second question is that both physical things and pure rights can be objects of real rights. Obviously, the scope of the latter is wider than that of the former. This is where a caveat is required when studying the civil law of real rights.

(3) The Numerus Clausus Rule

The numerus clausus rule states that real rights cannot be created at will, and only those provided for by statutes or customary law can be regarded as real rights (CivC Article 185). This means that both the types and content of any real rights must be pre-established by law. (As an aside, only a limited number of real rights with fixed content are available in the market.) Parties cannot privately invent new types of real rights or change the content of the existing real rights as they please. The rationale behind this rule is that the law should make the public know with certainty what kinds of real rights exist in the country so that they can check if any of such real rights are attached to a thing they intend to deal with. This protects third parties (i.e., potential buyers, etc.) from being prejudiced by any unexpected or unheard-of real rights. To sum up, the justification for the numerus clausus rule lies in the nature of a real right itself, its universal binding effect: If you want me to be bound by something, you should at least give me a chance to know of its existence in advance. As mentioned earlier, CivC recognizes eight real rights. Except for possession, they are the main focus of this chapter.

3. Ownership (*Soyugwon*) with Respect to Chattels

(1) Acquisition

Real agreement by way of transfer of possession. The first real right to be explored is ownership. Ownership of chattels involves the right to use, profit, and dispose of chattels within the scope of the law (CivC Article 211). Ownership is the most free and comprehensive real right that a person can enjoy, although it cannot be exercised in a way that the law does not permit (i.e., in an illegal way, such as harming another's body or property). To acquire ownership of a chattel, the following requirement must be met: a real agreement (*dingliche Einigung*) accompanied by the transfer of the chattel's possession. Say A wants to purchase a chattel from B. A and B must reach a real agreement with respect to the transfer of ownership of the chattel itself. Here, the real agreement involves B's intention to transfer ownership of the chattel to A and A's intention to obtain it from B. This is different from the obligational agreement arising from a contract. A contract generates only mutual obligations. That is, it involves only the parties' intentions to owe an obligation to each other. A real agreement, on the other hand, is an agreement that finalizes the transfer of ownership of the chattel to A. But how is this real agreement made? In principle, it is considered to be made at the time the chattel is physically delivered by B to A and A assumes physical possession of it. Thus, the transfer of ownership of a chattel takes effect when the possession of the chattel is transferred by the chattel's owner to the chattel's purchaser (CivC Article 188(1)) because that is when the real agreement is accomplished. In the aforementioned scenario, A thus acquires ownership of the chattel when B transfers its possession to him/her, not at the moment the contract is concluded.

Prescriptive acquisition. The second mode by which ownership can be obtained is through prescription. A person acquires ownership of a chattel belonging to another by operation of law if he/she, with the intention of owning the chattel, possesses it peaceably and openly for 10 years (CivC Article 246(1)). However, if a person obtains possession of a chattel belonging to another in good faith, not knowing that the chattel belongs to another (without any negligence in not knowing such), he/she acquires ownership of the chattel after 5 years of peaceable and open possession of it (CivC Article 246(2)). For example, if A bought chattel X from B but the deal is void and the ownership of X is not transferred to him/her (A), A does not acquire ownership of X. However, if A possesses X for 10 years knowing that the purchase deal was void, or for 5 years not knowing that the purchase deal was void, he/she acquires ownership of X. As the possessor of a chattel automatically acquires ownership of it after the passage of certain prescriptive periods, the acquisition is effectuated by operation of law. This ultimately deprives the original holder of the chattel of his/her ownership of it. The rule of prescriptive acquisition aims to secure legal stability by maintaining the status quo and sacrificing the original owner.

Accessio, *confusio*, and *specificatio*. Ownership of a chattel can also be acquired through *accessio*, *confusio*, or *specificatio*. If two chattels belonging to different owners are so combined that they can no longer be separated without being damaged or incurring excessive expenses, the ownership of the composite chattel, according to the rule of *accessio*, belongs to the owner of the principal chattel. Therefore, the owner of the accessory chattel loses his/her ownership of it. If no distinction can be made between the principal and accessory chattels, the owners of such chattels lose their original ownership of these but shall have shares (i.e., ownership in common) of the composite chattel according to the values of their respective chattels at the time these were combined (CivC Article 257).

If mixed things have identical natures and are thus mutually indistinguishable (e.g., beans, apples, rice), the rule of *confusio* applies. According to this rule, the owners of the chattels lose their original ownership of these but shall have shares (i.e., ownership in common) in the mixture according to the values of their respective chattels at the time these were mixed (CivC Articles 258 and 257).

Finally, if a person has processed a chattel belonging to another, the rule of *specificatio* applies, and the ownership of the processed chattel shall belong to the owner of the raw material. However, if the value of the processed chattel significantly exceeds that of the raw material, the person who processed the chattel acquires ownership of the processed chattel (CivC Article 259(1)).

When ownership or co-ownership is acquired through the three aforementioned rules, the acquisition is not consensual but is effectuated by operation of law. Those who lost ownership are entitled to claim compensation according to the rules of unjust enrichment (CivC Article 261).

Immediate acquisition. Ownership of a chattel can also be acquired via the rule of immediate (or bona fide) acquisition. This is a rule that enables a transferee to obtain valid ownership of a chattel even if the transferor has no good title to it. The legal rule *nemo dat quod non habet* (i.e., no one can transfer what he/she does not have) cannot defeat a bona fide purchaser's interest. Therefore, even if the transferor has no good title to the chattel disposed of or sold, the transferee can still acquire ownership of the chattel provided he/she (1) has started to possess the chattel peaceably and openly and (2) believed that the transferor was the genuine owner of the chattel at the time of the transaction, and was not negligent in believing so

(CivC Article 249). This is another case in which ownership is procured by operation of law. The main purpose of this rule is to protect the security of commerce. Chattels are generally not earmarked, and potential buyers do not know for sure who really owns a chattel under negotiation. The law therefore presumes that whoever is in possession of a chattel is its legal owner (CivC Article 200). Thus, potential buyers can proceed with their purchase deals, relying on the other party's possession of the chattel being bought as proof of such party's ownership of it. As long as the transferee is not negligent in believing that the transferor has a good title to the chattel, he/she acquires ownership of the chattel by virtue of the rule of immediate (bona fide) acquisition. That said, this may seem unfair to the true owner of the chattel, especially if the relevant chattel is a stolen or lost chattel. Thus, the law attempts to strike a balance by prescribing that the true owner can recover the chattel within two years after it was stolen or lost (CivC Article 250).

Discovery. Last but not least, whoever discovers an ownerless chattel acquires its ownership, provided he/she takes possession of it with an intention to own it (CivC Article 252). In other words, finders are keepers, and new ownership of the discovered chattel arises by operation of law. However, the rule of discovery does not apply to treasure troves or cultural heritage, whose ownership is vested in the state (CivC Articles 254 and 255).

(2) Rights

Ownership bestows upon its holder the right to use, profit from, and dispose of the chattel owned (CivC Article 211). Therefore, ownership involves a bundle of rights and is the most inclusive real right. The other real rights are carved out of ownership. If a person's ownership of a chattel is infringed upon or the chattel is taken by another, the owner has the right to demand the chattel's return (CivC Article 213). This is the so-called *rei vindicatio* claim rooted in Roman law. The owner can also eliminate another's interference in the chattel's ownership and in the exercise of the accompanying rights, or prevent another's imminent infringement on such (CivC Article 214). These three remedies are directly given by the Law of Real Rights itself, and the interferer's fault is irrelevant; the existence of infringement or imminent interference suffices for the owner to exercise such remedies. They are therefore demarcated from actions premised on tort law, which requires tortfeasor fault (CivC Article 750). A chattel owner can rely on the remedies awarded by both laws, although double compensation is not allowed concerning the chattel infringed upon. The two laws differ in requirements, but the remedies prescribed in the Law of Real Rights are preferable because they do not require the claimant to prove the interferer's fault.

(3) Extinction

Ownership of a chattel is extinguished once the chattel is completely destroyed, sold to another, or given up by the owner.

4. Ownership (*Soyugwon*) with Respect to Immovables

(1) Acquisition

Real agreement and registration. Ownership with respect to immovables can be acquired through a real agreement and registration. The owner of an immovable has the right to use, take profits from, and dispose of the immovable owned (CivC Article 211). As with chattels, however, to acquire ownership of an immovable, two requirements must be met: a real agreement (*dingliche Einigung*) and registration. Article 186 of CivC provides that the acquisition of a real right in immovables takes effect only when such immovables are registered. Ownership, being a real right, must also be registered if its object is an immovable: no registration, no title acquisition. Even though we can assume that a real agreement (i.e., the mutual agreement on the transfer of ownership)[6] is reached once the seller of an immovable (e.g., a piece of land) hands over all the relevant title documents to the buyer (because this is the moment when the seller intends to finalize the disposition), that is not sufficient. The real agreement must be supported by registration. Registration is a condition for a real agreement to take effect. That said, some exceptions may apply. Ownership with respect to immovables can be acquired shorn of a real agreement and registration, provided the immovables are acquired via inheritance, expropriation, a

6 This real agreement is different from a contractual agreement, which only creates the parties' personal obligations.

judgment, an auction, or other stipulated grounds (CivC Article 187). In these cases, ownership arises by operation of law. However, if a person who acquires ownership of an immovable through any of the aforementioned exceptional ways wants to dispose of the immovable or sell it to another, he/she has to register the relevant ownership under his/her name (CivC Article 187, proviso). Before a person can dispose of an immovable in the market, it must be ascertained that he/she is its owner. To sum up, the acquisition of ownership in immovables requires a real agreement and registration, subject to the exceptions prescribed in Article 187 of CivC.

Prescriptive acquisition. Ownership of an immovable can be obtained by satisfying the requirements of prescriptive acquisition. A person acquires a right to register ownership of an immovable belonging to another if he/she, with an intention to acquire ownership of the immovable, has been in peaceable and open possession of it for 20 years (CivC Article 246(1)). If a person has registered ownership of an immovable belonging to another but has done so in good faith and without any negligence in not knowing that the immovable belonged to another, he/she acquires ownership of it after 10 years of peaceable and open possession of it (CivC Article 246(2)). It must be noted that in the former scenario, the possessor is only entitled to request that the current registered holder of the immovable transfer its ownership to him/her. The nature of this claim is considered a personal right.[7] Therefore, technically, it is not a mechanism that generates ownership. In the latter scenario, however, ownership is acquired. Unlike with chattels, Korean law does not allow immediate acquisition of immovables. Hence, if a person purchases a piece of land from someone who is not its true owner, or if the purchase deal is void and thus no title transfer happens, such person cannot obtain a good title to the land despite his/her being a bona fide purchaser of it. However, relying on the rule of prescription enshrined in Article 246(2) of CivC, he/she can argue that he/she has now become the owner of the land. Again, the law endeavors to maintain legal stability because many interested parties may become involved in the matter after a certain period.

Accessio. Under the rule of *accessio,* the owner of an immovable acquires ownership of anything affixed thereto (CivC Article 256). For example, if wallpaper is attached to a building or a postbox is affixed to a

7 Supreme Court Decision 95Da34866, 34873, March 8, 1996.

piece of land, it becomes part of the building or land. Therefore, the owner of a piece of land or a building will acquire ownership of the wallpaper or postbox affixed by someone else to the building or land. The person who lost ownership of the affixed thing is entitled to claim compensation for it according to the rules of unjust enrichment (KTA Article 261). However, if the owner of the thing attached to an immovable retains the title to it, the rule of *accessio* does not apply (CivC Article 256, proviso). Thus, if a person grows some plants or crops on another's land, the land owner does not obtain ownership of the plants or crops because these belong to those who have taken care of them.[8] Furthermore, if a lessee has installed a new door lock, he/she retains ownership of it and can thus uninstall it when the lease ends. The landlord does not acquire ownership of the new door lock.

(2) Rights

If one's ownership of an immovable is infringed upon by another, the owner is entitled to demand the return of the immovable (i.e., the right of *rei vindicatio*) if it is illegally occupied by the infringer (CivC Article 213). The owner can also eliminate another's interference or prevent another's imminent infringement (CivC Article 214). That said, the right of *rei vindicatio* and that of elimination are identical remedies because they can be exercised only in the form of ejectment. (Unlike in the case of chattels, it is literally impossible to ask someone to return a piece of land.) The three aforementioned remedies are directly provided by the Law of Real Rights itself, and an interferer's fault is irrelevant. The existence of infringement or imminent interference suffices for the owner of the immovable to exercise any of such remedies. The three remedies are thus demarcated from those actions premised on tort law, which requires tortfeasor fault (CivC Article 750). The owner of the immovable can rely on the remedies awarded by both laws, although double compensation is not allowed with regard to the immovable interfered with. The two laws differ in requirements, but the remedies prescribed in the Law of Real Rights are preferable because they do not require the claimant to prove the interferer's fault.

8 Supreme Court Decision 79Da784, August 28, 1978.

(3) Extinction

Ownership of an immovable is extinguished once the immovable is completely destroyed, sold, registered under another's name, or given up by the owner.

5. Co-ownership

(1) Ownership in Common

There are three types of co-ownership. The first and most common type is ownership in common, by which two or more persons can own a thing in proportion to their respective shares of it (CivC Article 262(1)). Here, five matters merit mentioning. First, there is still only one ownership, but it is proportionally divided among the co-owners in the form of shares.[9] Second, the co-owners are not allowed to dispose of the thing co-owned (CivC Article 263) but are allowed to dispose of their respective shares of it (CivC Article 264). Third, each co-owner's share can be inherited by his/her heirs. Fourth, each co-owner can demand division of the thing co-owned (CivC Article 268(1)). The commonly adopted methods for this are physical division and monetary compensation. If the thing is indivisible or if the co-owners fail to reach an agreement regarding how to divide it, any co-owner can ask the court to decide how the division should be done (CivC Article 269(1). Fifth, the questions of management and whether to dispose of the thing co-owned are resolved by a majority of the co-owners' shares (CivC Article 265) rather than by a majority of the co-owners. For the expenses (repair costs or tax) incurred in relation to the thing co-owned, all the co-owners are liable for these in proportion to their respective shares of the thing co-owned (CivC Article 266(1)).

(2) Joint Ownership

The second type of co-ownership to be explored herein is joint ownership.

9 Supreme Court Decision 91Da27228, November 12, 1991.

This is a form of co-ownership that applies to the partners in a partnership or to the members of other relationships prescribed by law[10] (CivC Article 271(1)). The thing jointly owned is generally related to the common purposes pursued by the joint owners. Therefore, despite the fact that joint ownership and ownership in common are similar in that the owners have fixed shares of the thing co-owned or jointly owned, they are significantly different in the following respects. First, joint owners are not permitted to dispose of their shares of the thing jointly owned unless all the other joint owners agree to such (CivC Article 273(1)). In the case of the death of a joint owner, his/her heirs cannot succeed to the deceased shares of the thing jointly owned because they are irrelevant to the business purpose being pursued by the other joint owners. The rule of survivorship applies, and the other joint owners succeed to the share of the deceased. Second, joint owners cannot request the division of the thing jointly owned (CivC Article 273(2)) as such division may harm the execution of the business purpose being pursued by the joint owners. Third, the management or disposition of the thing jointly owned is determined by the unanimous consent of all the joint owners (CivC Article 272) unless otherwise provided for in the covenants made by the members' association.

(3) Collective Ownership

The last type of ownership is collective ownership. It applies to the members of unincorporated associations (CivC Article 275(1)). Unlike ownership in common and joint ownership, the members of unincorporated associations do not enjoy any share of the thing collectively owned by them. Thus, there are no shares of the thing collectively owned by them that can be transferred to another and that other persons can succeed to. As to the management or disposition of the thing collectively owned, this is determined in the general meetings of the members (CivC Article 276(1)), unless otherwise provided for in the articles of association or in the covenants made by the members of the association (CivC Article 275(2)). Even the use and enjoyment of the thing collectively owned must be done in accordance with the articles of association or with the covenants made by the members of the association (CivC Article 276(2)).

10 For example, trustees are joint owners of trust property (Trust Act, Article 50(1)).

6. Superficies (*Jisanggwon*)

(1) Acquisition

Real agreement and registration. Superficies is a real right that entitles its holder to use another's land for the purpose of establishing a building or structure or planting trees thereon and owning these (CivC Article 279). Furthermore, the space on or under the ground may be demarcated into upper or lower parts and may become the subject matter of superficies for owning a building or structure (CivC Article 289-2). The Supreme Court[11] goes further and states that even graves can be the subject matter of superficies. As with ownership in land, to acquire superficies with respect to land, two requirements must be met: a real agreement (an agreement on the grant of superficies itself) and registration (CivC Article 186).

Prescriptive acquisition. Superficies can be acquired by prescription. There is no need to explain this in detail here because what was mentioned earlier regarding the prescriptive acquisition of ownership also applies to superficies. Thus, Article 245 of CivC applies *mutatis mutandis* to the acquisition of superficies (CivC Article 248).

Acquisition by operation of law. If a piece of land and a building thereon belong to one and the same person but either the land or the building is later vested in another, the owner or the real-right holder of the building acquires superficies with respect to the land by operation of law. Say A owns land X and building Y thereon and B has a lump-sum lease over Y. B has a real right to use Y and the relevant part of X on which Y stands. However, A subsequently disposes of X to C. In this case, a superficies will arise by operation of law (CivC Article 305(1)) over the part of X on which Y stands. C thus cannot exclude B. The rationale behind the creation of superficies by operation of law is to protect B's reliance on the continuous use of the relevant part of X and to preserve the economic value of Y by preventing C, the new owner of X, from requesting B to tear down Y. Fundamentally, this problem results from the fact that land and the buildings thereon are considered two separate immovables.

11 Supreme Court Decision 86Daka2919, February 23, 1988.

(2) Rights

First, people use superficies to own buildings, structures, or trees. These are immovables and thus cannot be moved easily, and it will take a relatively long time for their owners to benefit from them. Thus, the law prescribes that the duration of superficies shall not be less than (1) 30 years if the superficies is for owning buildings made of stone, lime, brick, or other similarly strong materials, or for owning trees; (2) 15 years if the superficies is for owning buildings other than the aforementioned ones; and (3) 5 years if the superficies is for owning structures other than buildings (CivC Article 280(1)). Therefore, holders of superficies have a right to enjoy their immovables on another's land for a rather long period.

Second, if a building, other structure, or trees remain on another's land upon the termination of the superficies, the superficiary may request the renewal of the superficies (CivC Article 283(1)). If the superficies grantor refuses to renew the superficies, the superficiary can request the grantor to purchase the immovable on the land at a reasonable price (CivC Article 283(2)).[12] The holder of the superficies can demand the return of the immovable (i.e., the right of *rei vindicatio*) if it is illegally occupied by another (CivC Articles 290 and 213),[13] and can also eliminate another's interference with, or prevent another's imminent infringement upon, his/her use of the land (CivC Articles 290 and 214). Third, a superficiary, being a real-right holder, may transfer the superficies to another or lease out the land within the duration of the superficies. The transfer is allowed even if the superficies grantor does not give permission for such.[14]

(3) Extinction

The right of superficies is extinguished when the land on which the building, structure, or trees thereon that are the subject matter of the superficies are

12 However, the superficiary loses his/her right to request the superficies grantor to purchase the immovable on the land if the reason for the termination of the superficies is the superficiary's default in paying rent to the grantor (Supreme Court Decision 93Da39925, June 29, 1993).

13 This is done by ejecting the person occupying the land because it is impossible to return immovables.

14 Supreme Court Decision 90Da15716, November 8, 1991.

destroyed. It also ends when its duration expires. In such a circumstance, if the grantor of the superficies makes a request to purchase the relevant building, structure, or trees at a reasonable price, the superficiary may not refuse such request without justifiable reason (CivC Article 285(2)). The right of superficies is also terminated if the grantor claims termination when the superficiary defaults in paying the rent for two years (CivC Article 287). Last but not least, if the superficiary fails to exercise his/her right for 20 years, the rule of extinctive prescription applies (CivC Article 162(2)). The superficies therefore becomes extinct.

7. Easement (*Jiyeoggwon*)

(1) Acquisition

Real agreement and registration. Easement is a real right that entitles its holder (i.e., the dominant tenement) to use the land of another (i.e., the servient tenement) for the convenience and benefit of his/her own land for a certain purpose (CivC Article 291). To acquire superficies with respect to land, two requirements must be met: a real agreement (an agreement on the grant of easement itself)[15] and registration (CivC Article 186).

Prescriptive acquisition. Easement can be acquired by prescription. There is no need to explain this in detail here because what was mentioned earlier regarding the prescriptive acquisition of ownership is also applicable, *mutatis mutandis*, to easement. Thus, Article 245 of CivC applies *mutatis mutandis* to the acquisition of easement (CivC Article 248).

Acquisition by operation of law. If a piece of land has no access to a public road (which is necessary for the use of the land) without passing over the surrounding land, and the owner of the land thus cannot reach the public road without passing over the surrounding land, or if the cost of reaching the public road would be excessive, the owner of the land may pass over the surrounding land to reach the public road. This is the so-called right of way. However, the method and place of passing over must be so chosen as to cause the least possible damage to the surrounding land (CivC Article 219).

15 This real agreement is different from a contractual agreement, which only creates the parties' personal obligations.

No real agreement (i.e., the intention to grant an easement) is required between the servient tenement and the dominant tenement. The easement arises by operation of law simply because the latter's land is closed off and has no exit to a public road.

(2) Rights

The dominant tenement has the right to use the servient tenement's land. He/she can also eliminate another's interference with, or prevent another's imminent infringement upon, his/her use of the land for the purpose of passing over it to reach a public road (CivC Articles 301 and 214). It must be noted that the right to request the return of land has no application in easement because the dominant tenement is not in continuous possession of the servient tenement's land. Such right is left for the owner of the land (i.e., the servient tenement) to exercise. The aforementioned right to eliminate interference and to prevent imminent infringement shall suffice for the dominant tenement. The right of a dominant tenement has two characteristics worth mentioning. First, the dominant tenement's right under an easement is ancillary to his/her land. Therefore, if the dominant tenement disposes of his/her land or sells it to another, the easement follows. Second, the dominant tenement is forbidden from selling only his/her easement right to another (CivC Article 292).

(3) Extinction

Easement relationships come to an end when the land involved is destroyed. If the dominant tenement sells his/her land to another, he/she will lose his/her right of easement, but the new landowner will succeed to it as the easement follows the land it attaches to. Finally, if the dominant tenement fails to exercise his/her right under easement for 20 years, the rule of extinctive prescription applies (CivC Article 162(2)). The easement therefore becomes extinct.

8. Lump-Sum Lease (*Jeonsegwon*)

(1) Acquisition

Real agreement and registration. Lump-sum lease is a real right that (1) entitles its holder (i.e., the lessee) to possess and use the immovable of another (i.e., the lessor) by paying a lump-sum deposit[16] to the latter, and that (2) empowers the lessee to recoup his/her deposit on the immovable ahead of the lessor's other personal creditors should the lessor fail to return the deposit (CivC Article 303(1)). In this case, as the amount of the deposit is generally extremely high, the lessee does not have to pay any rent to the lessor, but the lessor takes the interest arising from the deposit. As the lessee can recoup his/her deposit from the leased immovable ahead of the lessor's other personal creditors if the lessor defaults in returning the deposit, lump-sum lease also has the nature of a security right. To acquire lump-sum lease of an immovable, two requirements must be met: a real agreement (an agreement on the grant of lump-sum lease itself)[17] and registration (CivC Article 186). This is the only way by which lump-sum lease can be created. It must be stressed that the subject matter of lump-sum leases in the market is generally a house or an apartment.

(2) Rights

The lessee, as a real-right holder, is entitled not only to possess, use, or take profits from the immovable leased, but also to exclude and prevent anyone from infringing upon these rights (CivC Articles 219, 213, and 214). However, some complications merit elaboration. First, if the lessor does not own the land on which the leased building stands and has a superficies on such land, then the lessee's lump-sum lease also enjoys the superficies attached to the lessor's building (CivC Article 304(1)). Second, if the lessor owns both the land and the building thereon and a lump-sum lease is created on the building, then a superficies will be created by operation of law if the lessor

16 In practice, the amount generally reaches 70% of the whole value of the immovable leased.

17 This real agreement is different from a contractual agreement, which only creates the parties' personal obligations.

sells the land to another (CivC Article 305(1)). Third, if the lessee has attached a thing (e.g., a new door lock or new curtains) to the immovable with the lessor's permission, the lessee has the right to request the lessor to purchase the thing attached (CivC Article 316(2)). Fourth, unless otherwise prohibited when the lump-sum lease is granted, the lessee has the power to transfer his/her lump-sum lease to another or to offer the lump-sum lease as security to his/her creditor (CivC Article 306). Finally, the lessee can recoup his/her deposit on the immovable to which the lump-sum lease is attached ahead of the lessor's other personal creditors should the lessor default in returning the deposit to the lessee (CivC Article 318).

(3) Extinction

The lump-sum lease relationship ends when the agreed-upon period for it expires. Moreover, the lessor can terminate the lump-sum lease if the lessee fails to use or take profits from the immovable according to the terms of the lease (CivC Article 311). Finally, the lump-sum lease is also extinguished when the relevant immovable is destroyed.

(4) Housing Lease Protection Act (HLPA)

In lump-sum lease, the lessee's right is a real right. It is attached to the immovable and is thus binding on third-party transferees. Lump-sum lease is widely used in South Korea, but some landlords are reluctant to use it as it accords a real right to the lessee. Such landlords alternatively choose to use a similar mechanism provided for in the law of contract: contractual lease. In contractual lease, the lessee generally provides the landlord (i.e., the lessor) with a smaller deposit (compared to that in lump-sum lease) and pays monthly rent. As the contractual lease, however, gives the lessee only a contractual right, it cannot bind the subsequent transferees. This allows the lessor to easily dispose of his/her immovable. Furthermore, in contractual lease, the lessee does not have a right to recoup his/her deposit ahead of the lessor's other personal creditors. This causes serious problems especially for those who need to rent a house or an apartment to live in but cannot afford lump-sum lease, which requires the payment of a large amount of money to the landlord up front. In other words, in contractual lease, the lessees are in a relatively weak position and at a higher risk of being ejected from the house or apartment they are leasing and living in.

In response to the aforementioned problem, a special statute was enacted in 1981: the Housing Lease Protection Act (HLPA).[18] Four points regarding this law merit mentioning. First, the minimum period for contractual lease is two years (HLPA Article 4(1)). This rule binds the lessor but not the lessee; the lessee can request a contract for less than two years. This rule was established to ensure the lessee's stability of residence and to prevent the lessor from increasing the rent every year. Second, once the lessee moves in, begins to possess the house or apartment, and completes the resident registration, his/her rights are binding on the subsequent third-party transferees of the rental property (HLPA Article 3(1)). Third, the lessee is entitled to recoup his/her deposit from the house or apartment ahead of the landlord's other personal creditors should the landlord fail to return the deposit (HLPA Article 3-2(2)). Finally, the lessor cannot refuse to renew the contract without justifiable grounds (HLPA Articles 6 and 6-3). To sum up, functionally, contractual lease has become akin to lump-sum lease despite the fact that the former is contractual and the latter is proprietary. It seems that the possibility of publicizing the lease (i.e., resident registration and possession) has made it possible for contractual lease to straddle two areas of private law.

9. Hypothec (*Jeodanggwon*)

(1) Acquisition

Real agreement and registration. Under a hypothec, the lender is entitled to recoup the money he/she has lent out, ahead of other creditors, from the immovable that the debtor or a third person furnished as security, without transferring its possession (CivC Article 356). The amount of the debt does not have to be fixed from the beginning as the line-of-credit hypothec is also valid (CivC Article 357). However, debt crystalizes when it comes due. The

18 The Housing Lease Protection Act (Official trans. Ministry of Government Legislation, National Law Information Center, Republic of Korea) at https://www.law.go.kr/engLsSc.do?menuId=1&subMenuId=21&tabMenuId=117&query=%EC%9E%84%EB%8C%80%EC%B0%A8%EB%B3%B4%ED%98%B8%EB%B2%95#.

line-of-credit hypothec then turns into a general hypothec[19] with ascertained debt. There are two requirements: a real agreement (an agreement on the grant of hypothec itself) and registration (CivC Article 186). The owner of the immovable furnished as a security can not only retain ownership of it but also continue to possess it. If the subject matter of the hypothec is provided by a third person, a real agreement is made not between the debtor and the creditor but between the third person and the creditor. Furthermore, the aforementioned superficies and lump-sum lease can also be the subject matter of a hypothec (CivC Article 370). In these cases, what is offered is a right to possess and use the relevant immovable (plus the lump-sum money in the case of lump-sum lease), creating a legal structure of right against right.

Acquisition by operation of law. A hypothec may be imposed by operation of law if the following two requirements are met: (1) if the contractual lessee who has a building on the leased land delays payment of rent for two years and (2) if the lessor seizes the building furnished as security to recoup the rent in default. In such a case, the law deems the seizure as having the same effect as a hypothec (CivC Article 649).

(2) Rights

The creditor's hypothec secures the principal and its interest, penalties, liquidation damages, and expenses for the enforcement of the hypothec. However, for the interest arising from a default, the hypothec can be exercised only as regards payments due within one year after their respective deadlines (CivC Article 360). When the value of the hypothec's subject matter has significantly decreased due to the debtor's fault, the creditor can require the debtor to recover it or to offer another reasonable security (CivC Article 362). The creditor can also exclude or prevent anyone from infringing upon the immovable offered as security (CivC Articles 370 and 214). However, the creditor does not have the right to ask for the return of the possession of the relevant immovable (i.e., *rei vindicatio*) because he/she does not have any power to possess and use it.

If the debtor defaults in paying his/her debt, the creditor is entitled to recoup it from the immovable ahead of the debtor's other personal creditors

19 Supreme Court Decision 97Da25521, December 9, 1992.

(CivC Article 356). However, some exceptions apply here, such as certain taxes (e.g., inheritance tax: National Tax Act Article 35(1)(iii)) and deposits of small amounts (e.g., HLPA Article 8). Furthermore, the rule of real subrogation applies (CivC Articles 370 and 342). Thus, if the subject matter of the hypothec is substituted for another thing (e.g., if the government expropriates the land under a hypothec and another piece of land is given as compensation) or right (e.g., a claim to payment against the insurance company when the land is damaged), the hypothec will become attached to that thing or right. Last but not least, if the debtor in a hypothec has constructed a building on the land after a hypothec was created over such land, and if the debtor defaults on the payment of his/her debt, the creditor may sell such building by auction, together with the land. However, the creditor has no right to recoup the money he/she has lent out from the proceeds of the building ahead of the debtor's other personal creditors (CivC Article 365). The purpose of this is to facilitate the sale of the land offered as security. The existence of a building may hamper its sale at an auction. However, the creditor is not prioritized in recouping the money he/she has lent out from the proceeds of the sale of the building because the building was not the subject matter of the debt *ab initio*. He/she is only a personal creditor with regard to the proceeds of the sale of the building.

(3) Extinction

As a hypothec is ancillary to the debt it secures, it is extinguished once the debt it secures becomes defunct due to extinctive prescription[20] or satisfaction (CivC Article 369). It is also terminated if the immovable offered as security is destroyed.

(4) Ownership-based Security Interests over Immovables

Hypothec is a security interest imposed upon an immovable (i.e., land or a building) belonging to the debtor (or a third person). Thus, the security interest granted to the creditor is a hypothec, and the debtor's ownership of the relevant immovable remains unchanged. However, the realization of a hypothec must be carried out through an auction and is thus time-

20 Extinctive prescription of a personal right occurs if it is not exercised for a period of 10 years (CivC Article 162).

consuming and incurs further expenses. This may not be favored by creditors or debtors.

To bypass the aforementioned cumbersome process, debts are sometimes secured by the following two ownership-based mechanisms: (1) provisional registration of the right to require the debtor to transfer ownership of the immovable offered as security to the creditor and (2) mortgage (*Budongsan-Yangdodambo*). Under the former, the creditor and debtor agree to the transfer of ownership of the immovable to the creditor for the purpose of securing the loan, followed by a provisional registration of the creditor's right to demand the transfer of ownership of the immovable to him/her. The creditor is then entitled to have the immovable's ownership registered under his/her name if the debtor falls into default. In the case of mortgage, the debtor simply transfers the ownership of an immovable to the creditor to secure the loan,[21] and the creditor gives the debtor an option to repurchase the immovable or to conclude a resale contract between them. In both cases, the creditor obtains ownership of the immovable if the debtor fails to repay the loan. The use of these ownership-based security mechanisms is obviously convenient and efficient for the creditor, but it may be seriously disadvantageous to the debtor if he/she loses ownership of the immovable immediately after the debt falls due and he/she is unable to pay it, especially if the value of the immovable exceeds his/her debt. Thus, the Provisional Registration Security Act (PRSA) states that the creditor can obtain ownership of the immovable offered as security only after paying the difference in value between the debt and the immovable. However, this can be processed only two months after the creditor informs the debtor of the amount of the difference in value between the debt and the immovable (PRSA Articles 3(1) and 4). These provisions aim to give the debtor another chance to redeem the immovable and to protect his/her interest by preventing the creditor from obtaining extra value or a value exceeding his/her debt to the creditor.

21 This can be done through a loan or sale. In the case of a sale, the purchase money that the seller (i.e., the debtor) receives from the buyer (i.e., the creditor) is *de facto* a loan in nature.

10. Pledge *(Jilgwon)*

(1) Acquisition

Real agreement and registration. A pledgee of movables is entitled to hold possession of the movable that he/she received from the debtor or a third person as security for the debt, and to recoup the money he/she has lent out from the movable ahead of the debtor's other creditors (CivC Article 329). Two requirements are required here: a real agreement (an agreement on the grant of pledge itself) and transfer of possession (CivC Articles 188 and 330). The creditor takes possession of the subject matter of the pledge.[22] Immovables, although capable of being possessed, cannot be the subject matter of a pledge; instead, hypothec is used for immovables. Objects not physical in form, such as intangible personal rights (e.g., debts), can also be the subject matter of a pledge (CivC Article 345). However, debts cannot be possessed as they are not corporeal. Instead, a notice must be given to the original debtor about the creation of a pledge over the debt (CivC Articles 345 and 450(1)). When the debtor has become aware of the existence of the pledge, he/she cannot defeat the new creditor's claim by arguing that his/her debt has already been paid.

Acquisition by operation of law. A pledge is sometimes created by operation of law. For example, if the lessor of a building seizes any movable owned by the lessee to secure a personal right arising from the lease relationship (e.g., rent or damages), it is deemed effective as a pledge (CivC Article 650).

(2) Rights

The creditor's security interest under a pledge secures the principal and its interest, penalties, liquidation damages, and expenses for the enforcement of the pledge. As to the interest arising from default, as mentioned earlier, a hypothec can be exercised only as regards debt payments due one year after their respective deadlines (CivC Article 360). There is no such qualification for a pledge. This is because a hypothec may have another creditor with

22 Thus, a pledge is a powerful security interest for creditors.

a second hypothec; thus, there is a need to limit the scope of the interest arising from the default. Otherwise, the second hypothec's holder might not be able to recoup the money he/she has lent out. However, such damage rarely arises in practice with regard to pledges because there are few cases in which multiple creditors hold a pledge over a single chattel.

The scope of the secured debt is thus wider than that of the pledge. The creditor under a pledge has the power to possess the relevant chattel (CivC Article 335) and can thus exclude or prevent anyone from infringing upon the movable offered as security (CivC Articles 204 to 206). Once the debtor defaults in paying the debt, the creditor is entitled to recoup the money he/she has lent out from the movable, ahead of the debtor's other personal creditors (CivC Article 329). To do this, the creditor may sell the pledged chattel at an auction (CivC Article 338(1)) or may apply to the court to have the pledged chattel appropriated to the extent of its value to recoup the money lent out, with appraisal by an expert (CivC Article 338(2)). If the subject matter of the pledge is a debtor's debt to another debtor, the pledgee/creditor may request the debtor's debtor to pay the debt he/she owes the debtor directly to the creditor, but only the portion of it corresponding to the amount of the debtor's debt to the creditor (CivC Article 353(1)(2)). It must be noted that the pledgor and pledgee are not allowed to agree that the pledgee obtains ownership of the chattel before the debt comes due because the pledgee can obtain ownership of the pledged chattel as an alternative method of paying the debt (CivC Article 339). This rule protects the debtor, who is generally in a relatively disadvantageous position. The rule of real subrogation also applies (CivC Article 342). Thus, if the subject matter of a pledge is substituted for another thing or right (e.g., a claim to payment against an insurance company when the chattel is damaged), the pledge becomes attached to that thing or right.

(3) Extinction

Possession is the core element through which a pledge takes effect; thus, a pledge is extinguished if the creditor no longer possesses the relevant chattel. Also, as a pledge is ancillary to the debt it secures, it may expire through extinctive prescription[23] or debt payment/ satisfaction. It is also terminated if the movable offered as security is destroyed.

(4) Mortgage and Charge over Chattels

Mortgage over chattels (Dongsan-Yangdodambo). Although a pledge is a powerful tool for securing the payment of a loan, the subject matter of a pledge may lose its use value because both the pledgor (i.e., the debtor) and the pledgee (i.e., the creditor) are not permitted to use the chattel offered as security. Therefore, mortgage with respect to chattels is sometimes adopted by the parties to a loan contract. Under this scheme, the debtor transfers the ownership of a chattel to the creditor to secure the debt, but unlike in a pledge, the debtor is allowed to continue to possess and use the chattel.

It is important to note that the doctrine of *Trëuhand* applies to the mortgage of chattels. Under this doctrine, as far as the creditor and debtor are concerned, the ownership of the chattel remains with the transferor (i.e., the debtor), but as far as the creditor and the third parties in the market are concerned, the chattel is fully owned by the creditor. The creditor is obliged to return the chattel to the debtor once the debt is paid, but the creditor can acquire full ownership of the chattel (i.e., even *vis-à-vis* the transferor/debtor) if the debtor fails to repay the debt. Therefore, the creditor can exercise the right of rei vindicatio against the debtor and request a transfer of the chattel's possession to him/her. However, there is a danger that the debtor, as a possessor of the mortgaged chattel, will dispose of the chattel by selling it to a bona fide purchaser or by setting up another mortgage or pledge conflicting with the existing mortgage. This can cause problems in the commercial world. Third parties in the market will have no reason to think that the creditor is the real owner of the chattel because the debtor has possession of it. There is thus a need for a system that informs people in the market that a security interest exists with respect to the chattel possessed by the debtor. The system of charge over chattels fulfills this function.

Charge over chattels. Under the charge system, the debtor does not have to transfer possession of the chattel offered for security to the creditor.[24] Neither does the debtor need to transfer the ownership of the chattel to the creditor.[25] The creditor can simply have a security interest over the chattel,

23 Extinctive prescription of a personal right occurs if it is not exercised for a period of 10 years (CivC Article 162).

24 Hence, charges are different from pledges.

25 Hence, charges are different from mortgages.

which continues to be in the possession of the debtor (the owner of the chattel). The creditor's security interest (i.e., charge) can be imposed upon the chattel, and registered. Also, unlike the land registration system, which is based on information about the property (e.g., address, size, type), the chattel registration system is based on information about the debtor.[26] The charge system also benefits both debtors and creditors as debtors can keep using the chattel and creditors can assert charges against anyone in the market. The danger of a debtor disposing of the chattel to a third party is significantly decreased as no one would purchase a chattel with a publicized security interest. If the debtor fails to repay his/her debt, the creditor can appropriate the chattel for him/herself if there are justifiable grounds for him/her to do so, or sell the chattel at an auction and take the proceeds therefrom (Act on Security over Movable Property, Claims, Etc. [SMPC] Article 21(1)-2)). Last but not least, the charge system can at present be used only by commercial legal persons (SMPC Article 3(1)).

11. Lien (*Yuchigwon*)

(1) Acquisition

Acquisition by operation of law. A lien arises when an obligee possessing a thing belonging to another person has a claim (i.e., a personal right) arising with respect to that thing, and the obligation owed by the obligor comes due. The obligee may then retain possession of the thing until the claim is satisfied (CivC Article 320). The lienee's right to retain the thing arises automatically under such circumstances. Thus, a lien arises only by operation of law. For example, if A has left his/her car in a garage for repairs, the garage can take possession of the car if A fails to pay the cost of the repairs done. The lien relationship is generated by law, and as such, no real agreement is involved in the creation of a lien. As the lienee can take possession of the thing with respect to which a claim arises until the claim is satisfied, a lien has the effect of compelling the lienor (i.e., the obligor) to fulfill his/her obligation.

26 Act on Security over Movable Property, Claims, Etc. (SMPC) Article 47.

Three issues merit stressing. First, the subject matter of a lien must be something that belongs to another. A lien could thus not arise for X in relation to a house if X builds the house at Y's request but Y fails to pay for the work completed, because the new house belongs to X (i.e., the construction company) before it is registered under Y's name. In other words, a lien does not arise for X with respect to the house as the house belongs to it. One cannot have a security interest over one's own property.[27] Second, the possession must be legal (CivC Article 320(2)). Thus, if X has stolen Y's bike, a lien would not arise for X even if X has in the meantime incurred some expenses in repairing the bike. A lien is not triggered by operation of law for the benefit of a tortfeasor. The tortfeasor cannot assert a lien and must return the bike to the owner. Third, the obligation that a lien aims to secure must be connected to the subject matter of the lien. Therefore, in the aforementioned car repair case, the garage cannot retain possession of the car if A's obligation to the garage is a debt that arose from another contract irrelevant with the repair of the car.

(2) Rights

Unlike other security rights, the creditor/lienee under a lien, although having the power to sell the subject matter of the lien by auction (CivC Article 322(1)), cannot take the proceeds from such sale ahead of the lienor's other personal creditors. However, he/she does have the power to retain all the proceeds until the obligation is completely fulfilled (CivC Article 321). Therefore, a lien is sometimes even stronger than other security interests in that a lienee can assert his/her security interest even against a third party who is the real owner of the subject matter of the lien.[28] For example, in the aforementioned car repair case, the creation of a lien is not influenced by the fact that the car is not A's but belongs to A's friend, B. The garage can assert the lien against B. Furthermore, the lienee may apply to the court to have the subject matter of the lien appropriated for the satisfaction of the lienee's claim, to the extent of the chattel's value as appraised by an expert (CivC Article 338(2)). The lienee is also entitled to collect the fruits of the retained thing, and may apply these to the satisfaction of its claim ahead of

27 Supreme Court Decision 91Da14116, March 26, 1993.
28 Supreme Court Decision 73Da746, February 10, 1975.

the lienor's other creditors (CivC Article 323).

It is also important to remember that the lienee can use the retained thing insofar as necessary for its preservation (CivC Article 324(2) proviso). For instance, the lienee may drive a car kept under a lien to prevent its batteries from failing.[29] Last but not least, if some necessary expenses have been incurred with respect to the retained thing, the lienee can request reimbursement from the lienor (CivC Article 325). Therefore, if a veterinarian has retained a cured dog and must feed it until the owner pays the treatment expenses, the vet (i.e., the lienee) can require the lienor to reimburse him/her for the cost of the dog food.

(3) Extinction

Possession is the core element through which a lien takes effect. Thus, liens are extinguished if the lienee loses possession of the thing retained (CivC Article 328). Also, as the lien is ancillary to the obligation it secures, it is extinguished if the obligation expires through extinctive prescription[30] or through fulfillment/satisfaction of the obligation. It is also terminated if the thing under a lien is destroyed.

12. Conclusion

This chapter explores the real rights recognized under CivC: ownership, usufruct rights (superficies, easement, and lump-sum lease), security rights (hypothec plus mortgage, pledge plus mortgage, and charge), and lien. These are the most fundamental and important real rights under CivC. Due to space constraints, the real rights stipulated in other special statutes shall be dealt with elsewhere. The list of real rights is nearly complete due to the numerus clausus rule. However, in the present era, which some define as the Fourth Industrial Revolution, we have seen new types of valuable objects emerge. The most important examples in terms of the economy are cryptocurrency and data. Under the current regime, these cannot be the subject matter of

29 Supreme Court Decision 2009Da40684, September 24, 2009.

30 Extinctive prescription of a personal right occurs if the right is not exercised for a period of 10 years (CivC Article 162).

ownership, but there is no denying that they can be owned. Furthermore, anything that is valuable may qualify as the subject matter of security rights. This issue, however, remains a theoretical conundrum[31] because the nature of the aforementioned non-material objects is still ambiguous under the law, other than the recognition that they possess value. This matter is one of the most important problems faced by the present generation of academics and practitioners, who confront and respond to it from both practical and doctrinal perspectives.

31 For more details, see Kelvin Low and Ying-Chieh Wu, *The Characterisation of Cryptocurrencies in Japan, South Korea and China*, THE PRIVATE LAW IMPLICATIONS OF CRYPTOCURRENCIES (David Fox et al. eds.), Oxford University Press (2019).

Chapter 4

Tort Law

Kye Joung Lee*

1. Introduction

The Korean legal system is a civil law system, which differs from the common law system. In Korea, the primary authority that legally binds court decisions is statutes, including the Korean Civil Code (CivC). Article 1 of the CivC articulates this point by stipulating that if there are no provisions applicable to certain civil affairs, customary law shall apply, and if no applicable customary law exists, sound reasoning shall apply. The provisions applicable to certain civil affairs are statutes, including the CivC.

It should be noted that the doctrine of stare decisis does not apply to civil law countries such as the Republic of Korea. However, precedents do affect a court's decision in a practical manner, since seminal decisions have persuasive authority.[1] The Korean Supreme Court's decisions have a *de facto* binding effect on lower courts' judgments since lower courts generally follow the Korean Supreme Court's decisions. Practically, the Korean Supreme Court itself tends to stick to its past decisions. It has developed its core legal principles through a substantial number of decisions rendered

* Professor, Seoul National University School of Law.

1 Regarding the issue of whether judicial precedent can be a legal source, see Chun-Soo Yang, *The Problem of Judicial Precedent and Legal Source Revisited - From the Perspective of Legal Theory* (판례의 법원성 재검토 -법이론의 관점에서), 52 JURIS 431, 434 et seq. (2020) (in Korean).

over the six decades since the CivC came to effect in 1960; as a result, judges tend to rely on precedents. Thus, it is imperative to refer to not only statutes but also Supreme Court decisions to understand tort law in Korea.

CivC Articles 750-766 and other special statutes such as the Product Liability Act define tortious acts. Korea adopts a comprehensive approach to tort law, basing its tort law on a general clause: CivC Article 750 provides that any person who causes losses to or inflicts injuries on another person by an unlawful act, whether intentionally or negligently, shall be bound to make compensation for damages arising therefrom. This comprehensive approach originates in the French Civil Code, Article 1240 of which prescribes that any act whatsoever of a person that causes damage to another obliges the one by whose fault it occurred to compensate it. Through the influence of the French Civil Code, Japan has also adopted the comprehensive approach: Article 709 of the Japanese Civil Code prescribes that a person who has intentionally or negligently infringed any right or legally protected interest of others shall be liable to compensate any damages resulting as a consequence.[2]

In contrast, the United Kingdom and the United States have adopted the categorical approach. Traditionally, the common law was organized around writs or forms of action, some of which were eventually classified as tort actions.[3] To win a case, the plaintiff had to fit the case within one of the existing writs. Germany also adopted the categorical approach. Article 823(1) of the German Civil Code prescribes torts regarding injury to life, body, health, freedom, property, or right of another,[4] Article 823(2) prescribes torts regarding the infringement of a statute,[5] and Article 826

2 Regarding Japanese tort law, see Emi Matsumoto, *Tort Law in Japan*, COMPARATIVE TORT LAW (Mauro Bussani and Anthony J. Sebok, eds.), Edward Elgar Publishing 359 et seq. (2015).

3 James Gordley, *The Architecture of the Common and Civil Law of Torts: An Historical Survey*, COMPARATIVE TORT LAW (Mauro Bussani and Anthony J. Sebok, eds.), Edward Elgar Publishing 174 (2015).

4 Article 823(1) of the German Civil Code stipulates that "A person who, intentionally or negligently, unlawfully injures the life, body, health, freedom, property or another right of another person is liable to make compensation to the other party for the damage arising therefrom."

5 Article 823(2) of the German Civil Code stipulates that "The same duty is held by a person who commits a breach of a statute that is intended to protect another person. If, according to the contents of the statute, it may also be breached without fault, then liability to compensation only exists in the case of fault."

prescribes torts regarding intentional damage contrary to public policy.[6] It must be noted that even though German tort law's approach differs from Korean tort law, the legal theory of German tort law has influenced the interpretation of the CivC, because a substantial number of Korean legal scholars have studied German law.

This chapter aims to describe Korean tort law. We first review the general clause, CivC Article 750 (2), co-tortfeasors' liability (3), employer liability (4), liability of the possessor or owner of a structures (5), liability caused by an automobile accident (6), and extinctive prescription (7). After addressing product liability (8), the chapter concludes with a brief outlook on the future (9).

2. Tort under Article 750 of Civil Code

(1) Elements to Be a Tort under Article 750

As noted above, CivC Article 750 is a general clause defining the kinds of acts that constitute a tort. Under that article, there are four elements of a tort: a wrongdoer's intention or negligence, the unlawfulness of a wrongdoer's act, damages, and the causal relationship between a wrongdoer's act and the damages. The burden of proof concerning all four elements lies with the plaintiff.

1) Wrongdoer's Intention or Negligence

The first element under Article 750 is a wrongdoer's intention or negligence. Whether there is negligence is closely connected to the extent to which an ordinary person would have been cautious under the circumstances in question. The issue lies in what "ordinary person" means. According to prevailing authorities and Supreme Court decisions, it refers to an average person at the time of each specific situation. Factors such as the individual's occupation, social status, and the concrete circumstances at the time of the act are also considered in determining an ordinary person.[7] For example,

6 Article 826 of the German Civil Code stipulates that "A person who, in a manner contrary to public policy, intentionally inflicts damage on another person is liable to the other person to make compensation for the damage."

in a malpractice case, whether the doctor was negligent or not is judged in light of the medical knowledge and skills a typical or average doctor should have.

2) Unlawfulness of a Wrongdoer's Act

The second element under Article 750 is the unlawfulness (*Rechtswidrigkeit*) of a wrongdoer's act, which means that a person's act is against a statute, good morals, or the social order more generally. It refers to the infringement of not only a right such as a right in rem but also legally protected interests such as economic interests,[8] the right to view, or the right to sunshine.[9]

There are many perspectives on how to define unlawfulness.[10] According to the theory of unlawfulness of conduct (*Verhaltensunrechtslehre*), assessing unlawfulness always relates to the human behavior involved and not to any damages that result. However, according to the theory of unlawfulness established by the result (*Erfolgsunrechtslehre*), whoever causes injury to an absolutely protected good or right (such as the right to bodily integrity or property rights) has acted unlawfully unless he or she had a special justification. The Korean Supreme Court held that in judging unlawfulness, it is not necessary to decide according to a unitary rule; rather, each act at issue should be judged individually and relatively.[11] The court has thus taken a categorical approach that establishes standards for judging unlawfulness according to type of conduct.

For example, regarding the installation by Korea Electric Power Corporation's (KEPCO) of a power transmission line on land owned by an individual, the Supreme Court recognized that KEPCO was liable for infringing on the individual's right to property.[12] Rights in rem, such as

7 Deok-Su Song, *The Law of Obligation: Particular* (채권법각론) (4th eds.), Parkyoungsa (2019), 506 (in Korean); Young-Joon Kwon, *Negligence in Tort Law and an "Average Person"* (불법행위의 과실 판단과 사회평균인), 68 JOURNAL OF COMPARATIVE PRIVATE LAW 91, 111 et sq. (2015) (in Korean); Supreme Court Decision 2000Da12532, January 19, 2001.

8 Young-Joon Kwon, *Pure Economic Loss: A Korean Perspective*, 10 JOURNAL OF KOREAN LAW 212, 225 (2011).

9 Supreme Court Decision 2008Da41499, December 24, 2008 (regarding a right to sunshine); Supreme Court Decision 2003Da64602, September 13, 2004 (regarding a right to view).

10 Helmut Koziol, BASIC QUESTIONS OF TORT LAW FROM A GERMANIC PERSPECTIVE, Jan Sramek 172-173 (2012).

11 Supreme Court Decision 2001Da734, June 27, 2003.

the right to property, are granted a strong degree of protection; therefore, the infringement itself constitutes unlawfulness in this case. On the other hand, regarding legally protected interests such as the right to view, mere infringement cannot be deemed unlawful. According to the Supreme Court, the extent to which one's interest has been harmed must exceed the limit of tolerance generally accepted according to society's norms in order for an infringement to be deemed unlawful.[13] In the ruling, the determination of whether the limit of tolerance was exceeded considered many factors, including the overall scenery subject to the obstructed view, the location and structure of both the obstructing and obstructed building, the process of how the obstructing building was built, and whether there was malicious intent in obstructing the view at issue. Adopting a policy that emphasizes the protection of the right to view as a legally protected interest would limit the ability of a neighbor to exercise his or her right to property, and the level of protection of the right to view varies depending on the specific locations of the buildings at issue. Therefore, it cannot be said that a mere infringement of the right to view is a legally protected interest sufficient to find unlawfulness.[14]

Unlawfulness is the key issue in determining whether privacy infringement constitutes a tortious act. Privacy must be protected, but that protection will inevitably conflict with other values. Thus, balancing is an important question in determining lawfulness.[15] In a case where an insurance company employee took photographs of a victim's daily activities for the purpose of collecting evidence against the victim's assertion regarding the seriousness of disability caused by an insured accident, the Supreme Court held that the final determination of unlawfulness should be made by balancing interests. The balancing test is to be a comprehensive examination of the overall circumstances in a concrete set of facts. First, factors regarding the infringing act must be considered, including the

12 Supreme Court Decision 2003Da5498, March 25, 2005.

13 Supreme Court Decision 2003Da64602, September 13, 2004.

14 Cheol-Hong Yoon, *A Study on the Endurance Limit* of the *Right to View* (조망권의 침해시 수인한도의 판단기준), 9(2) NORTHEAST ASIAN LAW JOURNAL 201 et seq. (2015) (in Korean).

15 Young-Joon Kwon, *Determining Unlawfulness through Balance of Interests Regarding the Right to One's Image and the Right of Privacy* (초상권 및 사생활의 비밀과 자유, 그리고 이익형량을 통한 위법성 판단), 31 JOURNAL OF PRIVATE CASE LAW STUDIES 519, 535 (2009) (in Korean).

content and gravity of the interests pursued by the act, the necessity and effectiveness of the act, the urgency of the act, and the reasonableness of the method of infringement. Second, it is also necessary to consider factors regarding the infringed interests, including the content and gravity of the infringed legal interests, the degree of damage suffered by the infringing act, and the degree of protection of the infringed interests.[16] The Supreme Court concluded that, considering the aforementioned factors, the acts committed by the defendant against the plaintiff were unlawful.

In addition, unlawfulness is the key issue in determining whether a media report can be a tortious act. The Supreme Court has held that, even when an expression of opinion or commentary based on a certain fact injures a person's reputation, the act is not unlawful if the act is related to the public interest, and the crucial parts of the aforementioned fact are true, or there are substantial grounds for media reporter to believe that the crucial parts can be true.[17] This decision is significant in in that it emphasizes the role of media companies and tries to determine a standard of evaluating unlawfulness for cases where the freedom of the press and the protection of a person's reputation were in conflict. The court also held that in achieving the delicate balance between ensuring freedom of press and protecting the reputation of an individual, the standard of evaluating unlawfulness should take into account whether the party whose reputation was damaged is a public or private figure, and whether the expression is in the public interest or belongs to a private, personal domain. It ruled that a greater degree of freedom of expression should be allowed if the expression concerns a media company, as the media company itself enjoys a wide degree of freedom of speech. In a decision where prosecutors filed suit against a broadcasting company on the grounds that the report injured the prosecutors' reputation, the Supreme Court held that a media company's ability to monitor or criticize public officials should not be easily restricted unless the report was made with actual malice or with reckless disregard for the truth.[18] Unlike *New York Times Co. v. Sullivan*,[19] in which the US Supreme Court held that a state is not liable to a public official for a defamatory falsehood relating to

16 Supreme Court Decision 2004Da16280, October 13, 2006.
17 Supreme Court Decision 2011Da86782, November 15, 2012.
18 Supreme Court Decision 2002Da63558, September 2, 2003.
19 376 U.S. 254 (1964).

that official's conduct unless the official proves 'actual malice,' the Korean Supreme Court case referred to above does not find it necessary for the media to have 'active malice' in order for a public figure to claim damages. Rather, a public figure can claim damages when there is a reckless disregard for truth in a media report.

3) Damages

The third element under Article 750 is damages, which refer to the harm caused by the fact that a right or legal interest was infringed; damages are essentially the gap between the state after the tortious act versus the state that would have existed if not for the tortious act. This is dealt with in depth later in this chapter, but for now it is enough to note that damages consist of actually incurred losses (positive losses), lost benefits (negative losses), and consolation.

The damages to be compensated must be definite damages that were actually suffered.[20] For instance, if an injured party has to take on debt due to a tortious act inflicted by the tortfeasor, the injured party must show that the burden of the debt is definite and is therefore of a quality that should be paid to the obligee.[21]

4) Causal Relationship between a Wrongdoer's Act and Damages

The fourth element of a tort is a causal relationship between the wrongdoer's act and the damages. A causal relationship can be found when the wrongdoer's act is a proximate cause, considering the objective circumstances and the wrongdoer's subjective consciousness. Proximate cause is determined based on the standard of high probability barring contingency.[22] In principle, the plaintiff bears the burden of proof concerning the existence of causation; thus, the plaintiff is obliged to produce evidence to establish causation.

In environmental lawsuits where plaintiffs file a suit for damages caused by water pollution, plaintiffs tend to find it difficult to collect

20 Supreme Court Decision 97Da4760, August 25, 1998.
21 Supreme Court Decision 2017Da278446, October 15, 2020.
22 Sun-Goo Lee, *Proving Causation With Epidemiological Evidence in Tobacco Lawsuits*, 154 JOURNAL OF PREVENTIVE MEDICINE AND PUBLIC HEALTH 80, 81 (2016).

evidence to prove the existence of causation since the damages in question can be caused by pollutants accumulated with the passage of time and because important evidence is controlled or managed by the defendant. Accordingly, requiring the victim to scientifically and strictly prove the existence of a causal relationship may lead to the denial of judicial relief from environmental pollution. On these grounds, the Supreme Court has adopted *res ipsa loquitur*, or the 'new probability theory,' to alleviate the burden of proof for plaintiffs. The Supreme Court holds defendants liable if the plaintiff can prove three things: first, that the defendant discharged the harmful substance; second, that the substance reached the damaged area or objects; and third, that damages actually occurred. In other words, the plaintiff's success in proving the aforementioned three things can make defendants liable unless defendants successfully prove that the substance in question is not actually innocuous.[23] This tendency to alleviate the burden of proof for plaintiffs extends to malpractice lawsuits.[24]

(2) The Scope of Compensation

1) The Principle of Pecuniary Compensation and Succession

The victim is entitled to be compensated once he or she has established the four elements of a tortious claim. The principle of pecuniary compensation means that harm inflicted by a tortious act will be compensated by money (CivC Article 763, 394).

The victim is entitled to compensation for actually incurred losses (positive losses), lost benefits (negative losses), and consolation. Some examples of actually incurred losses are medical expenses and nursing care fees that the victim has already paid due to the act. Lost benefits could be a

23 Supreme Court Decision 2012Da11661, October 11, 2013; Supreme Court Decision 2016Da233538, 233545, November 28, 2019; Supreme Court Decision 2019Da292026, 292033, 292040, June 25, 2020.

24 Supreme Court Decision 2004Da52576, September 30, 2005, held that when a medical accident occurs, if the victim proves, based on the general public's common sense, that (1) the patient did not have any health problem that could have caused the result before the medical practice, (2) the patient came to suffer from the injury or harm after the medial practice at issue, (3) no cause other than the course of medical care could have led to the result, the existence of a causal relationship between medical malpractice and the result is presumed, unless the medical staff proves that the result was due to a completely different cause.

victim's anticipated earnings, which can be calculated by examining the average salary of people in the same career as the victim during the average workable period. Finally, the victim is entitled to consolation. The scope of consolation in case of death of a car accident victim is approximately KRW 50,000,000–80,000,000 (≒ USD 41,290–66,050). The right to damages that a victim may claim succeeds to his or her heirs. Since the victim's right to damages is a pecuniary right, it is not just that individual alone who may claim this right; in the case of an individual's death, the heirs can also make a claim. Even in a case where the victim suffered instantaneous death, the consolation money to be claimed by the victim succeeds to his or her heirs. Note that in a case where a tort causes the death of the victim, the victim's spouse, lineal descendants, and lineal ascendants may claim their own consolation, separate from that of the victim (CivC Article 752).

In calculating consolation, damage to property that is difficult to estimate and thus cannot be easily compensated can be taken into account.[25] In these cases, consolation plays a complementary role.[26] Under certain circumstances, it may be difficult to provide a concrete estimate of damages even though it is clear that the injured party's property was damaged. Thanks to the complementary role of consolation, the injured party is allowed to receive appropriate compensation. However, the complementary function of compensation is limited in its application. Even in the absence of clear evidence, the court may fix the amount of damages to property to a reasonable degree by taking into consideration all circumstances based on the pleadings and by examining all evidence.[27] As such, courts have wide discretion in determining the amount of damages to property to be awarded to an injured party, which can make it often unnecessary to apply the complementary function of damages.

Whether the injured party can obtain an injunction is also a key issue. Unlike monetary compensation, an injunction requires a tortious act to be ceased or reverses the result of the tortious act. Currently, prevailing authorities and court precedents do not accept injunctions as a remedy for

25 Supreme Court Decision 84Daka722, November 13, 1984; Supreme Court Decision 2017Da229536, April 12, 2018.

26 Chang-su Yang and Young-joon Kwon, THE TEXTBOOK OF THE CIVIL LAW, Part 2 (민법) (4th ed.), Parkyoungsa 683 (2021) (in Korean).

27 Civil Procedure Act Article 202-2.

tortious acts, unless otherwise indicated by a provision of law.[28] However, if a report defames an individual's reputation, courts may still order the wrongdoer to release a corrected report and the holding of the court's decision containing this order. According to Article 764 of the CivC, courts may order a wrongdoer who has defamed another's reputation to take measures appropriate for repairing that party's reputation. In addition, in a case where there are acts infringing on another person's economic interests by taking advantage of his or her achievements obtained through substantial efforts—without permission and in a manner contrary to fair commercial practices—the court may grant an injunction.[29] There are many voices in favor of generally allowing the use of injunctions for injured parties, since they may allow them to efficiently prevent further damages caused by tortious acts.[30] At present, however, this expansion of the role of injunctions has not received legislative approval.

2) Punitive Damages?

Punitive damages are damages intended to deter the defendant and others from engaging in intentional torts by forcing the defendant to compensate in excess of the plaintiff's provable injuries. Punitive damages are usually imposed on wrongdoers who commit intentional, malicious, or antisocial torts. The concept is that repetitive wrongdoings and torts would be prevented in the same way that penal punishment prevents illegal behavior.

In principle, punitive damages are not acknowledged in Korea, so injured parties can only recover the actual harms they have suffered. However, punitive damages are exceptionally acknowledged by special acts such as the Product Liability Act and the Fair Transactions in Subcontracting Act. There are voices in favor of imposing punitive damages on media outlets that commit defamation with malicious intent, but that has not been enacted.

28 Supreme Court Decision 96Da10638, March 28, 1997.

29 Unfair Competition Prevention And Trade Secret Protection Act Article 2(1)(ta), 4.

30 Sang-Joong Kim, *Vorschlag zur allgemeinen bürgerlichrechtlichen Einführung eines deliktischen Beseitiguns- bzw. Unterlassungsanspruchs* (불법행위에 대한 금지청구권 규정의 신설 제안), 55 THE KOREAN JOURNAL OF CIVIL LAW 177 et seq. (2011) (in Korean).

3) Comparative Negligence

According to the rule of contributory negligence, if the victim was partially at fault for his or her injury in an accident, the other party who caused the injury is not liable for it, and the victim would not be able to recover damages. By contrast, under the rule of comparative negligence, if the victim is partially at fault for his or her injury, the amount the victim can recover in damages is reduced proportionally. As such, if a court finds the victim 20% responsible for an injury, the amount the victim would be able to recover will be reduced by 20%, Korea follows the comparative negligence rule (CivC Articles 763, 396).

Comparative negligence plays a conciliatory role by flexibly considering all details of the circumstances of an individual case, thereby allowing losses to be shared impartially among all relevant parties. Here, 'negligence' takes on a different meaning from negligence as an element of a tortious act (see above). Negligence, in the context of comparative negligence, includes disregarding the level of attention required by social norms in conducting one's own affairs. For instance, the failure to put on a seatbelt has to do with an individual's own safety and therefore cannot constitute 'negligence' as one of the four elements of a tortious act. However, the failure to put on a seatbelt can still constitute grounds for comparative negligence if it caused additional harm that could otherwise have been avoided.

The fundamental principle is that a person who intentionally commits a tortious act by taking advantage of a victim's carelessness cannot then ask for reduced liability on the basis of that carelessness.[31] If the wrongdoer commits fraud or embezzlement by taking advantage of a victim's carelessness, he or she may not claim that there was comparative negligence, because finding comparative negligence in such a context would will ultimately undermine fairness by tipping the scale to allow wrongdoers to benefit from tortious acts.

31 Supreme Court Decision 2005Da32197, October 7, 2005.

3. Co-tortfeasor Liability

(1) Elements Required for Co-tortfeasor Liability under Article 760

Article 760 of the CivC governs the liability of co-tortfeasors. According to this provision, if two or more persons have caused damages to the victim by their joint unlawful acts, they shall be jointly and severally liable to compensate such damages. The victim must prove that (i) each act of the co-tortfeasors satisfies the elements of a tort as described in Article 750 of the CivC and that (ii) co-tortfeasors' respective acts are objectively related to each other in causing damages.[32] Item (i) means that the victim must prove (a) each person's intention or negligence, (b) the unlawfulness of each person's act, (c) actual damages, and (d) a causal relationship between each person's act and those damages. Item (ii) requires that each person's act contributes to damages not subjectively but objectively. Accordingly, the victim does not need to prove collusion or conspiracy among co-tortfeasors.[33]

(2) Joint and Several Liability of Co-tortfeasors and Right of Contribution among Co-tortfeasors

Co-tortfeasors are held jointly and severally liable to the victim. There are two kinds of joint and several liability: statutory and non-statutory joint and several liability. Generally, a subjective co-relationship is required for the former but is not required for the latter.[34] According to Article 419 of the CivC, which lays out the legal doctrine regarding statutory joint and several liability, if two obligors (A and B) bear statutory joint and several liability, an exemption from obligation granted to one obligor (A) shall be effective in favor of the other obligor (B) only to the extent of A's share of the obligation. In other words, an exemption granted to A by a creditor reduces the amount of debt owed by B.

However, the Supreme Court and prevailing authorities have concluded that Article 419 of the CivC does not apply to non-statutory joint and

32 Supreme Court Decision 96Da46903, August 29, 1997.

33 Supreme Court Decision 87Daka2951, April 12, 1988.

34 Supreme Court Decisions 2009Da32409, August 20, 2009; 2012Da97420, 97437, August 20, 2014.

several liability. Since it is unjust to allow a co-tortfeasor to enjoy the benefit of an exemption granted to the other co-tortfeasor and there is no subjective relationship among co-tortfeasors, as explained above,[35] the Korean Supreme Court concluded that co-tortfeasors bear non-statutory joint and several liability.[36] As a result, an exemption granted to one co-tortfeasor does not affect the victim's claim for damages against another co-tortfeasor.[37] The non-statutory joint and several liability approach thus provides stronger protections for victims.

However, statutory and non-statutory joint and several liability do have several similarities. Both produce an identical legal result if one obligor makes payments to the creditor or victim. In such a case, the other obligors are relieved of the obligation to make payment to the creditor or the victim. In addition, the right of contribution is legally recognized in both kinds of liability. Thus, the Korean Supreme Court ruled that Article 425 of the CivC, which governs the right of contribution in the context of statutory joint and several liability, is applicable to the right of contribution of co-tortfeasors.[38]

In order to exercise the right of contribution in a joint tort, the following elements need to be established: i) there must exist a joint unlawful act by co-tortfeasors, and ii) the co-tortfeasor must have paid more than his or her share of joint liability to the victim.[39]

Assuming the above elements are met, one co-tortfeasor can claim the right of contribution against another co-tortfeasor up to the extent of the other co-tortfeasor's share of joint liability. For example, if A and B as co-tortfeasors caused damages of US$10,000, each is liable to pay the full amount to the victim. Assuming A pays US$10,000 to the victim and that B's share of the joint liability is four times higher than A's share,[40] A has a right to claim a contribution of US$8,000 against B.

The majority of the Supreme Court's decisions have held that the pro

35 As noted above, each co-tortfeasor's act is required to contribute to the damages not subjectively but objectively to find liability of co-tortfeasors; the victim does not need to prove collusion or conspiracy among co-tortfeasors.

36 Supreme Court Decisions 2009Da32409, August 20, 2009; 2012Da97420, 97437, August 20, 2014.

37 Supreme Court Decision 2005Da19378, January 27, 2006.

38 Supreme Court Decisions 90Da20244, October 22, 1991; 2005Da7085, October 11, 2007.

39 Supreme Court Decision 2000Da69712, September 24, 2002.

40 In other words, the ratio of A's pro rata share to B's pro rata share is 1:4.

rata shares for respective co-tortfeasors should be determined by the degree of negligence of each tortfeasor.[41] In other words, the court should first determine the degree of negligence of each co-tortfeasor in damaging the victim or which co-tortfeasor's negligence was the main cause of the damage and then apportion the pro rata shares based on those findings.

4. Employer Liability

Employer liability is a form of vicarious liability. The employer is alleged to be held liable not because of its own wrongdoing but because of an employee's wrongdoing. The idea is that an employer who earns profits through the activity of its employees should be responsible for any losses caused by the tortious acts of those employees.

CivC Article 756 states the following on employer liability:

(i) A person who employs another to perform a specific affair is liable for compensating for any loss inflicted on a third person by the employee in the course of performing the specific affair: this shall not apply where the employer has exercised due care in appointing the employee, and in supervising the performance of the specific affair, or where the loss has been inflicted even if the employer has exercised due care.

(ii) A person who supervises the performance of a specific affair on behalf of the employer shall also assume the same liability as prescribed in (i).

41 Supreme Court Decisions 98Da52469, February 26, 1999; 2000Da29028, August 22, 2000; 2002Da14112, May 24, 2002; 2000Da69712, September 24, 2002; 2005Da8125, July 8, 2005; 98Da52469, February 26, 1999 held that "co-tortfeasors are held jointly and severally liable to the victim. Each co-tortfeasor has his or her pro rata share of a joint liability, and his or her share depends on the degree of his negligence. A co-tortfeasor who has paid more damage than his or her share to the victim can claim the right of contribution against another co-tortfeasor on a pro-rata basis.

Where the plaintiff and the defendants are co-tortfeasors regarding the death of the deceased, and the defendants seek the right of contribution to the plaintiff after making compensation to the victim, the court should first find out what negligence each of the plaintiff and defendants respectively committed for the damage of the victim and apportion the pro rata shares based on those findings."

(iii) In cases falling under (i) and (ii), the employer or the supervisor may claim reimbursement from the employee.

(1) Elements of Employer Liability

The first element of employer liability is the existence of an employment relationship. The second element is that the tortious act must be 'related to the employee's execution of the undertaking.' In other words, if a particular act can be seen 'apparently and objectively' as a part of (or related to) the employer's business activity, the unlawful act will be seen as an act related to the employee's execution of the undertaking, without considering the employee's subjective state of mind. For example, if a bank employee accepts money from a customer and uses it for personal purposes, then the employee's subjective state of mind is not taken into consideration, and the act is deemed to be related to the execution of the undertaking. The rationale under the second element is to protect a victim to whom it reasonably appeared that the employee's act was related to the employer's business activity. Conversely, if a victim who transacted with the employee knew that the employee's act was not related to the execution of the business activity or was grossly negligent, the second element is not satisfied.[42] Under such a circumstance, there would be no reason to take measures to protect victims' trust in the appearance of employees.[43]

Sexual harassment during a banquet after work can be seen as related to an employee's execution of the undertaking. In a case where A, the head of welfare facilities, committed sexual misconduct against the victim (an employee under A) just after a banquet ended, the Supreme Court determined that A's acts of sexual misconduct constituted an unlawful act of invasion of the plaintiff's right to self-decision that took advantage of his status and power as the head of welfare facilities.[44] In addition, the court held that if an employee commits intentional sexual harassment against another employee, employer liability can be established, given that the harmful act is closely

42 Supreme Court Decision 83Da217, June 28, 1983.

43 For a detailed analysis of the second element of the employer's liability, see Hyoung-Seok Kim, *The Functional Limitation of the Employer's Vicarious Liability - a Comparative Approach* (사용자책임에서 사무집행관련성의 판단 - 비교법적 연구로부터의 시사), 163 SEOUL LAW JOURNAl 351 et seq. (2012) (in Korean).

44 Supreme Court Decision 2008Da89712, February 26, 2009.

connected to the employer's business in terms of time and place.

The third element is that the employee's act must constitute a tort under Article 750. In other words, negligence or intention on the part of the employee, the unlawfulness of the employee's act, the existence of actual damages, and a causal relationship between the employee's act and the damages are all needed.

The fourth element is that the employer was not successful in establishing a defense. If the employer successfully establishes a defense that it had exercised due care in appointing the employee and supervising the performance of the specific affair or that the loss would have been inflicted even if the employer had exercised due care, the employer will not be held liable. In practice, this defense is very rarely accepted by the court.

(2) Effects of Employer Liability

The employer and employee are held jointly and severally liable to the victim. The employer can bring a contribution claim against the employee after compensating the victim, although the amount claimed by the employer against the employee is often reduced by the court under the principle of good faith.[45]

(3) State Compensation Act

In cases where the government, whether national or local, is the employer, it is responsible for compensating for any harm caused by its employees (i.e., civil servants). According to Article 2 of the State Compensation Act, when public officials inflict damage, whether intentionally or negligently, on other persons in violation of statutes in performing their official duties, the government in question shall compensate such damages. Therefore, in situations where the national or local government is the employer, the State Compensation Act will apply instead of Article 756 of the CivC, which is discussed above.

45 Supreme Court Decision 91Da7255, May 10, 1991.

5. Liability of Possessor or Owner of a Structure

In cases where a victim has suffered damage due to a defective structure, the possessor (occupant) of the structure will bear primary responsibility, while the owner of the structure will bear secondary responsibility. Article 758(1) of the CivC states that "if any damages have been caused to another person by any defect in the construction or maintenance of a structure, the person in possession of the structure shall be liable for such damages: if the person in possession has exercised due care in order to prevent the occurrence of such damages, compensation for the damage shall be made by the owner."

The rationale of the above provision is the principle of risk responsibility, which is the idea that a person who manages or owns a high-risk structure should take sufficient precautions; if a risk materializes and causes damage, it is appropriate for that person to bear responsibility.

(1) Elements of Liability of Possessor or Owner of a Structure

The first element is that what caused damage must be a structure, which is a thing that was made through artificial work, including buildings, telephone poles, advertisement towers, and elevators.

The second element is the existence of a defect in the construction or maintenance of a structure. Defect in this context means that the structure is in a condition that lacks the safety normally required for its use.[46] Whether this standard for safety has been met is judged on the basis of whether the party that built or preserved the structure has fulfilled its duty to take the protective measures typically required by social norms.[47] The existence of a defect is judged by an objective standard; no consideration is given as to whether the defect was caused intentionally or negligently by the party that built or preserved the structure.

The third element is that the defect of the structure must have caused the damage suffered by the victim. When the cause of the damage is force majeure, a defect in the structure will not make the builder or preserver of the structure liable for a tort since causality between the defect of the structure and the damage cannot be established.

46 Supreme Court Decision 2004Da21053, January 26, 2006.
47 Supreme Court Decision 2015Da68348, July 12, 2018.

The fourth element is that the possessor (occupant) of the structure must fail to establish that he or she exercised due care in order to prevent the occurrence. Unlike torts under Article 750, where the victim bears the burden of proof in establishing the negligence of the wrongdoer, the possessor of the structure bears the burden of proof in establishing his or her exercise of due care. Once again, the principle of risk responsibility is reflected in this fourth element, which holds possessors liable for a tort in the event that danger in a high-risk structure materializes, with damage occurring as a result. If the possessor is successful in establishing that he or she exercised due care, the owner rather than the possessor of the structure is liable for damages. The owner of the structure bears strict liability since he or she is not entitled to raise the defense of having exercised due care.

(2) Effects of Liability of Possessor or Owner of a Structure

The possessor (occupant) of the structure bears primary liability in terms of compensating damages, but if the possessor is successful in establishing his exercise of due care, the owner of the structure is liable for damages. Furthermore, if there is an indirect possessor among several possessors, the direct possessor will first bear responsibility, after which the indirect possessor will bear responsibility if the direct possessor cannot be held liable.[48] For example, if a lessor leases a building and the lessee uses the whole building, then the lessee is the direct occupant. If the victim suffers damage due to a defect in the building, the direct possessor (i.e., the lessee) shall bear primary responsibility.

If a victim suffers damage as a result of a defect in a structure managed or owned by the national or local government, that government is responsible for compensating the victim. Article 5 of the State Compensation Act provides that in cases where any damages have been inflicted on another person due to the defective construction or management of a road, river, or any other public structures, the appropriate level of government shall redress such damage. Therefore, when defects in structures managed or owned by the national or local government are at issue, the State Compensation Act will be applied in place of CivC Article 758.

48 Supreme Court Decision 92Da10081, March 26, 1993.

6. Liability Caused by an Automobile Accident

Korea enacted a special act called the Guarantee of Automobile Accident Compensation Act (GAAC Act) to deal with torts resulting from automobile accidents. The gist of the GAAC Act is to broaden the liability of the owner or possessor of an automobile and to mandate that all owners or possessors are appropriately insured. Thanks to the positive effect of the GAAC Act, victims of automobile accidents can be compensated without much difficulty. The passage of the act has made an enormous contribution to expediting car purchases without fear of involvement in civil or even criminal trials.

(1) Elements of Liability

The first element of liability in the GAAC Act is that a person 'operates an automobile for his or her sake.' In order to be a person that operates an automobile for his or her sake, a person should control the operation of an automobile and enjoy the benefit therefrom.[49] The concept of a person that operates an automobile for his or her sake is different from that of the automobile owner. For example, when the automobile owner entrusts his or her automobile to a repair shop, the automobile owner temporarily loses control over the vehicle and during that period is not a person that operates an automobile for his or her sake. Therefore, if a repair shop mechanic causes an accident while driving the car, the automobile owner will not be responsible for that accident. On the other hand, the concept of a person that operates an automobile for his or her sake is not simply the equivalent of the person driving the automobile. If an individual or company employs a chauffeur who causes a car accident, then that individual or company will be liable under the GAAC Act, since in this situation the employer is the person operating the automobile for his or her sake.[50] In this regard, the GAAC Act is a special provision of employer liability prescribed in CivC

49 Supreme Court Decision 86Daka556, December 23, 1986; Supreme Court Decision 2009Da42703, 42710, October 15, 2009.

50 The automobile driver who is employed is also supposed to be liable for car accident based on CivC Article 750. As a result, the automobile driver and the employer shall be jointly and severally liable to compensate damages.

Article 765.

The second element of liability is that a victim has been killed or injured by the 'operation of an automobile,' which refers to the use or management of automobiles. This means the accident occurred by using various devices with which an automobile is structurally equipped according to the purpose of each device. If the driver of a car falls asleep after parking the car on a sloped lawn next to the road, and the car slides and falls into a pond, the accident did not occur while the car's devices were being used for their intended purpose. In this situation, the second element is not satisfied.[51]

The third element of liability is that a defendant is not successful in making a defense. The defendant must show the following: (i) the person who operated the motor vehicle was not negligent in its operation, that there were no structural defects or functional issues in the motor vehicle, or that a victim or a third party committed an intentional or negligent act; or (ii) the victim died or was injured due to his or her intentional or even suicidal act. In reality, it is very difficult to demonstrate the above, so liability under the GAAC Act can be seen as *de facto* strict liability.

(2) Actual Compensation by Insurance Companies

Under the GAAC Act, all motor vehicle owners are to purchase liability insurance that covers the amount prescribed by presidential decree that shall be paid to a third party who has died or been injured due to the operation of a motor vehicle (GAAC Act Article 5). If a motor vehicle owner purchases comprehensive insurance, a driver who caused traffic accident and thus committed a crime by inflicting bodily injury due to occupational or gross negligence shall not be prosecuted in principle.[52] For this reason, most motor vehicle owners tend to purchase comprehensive insurance so that the victim can be easily compensated by the insurance company.

51 Supreme Court Decision 93Da55180, April 29, 1994.

52 Concerning reasons for being exceptionally prosecuted, see the Act On Special Cases Concerning the Settlement Of Traffic Accidents Article 4(1).

7. Extinctive Prescription

The right to claim damages resulting from a tort lapses if not exercised within three years from the date on which the victim or his or her legal representative becomes aware of such damage and of the identity of the person who caused the damage (CivC Article 766(1)). The statute of limitations is triggered only if either the victim or his or her legal representative is aware not only of the injury but also that the defendant's conduct was tortious. In case of new damage unforeseen at the time of the act, the statute of limitations is triggered only after the cause of the additional damage is clearly confirmed.[53]

In addition, the right to claim damages resulting from a tort will expire if ten years have elapsed from "the time the unlawful act was committed" (CivC Article 766(2)). Here, "the time" does not refer to when that the unlawful act happened but rather the date on which the actual damage occurred.[54] Therefore, in claims for damages in which there is a time gap between the unlawful act and actual damage resulting from it, the time the unlawful act was committed actually means the time when a harmful result occurred.[55] In a case where a victim claimed he had contracted HIV from a blood product manufactured and supplied by the defendant, the Supreme Court ruled that in cases where the latency period of infection is long, or when it is difficult to predict how far the illness will progress, it would be wrong to have the statute of limitations begin to run on the date of the infection. Rather, it would be right to find the starting point for extinctive prescription run from the date when symptoms began to manifest or the illness progressed.[56] In one case, a victim was sexually assaulted by her tennis coach during elementary school and ran into the assailant fifteen years later. This triggered memories of the sexual violence and caused the victim to be diagnosed with post-traumatic stress disorder, after which the victim claimed damages against the assailant. The court held that the point at which the victim received a diagnosis was the point at which the actual

53 Supreme Court Decisions 99Da42797, September 14, 2001; 2009Da99105, April. 29, 2010.

54 Supreme Court Decision 2010Da54566, August 30, 2012.

55 Supreme Court Decision 2005Da55312, November 16, 2007.

56 Supreme Court Decision 2008Da16776, September 29, 2011.

damage resulting from the sexual violence occurred and that the statute of limitations should only start then, under CivC Article 766(2).[57]

Even if the statute of limitations on a victim's right to claim damages for tortious acts has expired, asserting it may be against the principle of good faith. For example, if the wrongdoer obstructs the victim's exercise of right to a significant degree, it can be said that it is a violation of good faith to deny the victim's exercise of right just because ten years have passed since the time the unlawful act was committed. The Supreme Court has recognized the doctrine of abuse of extinctive prescription. As such, the Supreme Court applies this doctrine, where the debtor makes it remarkably difficult or even impossible for the creditor (victim) to exercise his or her right; where the debtor performs actions that make the creditor (victim) believe that his or her exercise of right is unnecessary; where the creditor (victim) is obstructed from exercising his or her right due to objective impediment; where the debtor acts in a manner that makes the creditor believe that the debtor will not invoke extinctive prescription.[58]

In one case, plaintiffs filed suit against Nippon Steel Corporation (defendant), maintaining that they were forced by the defendant and the Japanese government to provide labor while they were deprived of their freedom.[59] The plaintiffs maintained that the defendant was liable for damages stemming from mental harm incurred by forced labor in the 1940s, during Japanese colonial rule. The Supreme Court found that the defendant's argument that extinctive prescription should block the plaintiffs from seeking damages contradicted the principle of good faith.[60]

57 Supreme Court Decision 2019Da297137, August 19, 2021.

58 Supreme Court Decision 2009Da103950, January 13, 2011. Regarding the doctrine on the abuse of extinctive prescription in Korea, see Jin-Su Yoon, *The Development of the Doctrine on the Abuse of Extinctive Prescription* (소멸시효 남용론의 전개), 93 THE KOREAN JOURNAL OF CIVIL LAW 3 et seq. (2020) (in Korean).

59 For a general analysis of the liability of Japanese companies for forced labor during the Japanese colonial era, see Kye Joung Lee, *The Supreme Court Decision on the Liability of Japanese Company for Forced Labor During the Japanese Colonial Era and its Implications*, 36 JOURNAL OF KOREAN LAW 335, 336 et seq. (2019).

60 Supreme Court Decision 2009Da68620, May 24, 2012. Concerning the issue of whether a defendant's argument based on the statute of limitations is barred by the principle of good faith, see Hyo-Soon Nam, *L'étude sur l'abus de la prescription extinctive de l'action contractuelle des dommages- intérêts contre l'entreprise japonaise née pendant la période coloniale du Japon* (일제징용시 일본기업의 불법행위로 인한 손해배상청구권의 소멸시효남용에 관한 연구 - 대법원 2012. 5. 24. 선고 2009다68620 판결), 168 SEOUL LAW JOURNAL 393, 394 et seq. (2013) (in Korean); Eun-

During the Korean War and South Korea's dictatorship period, there were cases in which human rights were violated by the government. As Korea democratized after 1987, victims of human rights violations filed claims for damages against the government on the basis of tortious acts. Defenses of extinctive prescription against such claims were often denied on the basis of good faith, but there were circumstances under which that defense was accepted. For this reason, the Constitutional Court was called on to decide whether it was constitutional to apply the 10-year statute of limitations under CivC Article 766(2) to "civilian massacres" and "grave human rights abuses." The Korean constitutional court ruled that applying extinctive prescription of 10 years to the right to claim damages suffered in these massacres and abuses would infringe the victims' rights and thus violate the constitution.[61] Since this ruling, victims of civilian massacres and grave human rights abuses do not need to defend themselves against extinctive prescription, since the government (defendant) are not allowed to raise the defense of extinctive prescription. If a lower court were to apply CivC Article 766(2) to incidents concerning civilian massacres and grave human rights abuses, it would commit an error in applying the law.[62]

A new paragraph, CivC Article 766(3), was recently added to protect minors in 2020; it states that when a minor suffers from sexual violence, sexual molestation, sexual harassment, or other sexual infringement, the extinctive prescription of the right to claim compensation for damages shall not begin until such a minor becomes an adult, which in Korea means age 19. Before this revision, if a 15-year-old minor was sexually assaulted, and his or her parents did not file a lawsuit for three years—even after knowing who the perpetrator was—any claim for damages would expire before the minor reached adulthood due to the statute of limitations. This was a problem since minor victims would be denied the right to claim damages

Kyung Lee, *The Right of Civilian Claim to Japan & Extinctive Prescription in Forced Enforcement* (강제징용 배상판결에서 나타난 대일민간인청구권과 소멸시효 - 대법원 2012.05.24.선고 2009다68620 판결을 중심으로), 41(2) HUFS LAW REVIEW 291, 292 et seq. (2017) (in Korean); Hong-Ryeol Lee, *A Study on the Forced Labor Victims and Compensation for Damage* (강제징용피해와 손해배상책임 - 대판 2012.5.24, 2009다22549를 중심으로), 10 THE KOREAN AGGREGATE BUILDINGS LAW 189, 190 et seq. (2012) (in Korean).

61 Constitutional Court Decision 2014Hun-Ba148 · 162 · 219 · 223 · 290 · 466, 2015Hun-Ba50 · 440, 2016Hun-Ba419 (consolidated), August 30, 2018.

62 Supreme Court Decision 2019Da220380, May 14, 2020.

if their parents decided not to file a lawsuit, which they might do to avoid the harm that a lawsuit might cause their children or in consideration of their relationship with the perpetrator. Accordingly, the law was amended to include CivC Article 766(3), which ensures that minors who have been sexually assaulted have the right to claim damages once they reach the age of majority.

8. Product Liability

Product liability is a type of liability in tort law whereby manufacturers, suppliers, and the like are liable if the products they make available to the public are defective and cause injuries. Courts in common law jurisdictions developed the idea of product liability to counteract a common defense in contract law regarding a lack of privity in cases where plaintiffs had not directly transacted with the manufacturer.[63] Recognizing the hurdles in the existing system with regard to protecting consumers, Korea also enacted the Product Liability Act (PL Act) in 2002; it adopted the common law jurisprudence of product liability.[64]

(1) Elements of Product Liability

The PL Act is applied in relation to movables that are industrially manufactured or processed; it does not cover immovables such as condominiums. A "manufacturer" refers to a legal person engaged in the business of manufacturing, processing, or importing products. The manufacturer is held primarily liable; suppliers of products may become secondarily liable if the manufacturer cannot be identified (PL Act Article 3(3)).

1) First Element: Defect in Product

'Defect in product' means that a product does not satisfy the ordinarily

63 Mathias Reimann, *Product Liability*, COMPARATIVE TORT LAW (Mauro Bussani and Anthony J. Sebok, eds.), Edward Elgar Publishing, 251 (2015).

64 For a general analysis of the Product Liability Act, see Dong-Jin Park, *Study on the Issues of the Amendment to the Product Liability Act* (현행 제조물책임법의 문제점과 개정방향), 57 ADVANCED COMMERCIAL LAW REVIEW 121, 136 et seq. (2012) (in Korean).

expected level of safety. The key in determining whether a defect in a product exists has to do with its safety. There are three kinds of defects: defect in manufacturing, defect in design, and defect in indication.

❶ Defect in Manufacturing

In order to determine whether there is a defect in manufacturing, it is pivotal to find out whether the product in question deviates from the originally intended design. A defect in manufacturing is a lack of safety caused by the failure to conform with the originally intended design of the product, regardless of whether the manufacturer faithfully carried out its duty of care with respect to the manufacturing or processing of the product.

❷ Defect in Design

Defect in design refers to a lack of safety caused by the failure of a manufacturer to adopt a reasonable alternative design. Determining whether there is a defect in design takes into account a number of factors, including the characteristics and usage of the product, users' expectations of the product, the expected risk associated with the product, users' perceptions of that risk, the possibility of risk avoidance by users, the feasibility of a reasonable alternative design and its financial costs, and the relative merits and demerits of the adopted and reasonable alternative designs.[65] Considering these factors, the Hand rule may serve as a model to decide whether a defect in design exists. According to the Hand rule, it is necessary to compare three factors: the costs of taking precautions (B), the probability of loss (P), and the damage caused by the incident (L). If $B < (P \times L)$, one can infer that there is a defect in design, since possible preventive measures were not taken.

In so-called '*Agent Orange* case', Vietnam War veterans sought damages, alleging that various diseases had been caused due to the US military's practice of spraying the defoliant Agent Orange. The Korean Supreme Court recognized a defect in design;[66] the court held that if a manufacturer designs and manufactures a chemical product containing toxic substances harmful to the human body, it is possible that users of that product or people around those users may be continually and repeatedly exposed to the toxic substance, given its intended use. If the functional utility of the toxic

65 Supreme Court Decision 2011Da22092, April 10, 2014.
66 Supreme Court Decision 2006Da17553, July 12, 2013.

substance is absent or extremely insignificant, and the risk that repeated and continuous exposure to the substance will cause harm to the body is present, then the manufacturer has a high level of obligation to prevent that risk from materializing. Furthermore, the Supreme Court held that in such a case, the manufacturer must minimize or eliminate the risk of the harmful substance by thoroughly verifying the safety of the product with the most advanced technology available at the time of manufacture. No chemical product should be distributed unless it is confirmed that the risk has been eliminated or minimized to a level that verifies the safety of the product. If a manufacturer violates this obligation and manufactures and sells a product that has a risk of causing harm to human health, then the product will be viewed as having a defect in design.

Meanwhile, the Supreme Court did not affirm that there was a defect in design in a tobacco case in which plaintiffs with a history of more than 30 years of smoking were diagnosed with lung cancer and sought damages against the manufacturers and sellers of cigarettes. The Supreme Court affirmed the judgment below, which refused to acknowledge a defect in design in tobacco products. The Supreme Court held that the taste of tobacco varies depending on the quantity of nicotine and tar contained in tobacco smoke. Consumers of tobacco choose and smoke tobacco products with the taste and smell they prefer and with nicotine's pharmacological effect in mind. In light of these factors, a failure to eliminate nicotine by itself cannot be deemed to constitute a defect in design.[67]

Demonstrating a defect in a product can be difficult, since the plaintiff has to present an alternative design that would have been reasonable at the time of the manufacture and distribution of the product.

❸ Defect in Indication

Defect in indication refers to cases where damages or risks caused by a product could have been reduced or avoided if the manufacturer had provided a reasonable explanation, warnings, or other indications on the product. In determining whether a defect in indication exists, factors such as product characteristics, conventional form of usage, users' expectation of the

67 Supreme Court Decision 2011Da22092, April 10, 2014. For a general introduction to the tobacco case in Korea, refer to Kye Joung Lee, *Notable Supreme Court Cases: Civil Law*, 28 JOURNAL OF KOREAN LAW 213, 221 et seq. (2015).

product, expected risks, users' perception of those risks, and the possibility of risk avoidance by users should all be taken into account.[68]

In a case in which a person who took the cold medication Contac 600, an over-the-counter medication containing phenylpropanolamine, died of a hemorrhagic stroke, the Korean Supreme Court did not find a defect in indication. The cold medication packaging indicated hemorrhagic stroke as a potential side effect and added that Contac 600 should not be taken by patients with a history of hemorrhagic strokes.[69]

In the tobacco lawsuit, one of the key issues was whether there was a defect in indication. Interestingly, the Korean tobacco company used to put mild warnings like "moderate smoking for your health" on its products in the 1970s. As more scientific reports cited the serious diseases caused by smoking, the company intensified its warnings around 1989, stating that smoking could lead to lung cancer and was especially harmful to the health of pregnant women and young people. The Supreme Court refused to recognize a defect in indication in tobacco products, holding that media reports and statutes had raised awareness among the general public of the fact that tobacco consumption can cause various respiratory diseases, including lung cancer. In addition, the Supreme Court noted that a determination of whether to continue smoking was a matter of personal choice based on each individual's free will; furthermore, it was widely known among cigarette smokers that it might be difficult to quit smoking once one starts.

2) Second Element: Damages Due to Defect (Causation)

One of the difficulties a victim faces in seeking damages for product liability is the establishment of causation. Due to the structural maldistribution of evidence, victims often find it difficult to collect enough evidence to establish causation between the defect and the damages. Previously, the Supreme Court adopted the *de facto* presumption legal approach in a case in which a television exploded while the victim was watching it.[70] The Supreme Court clarified the theory of *de facto* presumption by stating that the good is presumed to be defective and the accident is presumed to have occurred

68 Supreme Court Decision 2002Da17333, September 5, 2003.
69 Supreme Court Decision 2007Da52287, February 28, 2008.
70 Supreme Court Decision 98Da15934, February 25, 2000.

due to the defect if the following conditions are met: first, the accident occurred in the normal process of use of the good by the consumer; second, the consumer proves that the accident occurred in a realm under the manufacturer's exclusive control; and third, it seems that the accident normally would not have occurred without manufacturer's fault. An exception applies if the manufacturer can prove that the accident resulted from causes other than the defect. Such an alleviation of the burden of proof for injured parties complies with an ideal underlying the system of the tort law, which is to apportion damage equitably.

De facto presumption was codified in 2017 following the above precedent. PL Act Article 3(2) prescribes that when an injured person demonstrates the following, it shall be presumed that the product had a defect at the time it was supplied and that the damage was caused due to the defect: first, that the damage was incurred during the product's normal use; second, that the damage was attributable to a cause substantially under the manufacturer's management; and third, that the damage would not ordinarily have occurred if it were not for the relevant defect of the product. However, this provision does not apply to cases where the manufacturer has proven that the damage is attributable to causes other than the defect.

Another issue concerning causation is whether epidemiological causation can be used to determine legal causation. Epidemiology is a method used to study causes of health outcomes and diseases in populations. Epidemiology has also been defined as the study of the distribution (frequencies and/or patterns) and determinants (e.g., causes and risk factors) of health-related circumstances or phenomena in specified populations.[71] Thus, epidemiological causation can be defined as a statistically determined correlation between exposure to certain materials and the occurrence of certain diseases and the quantification of the degree of such a correlation. The key question is whether epidemiological causation can be used to support legal causation. Since epidemiological causation only deals with the factors that may have caused the disease in question rather than the factors that *actually* resulted in a given plaintiff's disease, it is difficult to conclude that epidemiological causation can be used to establish legal causation. The Korean Supreme Court holds this view. In the tobacco case, the Supreme

71 https://www.cdc.gov/careerpaths/k12teacherroadmap/epidemiology.html (accessed on February 4, 2022).

Court affirmed the lower court's judgment that refused to acknowledge a causal link between plaintiffs' smoking and lung cancer, holding that even if epidemiological causation between smoking and cellular cancer is acknowledged, this alone does not prove causation between a given individual's smoking and the disease, particularly as cellular cancer is a non-specific disease.[72]

3) Third Element: Lack of Grounds for Exemption

Where a manufacturer or supplier that is liable for damages proves any of the following facts, it is exempt from any liability for damages: first, the manufacturer did not supply the product; second, the existence of the defect could not be identified by the scientific or technical knowledge of the time when the manufacturer supplied the product (this is known as the development risks defense); or third, the defect is attributable to the fact that the manufacturer complied with standards prescribed by an act or a subordinate statute in force at the time when it supplied the product (this is known as the defense of compliance to regulation).

The development risks defense is often the key issue in litigation; it is accepted in order not to curb technological development, since burdening manufacturers with the responsibility of development risk could hinder future technological advances. In judging whether a development risks defense is valid, courts are to apply the standard in force when the manufacturer supplied the product—judges should not decide based on the time of the lawsuit or based on hindsight.

In reality, these grounds for exemption are hard to establish, and thus product liability can be seen as strict liability.

(2) Effects of Product Liability, Including Punitive Damages

Under the PL Act, a victim can claim compensation limited to consequential damages. A victim shall be compensated for damages to a person's life, body,

72 Supreme Court Decision 2011Da22092, April 10, 2014. Concerning the assertion that the probability of causation calculated by epidemiological study can show a high degree of probability so that the determination of epidemiological causation can equate proof of causation, see Sun-Goo Lee, *Proving Causation With Epidemiological Evidence in Tobacco Lawsuits*, 154 JOURNAL OF PREVENTIVE MEDICINE AND PUBLIC HEALTH 80, 87 (2016).

or property caused by a defect of a product. This means the victim cannot be compensated for damages to the product itself under the PL Act; those can be sought under the general tort law in CivC Article 750.

One of the characteristics of the PL Act is that, exceptionally, it introduced punitive damages.[73] If an unspecified number of people are harmed by a defective product, and if manufacturers are only obliged to compensate damages suffered by those who file suit (and not for damages suffered by others who did not take legal action), then the overall result is that the manufacturer would have gained a net profit from the distribution of defective goods. In order to correct this unreasonable and unfair result, punitive damages are introduced.

If a manufacturer, despite its knowledge of a defect of a product, causes serious damage to a person's life or body as a result of not taking necessary measures against the defect, the manufacturer shall be liable for up to three times the actual damages sustained by victims (PL Act Article 3(2)). The court shall consider the following factors when determining punitive damages: the degree of malice in the intention, the extent of damages caused by the defect, the financial gains obtained by the manufacturer by supplying the product, the degree of criminal punishment or administrative measures inflicted on the manufacturer due to the defect, the period during which the product was supplied and the scale of such supply, the financial status of the manufacturer, and finally any endeavor by the manufacturer to compensate victims' damages. If a victim shows that the defendant intentionally or recklessly disregarded the defect and caused grave injury, he or she is likely to be entitled to punitive damages.

(3) Extinctive Prescription

The right of claim for damages under the PL Act expires three years from the date on which the injured person or his or her legal representative becomes aware of both the damage and the person liable for the damage (PL Act Article 7(1)).

In addition, the right of claim for damages under the PL Act shall expire ten years from the date on which the manufacturer supplied the

73 Chang-Hyun Lee, *Product Liability and Punitive Damages* (제조물책임과 징벌적 손해배상), 172 JUSTICE 5 et seq. (2019) (in Korean).

product which caused the relevant damages (PL Act Article 7(2)). With respect to damages by substances such as asbestos or medicines that accumulate in the human body and damage a person's health, or any other damages whose symptoms appear after a significant latency period, extinctive prescription shall run from the date on which the actual damages occur (PL Act Article 7(2)). In case lawsuits were filed by patients whose illnesses had a latency period due to a defect of a product, extinctive prescription shall run from the date on which the victim was diagnosed by a doctor.[74] This makes extinctive prescription similar to the discovery rule, a rule of common law indicating that the statute of limitations on bringing a claim does not begin until the date on which a claimant actually discovers or should have discovered an injury or loss.[75]

9. Conclusion

Korea has surprised the world by simultaneously establishing a solid and stable democratic system and achieving remarkable economic development. This achievement can be attributed to the dynamic aspects of Korean society and the country's ability to cope with new circumstances and phenomena. As this article has detailed, the legal theory behind torts and the practice of tort law also show these characteristics; they demonstrate flexibility in terms of handling new social problems as they emerge. However, it remains to be seen how tort law in Korea will progress to deal with new challenges such as artificial intelligence and the fourth industrial revolution. Based on this examination of the historical path that Korean tort law has traversed thus far, it is reasonable to have an optimistic outlook.

74 Supreme Court Decision 2019Da297137, August 19, 2021.

75 Naomi Berkowitz, *Balancing the Statute of Limitations and the Discovery Rule: Victims of Incestuous Abuse Are Denied Access to Washington Courts - Tyson v. Tyson*, 10 SEATTLE UNIVERSITY LAW REVIEW 721, 747-757 (1987).

Chapter 5

Civil Procedure Law

Wonyol Jon*

1. Introduction

(1) Features of Korean Civil Procedure Law

Civil procedure is the body of law that sets out the rules and standards that courts follow when adjudicating civil lawsuits. These rules govern how a lawsuit or case may be commenced; what kind of service of process is required; the types of pleadings or statements of case, motions or applications allowed in civil cases; hearings and trials; the process for issuing a judgment; the process for post-trial procedures; various available remedies; and how the courts and clerks must function.

The most notable feature of Korean civil procedure law might be that the Court of Appeal, which is situated between district court of first instance and the Supreme Court, deals with fact-finding as well as questions of law. In the United States and many European countries, the second instance courts deal only with questions of law, or deal only to a limited extent with factual issues. In Korea, however, the Court of Appeal is fully empowered to re-establish issues of fact.

Another aspect of Korean civil procedure is that trials are not concentrated. In other words, trial hearings are held sporadically, often

* Professor, Seoul National University School of Law.

reconvening every four weeks. This style of hearing schedules can also be often found in the continental civil procedure system, for example in the German or French civil procedure practices. In contrast, the common law civil procedure typically calls for a more concentrated trial once the initial pleadings and discovery have taken place.

(2) History

As in any sophisticated society, Korea for the past thousand years has had a well-defined legal system. There have been written rules for administrative and criminal law, and adjudicators have been expected to follow such rules. There has also been a robust procedural law and adjudication system since before the medieval age, starting under the Koryeo dynasty and reinvigorated during the Chosun dynasty, which lasted until the modern era. That said, the rules governing civil transactions were slow to develop, and the administrative and judicial powers were not separated during those times. Korea's modern judicial system, which is based on the separation of powers, was imported from Europe through Japan during the so-called Korean 'modernization period', which took place roughly from the late 19th to the early 20th centuries.

In July 1894, King Gojong separated Korea's judicial affairs from his central administrative apparatus by proclaiming that punishment could henceforth be levied as the result of a trial only by a specialist entity. He also banned the arrest of suspects by administrative agencies. Under the Court Organization Act, five different courts were established on March 25, 1895. When the Korean government was put directly under the supervision of Japanese colonial occupiers in 1905, Japan began to intervene in Korea's judicial affairs by sending Japanese judges and prosecutors and their assistants to Korea to "advise" its court system. In October 1909, all the judicial organizations of Korea, including its courts and jails, were placed under the direct control of the Japanese colonial power. About a year later, on August 29, 1910, Korea was finally formally annexed to Japan, and Korea's three-tier, three-instance court system was then introduced on March 18, 1912. The model has remained to this day.

On August 15, 1945, at the end of World War II, the United States placed Korea under its military rule after liberating the Korean Peninsula from Japanese colonial rule. However, the Americans temporarily maintained the old Japanese legal and judicial systems. The Korean judiciary was formally reborn on July 17, 1948 with the promulgation of a new constitution for the Korean government.

The Korean Constitution guarantees the independence of the judiciary. The Court Organization Act, enacted in 1949, provided for a modern legal system based on the concept of a three-tier court system. The Korean Constitution has undergone several amendments since those early days, many of which have been translated into revisions of the Court Organization Act. The three-tier organizational structure, however, remained intact throughout that period.

The Korean judiciary, which began with one high court and three district courts in 1948, now consists of a Supreme Court, six high courts, one patent court, one administrative court, one bankruptcy court, eight family courts, and eighteen district courts. In addition, the judiciary has a Judicial Research and Training Institute and a Training Institute for Court Officials.

The basic source of law for Korean civil procedure is the Civil Procedure Code (CPC), which consists of 502 articles. Other important sources of civil procedure law include the Civil Enforcement Act, the Small Claims Act, and the Bankruptcy Act.

(3) Outline of Civil Procedure

The procedures for filing a lawsuit, case management and deliberation protocols under the CPC are as follows.

A civil complaint is initiated when a plaintiff who wants his/her right to be upheld through a trial files a lawsuit or complaint. When the court receives such a complaint, it must first conduct a simple review thereof. If there is no defect in format, the court immediately serves a copy of the complaint on the other party (the defendant) through the regular post system. The defendant then has 30 days to submit his/her response to the initial complaint. If a copy of the complaint cannot be served on the defendant for some reason, the plaintiff is required to provide the court with another valid address of the defendant. In some instances, a complaint can also be served by way of public notice.

Once a complaint is served on the defendant, the defendant's answer (or lack thereof) determines the subsequent procedural posture of the case. If a defendant fails to submit an answer within the specified 30 days, or admits the allegations levied against him/her, the case will be referred to judgment without any hearing. In many cases, however, the defendant submits an answer refuting the plaintiff's allegations. In such cases, the presiding judge sets the earliest possible hearing date to allow the parties to have an in-person meeting with him/her. Unlike in the United States, there are no strict distinctions between the various phases of a civil trial in Korea. New claims may be submitted even when the initial complaints and answers have been exchanged or some evidence taking has already been conducted. In other words, the parties may submit evidence on numerous occasions throughout the proceedings.

The initial hearing date is set at an early stage. Subsequent hearings are held by piecemeal, usually every four to five weeks. The hearings themselves are oral in nature. Each party is given the opportunity to narrow down the issues under dispute before the judge, and allowed to rebut the other side's arguments. This process allows the parties to exhaust their assertions and arguments, and the Court can arrive at its decision in a transparent manner by means of oral examinations in open court. The aim is for the proceedings to operate in a way that enhances the participants' trust and sense of procedural justice. Once the parties' positions become clear, the ensuing application for evidence and its examination by the Court can then focus on those remaining issues under dispute.

In addition to the oral arguments in open court, each party must submit or file legal briefs (written documentation of its pleadings and supporting evidence) throughout the litigation process. To substantiate its claims, each party must complete an application for evidence or produce relevant evidence on its own. Relevant documentary evidence should be submitted together with the legal briefs, along with other necessary submissions, such as requests for document production orders and applications for witness or expert testimony.

During the evidentiary examination hearing, witnesses may be examined one by one. However, as hearings are not concentrated in the Korean civil adjudication process, only one or two witnesses are usually examined at a particular hearing date, with the subsequent witness testimonies examined at the next hearing date.

When both sides have submitted sufficient arguments and evidence, the court closes the trial and sets the date for the delivery of the judgment, usually four or five weeks after the final hearing date.

2. Jurisdiction

(1) Concepts

The social purpose of a judicial procedure is for there to be an effective and efficient system for resolving disputes. For a court to be effective, it must have a system of rendering a binding adjudication and a corresponding capacity to enforce its judgments. This raises the question of power: the power to command the parties to a case to appear before the court and the power to enforce the court's judgment. The court's power to enforce its judicial judgment ultimately hinges on the authority of the judges to coerce resistant or reluctant parties to appear before them and abide by their commands. Such authority is termed the "jurisdiction" of the court.

Conceptually, a court's jurisdiction can be further divided into a few sub-issues. First, the parties to a case must be subject to the reach of the Korean courts (jaepankwon in Korean) and not subject to some civil-liability exemption. Second, the case should have a "reasonable link" to Korea so that the Korean courts could exercise their jurisdiction over it under international procedure law. Third, there must be a district or special court within Korea that enjoys both subject and territorial jurisdiction over the parties to a case (kwanhalkwon in Korean).

(2) Exemption of Jurisdiction and International Jurisdiction

In principle, the Korean courts' power to adjudicate civil complaints applies to all those who are physically present in the Korean territory, except those who are exempt from such power. Diplomats are one category of individuals exempted from such power by virtue of the Vienna Convention on Diplomatic Relations. A difficult question is whether foreign governments are exempt from the Korean courts' civil jurisdiction. In the 1970s, the Korean Supreme Court held that foreign governments are not subject to the jurisdiction of the Korean courts. However, the Supreme Court changed its position in 1998 and held that the Korean courts may exercise jurisdiction over a foreign government acting as a defendant in a transactional complaint unless the dispute is, for some reason, closely related to a sovereign activity of that foreign state.[1] Despite this pronouncement by the Korean Supreme Court , it is still unclear whether a court can easily establish jurisdiction over a foreign government because the courts themselves do not seem to adhere to the above principle in all cases.[2]

Even if the parties to a case are not exempt from the jurisdiction of the Korean courts, the courts do not always exercise their power to adjudicate. A Korean court can assert international jurisdiction over a case only if the plaintiff's complaint or the defendant has a reasonable link to Korea (i.e., a significant connection to Korea). To establish such reasonable link, the Act on Private International Law (APIL) of Korea requires a case to have a "substantial relation" to Korea (Article 2(1)). The Korean Supreme Court has held that this means that the parties and the object of dispute must have a relation to Korea that could justify the Korean courts' exercise of such jurisdiction.[3] This issue is discussed in greater detail in the section on international jurisdiction under the topic of international civil procedure law.

(3) Territorial Jurisdiction

People who want to file a lawsuit before a Korean court must first ensure that the court has territorial and subject matter jurisdiction over the case.

The rules delineating territorial jurisdiction are stipulated in Articles 2 to 24 of CPC. At its most basic level, territorial jurisdiction is decided on the basis of the defendant's residence. If the defendant is a corporation, its residence is the place where its main office is located. Territorial jurisdiction can also be established in places where business is conducted, places where a financial or transactional duty is or should have been performed, places where the defendant controls real property, and places where an alleged tortious offense was committed, among others. In cases where multiple territorial jurisdictions can be established, the plaintiffs may choose to bring

1 Supreme Court Decision 97Da39216, December 17, 1998.

2 See, e.g., Supreme Court Decision 2009Da16766, December 13, 2011.

3 In contrast, the US Supreme Court requires only "minimum contact" for the US courts to exercise international jurisdiction over a case (International Shoe Co. v. Washington, 326 U.S. 310 (1945)).

their cases to any of the applicable courts.

(4) Subject Matter Jurisdiction and Venue

In contrast with the courts of first instance in the Anglo-American system, where a single judge usually hears civil cases, in the Korean courts, there are two models of judicial panels. A court can be composed of either a three-judge panel chamber or a single-judge chamber. This corresponds with the continental system's tradition. The three-judge chamber, which consists of a presiding judge and two associate judges, is usually reserved for larger lawsuits where the damages claimed exceed KRW200 million.

Even for three-judge panel chamber cases, however, the parties need not be represented by a lawyer, and *pro se* litigation is permitted. However, if a party chooses to hire a representative, that person must be a licensed lawyer if the case is being heard by a three-judge panel. In cases handled by a single judge, non-lawyers are allowed to represent the parties under certain circumstances, but only with the courts' express approval. The representatives in such cases are limited to family members who have close relationships with the litigants or those hired by the parties and have already executed matters directly relating to the cases at hand.

Small claims cases are those in which the amounts in dispute do not exceed KRW30 million and the plaintiffs seek no form of redress other than either payment of money or delivery of a certain quantity of monetary securities. (This threshold may seem quite high.) In small claims cases, the spouses, parents, and siblings of the parties may represent them without the courts' approval.

3. Initiation of an Action

(1) Filing a Complaint

A person can commence an action against another by filing a "complaint" with a district court (CPC Article 248). A complaint is a document containing a statement of claim in which the plaintiff details the relevant parties, any legal representative or counsel authorized to speak on their behalf (if applicable), and the relief sought by the plaintiff. The complaint sets the boundaries of the subject matter of the proposed adjudication. Depending on the amount of damages sought by the plaintiff, the complaint is then passed to either the three-judge panel chamber or the one-judge chamber for further processing.

When submitting a complaint, the plaintiff must also prepay the delivery and stamp fees. The stamp fee increases proportionally to the size of the case.

Under Korean civil procedure law, it is vital to accurately describe the object of the claim (i.e., the conclusion or demand of the complaint). The plaintiff must always define and describe his/her concrete demands. Even in a personal injury case following a traffic accident, for example, in which the plaintiff is unable to continue working and the actual monetary damages can be properly calculated only after physical assessment by a doctor (which typically occurs later in the judicial process), the plaintiff's complaint submitted to the court must state the concrete amount claimed as compensation. In such cases, the plaintiff usually indicates a provisional amount of claimed damages and later revises the object amount of the claim when he/she has already undergone a physical examination by a doctor.

According to CPC, evidence (e.g., copies of written contracts in contract-related disputes or title registrations in land-related disputes) need not be included or attached to the initial complaint. Nonetheless, the court often recommends that the plaintiff does so to expedite the legal proceedings.

(2) Assignment of a Case

The chief judge or deputy chief judge assigns cases to several chambers of the district court. This is typically done in accordance with a workload allocation plan, which is usually promulgated in late February of each year, when district court judges are usually rotated or promoted. (Korean judges do not serve at one district court for their entire careers. They usually serve at one district court for two to four years, after which they are usually assigned to another district court pursuant to the personnel requirements of the judiciary, as detailed in an order issued every February by the Supreme Court.)

(3) Review of Formalities

When the chief judge or deputy chief judge has assigned a case to either a three-judge panel chamber or a single-judge chamber, the case is passed to such chamber. Most civil cases are handled by judges sitting alone. In single-judge cases, the singular judge is the presiding judge. In three-judge panels, the most senior judge on the panel usually becomes the presiding judge.

The presiding judge first reviews the complaint to check if the statement of claim meets the requirements. These requirements are as follows: (1) the statement of claim must state all the elements required by Article 249 of CPC (e.g., the names of the parties, the names of the representatives, the type of relief and the claim amount sought by the plaintiff) and (2) the relevant stamp fees must be attached to the written complaint. If any of these requirements are not satisfied, the presiding judge will order the plaintiff to amend his/her complaint within a designated period of time. Failure to do so may lead the presiding judge to either reiterate the order or dismiss the complaint at his/her discretion (CPC Article 254(2)). Once dismissed, a complaint can be refiled when the plaintiff subsequently cures the previous defects.

(4) Service of Process

If a written complaint has satisfied all the necessary requirements, the court serves the complaint on the defendant or gives the defendant a copy of the complaint (CPC Article 255(1)). Here, the defendant must be given sufficient time to take effective action in his/her defense. Other relevant documents, such as instructions regarding the Korean civil procedure and the Order to Submit a Written Defense, are usually enclosed with the original complaint and served together with it.

Service is an official act that is to be effectuated ex officio by the court. It is usually delivered via a special kind of registered mail through the Korean Post Office. In the United States, the plaintiff is personally responsible for effectuating service, and service must be made within the court's territorial jurisdiction. The rule in Korea is quite different. In the Korean court procedure, the court is responsible for serving notice of litigation, and there are no "territorial limits of service."

As mentioned above, in Korea, service is effectuated through registered mail. In certain instances, however, a designated court official or bailiff can also serve the documents, usually after the issuance of a court order or after a request for such is made by the plaintiff. This is usually done when the first attempt to serve notice through the postal system has failed. The details of how to serve notice are largely the same regardless of the nature of the litigation or the relief sought, varying only slightly on the basis of whether the defendant is a natural or juridical person and whether the defendant's residence, domicile, place of business, or whereabouts are known or unknown to the plaintiff and court.

In the event that the notice of litigation cannot be served due to the unavailability of the recipient, unanswered door knocks, an unclear recipient, an unclear address, relocation of the defendant, or another reason, the service will have to be tried again. The presiding judge in such situation then orders the plaintiff to correct the defendant's address within a few days, usually seven business days. Failure to comply with this order may result in dismissal of the complaint.

Depending on the reason for the failure of the initial service attempt, the following methods for retrying service can be used: attempting to serve the same complaint at the same address again, attempting service with the support of a court bailiff, or service by public notice. If it becomes obvious that it is impossible for the plaintiff, acting without fault or negligence, to specify the defendant's actual address, the presiding judge may allow service to be effectuated through public notice as an alternative means of service (CPC Article 194). In such situations, the plaintiff must first apply for service by public notice, and once the application is approved, a public notice of service is posted. The first public notice takes effect 14 days after the posting. From the second public notice, the period before the notice takes effect is shortened to one day (CPC Article 196). After the public notice of the complaint takes effect, the first hearing date is set by the court. Most of these cases are typically closed after the first hearing and subsequently directly proceed to judgment rendering.

In previous decades, public notices were posted on the district court's bulletin board. Today, they are posted on the court's website.

(5) Computerization and Text Message Notice System

Korea has one of the world's most sophisticated digital case management systems (CMSs). All the judges and court officials in any Korean court nationwide today use the judiciary's CMS to digitize all case documents. CMS was introduced in 1998 and has since been updated numerous times. It was initially used only for civil cases but has since also been used for family, administrative, and insolvency cases.

CMS, however, is used not only by judges and court personnel but also by outside stakeholders, including the litigants themselves. The general citizenry can also discover a wide array of information on the judiciary's website, including relevant hearing dates, documents that have been submitted as evidence in certain cases, and procedural orders issued by the court.

One of the most useful features of CMS is the text message notice system. This system allows litigants to expediently learn via text messages if there is an update regarding their case, such as when a hearing date has been set and when documentary evidence has been filed. Anyone with a civil case pending before a Korean court (including the branch and municipal courts) and his/her representatives may make use of this system after paying a modest service fee.

4. Subsequent Pleadings and Hearings

(1) The Answer

The disposition of a case is generally the same regardless of whether it is handled by a single judge or by a three-judge panel. Upon receiving a copy of a written complaint, the defendant is required to file a written defense within 30 days. The answer should be a Statement of Defense.

If the defendant accepts the allegations and/or admits all the facts as stated in the complaint, the court may directly proceed to summary judgment, without conducting a hearing. Defendants who fail to object to the written complaint as served are considered by the court to have admitted all the relevant facts and allegations, therefore leading to the same result. These provisions are designed to ensure a swift trial in cases where there are no relevant legal or factual disputes.

However, defendants typically contest the facts alleged in the complaints. In such cases, after receiving the defendant's answer, the plaintiff can submit a new set of written pleadings elaborating in greater detail the grounds for his/her original "Demand of Complaint." This document is described as a "preparatory writing." After receiving a preparatory writing from the plaintiff, the defendant can submit his/her own written pleading in response. This document is also called preparatory writing.

(2) General Pattern of Hearings

The idealized image of proceedings before the court is that of a series of well-prepared oral arguments. In reality, however, the parties' oral arguments are delivered on the basis of their writings and usually before hearings. After the oral arguments, the court initiates proof taking to determine any facts that may have been disputed in the various exchanges. Further oral arguments to size up and assess the entire case are often made, after which the case proceeds to the final judgment.

The idealized image of court proceedings again suggests that the exchanges described above are carried out intensively during one or two hearings. In reality, however, even in simple cases, this ideal is often not achievable. More commonly, the courts schedule several hearings for oral argumentation and proof taking in any given case. Cases are frequently adjourned for the convenience of the litigants, experts, witnesses, and court, which tends to prolong civil proceedings.

The Korean courts will often set the first hearing date when the parties have exchanged their initial pleadings. After one or two exchanges of written arguments between the parties, the court designates an initial hearing date. The hearings follow a relaxed schedule, and a second hearing is usually held four or five weeks after the first hearing. The litigants use the intervening time to prepare evidence for the second hearing. Depending on the complexity of the case, there can be several hearings scheduled in this way, separated by a period of four or five weeks so that the parties can prepare additional evidence. At each hearing, the court asks both parties to make their arguments and submit their relevant evidence.

The proceedings unfold across a number of sessions, spanning the time from the initiation of the case to the final judgment. This model, as already alluded to above, stands in contrast to the more concentrated trial procedure that can be observed in many common law systems, such as those in the United States and the United Kingdom.

The presiding judge may also order the litigants in a case to go through "preliminary proceedings" to clarify the relevant legal and factual issues of the case. The judge may do this at any point when he/she wishes to classify the case, usually at the earlier stages of the case but sometimes also after several hearings. Preliminary proceedings are designed to clarify and narrow down the facts and legal issues that will be examined in the trial. This is often necessary in complex cases in which the judge feels that there is a need for a separate set of proceedings to map out the structure and logic of the trial.

There are two kinds of preliminary proceedings. The first requires the litigants to exchange legal briefs about the factual disputes and legal issues at play. This is called a written preliminary proceeding. The second requires that the parties appear in court to establish their claims and evidence. This is called an oral preliminary proceeding.

The preliminary proceedings in the Korean system may be loosely equated with the pre-trial proceedings in US civil procedure. However, unlike in the United States, where every case must go through a pre-trial proceedings phase, in Korea, preliminary proceedings are optional, and the court can either order them or proceed directly with the regular trial proceedings.

(3) Principles of Pleading and Orality

The iterative sequence of discussions and conferences, collectively referred to as oral arguments, is progressively designed to structure and clarify the content of a case and advance the process of litigation. The procedure is under the "principle of orality".

In addition, as in most other modern civil procedure codes, the "principle of pleading" serves as a fundamental legal principle in CPC. This means that a Korean court must also generally take a case as it is presented by the parties themselves. The Korean courts cannot address claims that have not been raised by the plaintiff. It is the parties that must raise pertinent allegations and offer relevant proof for these, including which witnesses to call. The court, on its own, cannot dig up and present evidence in a trial.[4]

However, there are two important caveats to the principle of orality and

4 A notable exception exists in some "family" actions, where the court has extensive sua sponte powers, including the power to call witnesses not nominated by the parties.

pleading in Korea. The first is the observation that, *de facto*, the principle of orality is actually quite impaired in the Korean system. In actual court cases, the litigating parties, their attorneys, and the judges do not depend much on oral arguments. Rather, they depend heavily on the written submissions by the parties. This phenomenon is intensified by the piecemeal hearing practice described earlier. American lawyers observing a Korean trial will likely feel that the oral arguments lack the intensity of those in a US courtroom.

Second, the judges in Korea tend to intervene much more actively during oral arguments than their US counterparts. The Korean judges tend to take a more active role in courtrooms. Thus, Korean civil procedure feels more like a collective discussion than an adversarial argument. That said, the atmosphere in the Korean courtrooms differs on the basis of a number of factors, including the judge's personal temperament and imagination, level of understanding of the case, and assessment of the overall capacity and energy of the counsel, of the complexity or novelty of the case, and of the overall relevance of the case from an equity or public-interest perspective.

In three-judge court panels, the presiding judge is usually the one who intervenes in the oral arguments. Presiding judges typically prepare themselves to direct oral argumentation and gather the necessary evidence. The two associate judges are generally less vocal during oral arguments. It is the presiding judges who serve as the principal actors for the court, although they may order recesses to deliberate and consult with the two associate judges.

Article 136 of CPC enables judges' active involvement in oral argumentation. It states that "[t]he presiding judge may, to clarify the litigation relations, ask the parties questions, and urge them to prove, on the factual or legal matters." The same article of CPC also empowers the associate judges to do the same "after informing the presiding judge thereof." This is called clarification right. It is also the judges' "clarification duty" inasmuch as it is what is right.

(4) Deciding on and Changing the Hearing Date

As mentioned above, the presiding judge unilaterally sets the first hearing date, but such date can be changed with the consent of both parties. For this, the parties must submit a hearing date change application, along with the written consent of the other party, to the relevant court prior to the hearing date.

The second hearing date is set during the first hearing, after consultation with the parties. The subsequent hearing dates are set in the same way. Changing the second or subsequent hearing date, therefore, is allowed only with the court's permission and only when a substantial reason justifying such a hearing date change arises (e.g., a funeral or marriage of a family member of one of the litigants, a summons from a different court prior to receiving the notice for hearing). To request such an extraordinary hearing date change, the parties must submit a hearing date change application to the court along with the necessary documentation to demonstrate the extraordinary circumstances leading to the request.

(5) Change in Claim

After the initial pleadings are made, the case begins to flow and take shape on the basis of the arguments and evidence presented by both parties. However, it sometimes happens that, during the process, it becomes necessary to amend or change the cause of action or alter the concrete remedies (objects) of the claim.

Each jurisdiction's procedural law has its own unique approach for allowing such alterations. CPC is designed not to hold the parties to their initial claims and evidentiary arguments; rather, it allows the parties to amend their claims as the case develops. Korea has one of the most accepting approaches to such modifications (CPC Article 262). Due to this flexibility, plaintiffs frequently change their causes of action or the objects of their claims.

(6) Effects of Non-Attendance in Hearings

1) Plaintiff's Failure to Attend a Hearing

If the plaintiff fails to make an appearance in court but the defendant makes an appearance, the defendant's attitude can determine the subsequent disposition of the case. If the defendant (often intentionally) fails to provide any legal or factual argument or evidence to support his/her non-liability, the presiding judge sets a new hearing date. If both parties fail to appear at the rescheduled hearing or if only the defendant makes an appearance but again fails to produce any legal defense or exculpatory evidence, the court may abandon the case rather than set another hearing date. If, within one month, the plaintiff fails to apply for the setting of a new hearing date, the court will deem the lawsuit to have been effectively withdrawn (CPC Article 268).

If, on the other hand, the defendant makes an appearance in court and provides legal or factual arguments in his/her defense, the case may proceed even if the plaintiff fails to appear in court.

2) Defendant's Failure to Attend

If the plaintiff makes an appearance in court and provides arguments supporting his/her original complaint but the defendant fails to make an appearance or submit any exculpatory response, the court may find that all of the plaintiff's claims have been confirmed (CPC Article 148). This rarely happens in reality, however, because the court typically moves for "summary judgment" without conducting a hearing whenever the defendant fails to submit an answer within 30 days from his/her receipt of the initial complaint (CPC Article 257).

In such situations, a defendant can always file a petition to resume the case by submitting an answer at any time prior to the judgment hearing.

5. Evidence

(1) Features of Korean Evidence Law

Korean evidence law has several peculiarities. The first pertains to discovery or disclosure during litigation. Here, Korea finds itself at the opposite end of the spectrum from the United States. The United States seems to have one of the most permissible systems globally with regard to evidence gathering and broadly permits the parties themselves to search for evidence confirming their allegations during discovery. The US discovery system was enacted in 1938 with the passage of the Federal Rules of Civil Procedure. The German system seems to have a more moderate approach. In Korea, the parties have great difficulty gathering their own evidence if such evidence happens to be in the possession of the opposing party. CPC's provisions focus primarily on evidence taking by the court and hardly dwell on the gathering of evidence by the parties themselves. This is based on the philosophy that each party should carry out lawsuits on his/her own risk.

The foregoing makes it more challenging for Korean plaintiffs who do not possess crucial evidence prior to the commencement of a trial to adequately justify their allegations. There are many instances in which only one side of a dispute has access to the necessary evidence, especially in cases of alleged medical malpractice, intellectual property cases, pollution cases, and others. Without a proper discovery procedure in place, the plaintiffs in such cases cannot always obtain the information and evidence they need to support their claims, and the judgments sometimes fail to uphold justice. Because there is no developed system of pre-trial discovery in Korea, some major industrial disputes between Korean companies have even been litigated before US courts by virtue of forum shopping.

The second peculiarity has to do with the nature of the evidence that may be submitted to the court. Due to the system of trial by jury employed in many US trials, the US system is rigid about the kinds of evidence that are admissible in court. CPC, on the other hand, is quite tolerant of the kinds of evidence that may be brought before a court. Korean law assumes that judges, acting as professional and legally trained adjudicators, are capable of making nuanced decisions about the reliability of the evidence presented.

As is well known, US courts do not permit the use of hearsay evidence in court cases. Korea has a similar evidentiary rule for criminal cases but not for civil cases. CPC allows the parties to submit hearsay evidence without limit, and the judges have the responsibility of determining the evidentiary weights of such submissions.

(2) Submission and Taking of Evidence

Each party must present relevant evidence to the court to establish the various factual claims in their allegations. The only exceptions to this rule are (1) the facts admitted by the opposing party and (2) publicly known facts. Whenever the opposing party fails to contest a claim, it is taken as admitted. The parties must declare themselves in opposition to any of their opponents' assertions if they wish to prevent such assertions from being admitted.

The provisions for evidence in CPC pertain primarily to motions to examine relevant evidence before the court. The parties themselves must initiate any motion to examine the evidence, and the party seeking to support a claim must submit documents or other items as evidence or seek witness testimony, expert appraisals with the motion. Whenever a party makes such a motion, the court must decide whether to grant it. As discussed above, Korean civil procedure is committed to the doctrine of pleading, the principle that the court must generally take a case as the parties plead it. Consequently, the court will not examine any evidence that the parties have not motioned to have examined. Furthermore, as the hearings are scheduled piecemeal, the court will not seek all the relevant evidence on contested issues to be presented in one sitting but will sequence the presentations over time.

Although the parties are usually expected to attach all relevant documentary evidence to their initial complaint or answers in the initial exchange of letters, such exhibits are often not exhaustive, and the parties are usually given opportunities later to produce further documentary evidence or witnesses if a need for such arises.

CPC states that all evidence must be submitted in a timely manner (CPC Articles 146, 147). In reality, however, this is often not properly observed. In such cases, the presiding judge may set a deadline for the production of certain evidence. If such period lapses without compliance, the non-compliant parties may lose their right to submit such evidence even if they attempt to do so at a later date.

(3) Witness

1) Comparative Analysis

With regard to the examination of witnesses, the Korean system focuses more on the "totality of the evidence" and is far less preoccupied than the American system with a minute investigation of individual factual details or the reliability of individual witnesses. Experienced judges in Korea constantly warn against overreliance on oral testimony. Accordingly, they tend to value the testimony of an individual witness less than their counterparts in the United States do. Nonetheless, witnesses still play an important evidentiary role in Korean civil trials.

2) Submitting an Application for Witness Testimony

A party that wants to bring a witness before court must, before the hearing date, formally apply for such witness to appear in court. A witness will not be heard in ordinary litigation unless the presenting party petitions the court to allow such witness's testimony. However, only the court itself can call a witness to the witness stand, and it has the discretion to do or not do so and how often to do so over the course of litigation.

When requesting a witness to be called to the witness stand, the applicant should clearly state the purpose for the witness's testimony and the witness's relationship to the matters at play in the litigation. The applicant should also indicate that the witness will appear in court without coercion and provide the witness's telephone number and/or other contact information.

3) Conducting a Witness Examination

Witnesses may take the witness stand only after they are called to testify. When their turn to testify comes, the court asks them to state their name, age, occupation, and place of residence. It also warns them of their duty to speak the truth before the court, reminding them of the penalties for perjury. Finally, all witnesses are asked to swear an oath of truthfulness. The oath is similar to one that a witness might be asked to swear in other countries: "I swear on penalty of perjury to tell the whole truth and nothing but the truth, in accordance with my conscience."

CPC specifies that witnesses shall first be invited to speak in narrative form, without undue interruption, regarding what they know about the matter on which they have been called to testify. Again, this provision of CPC is not always observed, and some attorneys ask the witnesses long-winded and complex questions, demanding only succinct responses from them in return.

In the past, no verbatim report of the witness testimony was made, and only summaries of the witness's testimonies were entered into the minutes. These summaries, however, were typically detailed. One cannot help but admire the skill with which experienced judges captured the essence of a witness testimony in the trial minutes. The production of such witness testimony summaries certainly made it easier for judges to repeatedly refresh their memories about what happened in the previous trial sessions or proceedings. However, such old system also had serious disadvantages, foremost of which was that nuanced factual details were likely to be lost when the witnesses' stories were only being summarized and not reported verbatim. Often, the color of the witnesses' testimonies was drained in such summaries. For this reason, most witness testimonies today are electronically recorded.

4) Compelling the Appearance of a Witness in Court – Penalties and Imprisonment for Non-Appearance

If a witness fails to appear in court without a reasonable excuse, the court may issue summons to compel him/her to come before the court or to appear in another place where he/she may be examined. A witness who ignores the court's summons without reasonable cause may be fined up to KRW5 million or sentenced to seven-day imprisonment by a civil court. Furthermore, witnesses and experts are criminally liable if they provide false testimony under oath. The litigants themselves, on the other hand, are not criminally liable if they provide false testimony on their own behalf (see section 6).

Court summons may be generally enforced by the police or by an enforcement officer (analogous to a sheriff in the United States). In such cases, the travel expenses of the enforcement officer must be deposited with the court by the party that applied for the summons.

A litigant's spouse or close relative by blood or marriage may also refuse to testify before the court and need not provide any reason for such refusal (CPC Article 314). The court must also inform any such witnesses of their right to refuse to testify in court.

5) Cross-Examination of Witnesses

The party that originally requested the appearance of a witness is entitled to examine the witness first ("direct examination"). Afterwards, the opposing party is given the chance to examine the same witness ("cross-examination"). The purpose of cross-examination is to verify the integrity of the testimony offered during direct examination. Cross-examination, therefore, may not focus on any matter other than those that arose in the direct examination.

It can sometimes happen that the opposing party fails to understand the nature of the witness testimony offered under direct examination and is therefore unable to conduct an effective cross-examination. The opposing party should therefore listen carefully to the direct examination, note the questions to ask during the cross-examination, and subsequently ask such questions in the proper sequence during the cross-examination.

6) Party Testimony

In common law civil procedure, party testimony is a part of witness testimony; that is, the parties can themselves also provide witness testimony. In Korea, however, as in other civil law systems, the litigants themselves are not considered witnesses. Thus, even though they can take the witness stand to explain their understanding of the facts of the case, their testimonies are deemed to fall under a different category of evidence called party testimony. In reality, however, the process of taking evidence from the litigants is similar to the process of taking evidence from witnesses.

Due to the presumption that the litigants may have a distorted or biased recollection of the facts of the case, party testimony is generally considered to have lower evidentiary weight than other forms of evidence and is therefore deemed to be the evidence of last resort. In addition, the constitutional principle of prohibition of self-incrimination is interpreted to extend to the area of party testimony; thus, Korean litigants are not criminally liable for perjury even if they provide what may later be proven to be false testimony.

(4) Documentary Evidence

1) Submission of Documentary Evidence

"Documentary evidence" refers to any document submitted to the court as evidence. In most Korean civil trials, this is the most relevant type of evidence. Both parties submit any documents in their possession that may serve as evidence of their claims. A party may also petition the court to compel the opposing party to submit documents in its possession that may serve as evidence for the petitioning party's claim. Such motion is called Application for a Document Production Order (see section 4).

Further, on the basis of a party's motion to produce relevant documentary evidence, the court can request the appropriate public authority or institution to supply documents to which the party does not have easy access.

On the relevant hearing date, a party should submit a hard copy of each document to the court. The party should also provide the opposing party with copies of all the documentary evidence it submits to the court.

Each documentary evidence submitted by the plaintiff shall be assigned a unique sequence number ("*GAP* Evidence No."), and that submitted by the defendant shall also be assigned a similar unique identifying number ("*EUL* Evidence No.").

Any document submitted into evidence that is only a copy and not a transcript or an original document should be certified. For document certification, in addition to numbering the document as documentary evidence as described above, each individual page of the document should bear an overlapping seal, proving that no pages have been inserted between those certified to be true copies of the originals. At the bottom of the last page, there should be a line stating "[t]his is a true copy of the original" certified by the seal of the submitter. Legal practice requires doing this not only for the document copies to be given to the court but also for the document copies provided to the defendant. In addition, although it is not essential especially when there are only a few pieces of documentary evidence to be submitted, it is considered a best practice to generate a "documentary evidence list." Such a list can also be used as a cover page for the documentary evidence to be submitted.

2) Admission/Denial of Documentary Evidence

Whenever documentary evidence is submitted to the Court, the Court then must ask the opposing party whether they accept that evidence as authentic. The opposing party may admit or deny the authenticity of the documentary evidence or may profess its ignorance of such.

When the opposing party admits the authenticity of the documentary evidence, it affirms that the evidence was indeed produced by the draftsperson whom the party seeking to enter the evidence into the record claimed to have produced it. When the opposing party denies the authenticity of the documentary evidence, it contests the claim of the party seeking to enter the evidence into the record that the document was drafted by the alleged drafter. In other words, the opposing party claims that the document is a forgery. Finally, when the opposing party professes its ignorance of the authenticity of the documentary evidence, it is stating that it does not know if the document is authentic or a forgery.

3) Submission of Elucidation of Evidence

In addition to the evidence itself, the parties to a case may sometimes also need to submit an "Elucidation" (clarification) of their previously submitted evidence. This is particularly important when the volume of documentary evidence has become so large that it has become difficult to assess the relevance of each piece of evidence submitted, when the documentary evidence is difficult to understand, when the purpose of the evidence is unclear, or when the drafter of the documentary evidence or the date of its drafting is unclear.

The elucidation of evidence must detail the name of the document, the date of its drafting, the name of the drafter, the purpose of the evidence, and the location of the original document. When describing the "purpose of the evidence," the party concerned must detail the central facts to be proven by the evidence and, depending on the issue, why and how the document was originally drafted.

4) Document Production Order

As mentioned earlier, a party to a case may seek an order from the court compelling the opposing party to produce documents the latter referred to in its writings or at the relevant oral argument, and which are in its possession. The court may also order the opposing party to produce documents that a party has a right to demand or inspect under the rules of private substantive law, such as those set out in the Civil Code.

The court may issue document production orders for documents under the control of either the opposing party or a third party. Such orders must state the document title and purpose, who or what institution has possession of the document, the facts to be proven with the document, and the reason that such evidence must be gathered.

The amended CPC has expanded document holders' duty to submit relevant documents; now, all documents ordered to be produced must be submitted by their holders except when there exist valid reasons for refusing to submit them into evidence. Some examples of valid reasons for rejecting an otherwise valid document production order are threats of criminal prosecution, personal reputational concerns, occupational confidentiality, and fear of revealing a trade secret. Some public documents maintained by public servants are also covered by such privileges.

CPC stipulates that absent the aforementioned privilege, failure to comply with a document production order may result in the court's acceptance of the allegations of the other party concerning the content of the relevant document (CPC Article 344). In reality, however, the meaning of this provision is not clear, and many courts are thus reluctant to apply it.

(5) Expert Appraisal

A final category of evidence pertains to expert appraisals. Such appraisals are intended to supplement a judge's capacity to render a judgment. In such situations, third parties with knowledge about and experience with the relevant topic are asked to examine certain pieces of evidence and apply their specialized knowledge thereto and share their expertise with the court (CPC Article 333).

When a party's application for an expert appraisal to the Court is approved, the applicant must also confirm the cost of the hoped-for appraisal, and confirm that he/she is capable of covering such costs. If money covering the cost of the expert appraisal is not deposited with the court in advance, the appraisal may not be authorized.

6. Closure Procedure

(1) Closure of Trial or Hearings

When the court determines that the parties' arguments and submitted evidence have been sufficiently scrutinized, the court closes the trial. The trial's last session date is the point at which the new legal relationship between the parties flowing from the judgment is deemed to begin.

Occasionally, after a judge moves to close the trial, one or both parties express the desire to continue making arguments or submitting evidence, usually miscellaneous ones. In such situations, many judges try to negotiate with the parties concerned to limit their future submissions and grant only one more trial session. However, the final decision as to whether to close or extend the trial lies exclusively with the judge or judges.

After the trial is closed, a dissatisfied party may submit a "Request for Reopening." Such requests are usually not granted, but if the court, upon evaluating such a request, agrees that the case has not been fully explored despite the trial's closure (i.e., if the court thinks that additional oral arguments or evidence submissions are required to fully understand the dispute), it may reopen the trial without limit. There are no procedural hurdles preventing a court from reopening an already closed trial for further oral argumentation.

In common law systems, the responsibility of providing a legal basis for a claim lies entirely with the party that has the burden of making an actionable claim. Common law judges typically do not hesitate to render a judgment unfavorable to a party that fails to put forward an applicable legal theory of liability. In Korea, however, there is no such obligation,[5] and the Korean judges are typically reluctant to render an unfavorable verdict only on such basis. They usually feel that it is their duty to imply or suggest a basis for potential legal reasoning to the parties during oral argumentation, if only to avoid surprising the parties at the conclusion of the trial. Even while reviewing requests to reopen an already closed trial, judges often look to see if there may have been a potentially relevant legal theory that the parties failed to raise and will sometimes reopen a trial on the basis of this.

(2) Trial Closure without a Judgment

Most people believe that the purpose of initiating a lawsuit is to obtain a favorable judgment. In the real world, however, many cases are closed without a judgment from the court. The most common causes of such instances are withdrawal and settlement.

1) Withdrawal

A plaintiff may withdraw a case voluntarily at any time after filing a Statement of Claim. However, if the defendant has already made pleadings on the merits of the case, the plaintiff must obtain the defendant's consent to withdraw the case before withdrawing it. The defendant can either agree to or reject the case withdrawal request within two weeks from his/her notification of such; if the defendant fails to do so within such period, he/she is deemed to have consented to the withdrawal of the case (CPC Article 266(2)). Voluntary withdrawal of a case is without prejudice unless it was made when a judgment had already been issued (CPC Article 267). That is, while a plaintiff may still withdraw the case even when a judgment has been made, the judgment will nonetheless stand despite the plaintiff's withdrawal of the case. After the period during which a plaintiff can file an appeal lapses, his/her power to withdraw a case also lapses.

5 However, explicit statements about the law, even argumentative statements, are in reality not proscribed and are frequent in writings for Korean litigation.

2) Settlements

Frequently, the parties to a case manage to reach an informal negotiated settlement while litigation is playing out in court. In many cases, the court encourages the parties to attempt to reach such out-of-court settlements. The intensity and candor with which a Korean court urges parties to seek out-of-court settlements may sometimes astonish a foreign observer. Few cases proceed without the judge urging the parties to seek an informal negotiated settlement. Judges often set a conference at the courthouse for the parties to the case to attempt to reach a settlement prior to the closing of the hearing. At such conference, the judge may aggressively recommend that the parties negotiate a settlement. Here, the judge often acts as a quasi-mediator, but he/she often sends the case to an appropriate mediator who is a member of a registered panel of court-associated mediators. If the parties manage to reach a settlement, the details of such are incorporated into the minutes of the trial, thus assuming the weight of a formal judgment or verdict of the court.

When the judge feels that a compromise is either feasible or advisable, he/she may even enter the proposed settlement into a formal document ("Decision of Settlement Recommendation") and give the parties two weeks to consider the matter. When the parties fail to make decisions regarding the recommendation after the two-week period expires, they are deemed to have agreed to the recommendation. The Decision of Settlement Recommendation, then assumes the weight of a formal judgment or verdict of the court.

In the United States, the pre-trial period is very long and the discovery procedure is quite intensive. Furthermore, there are long waiting periods before a case is heard. Perhaps for these reasons, the ratio of cases that get settled out of court is quite high. While there are certainly also some civil cases in Korea that are settled out of court, the ratio of cases that go to trial in Korea is much higher than that in the United States. This pattern of ratio is in keeping with that also found in other civil law systems, such as those in Germany and Japan.

In Korea, a negotiated settlement incorporated into the minutes of a trial has the same legal weight as a formal judgment for the purpose of execution. Here, the Korean system departs from other civil law systems: in Korea, the agreement or settlement reached by the parties to a case before a court is as binding as a court's adjudication on the case in a formal trial.

Negotiated settlements before a court in Korea are held to be *res judicata* or final and binding. Other civil law systems, such as those in Germany and Japan, also prescribe some binding effect to negotiated settlements but do not consider them *res judicata*.

(3) Judgment

1) Establishing and Rendering Judgments

For cases that proceed to formal judgment, the judgments are not rendered immediately after the final trial session. Usually, a new trial date is set for the issuance of a judgment order, similar to the practice in other civil law systems.

CPC prescribes that no more than two weeks should separate the final oral argument from the pronouncement of a judgment. However, this time limit is without sanction, and most judgments take a longer period to be issued. The time between the final oral argument and the judgment varies from case to case, but the average is four weeks. Even when the date for the issuance of a judgment is set, the court may postpone the session or even order further oral argumentation when it realizes that it needs additional input before it can reach a verdict.

Once oral arguments are closed, the judge or judges review the case record to formulate their conclusions. If the case has been brought before a judge sitting alone, he/she then begins to draft the judgment. Judges sitting on three-person panels, however, must first meet in private to deliberate on the case so that they can arrive at a collective judgment. The presiding judge is likely to lead such deliberations.

At the aforementioned conferences, the reporting judge, usually the associate judge in charge of maintaining the trial record, is expected to have detailed knowledge of the case and to fully express what he/she knows about it. The other associate judge is likely to have followed the proceedings without keeping a written record of them or to have rarely studied the trial record. Furthermore, his/her knowledge of the case and recommended legal interpretations is likely limited compared to those of the other judges. Thus, the presiding and reporting judges on the panel are likely to dominate the discussion.

After the discussion, the judges will reach an agreement among themselves on how to dispose of the case. When the judges fail to reach a consensus, a series of rules defining what position should be taken as the "majority consensus" verdict will apply. It is the reporting judge who usually writes the final judgment even if he/she personally dissents to it. The presiding judge usually edits the written final judgment.

All the three judges sign the written final judgment, which is then presented as the collective decision of the court, without an identifying author. In courts of first or second instance, there can be no public dissenting opinion or any published opinion other than the court's official judgment. Dissenting opinions are published only in judgments issued by the Supreme Court.

Judgments are structured to include a summary of the litigants' demands, allegations made, evidence put forward by the parties, and evidence gathered over the course of the trial. The grounds for the decision are also presented, setting forth the court's findings of fact and legal evaluation of the facts of the case. Judgments must be compendious (concise but also comprehensive) and must state the relevant facts and the legal standards serving as grounds for the judgment. Abbreviated judgments are allowed for default judgments. The judges' paperwork burden is quite heavy, driving many district court judges to spend approximately only two days a week conducting trials and the rest of their time processing paperwork and writing judgments at their desks.

2) *Res Judicata*

After the court renders a judgment, a certified copy of the judgment is given to each party. The losing party has two weeks to file an appeal. The judgment is "validated" (finalized) either when the judgment is of a type that cannot be appealed or when the time for filing an appeal has expired without an appeal being made.

Once the judgment is finalized, it cannot be overturned through the ordinary method of appeal, and a party cannot relitigate the case by filing a new lawsuit. From this point onward, the judgment is said to regulate the legal relationship between the former litigants and is therefore referred to as *res judicata* (literally, the thing that is settled).

The only way to break *res judicata* is to motion the court for a "Resumption of Proceedings," as described in Article 451 of CPC. A party can seek a "Resumption of Proceedings" only on narrow statutorily prescribed grounds and only after showing that the applicant is free from fault for not having raised his/her objections earlier. A motion for a "Resumption of Proceedings" is possible only within one month from the date on which the applicant learns of the facts justifying the motion, and no later than five years after the date of issuance of the original judgment. Such requests are rarely granted.

(4) Enforcement of Judgments

A plaintiff in a civil lawsuit may seek various remedies, including delivery of an item or real property, injunctions, declaratory relief, punitive remedies, and others. Nonetheless, monetary damages remain the predominant remedy granted in Korean civil litigation.

Specific performance and monetary remedies are preferred to declaratory relief. The latter is clearly available under Korean law, but in practice, it is usually not granted. To secure a declaratory remedy, the plaintiff must establish a justifiable legal interest in obtaining such relief at the time of the trial. If other forms of relief can better satisfy the plaintiff's interests, the court will likely infer that no such declaratory relief is necessary.

A judgment can be executable in the fullest sense only when it has been validated or finalized. At this point, the plaintiff is deemed to become a judgment creditor, and the defendant, a judgment debtor.

A judgment can have "provisional executability" even before it is finalized, but only if the court specifically declares this as part of the judgment. As a general rule, judgments are to be declared provisionally subject to execution even without a motion to this effect. Such executability declarations may be suspended later, when the appellant furnishes security.

The actual process of executing a judgment can begin as soon as the service of judgment is made and the creditor secures a certified copy of the judgment with a distinctive execution clause. In judgments for monetary relief that can be satisfied from the debtor's ordinary personal possessions, the court's execution officer can immediately order the attachment or sale of the defendant's property at the creditor's request.

When the execution of a judgment concerns the debtor's claims on third persons or his/her title to real property, the remedies are usually handled by the execution court even when the original judgment was issued by another court. This kind of execution (i.e., the sale of a judgment debtor's real property) is the most frequently used form of compulsory execution. The proceeds of these sales are distributed among the judgment creditors.

7. Appeals

(1) Overview

A final noteworthy feature of Korean civil procedure is its appeal system. To understand the uniqueness of the Korean system in this regard, one must compare it with other legal systems.

In most common law systems, there is no right to have a case relitigated on appeal. The federal court system in the United States began as a two-tier court system with district courts as trial courts to examine evidence and apply the law and one centralized Supreme Court to adjudicate questions of law on appeal. Only when the workload of the Supreme Court in such system became unmanageable were permanent circuit or appellate courts established. At the state level, however, some US states still have the original two-tier system. Even in many so-called continental procedure countries, such as Germany and France, it seems that there is no existing provision guaranteeing a three-tier court system. The Constitutional Court of Germany once ruled that appeals are not guaranteed under the German Constitution and that the constitutional rights protection system "assumes the risk of the law being incorrectly applied" to give greater weight to the principle of legal certainty and legal peace.

In Korea, by contrast, there is a strong attachment to a three-tier court system. An appeal against a judgment issuing from a court of first instance (*Hang-so*) is even termed differently from that contesting a judgment of a court of second instance (*Sang-go*).

(2) Appeal against First-Instance Judgment (*Hang-so*)

Litigants who want to contest the findings of fact or judgments rendered by a court of first instance are allowed to appeal such judgments. The appeal may be filed either before the issuance of a written judgment or within two weeks from the date on which the judgment is served. To file an appeal, the appellant must submit a Document of Appeal to the court that issued the original judgment.

In general, high courts serve as the primary courts of appeal in the second instance. The only exception to this pertains to the appellate divisions of district courts in cases where the first-instance trial was presided over by a single judge.

The notice of appeal must clearly indicate the name of the appellant, the judgment issued by the lower court, and a statement regarding why such judgment is being appealed. The lower court's judgment typically details the name of the lower court and the case number, case name, date of issuance of the judgment, and the decisions of the court. An appeal may include the detailed reason for the appeal, but this may also be reflected in a written brief to be submitted later. In situations in which the parties have agreed not to file an appeal, they would subsequently have no right to appeal.

In Korea, the appellate proceedings in the court of second instance are broadly similar to those in the court of first instance. The parties are granted an opportunity to make new allegations and produce new evidence. This is an important difference between the Korean civil procedure and the civil procedure of most other modern judicial systems. Common law jurisdictions do not allow the submission of new evidence in appellate proceedings. Even in many continental jurisdictions, such as Germany and France, the appellate courts typically set stringent limitations on the ability of the parties to introduce new allegations or evidence into the case. Only Japan seems to have an appellate system model similar to that of Korea.

Consequently, hearings before a high court or the District Court Appellate Division can again stretch across several trial dates. Although fewer in number than in the initial trial, the hearings in a high-court appeal trial can easily be more than 10.

(3) Appeals to the Supreme Court (*Sang-go*)

A party that is dissatisfied even with the judgment of the court of second instance may again appeal the judgment, this time to the Supreme Court, Korea's court of last resort. Appeals to the Supreme Court must be made within two weeks from the date on which the lower appellate court's judgment is served. The appeal should again state the names of the appellant and appellee, their respective addresses, the appellate court's decision, and the extent of purpose to change the judgment.

The Supreme Court will entertain only matters of law. Therefore, all appeals lodged before the Supreme Court must allege that the appellate court erred in its application of the law to the facts or that the appeal process itself was in grave contravention of the law.

Appeals to the Supreme Court may be made to contest alleged violations of the Korean Constitution, applicable statutes, or any orders or rules that may have somehow figured in the appellate court's decision. The Supreme Court will not involve itself in any renewed fact finding.

The appellant must state the reason for his/her appeal to the Supreme Court in the appeal document to be submitted. Failing that, the appellant must submit an adequate statement of the reason for the appeal within 20 days after he/she receives notice that the trial records have been received by the Supreme Court. This period must be observed, and the court will not tolerate any delay in articulating a proper reason for an appeal. Failure to comply with this requirement will result in dismissal of the appeal.

8. Conclusion

As we have seen so far, Korean civil procedure law is primarily based on the European continental civil law tradition. The three-tier appellate system and sporadic hearings for a trial are only two examples of the similarities between the two. However, there are a few peculiarities in Korean procedural law that distinguish it from the procedural laws of other continental jurisdictions, such as the de novo review of a case by an appellate court over new allegations and/or evidence. A comparative analysis of civil procedure laws, as is done in this chapter, may contribute to the improvement and reformation of Korean civil procedure law.

Chapter 6

Criminal Law

Jinyoung Hong*

1. Introduction

Substantive criminal law is a complete set of legal norms that define criminal offenses and prescribe the categories and scope of criminal sanctions applicable to individual offenses. To put it concisely, criminal law deals with crime and punishment (and other criminal sanctions). A national regime of substantive criminal law performs two important functions. First, it protects the legal interests of citizens by deterring criminal behavior. Second, it should guarantee citizens freedom from undue government interference. The history of modern Korean criminal law can be summarized as the struggle to reconcile these two conflicting goals.

The main purpose of this article is to provide an overview of substantive criminal law in Korea.[1] First, the sources of Korean criminal law are identified, accompanied by a discussion of issues around the principle of legality. Second, some of the basic concepts and principles set out in the Criminal Act of 1953 (CA), the most important source of Korean criminal law, are outlined. Third, new trends and transformative efforts to modernize the CA and other criminal statutory provisions are briefly discussed.

* Associate Professor, Seoul National University School of Law.

1 In this chapter, Korea refers to the Republic of Korea (South Korea), unless otherwise specified.

2. The Sources of Korean Criminal Law

(1) Statutory Provisions

1) The Principle of Legality

The sources of criminal law have to be understood in the context of the most fundamental principle of modern criminal law; that is, the principle of legality or *nullum crimen sine lege, nulla poena sine lege* (*nullum crimen sine lege* below), which means "no crime without law, no punishment without law."[2] The main purpose of this principle is to protect citizens from the arbitrary governmental exercise of penal power, and it is achieved by separating legislative power from executive and judicial powers. The principle also aims to give citizens fair notice of what activities are prohibited and the consequences of committing a crime, thereby providing them with sufficient information on whether to proceed with a certain activity. Four sub-principles of the principle of legality have traditionally been identified: *lex certa* (the principle of certainty), *lex praevia* (the principle of non-retroactivity), *lex stricta* (the principle against analogy), and *lex scripta* (the principle against uncodified or unwritten criminal provisions).[3]

The principle of legality has its own constitutional grounds in the Korean Constitution. Article 12(1) provides that no person shall be punished, placed under measures of correction and prevention, or subject to involuntary labor except as provided by "act." In addition, Article 13(1) declares *lex praevia* by stipulating that no citizen shall be prosecuted for conduct that does not constitute a crime under an "act" in force at the time the conduct was committed.[4] In these clauses, "act" means a formal statute passed by the National Assembly, Korea's legislative authority. Therefore, in principle, the statutory provisions that define criminal offenses and

2 For an overview of this principle in Korean criminal law, see Kuk Cho, *Nullum Crimen, Nulla Poena Sine Lege in Korean Criminal Law*, 6(1) JOURNAL OF KOREAN LAW 147-161 (2006).

3 Claus Kreß, *Nulla poena nullum crimen sine lege*, Max Planck Encyclopedia of Public International Law, Max Planck Institute for Comparative Public Law and International Law, Heidelberg and Oxford University Press (2010); Kuk Cho, *supra*, 148.

4 CA Article 1(1) also asserts *lex praevia* by providing that "the criminality and punishability of an act shall be determined by the law in effect at the time of the commission of that act."

prescribe criminal sanctions are the only source of criminal law.

According to the Korean Constitutional Court, determining what conduct should be deemed criminal and how to punish such crimes is for the legislature to decide, with full consideration of the nation's history and culture, the times in which the legislation is drafted, the values or legal sentiments of the general public, criminal justice policies on preventing crimes, as well as the nature of the conduct and the protectable legal interests.[5] However, legislators' discretion is limited by the constitutional mandate of *nullum crimen sine lege* as well as the principles of criminal law as *ultima ratio* and the principle of proportionality. The criminal law as *ultima ratio* means that "the exercise of criminal punishment should be the last resort for the clear danger against substantial legal interests and should be limited at least."[6] Under the *ultima ratio* principle, legislators are to consider whether less restrictive alternatives than criminal sanctions exist. The principle of proportionality means that punishment is balanced with the gravity of the crime and the character of the criminal in question. These principles have a constitutional basis in Article 10 (the protection of human dignity and values) and Article 37(2) (the prohibition of excessive legislation) of the Korean Constitution.

2) The Criminal Act of 1953 (CA)

The CA of 1953 was proclaimed on September 18, 1953, and came into force on October 3, 1953, superseding the Japanese Criminal Code of 1908, which had been imposed upon the Korean people during the Japanese colonial period and had remained in effect after liberation. The CA was the first congressional act passed by the National Assembly after the establishment of the Korean government in 1948. Despite several amendments and repeals of provisions declared unconstitutional by the Constitutional Court, the basic structure and content of the CA have remained largely unchanged. To this day, it is still the most important source of criminal law in Korea.

3) Special Criminal Statutes

Although serving as the state's last resort to prevent undesirable behavior, criminal law is not impervious to changes in society—including the

5 Constitutional Court Decision 2008Hun-Ba84, March 25, 2010.
6 Constitutional Court Decision 2009Hun-Ba17, February 26, 2015.

emergence of new dangers created by technological developments or innovative types of commerce, evolving ideas about justice, and changes in social values and community standards as to what constitutes an intolerable moral wrong. Considering the "fair notice" function of criminal provisions (under the principle of legality), it is desirable that all types of crimes and their sanctions be collated in a single statute. However, the situation in Korea is opposite to this desirable statutory framework. Korean legislators prefer amending or creating special criminal statutes rather than amending the CA directly, because the former approach is convenient and speedy, whereas the latter calls for a prudent inquiry and careful deliberation.[7] It has also been said that legislating special criminal statutes can call the public's attention to the seriousness and urgency of preventing those newly introduced crimes. This kind of legislative motive, which is known as penal populism, is easily combined with people's sentiments against heinous crimes.

Consequently, there are numerous special statutes other than the CA that deal with various criminal offenses and criminal sanctions. These special statutes can be divided into three categories.

First, there are special statutes criminalizing various types of unlawful activities that are not specifically covered by the CA of 1953. For example, the National Security Act[8] criminalizes a range of dangerous activities undertaken by "anti-government organizations."[9] These types of statutes also provide specific procedures deemed to be adequate to try those special crimes. Article 19 of the National Security Act, for example, allows for longer detention periods for those suspected of breaching the act.

Second, there are special statutes that aim to stipulate aggravated punishments for specific crimes that are already included in the CA. For example, the Punishment of Violence Act increases the punishments for crimes such as assault, injury, and intimidation when such an act meets

7 However, there is a criticism to this view, which notes that there is no procedural difference between introducing a special criminal statute and revising the CA.

8 On the controversy surrounding the National Security Act, see Kuk Cho, *Korean Criminal Law under Controversy after Democratization*, 6(2) THE REVIEW OF KOREAN STUDIES 50-53 (2003).

9 According to Article 2 of the National Security Act, "anti-government organization" is defined as a domestic or foreign organization or group that fraudulently uses the title of the government or aims at a rebellion against the State and which is equipped with a command and leadership system. Practically speaking, it refers in most cases to the North Korean government.

certain additional requirements. According to Article 2(2) of the act, for instance, if two or more people jointly commit a crime listed in CA Articles 257(1) (inflicting bodily injury), 257(2) (inflicting bodily injury on lineal ascendant), 260(1) (assault), 260(2) (assault on the lineal ascendant), 276(1) (unlawful arrest), 276(2) (unlawful arrest on the lineal ascendant), 283(1) (intimidation), 283(2) (intimidation on the lineal ascendant), 319 (trespass), 324(1) (coercion), 350 (extortion), and 366 (destruction of property), the punishment can be increased by up to one half of the punishment prescribed in the relevant CA provision.

Third, there are statutes whose primary aim to implement public policies by administrative means but also criminalize some unlawful activities for which regulation by solely administrative means is deemed insufficient. For example, the purpose of the Road Traffic Act is to ensure the safe and smooth flow of traffic by preventing and removing all dangers and obstacles to traffic on roads. To fulfill this purpose, the Act imposes various duties on pedestrians and drivers to maintain a safe and smooth flow of traffic and regulates driver's licenses and traffic signs. Criminal sanctions are imposed only for breaches of the most important duties, for example, DUI (Driving Under the Influence), unlicensed driving, injury caused by dangerous driving, and so on. For other kinds of infractions, only administrative sanctions are imposed.

All told, Korea has more than 1,000 individual statutes that have at least one provision regarding criminal offenses. This situation is problematic from the perspective of the principle of legality. Because criminal provisions are not concentrated in one statute, it is not possible for ordinary people to find all the statutes that may apply to an activity they are considering. The criminal law is thus hindered from serving the purpose of general prevention because it cannot be the basis for decision making. It also endangers the principle of *ultima ratio*, because in reality not all its myriad criminal provisions are applied, which means that those statutes are rather symbolic. Therefore, it can be said that Korean criminal law suffers from the phenomenon of "over-criminalization."[10] While enacting symbolic criminal provisions may serve to temporarily direct people's attention to certain social problems, it may weaken the deterrence effect of the criminal

10 This situation is not unique to Korean criminal law; see Douglas Husak, *The Criminal Law as Last Resort*, 24(2) OXFORD JOURNAL OF LEGAL STUDIES 207-235 (2004).

statutory regime as a whole because over-criminalization is inevitably followed by underenforcement problems. In spheres of special statutes on aggravating crimes, the anti-proportionality problem is exposed, because those statutes tend to impose severe punishments to satisfy the demands of penal populism. Fundamental reform of Korea's criminal statutory regime is needed to overcome the domination of special statutes.

(2) Administrative Rulemaking and Municipal Ordinances

The legislature is responsible for establishing policies across a wide range of areas but does not have the in-depth expertise to carry out those tasks in their entirety, so the executive branch must sometimes be granted rulemaking authority to implement statutory programs in detail. Therefore, Articles 75 and 95 of the Korean Constitution allow presidential decrees and ordinances of the prime minister and other ministers to regulate matters delegated to them by congressional acts. This delegation authority enables the National Assembly to focus on fundamental issues rather than debating every technical detail required to fully implement complex public policies. While the area of criminal law is no exception in this regard, delegation is less desirable in light of the principle of legality. Therefore, the legislature can delegate authority to the executive branch to supplement statutory criminal provisions in what is known as the parental statute by administrative rulemaking only when the following requirements are strictly met: (i) there must be an urgent necessity or an unavoidable circumstance that makes it unable to provide precise details in the parental statute; (ii) the statutory description of the elements of crimes must be specific enough for ordinary people to infer the scope of the punished conduct; (iii) the parental statute must clearly prescribe the type, maximum severity, and scope of the applicable penalties.[11] When the legislature's delegation is legitimate and valid, administrative rulemaking combined with the parental statute can be regarded as a valid source of criminal law.

According to Article 22 of the Local Autonomy Act, local governments may impose penalties if there is a delegation of authority by legislation. Therefore, municipal ordinances can be a source of criminal law if legislated

11 Constitutional Court Decision 94Hun-Ba22, May 29, 1997.

under a legitimate and valid delegation. However, concrete examples of municipal ordinances with criminal penalties are rare.

(3) Are Precedents Source of Law?

Precedents refer to Supreme Court judgments regarding the interpretation and application of legal norms. Many provisions in the CA and other criminal statutes need to be interpreted by the criminal courts in order to be applied to specific cases. Because the principle of legality prohibits judge-made criminal sanctions and unwritten customary criminal law, precedents *per se* cannot be the source of criminal law. Therefore, a new judicial interpretation that criminalizes a defendant's conduct may be retroactively applicable even if the conduct was not punishable according to the judicial interpretation prevailing when the act was committed. The Supreme Court has explained that "the change of judicial decision regarding a criminal provision does not change the provision itself but just confirm the contents of the provision."[12] There have been many instances in which the Supreme Court retroactively applied a new judicial interpretation to a criminal provision. For example, the Supreme Court retroactively modified the meaning of "document" in Article 231(1) (counterfeit or alteration of a private document) to include photocopied documents, on the grounds that photocopied documents are duplicated with complete accuracy and regularly function as substitutes for original documents in important matters.[13]

The principle of *lex certa* requires criminal statutes to prescribe the criminal offenses and their penalties clearly enough so that anyone can predict what kind of acts are punishable and how they are punished and act accordingly. Too much dependence on judicial interpretations may erode this principle because it suggests that statutory provisions themselves do not adequately guide citizens in their actions. While the phenomenon of dependence on case law is hardly unique to Korean criminal law,[14] the CA's

12 Supreme Court Decision 97Do3349, September 17, 1999.

13 Supreme Court Full Bench Decision 87Do506, September 12, 1989. In the amendment of the CA in 1995, Article 237(2) was introduced to codify the Court's interpretation into the CA itself.

14 For similar situations in German criminal law, see Introduction to German Law (Joachim Zekoll and Gerhard Wagner eds.), KLUWER LAW INTERNATIONAL

frequent use of ambiguous and abstract terms exacerbates the problem. When the legislators of the National Assembly were drafting the first statute of the newly independent nation during the Korean War (1950-1953), they did not have the time, expertise, and resources to prepare a finely articulated statute that would meet the demands of the principle of legality. Therefore, strictly applying the principle of *lex certa* would mean that many provisions in the CA would not clear the hurdle of constitutionality, because the CA makes it difficult to understand what activities are prohibited by its statutory provisions without referring to the case law of the Supreme Court.

However, the Constitutional Court does not tend to strictly apply the principle of *lex certa*. Rather, it adopts a compromised approach, arguing that "somewhat broad concepts requiring supplementary judicial interpretation are not necessarily against the rule of clarity insofar as any person equipped with sound common sense and conventional legal awareness may understand the concepts with general methods of interpretation."[15] The Court added the following:

> Whether a legal norm is clear or not is determined by whether it provides predictability through a fair notice of its definition and whether it prevents law enforcement from arbitrary interpretation or enforcement through sufficient clarification of its meaning in the norm itself. The implication of a legal norm takes concrete shape when its texts are interpreted with full consideration of their legislative purpose, history, systematic structure, etc. Thus, whether a norm is against the rule of clarity will depend on whether that interpretation method can provide for a reasonable interpretation of its meaning.[16]

The Constitutional Court takes this approach for somehow understandable reasons, considering the serious effects of declaring the ambiguous provisions of the CA unconstitutional. According to Article 47(3) of the Constitutional Court Act, criminal statutory provision

537 (2018).

15 Constitutional Court Decision 2006Hun-Ba109, May 28, 2009.

16 Constitutional Court Decision 2009Hun-Ba27, November 25, 2010.

deemed unconstitutional lose their effect retroactively.[17] This means that all convictions obtained under an unconstitutional provision since 1953 (or the date of amendment, if any) could be vacated in the retrial procedures established in Article 47(4) of the Act, which is not desirable in terms of legal stability. One cannot still deny that its approach deviates from the core meaning of the *lex certa* principle.

One example of a provision that lacks clarity is Article 311 (insult), which punishes a person who publicly insults another by imprisonment for not more than one year or a fine not exceeding KRW 2 million. The Constitutional Court found this article constitutional.[18] According to the court, it does not appear to be significantly difficult for an ordinary citizen with common sense and a conventional legal mind to predict what kind of acts are banned. The court wrote that "the Supreme Court sets forth an objective standard for interpreting what insult means, which poses no concern for arbitrary interpretation by law enforcement agencies." However, it cannot be readily said that the Supreme Court provides a reliable standard for reasonable interpretation. The Supreme Court interprets "insult" as "the expression, without factual specification, of an abstract judgment or contemptuous sentiment deemed likely to undermine the victim's external reputation."[19] According to the court, expressions such as "a pathetic and pitiful person"[20] and "a trashy journalist (*ki-re-gi*)"[21] do fit the concept of "insult," but it ultimately found the defendants in both cases not guilty because those expressions can be justified under Article 20 of the CA. It thus seems in practice that "sound common sense and conventional legal awareness" do not help predict what expressions are—or are not—insults.

17 When there was a previous ruling that declared the contested provision constitutional, the scope of retroactivity is limited to the time period after the date on which the previous ruling was made, according to the proviso to Article 47(3).

18 Constitutional Court Decision 2012Hun-Ba 37, June 27, 2013.

19 Supreme Court Decision 2003Do3972, November 28, 2003.

20 Supreme Court Decision 2008Do1433, July 10, 2008.

21 Supreme Court Decision 2017Do17643, March 25, 2021.

3. Basic Structure and Core Concepts of the CA

(1) Basic Structure of the CA

The CA is divided into two parts. Part I (Articles 1 to 86) sets out general principles of criminal liability and punishment. The principles set out in Part I apply not only to the offenses described in the CA itself but also to offenses described in other special criminal statutes. Part II provides the elements of individual offenses and the scope of punishments for those offenses.

Part I of the CA consists of four chapters. Chapter I deals with the temporal and geographic applicability of Korean criminal statutes. Chapter II presents the general principles of criminal liability, while Chapter III prescribes the types of punishments, sentencing principles, and matters related to the enforcement of punishments. Chapter IV, which has the fewest provisions, deals with rules on calculating prison sentence terms.

Part II of the CA consists of 42 chapters, each of which contains offenses grouped by the common legal interest that they offend. Offenses are divided into three categories according to the nature of legal interest – crimes against the state (e.g., insurrection, aiding the enemy, spying, abandonment of duties by public officials, abuse of authority, unlawful arrest, bribery, assaulting or deceiving public officials, perjury, false accusation, escaping from lawful detention); crimes against society (e.g., arson, obstruction of traffic, counterfeiting of currency, securities, or documents, distribution of obscene materials, public indecency, gambling); and crimes against individuals (e.g., homicide, assault, abandonment, kidnapping, intimidation, rape, defamation, insult, trespass, larceny, robbery, fraud, embezzlement, extortion, destruction of property).

As it is impossible to cover all the CA's provisions in this brief introduction to Korean criminal law, only some of the core principles and concepts in Part I are discussed below.

(2) The Geographic Applicability of Korean Criminal Statutes

As for the scope of the geographic application of Korean criminal statutes, including the CA, the CA adopts the territoriality principle (Article 2), the active nationality principle (Article 3), the flag state principle (Article 4), the passive nationality principle (Article 5), and the protective principle (Article 6).

These principles are collectively referred to as principles of jurisdiction.

Article 2 stipulates that the CA is applicable to all offenses committed on Korean territory, which means that foreigners can be prosecuted in Korea, even if the activity in question is not a crime in their home country. An interesting relevant issue is the meaning of "Korean territory" in regard to North Korea. This issue arises because Article 3 of the Korean Constitution declares that the territory of the Republic of Korea shall consist of the Korean peninsula and its adjacent islands. In the past, the dominant view has held that South Korean criminal provisions applied to the North Korean area, even though the South Korean government was not able to enforce those statutes because the area was illegally occupied by the North Korean government, which is regarded as an anti-government by the South Korean government. However, the opposite view, which argues that Article 4 of the Korean Constitution on the state's duty to pursue peaceful unification[22] should be considered to interpret the term "Korean territory" in Article 3 appropriately, is gradually gaining support. Under the latter view, Korean criminal statutes do not apply to activities in the North Korean area, because it is considered analogous to any other area outside the territory of Korea.

Article 3 stipulates the Act is applicable to all Korean nationals who commit crimes outside the territory of Korea. Therefore, Korean nationals who commit activities prohibited under Korean criminal statutes can be prosecuted in Korea, even when an activity is not prohibited by the criminal statutes of the country in which the activity was committed. For example, if a Korean national smokes or even possesses marijuana for the purpose of smoking it in a country where the drug has been legalized, he or she can still be prosecuted for breaching the Narcotics Control Act.

Articles 5 and 6 serve to protect Korean nationals and the state by making it possible to prosecute offenses against Korean nationals and the state. The offenses enumerated in Article 5, including crimes concerning insurrection and foreign aggression, are unconditionally punishable, whether they are committed inside or outside Korean territory and regardless of whether Korean nationals or foreigners (or both) are involved.

22 Article 4 provides that the Republic of Korea shall seek unification and shall formulate and carry out a policy of peaceful unification based on the basic principles of a free and democratic order.

The other offenses not enumerated in Article 5 are punishable on the condition that a given offense is also punishable by the criminal law of the country in which it is committed.

While the universality principle is not mentioned in Part I, there are several provisions that individually adopt this principle in the CA and other criminal statutes. Under the universality principle, an offender can be prosecuted in Korea even when there is no link between the offense and the state, unlike other principles of jurisdiction. The universality principle applies to offenses in which all states share a common interest in prosecuting the wrongdoer and offenses that harm humanity as a whole. Human trafficking offenses (Articles 287 to 292 of the CA), crimes of genocide, crimes against humanity, and war crimes (Articles 8 to 14 of the Act on Punishment of Crimes under Jurisdiction of the International Criminal Court) are examples of offenses that fall under universal jurisdiction.

(3) General Principles of Criminal Liability

1) Three-step Test of Criminal Liability

❶ Framework

To convict a person of a crime, the court has to complete a three-step test: (i) the elements of the crime, (ii) its unlawfulness, and (iii) the person's guilt. This test originated in German criminal law doctrine.

First, an offender has to fulfill all the objective elements of an offense as provided in the relevant provision in Part II of the CA or in other special criminal statutes as well as the relevant provisions in Part I of the CA, if applicable; this is known as the *actus reus*. Additionally, the requisite subjective elements, such as intent or negligence (*mens rea*), must be fulfilled.

Second, it must be confirmed that the offender acted unlawfully. An act that meets all the elements of *actus reus* and *mens rea* is presumed to be unlawful. However, an offender can be acquitted if there is a cause of justification such as self-defense or necessity.

Third, the offender must be held personally accountable for the act. Personal guilt can be rejected if there is an acceptable excuse such as insanity or duress.

As in German criminal law, questions of unlawfulness or justification and questions of guilt or excuse are strictly distinguished in Korean criminal law, an approach that stands in contrast to common law jurisdictions. When a person is excused due to a lack of guilt, the conduct is still deemed a legal wrong. The distinction between justification and excuse has both theoretical and practical importance. For example, self-defense is not allowed against an offender whose act is justified, but it is allowed against an offender whose act is not justified but is excused. Section 1, Chapter II of the CA provides principles related to the components of the three-step test.

❷ Elements of Crime—*Actus Reus*

In Section 1 of Chapter II, there are three provisions on the general objective elements of crimes: Articles 17 (causation), 18 (crimes committed through omission), and 19 (concurrence of independent acts).

Many criminal offenses require the offender to bring about a specific unlawful result. Article 17 declares that causation is needed for these types of offenses. That is, it shall be confirmed that the result was caused by the offender's act in order to blame the offender for the unlawful result. Sometimes, however, it is not possible to identify which precise act among concurrent acts that are independent of each other actually caused the unlawful result. Article 19 provides that each offender shall be punished for an attempted crime in this situation. Article 263 establishes the only exception to the principle in Article 19 by providing that two persons using violence against a victim shall be deemed co-principals of the crime of injury if it is not possible to identify precisely who or which act caused the injury. Five of nine justices of the Korean Constitutional Court argued that Article 263 is unconstitutional because it unduly shifts the burden to prove causality from the prosecutor to the defendant.[23]

Crimes are normally committed through actions, but they are at times committed through omissions, and some criminal offenses can only be committed through omission. For example, Article 319(2) criminalizes the refusal to leave a certain place such as a private home in spite of a request to leave from the legitimate occupier. Beyond cases like that, Article 18 provides for general liability for omissions that cause harm; it stipulates that a person who—having a duty to prevent danger from arising or having

23 Constitutional Court Decision 2017Hun-Ka10, March 29, 2018. However, the provision is still valid because six votes are needed for unconstitutionality to be declared.

brought about jeopardy by his or her own act—does not prevent danger from arising shall be punished for the results of such danger. For instance, a person can be convicted of homicide by failing to prevent the death of a victim incapable of self-protection, despite the fact that he or she had a duty to do so and had enough control over the situation that caused danger to the victim's life that death could have been prevented. In this vein, the Supreme Court affirmed the homicide conviction of Jun-seok Lee, the captain of the ferry *Sewol* because he quickly abandoned the sinking ship without carrying out any rescue efforts for passengers who were waiting inside the ship, thereby causing the death of 152 victims who could not escape before the ferry sank into the sea.[24]

❸ Elements of Crime—*Mens Rea*

Mens rea is needed to constitute a crime because it is wrong for society to punish those who have innocently caused harm. Part I of the CA provides two categories of *mens rea*: intention and negligence; one or the other is necessary for a crime to have been committed.

Most of the offenses in the CA are crimes of intention, which is the default mode of *mens rea*. If there is no mention of *mens rea* in the description of a certain criminal offense, this implies that intention is required to constitute the crime. For example, intention is necessary to constitute the crime of intentional killing in Article 250[25] because there is no specific mention of *mens rea* in that provision. Under Korean criminal law, intention does not necessarily mean purpose[26] or desire to commit a crime. It suffices that the actor foresaw the possibility of fulfilling all the elements of *actus reus* and still acted in a way that led to the result that constitutes the offense.

In contrast to crimes with intention, the element of negligence is specifically mentioned in the description of crimes with negligence. For

24 Supreme Court Full Bench Decision 2015Do6809, November 12, 2015.

25 In Korea, there is no distinction between murder and manslaughter. Therefore, Article 250 encompasses both voluntary manslaughter and murder as defined in common law countries.

26 There are crimes that specifically require purpose in addition to intention as *mens rea*. For example, to constitute a crime of insurrection under Article 87, the purpose of usurping the national territory or subverting the Korean Constitution must be established.

example, Article 267 (death by negligence) provides that a person who causes the death of another through negligence shall be punished by imprisonment for not more than two years or by a fine not exceeding KRW 7 million. In crimes with negligence, the actor must have disregarded a duty to foresee and prevent a harmful outcome. Although Article 14 of the CA only specifically mentions inadvertent negligence, the concept of negligence also encompasses advertent negligence, which means that an actor foresaw the possibility of a harmful outcome but honestly intended to cause no harm.

❹ Justificatory Defenses

Justification means that an act is exceptionally lawful, even though it fulfills all the *actus reus* and *mens rea* elements of a specific criminal offense. There are five provisions on justification in the CA: Articles 20 (justifiable acts), 21 (self-defense), 22 (necessity), 23 (self-help), and 24 (consent of victim). Justifiable acts, self-defense, and necessity are discussed briefly below.

Article 20 provides a general provision of justification by stipulating that an act that is conducted in accordance with relevant statutes or in pursuance of accepted business practices or does not violate social norms shall not be punishable. This provision, especially the part regarding social norms, functions as an antidote to the absurd expansion of punishment that may follow from criminal statutes but does not accord with the common sense of ordinary people as to what is morally right and wrong.

Self-defense is justified when there are reasonable grounds for an act that is performed in order to prevent an impending and unjust infringement of one's own or another's legal interest (Article 21(1)), while necessity is justified when there are reasonable grounds for an act that is performed in order to avoid impending danger to one's own or other's legal interest. Self-defense and necessity both deal with exigent circumstances in which it is imperative that actors protect their own legal interests or those of others. The main difference between self-defense and necessity is whether an attack against the act of the offender which is ultimately justified is unlawful or not. Self-defense is only allowed against unlawful attacks. Because this situation involves "right versus wrong," the protected interest of the defender need not outweigh the infringed interest of the attacker. In other words, strict proportionality is not necessary. However, there has been criticism in both academia and the wider society that Korean courts tend to require quite strict proportionality to recognize self-defense, which means that such claims are rarely accepted. By contrast, necessity is allowed against lawful attacks under the rationale that there is an obligation to show solidarity with fellow citizens. In this situation of "right versus wrong," strict proportionality is required because no one can be coerced to sacrifice his or her own interests to protect the less important interests of others.

❺ Excusatory Defenses

An excusatory defense is allowed when the act is unlawful but the actor ultimately does not bear any criminal responsibility or bears only diminished criminal responsibility. Because of the free will of human beings, it is always presumed that a given offender could have acted in a different way than committing an unlawful activity. However, there are situations when it is not proper to blame an actor because that actor's ability to exercise free will is substantially diminished. There are five provisions for these excusable situations: Articles 9 (criminal minors), 10 (insanity), 11 (speech and hearing impairments), 12 (duress), and 16 (mistake of law). The degree of criminal responsibility of minors, those suffering from insanity, and speech and hearing impairments are discussed briefly below.

According to Article 9, children under the age of 14 cannot bear criminal responsibility. However, children aged at least 10 but under 14 years may be referred to juvenile proceedings for the purpose of rehabilitation and education. Juvenile proceedings are conducted by judges affiliated with the family courts. While juveniles aged at least 14 and under 19 can bear criminal responsibility, they also may be referred to juvenile proceedings, depending on the nature of the crime, the character of the offender, and other relevant considerations. Even though these cases do go through criminal proceedings, special provisions stipulated in the Juvenile Act are applied to the conduct of such proceedings to account for the distinctive traits of juveniles who are not fully developed.

Article 10 deals with the legal effect of insanity. According to Article 10(1), the act of a person who, because of a pathological mental disorder, is unable to discern situations or exercise control one's will, shall not be punished. Instead, the individual may be subject to medical treatment and custody if there is an application from the prosecution for those measures, as provided in the Act on Medical Treatment and Custody. However, if the offender is not totally lacking but only deficient in the above-mentioned abilities, punishment may be mitigated under Article 10(2). These articles do not apply to the act of a person who, in anticipation of the danger of a crime, has intentionally incurred the relevant mental disorder (Article 10(3)). Previously, Article 10(2) provided for mandatory mitigation of punishment. However, the courts came in for strong criticism that they were abusing this provision by treating intoxicated offenders leniently. Efforts to limit the scope of this provision emerged in the context of sex crimes against children, after Doo-soon Cho, who brutally raped an eight-year-old girl, was sentenced to 12 years of imprisonment with mandatory mitigation because he was drunk at the time.[27] After this incident intensified the controversy over undue leniency for drunken sex offenders, a newly introduced Article 19 of the Act on the Protection of Children and Youth Against Sex Offenders provided that Articles 10(1), 10(2), and 11 of the CA would not apply to sexual violence against a child committed in a state of physical or mental incapacity induced by alcohol or drugs. Ultimately, Article 10(2) was amended to provide for only discretionary mitigation of the punishment; that provision remains in force.

In addition, Article 11 provides that punishment should be mitigated for acts committed by those with hearing and speech impairments. However, this provision has been heavily criticized for its discriminatory stance toward people with disability, because it automatically deems a physical handicap to be a psychological handicap that impairs one's ability to discern situations or to exercise control over self-will.[28]

2) Inchoate Crimes

❶ Attempt

Criminal attempts refer to a situation in which an offense, as prescribed in the relevant provision, was not completed. Not every attempted crime is punished; only those for which there are specific provisions that criminalize such attempts carry the risk of punishment.

Section 2, Chapter II, Part I of the CA outlines three types of attempts:

27 *South Korea seeks new laws after brutal rape of child*, Reuters, November 9, 2009 at https://www.reuters.com/article/idINIndia-43802720091109.

28 Japan repealed a similar provision in 1995, in response to calls for equal treatment from people with disability; Koya Matsuo, *The Development of Criminal Law in Japan since 1961*, LAW IN JAPAN: A TURNING POINT (Daniel H. Foote ed.), University of Washington Press 318 (2007).

attempted crime (Article 25), voluntarily ceased crime (Article 26), and impossible crime (Article 27). If an intended crime is not completed or the intended result does not occur due to an obstacle contrary to the offender's intention, the punishment for that attempted crime may be mitigated (Article 25). If a person voluntarily ceases the criminal act that he or she began or prevents the result that would arise from its fulfillment, punishment shall be mitigated or remitted (Article 26). If completing a crime is impossible because the means adopted for committing the crime are not suitable or there was mistake in objects , the punishment may be mitigated or remitted. (Article 27). If it is absolutely impossible to complete a crime and there is no possibility of danger, even Article 27 is not applied, and the offender is acquitted.

❷ Crimes of Conspiracy and Preparation

According to Article 28, a conspiracy or preparation to commit a crime that has not reached the stage at which the crime has begun to be carried out is punished only when there is a specific statutory provision such as Article 255 (preparations or conspiracies for intentional killing). In the CA, 13 of 42 crime types criminalize conspiracy or preparation. Conspiracy means a secret agreement between two or more persons to attempt to commit a crime. Preparation is regarded as a set of actions undertaken before commencing a crime. While conspiracy focuses on internal plot by two or more actors, preparation focuses on concrete activities intended to enable a crime to be carried out.[29]

(4) Punishment

1) Types of Punishment

Influenced by German criminal law, Korean criminal law adopts a twin-track system of criminal sanctions,[30] by distinguishing 'punishments' (*hyeongbeol*; German *Strafen*) and 'measures of correction and prevention' *(boan*

29 For a critical view of the expansive use of conspiracy and preparation in the CA, see Il-Tae Hoh, *Criminal Punishment for Inchoate and Thought Crimes: A Critical Analysis of South Korean Criminal Law*, 5 YONSEI LAW JOURNAL 41 (2014).

30 For a concise description of Germany's twin-track system, see Johannes Kaspar, *Preventive Detention in German Criminal Law*, 4 PEKING UNIVERSITY LAW JOURNAL 1, 80-83 (2016).

cheobun; German *Massregeln der Besserung und Sicherung*). Punishments include sanctions that deprive convicts of their legal rights for the compensation of guilt. Thus, punishments presuppose the offender's culpability, which means the capability to recognize the illegality of a deed and to act accordingly.[31] By contrast, measures of correction and prevention are focused preventing recidivism and reoffending by reducing or eliminating the danger posed by an offender. The culpability of an offender is not a prerequisite for such measures. While the CA defines every kind of punishment available to the state, the statutory grounds for various measures of correction and prevention are distributed throughout special criminal statutes[32] and in the CA itself.[33] Punishments and measures of correction and prevention are not mutually exclusive; rather, they are complementary in many circumstances. For example, a sex offender who victimized a minor or minors will be punished by imprisonment for a certain period of time and sanctioned with measures such as disclosure of personal information and restriction on certain kinds of employment.

Article 41 of the CA prescribes nine types of punishments: the death penalty, imprisonment with prison labor, imprisonment without prison labor, deprivation of qualifications, suspension of qualifications, fine, detention, minor fine, and confiscation. Among these, the death penalty, punishments restricting physical freedom, and monetary punishments are discussed below.

The death penalty is the greatest possible punishment and reserved for the gravest offenses, such as murder, murder after rape, murder after robbery, insurrection, inducement of foreign aggression, espionage, and acts benefiting the enemy. Since the establishment of its independent government, the Republic of Korea has executed 902 people, mostly by

31 Johannes Kaspar, *supra* note 30, 82.

32 E.g., protective detention and other measures for juveniles under Article 32 of the Juvenile Act, medical treatment and custody under the Act on Medical Treatment and Custody, disclosure of personal information and restriction on employment under the Act on the Protection of Children and Youth Against Sex Offenses, pharmacologic treatment (frequently called 'chemical castration') under the Act on Pharmacologic Treatment of Sex Offenders' Sexual Impulses, and electronic monitoring orders under the Act on Probation and Electronic Monitoring, etc., of Specific Criminal Offenders.

33 E.g., probation orders (Article 59-2, 62-2, 73-2), social service orders (Article 62-2), and orders to attend lectures (Article 62-2).

hanging.[34] The last execution took place on December 30, 1997,[35] when 23 death row inmates were executed at once on short notice. Since the late former President Kim Dae-jung took office in February 1998, Korea has not carried out any executions and has been categorized as "abolitionist in practice"[36] by Amnesty International. Despite this *de facto* moratorium on carrying out the death penalty, courts have continued to impose the death penalty, although not frequently. The Supreme Court requires lower courts to sentence a person to death only when there are special circumstances in light of an offender's degree of criminal liability and the purpose of criminal punishment and after thoroughly examining the sentencing conditions under Article 51.[37] An analysis of cases in which the death penalty was affirmed reveals that courts tend to impose the death penalty when (1) the crime was very dangerous because it was committed by at least two people, (2) there are no mitigating factors as to motive, (3) the crime was committed with premeditation, (4) the crime was committed in a cruel manner, resulting in serious harm, and (5) the defendant does not show any remorse during the trial.[38] The most recent death penalty affirmed by the Supreme Court was in 2016.[39] As of February 2022, it is believed that Korea has 59 prisoners on death row, all of whom had been convicted of murder or aggravated murder. The constitutionality of the provisions regarding the death penalty has been challenged three times. While the first two challenges were unsuccessful,[40] the last one is still pending in the Constitutional Court. The

34 Sangmin Bae, *South Korea's De Facto Abolition of the Death Penalty*, 82(3) PACIFIC AFFAIRS 412 (2009). Hanging is the only form of execution permitted by Article 66 of the CA.

35 For the history of death penalty policy in Korea, see Byung-Sun Cho, *South Korea's Changing Capital Punishment Policy: The Road from De Facto to Formal Abolition*, 10(2) PUNISHMENT & SOCIETY 171-205 (2008).

36 "Countries that retain the death penalty for ordinary crimes such as murder but can be considered abolitionist in practice in that they have not executed anyone during the last 10 years and are believed to have a policy or established practice of not carrying out executions" are abolitionist in practice. *Death Sentences and Executions*, AMNESTY INTERNATIONAL GLOBAL REPORT 58 (2020).

37 Supreme Court Decisions 2006Do354, March 24, 2006; 2012Do8980, January 24, 2013.

38 Kwoncheol Lee, *Criminal Law and Procedure*, INTRODUCTION TO KOREAN LAW (Korean Legislation Research Institute ed.), Springer, 163 (2013).

39 Supreme Court Full Bench Decision 2015Do12980, February 19, 2016. The defendant was a sergeant surnamed Lim, who intentionally killed five soldiers and wounded seven others during a shooting rampage in a border unit of the Army's 22nd Division in Goseong, Gangwon Province, in 2014.

second ruling from the Constitutional Court observed that the decision of whether to maintain or abolish the death penalty is not a matter for judicial review but a matter of legislative policy. Further, it noted that the death penalty effectively serves several legitimate legislative purposes, including deterrence of crime, by posing a psychological threat to people, rendering justice through the fair punishment of criminals, and protecting society by permanently blocking the possibility of recidivism by certain criminals. The court concluded that it cannot be determined that there exists any other penalty with the same effect as capital punishment in accomplishing the legislative purpose of crime deterrence. However, it is notable that four of nine justices dissented from the ruling and wrote individual opinions to that effect. Former President Moon Jae-in administration's position on the death penalty was ambivalent. The government voted in favor of a moratorium on the use of the death penalty at the Third Committee of the 75th UN General Assembly held on November 17, 2020. This was the first time that a Korean government voted in favor of a death penalty moratorium in the international community. However, the Ministry of Justice explained that "the vote does not mean the Korean government should abolish the death penalty or is liable to change its legal system."[41] Furthermore, the ministry filed a written opinion with the Constitutional Court, arguing that the death penalty is constitutional and should be retained "as a necessary evil".[42] In October 2021, lawmakers Sang-min Lee and others proposed a bill replacing the death penalty with imprisonment for life without parole. It remains to be seen whether the legislative branch will ultimately take the initiative of abolishing the death penalty or pass the issue to the Constitutional Court, taking into account public opinion, which is not favorable to the abolition movement.

There are three types of punishment that restrict physical freedom. The first is imprisonment with labor. The second is imprisonment without labor, which is regarded as less severe than imprisonment with labor. This is

40 Constitutional Court Decisions 95Hun-Ba1, November 28, 1996; 2008Hun-Ka23, February 25, 2010;

41 Ministry of Justice, *Korean Government votes in favor of the resolution on a moratorium on the use of the death penalty at the 75th session of the UN General Assembly*, 34 RECENT TRENDS OF LAW & REGULATION IN KOREA 25 (2020).

42 *Horrific crimes reignited debate over death penalty*, THE KOREA TIMES, September 1 2021 at https://www.koreatimes.co.kr/www/nation/2022/03/251_314858.html.

imposed upon convicts who are found to have committed political crimes or crimes involving negligence. In the case of these convicts, labor may be allocated on a voluntary basis. Imprisonment with or without labor may be imposed for life or for a fixed term, which ranges from one month to 30 years and can be increased to 50 years if the offender committed multiple offenses or meets the requirement of a repeat criminal under the CA (Articles 35 and 42). A serving prisoner who has demonstrated good behavior and shown sincere contrition may be provisionally released by the parole committee within the Ministry of Justice when 20 years of a life sentence or one third of a fixed term has been served (CA Article 72(1)). Therefore, life imprisonment without the possibility of parole, as sentenced by a court,[43] is only a recommendation rather than a binding order under current law. The last and least severe type of punishment restricting physical freedom is detention, which applies to offenders who have committed minor offenses; detention terms are limited to fewer than 30 days (CA Article 46).

There are three types of punishment that deprive the offender of property: fines, minor fines, confiscation. Most typical are fines. These begin at a minimum of KRW 50,000 (CA Article 45) and must be paid within 30 days from the date when a judgment becomes final (CA Article 69(1)). A person who fails to pay a fine in full by the deadline is to be detained in prison and compelled to work for a term of not less than one day and no more than three years as a substitute for payment (CA Article 69(2)). When levying a fine, the court shall simultaneously determine and decree a substitute term of prison labor (CA Article 70(1)). While one day of prison labor is normally calculated at KRW 100,000 (approximately US$80), there are cases where one day's labor is valued at significantly more than that, due to the three-year cap established in Article 69(2). However, if the ratio between offenders serving time because of high fines and normal offenders becomes unreasonably high, it can arouse suspicion of unfairness and erode public confidence in the criminal justice system. After the notorious "emperor's labor" case[44] drew that kind of criticism, the National Assembly introduced

43 In March 2021, an appellate panel of the Seoul High Court insisted that a murderer who killed three women in the same family should be sentenced to life imprisonment without the opportunity of parole, although it recognized that the sentence was not binding.

44 *Judge resigns over 'emperor's labor'*, The Korean Herald, March 30, 2014 at http://www.koreaherald.com/view.php?ud=20140330000377#.

Article 70(2) to the CA, which provides a lower limit for the substitute term when the courts assess a fine of not less than KRW 100 million. Minor fines, which are imposed for lesser crimes, range from KRW 2,000 to KRW 50,000 (Article 47). In addition to other punishments, confiscation is imposed to deprive the offender of property such as (1) goods used or sought to be used in the commission of a crime, (2) goods produced by or acquired by means of criminal conduct, (3) and goods received in exchange for the above items (Article 48). It is not mandatory for the court to order confiscation, except when a specific provision orders it, as is the case with Article 134.[45]

2) Sentencing[46]

The different types of punishment and their ranges are stipulated in specific provisions on individual offenses in Part II of the CA. Within the range of prescribed punishments, judges enjoy broad discretion in sentencing because Article 51 requires judges to consider several factors: (i) the age, character and conduct, intelligence, and environment of the offender; (ii) the offender's relation to the victim; (iii) the crime's motive, means, and results; (iv) and the circumstances following the commission of the crime. However, the CA does not offer more specific guidelines on how to interpret and apply these considerations in individual cases. While it is legitimate to give judges discretion to enable decisions that are appropriate for individual cases, discretionary sentencing has drawn criticism because of the variation in sentences for similar crimes. That is, leeway in sentencing aroused the suspicion of corruption (*Jeon-kwan-ye-woo*, which suggests that judges gave lenient sentences to defendants represented by counsel who were former judges) and contributed to the public distrust of the judiciary. Alleged leniency toward white-collar crime offenders in particular has been heavily criticized.

In 2006, the National Assembly revised the Court Organization

45 Article 134 (Confiscation and Subsequent Collection). A bribe received or money or goods to be received as a bribe by an offender or by a third party having knowledge of its nature shall be confiscated, or, if confiscation is impossible, the value thereof shall be collected.

46 For a useful explanation of the process of establishing the Sentencing Commission of Korea and its historical background, see Hyungkwan Park, *The Basic Features of the First Korean Sentencing Guidelines*, 22(4) FEDERAL SENTENCING REPORTER 263 (2010). For the basic concepts and principles of sentencing guidelines, see Sentencing Commission of Korea, *Sentencing Guidelines Manual Commentary* at https://sc.scourt.go.kr/sc/engsc/guideline/manual/introduction/introduction_01.jsp.

Act (COA) to establish the Sentencing Commission of Korea, which bears responsibility for setting and revising sentencing guidelines. It was established to ensure fair and objective sentencing and restore public confidence in the judiciary (COA Article 81-2). Although the commission was established as a court-affiliated institution (COA Article 81-2(1)), it carries out its duties independently (COA Article 81-2(2)). It consists of 13 commissioners appointed by the Chief Justice, including one chairperson and one standing commissioner; they serve two-year terms and are subject to unlimited reappointment (COA Article 81-3(1), (4)). The Commission is to include four judges, two prosecutors recommended by the Minister of Justice, two defense attorneys recommended by the president of the Korean Bar Association, two law professors, and two non-lawyers with relevant expertise and experience (COA Article 81-3(3)).[47] Although sentencing guidelines are not mandatory, judges are presumed to respect guidelines when selecting punishments and determining specific terms or amounts (COA Article 81-7 (1)). A judge who wishes to deviate from the sentencing guidelines must justify that decision in writing (COA Article 81-7 (2). There was a lively debate on which approach should be adopted: the one used by the UK Sentencing Council or the US Federal Sentencing Commission's approach. The Sentencing Commission of Korea chose the former by crafting separate sentencing guidelines for each offense, starting with the most frequently occurring and socially important offenses.[48] The first sentencing guideline, encompassing eight categories of crime (homicide, bribery, sex crimes, perjury, false accusation, embezzlement, misappropriation, and robbery), took effect on July 1, 2009. As of 2020, the commission had established sentencing guidelines for 41 types of offenses.[49]

47 This structure of the commission allows for a significant influence of the judiciary, despite its independent status, a point that has been a criticism of the commission; see Daniel Fiedler, *Sentencing Guidelines in South Korea: Lessons from the American Experience*, 10 JOURNAL OF KOREAN LAW 133 (2010); Hyungkwan Park, *supra* note 46, 269.

48 Sentencing Commission of Korea, *Sentencing Guidelines: Introduction* at https://sc.scourt.go.kr/sc/engsc/guideline/intro/introduce.jsp.

49 Sentencing Commission of Korea, *2021 Sentencing Guidelines at* https://sc.scourt.go.kr/sc/engsc/guideline/down/down.jsp.

4. Transformations and New Trends in Korean Criminal Law

(1) Overview

While the legislators who crafted the CA were aiming to modernize Korean criminal law in accordance with western democratic countries, the CA also incorporated some basic Confucian moral concepts.[50] As Korea has gradually become a more liberal society, provisions founded on the moralism of the old era became increasingly out of touch with the views of people living in the 21st century. In addition, ambiguous and abstract terms used to describe specific criminal offenses opened the way for the courts to overly restrict people's individual rights. To cope with these problems, the Constitutional Court has actively reviewed the constitutionality of criminal provisions, leading to a considerable number of rulings declaring unconstitutionality. The Supreme Court also exerted some effort to apply provisions with broad legal terms in a way that respects diverse modes of living and doing business while not deviating exceedingly from the common sense of the people. Some of the transformations and new trends led by Korea's Constitutional Court and the Supreme Court are briefly discussed below.

50 Paul Kichyun Ryu, *The New Korean Criminal Code of October 3, 1953 – An Analysis of Ideologies Embedded in it*, 48(3) JOURNAL OF CRIMINAL LAW AND CRIMINOLOGY 278 (1957). The most vivid example of provisions reflecting Confucian moralism is Article 250(2), which aggravates the penalty of intentional killing when a person kills his own or his legal spouse's lineal ascendant. However, the Constitutional Court declared this article to be constitutional. According to the Court, "descendants' respect and love for ascendants are core values constituting essential elements of our social morals, rather than a cultural heritage of the feudal family system. It is especially emphasized in our nation that has succeeded and developed traditional cultures based on Confucian ideas." Constitutional Court Decision 2011Hun-Ba267, July 25, 2013.

(2) Transformations Led by the Constitutional Court

1) Repealing Outmoded Provisions Restricting Individual Liberty Protected by the Constitution

❶ Adultery

According to the repealed Article 241 of the CA, a married person who committed adultery could be punished by imprisonment for not more than two years. The same applied to a person who had sex with that married person. That is, a case of criminal adultery could be established if only one married person were involved. Since 1953, almost 100,000 people have been convicted of adultery, of whom more than 30,000 people were detained awaiting trial. Four constitutional challenges to Article 241 proved unsuccessful, with the Constitutional Court determining that the provision was constitutional in 1990, 1993, 2001, and 2008. However, people's attitudes toward adultery had evolved to a great degree. This change was reflected in the sentencing practices of trial courts, which began suspending terms of imprisonment[51] rather than having them enforced immediately. The Constitutional Court ultimately overruled its own precedent and declared the adultery provision unconstitutional in 2015, finding that it is an excessive restriction on people's rights to sexual self-determination, protected by the Korean Constitution Article 10, and the right to privacy protected by Article 17.[52] The reasoning of the majority opinion of five Justices is as follows:

> There is no longer any public consensus regarding the criminalization of adultery, along with the change in public perception of social structure, marriage, and sex and the spread of the idea of valuing sexual self-determination. In addition, the tendency of modern criminal law directs that the state should not exercise its authority

51 Article 62 of the CA enables suspending a sentence of imprisonment up to three years when extenuating circumstances exist, for a period of at least one year up to five years, except when the crime was committed during a period of three years after a final judgment sentencing imprisonment was completely executed or discharged.

52 Constitutional Court Decision 2009Hun-Ba17, February 26, 2015. For an in-depth analysis of the reasoning and legal consequences of this ruling, see Seokmin Lee, *Adultery and the Constitution: A Review on the Recent Decision on 'Criminal Adultery'*, 15(2) JOURNAL OF KOREAN LAW 325-353 (2016).

in the event that an act, in essence, belongs to the sphere of personal privacy and is not socially harmful or in evident violation of legal interests, despite the act being in contradiction to morality. According to this tendency, it is a global trend to abolish adultery crimes. It should be left to the free will and love of people to decide whether to maintain a marriage, and the matter should not be externally forced through criminal punishment.

It should be noted that adultery remains a breach of marital duty that establishes a cause for divorce and non-pecuniary damages. The Court's ruling clarified that any criminal sanction must remain a last resort, only being invoked when other means are insufficient.

❷ Abortion

The CA prohibited abortion without exception and regardless of timing, punishing both women who terminated their pregnancies and doctors or others who performed abortions with or without consent of the pregnant women. This strict and general ban on abortion had been somewhat eased by Article 14 (limited permission for abortion operations) of the Mother and Child Health Act, which allowed abortion when (a) the woman or her spouse suffers from a eugenic, genetic, or mental handicap or physical disease; (b) the woman or her spouse suffers from an infectious disease; (c) the woman is impregnated by rape; (d) the woman and her spouse are relatives who are unable to marry legally; or (e) the maintenance of the pregnancy injures or might injure the health of the mother's body. The law prohibiting abortion was enforced arbitrarily, based on the contemporary social atmosphere. The state did not strictly enforce the abortion law, especially when abortion contributed to implementing its birth control policy during the baby boom era. The underenforcement of the abortion law was also due to the dominant patriarchic culture preferring a son to a daughter, which was less of a concern to the state. However, as religious groups' pressure against abortion became stronger, more and more doctors were indicted for performing illegal abortions. As for women, many protested that access to safe and affordable abortion in the formal health system was not possible; as a result, women's health and right to self-determination were under-protected. In consequence, the constitutionality of the abortion law faced challenges from both doctors and women.[53]

The first challenge was not successful. In 2012, the Constitutional Court denied the petition of a midwife who challenged the constitutionality of the relevant law.[54] Emphasizing that the right to life is the most fundamental right of human rights, the court recognized the fetus's right to life as a fundamental right protected by the Korean Constitution. After balancing the right to life of the fetus and the right to self-determination of a pregnant woman under the proportionality analysis, the court concluded that it was not an excessive restriction on the latter that the relevant provision did not permit abortion based on social or economic grounds and that the provision therefore did not violate the constitution.

However, the court overruled its previous decision in 2019, declaring those provisions unconstitutional on the ground that a complete and uniform ban on all abortions throughout pregnancy, regardless of the developmental stage or viability of the fetus, excessively restricts a pregnant woman's right to self-determination.[55] Further, the court pointed out that the exceptions provided by Article 14 of the Mother and Child Health Act are extremely limited and therefore unable to encompass the myriad social and economic reasons for seeking an abortion. However, rather than simply striking down the abortion law, the court rendered a decision of nonconformity to the constitution, ordering that the relevant provisions continued to be applied until the legislature amended them by December 31, 2020. Because no legislation was passed by the deadline set by the court, there is currently no criminal sanction attached to abortion, regardless of the timing of termination or the circumstance leading to abortion.

❸ Sexual Intercourse under the False Promise of Marriage

Article 304 provided that a person who induces "a woman free from habitual debauchery" into sexual intercourse through the false promises of marriage or other fraudulent means shall be punished by imprisonment for

53 For a more detailed explanation on the abortion law before the Constitutional Court's ruling in 2020, see Hyosin Kim and Hyun-A Bae, *A Critical Assessment of Abortion Law and Its Implementation in South Korea*, 24(1) ASIAN JOURNAL OF WOMEN'S STUDIES 71-87 (2018).

54 Constitutional Court Decision 2010Hun-Ba402, August 23, 2012.

55 Constitutional Court Decision 2017Hun-Ba127, April 11, 2019. For an overview of this case, see Sang-Hyeon Jeon, *Notable Cases on Constitutional Law*, 19(1) JOURNAL OF KOREAN LAW 63-70 (2020).

not more than two years or by a fine not exceeding KRW 5 million. The "false promises of marriage" part of this provision was declared unconstitutional in 2009.[56] The Constitutional Court reasoned that the legislative purpose of that provision could not be regarded as legitimate for the following reasons.

First, it is totally within the realm of privacy for a man to have a sexual relationship with a female partner, against which the state's interference should be as minimal as possible if no coercion or violence is involved. Second, if a woman, after voluntarily deciding to have a pre-marital sexual relationship with a man who requests it, later asks the court to punish him by arguing that her decision was made by mistake, that is an act of denying her own right to sexual self-determination.

Third, under the provision, the subjects of protection were limited to women free from habitual debauchery, while all other women who had sexual relationships with multiple partners were stigmatized as sexually promiscuous and excluded from protection, which forces a sexual ideology based on patriarchy and moralism on women. In this regard, the provision not only ran afoul of the state's constitutional duty to create and maintain a gender-equal society (Constitution Article 36, Section 1) but also denied women's right to self-determination regarding sexual activity under the guise of protecting them by treating them as not mature enough to have the capacity to voluntarily make such a decision.

Although the court did not declare the "other fraudulent means" provision of Article 304 unconstitutional, the National Assembly deleted Article 304 in its entirety after the court's ruling. As a consequence, there remains no provision criminalizing rape by deception committed against adults without any mental incapacity or except under special circumstances provided by Article 303.

2) Efforts to Fulfill the Principle of Proportionality in Punishment

The principles of proportionality and criminal law as the last resort require legislators to act so that the criminal law shall not intervene if there are other adequate means for deterring specific activities. Even when the criminal law does intervene, proportionality between responsibility and punishment shall be maintained. This is needed because punishment is a stigma; that is,

56 Constitutional Court Decision 2008Hun-Ba58, November 26, 2009.

a marked condemnation that is publicly communicated. The entire criminal justice system involves severe infringements of personal autonomy by means of arrest, search, seizure, detention, interrogation, public court hearings, conviction, and punishment. Therefore, even when an accused person is ultimately acquitted, being subject to a criminal trial itself can cause tremendous suffering.

However, the reality of legislation in the criminal law area ran counter to these principles. Legislators' eagerness to gain public support often produced new criminal provisions with harsh punishments in order to respond to public anxiety about crimes, without meticulously examining the effectiveness and long-term practicality of the punishment. What made matters worse was that legislators simply added new provisions with harsher punishments to special criminal statutes, leaving the provisions punishing the same crimes in the CA as they were. As a result, the unity and coherence of the criminal statutory regime have been seriously impaired.

The Constitutional Court put a brake on this legislative practice by declaring unconstitutional a large number of special criminal statutes that aggravated the punishment of certain crimes already covered in the CA. The reasoning behind those rulings was twofold. First, those aggravated punishments were so severe that the proportionality between criminal responsibility and punishment was not maintained. Second, the overlap of those provisions with existing provisions in the CA could lead to arbitrary justice because it was entirely within a prosecutor's discretion to choose which one to apply. One example is the so-called "Jean Valjean" law, Article 5-4(1) of the Act on the Aggravated Punishment of Specific Crimes. The article provided that any person who habitually commits larceny shall be punished by life imprisonment or imprisonment not less than three years. It meant that even if a person with previous convictions of larceny stole a piece of bread only because of hunger, a prison term of at least 18 months (when mitigated by Article 53 of the CA) could result automatically. In comparison, Article 332 of the CA punishes the same offense by imprisonment of not more than nine years or a fine not exceeding KRW 15 million. The court declared the Jean Valjean article to be unconstitutional.[57]

57 Constitutional Court Decision 2014Hun-Ka16, February 26, 2015.

(3) Transformations Led by the Supreme Court Reflecting Social Changes in the Interpretation of Specific Provisions

1) Narrowing the Scope of Defamation in Favor of Protecting the Right to Expression

The CA criminalizes defamation, regardless of whether the alleged facts are true or false. Article 307(1) punishes a person who defames another by publicly alleging facts with imprisonment or imprisonment without prison labor for not more than two years or a fine not exceeding KRW 5 million. Article 307(2) aggravates this punishment when the alleged facts are false, punishing by imprisonment for not more than five years, suspension of qualifications for not more than ten years, or a fine not exceeding KRW 10 million. According to Article 310, defamation can be justified when the facts are true and solely in the public interest. Therefore, if a person says something true about another person and it harms another person's reputation without a purpose related to the public interest, the first person can be convicted even though the reputation is a "false reputation." This framework designed by the CA was heavily criticized by scholars and activists as excessively infringing the right to expression protected by Article 21 of the Constitution. However, the Constitutional Court determined such framework constitutional in 2021.[58]

The Supreme Court has developed several jurisprudential techniques for the purpose of narrowing the scope of defamation that would adopt a more balanced approach between protection of reputation and protection of the right to expression, especially regarding defamation of public officials. Because such officials have the right to enjoy human dignity, they can be victims of defamation, whereas the state itself cannot be a victim. However, if public officials actively accuse citizens or even simply turn a blind eye to an investigation triggered by a third party's complaint,[59] defamation charges can be used for the purpose of stifling criticism of the government. To cope with this problem, two approaches were taken by the Supreme Court.

58 Constitutional Court Decision 2017Hun-Ma1113, 2018Hun-Ba330 (consolidated), February 25, 2021.

59 According to Article 312(2) of the CA, defamation shall not be prosecuted over the express objection of the victim; that is, if the victim does not clearly state a positive objection to the investigation and prosecution of defamation, those processes are allowed.

First, the court tried to narrow the scope of "alleging facts" to ensure that freedom of expression regarding public figures or public matters could be protected as broadly as possible. Recently, the court ruled that publicly saying "presidential candidate Moon Jae-In is a communist" is not defamation because it is simply an opinion about a candidate's political views.[60] Another recent case dealt with a critical comment about an incumbent president. According to the court, raising the suspicion that President Park Geun-hye was taking drugs when she did not appear for seven hours after the *Sewol* ferry accident was reported to the President's Office did not defame her because it was an opinion that emphasized the need for transparent disclosure of the president's activities at the moment when hundreds of people were about to drown due to the failure of the maritime police to rescue them.[61]

Second, the Supreme Court declared that defamation against a public official is only punishable when that statement is made with "actual malice," even if it is false.[62] This jurisprudence appears to have been influenced by *New York Times Co. v. Sullivan* (1964), a landmark US Supreme Court decision ruling that the freedom of speech protections in the First Amendment to the US Constitution restrict the ability of American public officials to sue for defamation.

On the other hand, the Supreme Court has maintained a broad interpretation of the term "publicly" by adopting the "theory of propagation possibility." According to this theory, even when a defamatory remark about a person was made to only one other person, it can meet the requirement of "publicly" if there is a sufficient possibility that the other person will relay the defamatory remark to other people. The recent full bench decision of the Supreme Court in 2020 reaffirmed this theory as firmly grounded precedent.[63] However, three justices who joined a dissenting opinion criticized this theory on the ground that it relies on an analogical interpretation that is prohibited under the principle of legality.

60 Supreme Court Decision 2020Do12861, September 16, 2021.
61 Supreme Court Decision 2016Do14995, March 25, 2021.
62 Supreme Court Decision 2010Do17237, September 2, 2011.
63 Supreme Court Full Bench Decision 2020Do5813, November 19, 2020.

2) Expanding the Scope of Rape by Recognizing Marital Rape as Punishable under Article 297 of the CA

At times, the Supreme Court has expanded the applicable scope of specific criminal offenses to protect the legal interest of citizens more thoroughly. One example is the case of marital rape. In the past, Article 297 was interpreted as not including marital rape, because "female" as a victim of rape only meant women other than the offender's legally married wife in the traditional view of a majority of scholars. The Supreme Court also followed this traditional position. In 2013, however, the court overruled precedent and declared that the legal spouse of an offender can also be protected as a victim of rape under Article 297, because 'female' in that provision refers simply to a 'woman,' whether adult or minor, married or single.[64] Furthermore, this provision does not expressively exclude a legal spouse from the scope of being a victim. The court therefore concluded that there are no restrictions to interpreting an offender's legally married wife as included withing the possible range of rape victims. The court wrote as follows:

> Even when we recognize a married couple's duty to cohabit under the Civil Act, it can hardly be deemed to include the duty to endure sexual intercourse coerced by violence or intimidation. This is because a marriage can hardly mean the abandonment of an individual's sexual autonomy, nor can it be a process of enduring a sexually repressed life.

At the same time, the court emphasized the necessity of strictly interpreting the concept of 'force or intimidation' in marital rape cases, in full view of all relevant circumstances, including whether the content and degree of violence or intimidation have reached such a point as to essentially infringe upon the wife's sexual autonomy, the circumstances leading up to the husband's use of tangible force, the patterns of the couple's married and sexual lives, and the situation during and after the sexual intercourse at issue.

64 Supreme Court Full Bench Decision 2012Do14788, May 16, 2013.

5. Conclusion

As we have seen above, the CA had inherent limitations in strictly pursuing the principle of legality. In addition, for the past several decades, public sentiment demanding harsh punishment of criminal offenders produced a substantial number of special criminal statutes that called for severe punishments. As a consequence, the Constitutional Court and the Supreme Court have taken up the task of making Korean criminal law more understandable and proportionate. Beyond these efforts from the judicial authorities, however, fundamental reform is needed to make Korean criminal law more coherent and reasonable.

First, the heavy dependence on special criminal statutes must be overcome. The CA has to regain its status as the basic criminal statute of Korea by providing a complete set of punishable crimes and thus adequately fulfilling the function of fair notice.

Second, the excessive reliance on judicial interpretations of statutory provisions needs to be addressed. Of course, supplementary interpretations by courts are not completely avoidable because of the intrinsic ambiguity of language. However, the pervasiveness of judge-made law in the criminal law area has become incompatible with the principle of legality.

Third, legislators should conduct an in-depth constitutional analysis before submitting any bill with criminal provisions for consideration. An *ex post facto* ruling of unconstitutionality from the Constitutional Court is sometimes too late to prevent the infringement of individual liberty and the social costs that arise from implementing hastily introduced criminal provisions.

Chapter 7

Criminal Procedure Law

Sang Won Lee*

1. Introduction

The Korean criminal justice system has a long history. It traces back to the ancient *Gochosun* Dynasty which mythology says was founded in the 24th century B.C. and lasted until the 2nd century B.C. Since then, various systems came up and went down on the Korean Peninsula. However, those traditional systems were quite remote from the current system. Around the end of the 19th century, Korea (the *Chosun* Dynasty) introduced a modern justice system, which can be a root of the current system. Nevertheless, Koreans' efforts to establish a modern system was thwarted by the Japanese forced annexation in 1910. Imperial Japan forced Japanese law on the Korean Peninsula and the criminal justice system of the latter was regulated by Japanese Criminal Procedure Code, which was initially influenced by French law and then German law after 1922. In addition to the code, the colonial government enacted special regulations that applied only to Koreans, which gave the police enormous power. This characterized the criminal justice system as a police-oriented one. Law was nothing but a tool of reign at the time.

Having restored sovereignty in 1945, Korea built a new country as a republic. Before the official establishment of the government of the Republic

* Professor, Seoul National University School of Law.

of Korea in 1948, the military and provisional government made efforts to erase the traces of the colonial rule. In particular, this government repealed many harsh colonial criminal rules. Among the most meaningful changes was the introduction of the judicial warrant system, which had been denied during the colonial period. The new republic began to make laws including criminal procedure code. However, it took many years for the Criminal Procedure Code (hereinafter CPC) to be enacted due to the Korean War. The CPC was first enacted in 1954. From then until now (2022), the CPC has been revised 40 times. Looking back, the history of the Korean criminal justice system after 1945 can be divided into the following four periods.[1]

The first period, from 1945 to 1972, can be referred to as the "foundation period." The newly formed republic adopted the civil law system as the basic structure, but with shades of the common law. Considering the need to build a system within a limited period of time and the side effects of drastic changes, it reflected many aspects of the then existing law, leaving the transition toward a more ideal stage as a future challenge. Nevertheless, the protection of human rights was a manifest goal of the founding legislators.

The second period came with *Yushin* in 1972, which involves a kind of palace coup. Through the amendment of the constitution in 1972 and that of the CPC in 1973, the government strengthened criminal control over the people. Investigatory power, particularly the prosecution, gained more strength than earlier, and the prosecution became the substantial center of the criminal justice system. This period, from 1972 to 1987, can be called the "controlling period or authoritarian period," with a so-called prosecution-oriented system.

Although the government oppressed political dissidents, pro-democracy movements continued. In 1987, two torture crimes committed by investigators against student activists triggered a nationwide protest asking for democratization, which led to the constitutional amendment of 1987. This amendment is the current constitution, which provides strong protection of human rights. It also has many clauses directly stipulating

1 For more details of the Korean experience, see Sang Won Lee, The Influence of the Judiciary on the Criminal Legislation and Its Impact on the Transformation of Models: An Analysis of the Korean Experience, in RELATIONSHIP BETWEEN THE LEGISLATURE AND THE JUDICIARY (Jan von Hein et al. eds.), Nomos 169-193 (2018).

criminal procedures, which constitute the constitutional criminal procedure. The third period from 1987 to 2007 brought a paradigm shift to the criminal procedure, with a clear direction to protect human rights rather than social order. Further, the reform of the arrest warrant system in 1995 is one of the most notable changes during this period. Up until then, judges had been issuing warrants based only on documents. Hearings were not needed and arrestees did not have the right to appear before judges. Considering that the evidentiary documents were mainly prepared by the investigators, it was not difficult for the investigators to obtain a warrant. The amendment of the CPC in 1995 introduced warrant hearing and judges began to examine suspects in person before issuing warrants. This made substantial judicial review of investigatory arrest, which shifted the central axis of the arrest procedure from the prosecution to the court. Thus, the third period can be called the "taking off democratic period."

2007 was a notable year, as it brought about big changes in the trial system. The first is trial centralism. Shedding the traditional method, trials were given a substantial function because the 2007 CPC made courtrooms the central fora, in which guilt or innocence are substantially decided by argumentation and proof of parties. Until then, trials had mostly relied on documents rather than oral arguments in courtrooms, and judges usually made up their minds in their offices reading these documents after court hearings. Even before the amendment, the court had made efforts to change this document-based trial practice, but the 2007 amendment strengthened and provided institutional realization. The second is citizen participatory trial. It was introduced by the Act on Citizen Participation in Criminal Trial of 2007. The participatory trial is similar to the US jury trial, but differs in that the jury verdict has no binding force. The third is sentencing guidelines. The amendment of the Court Organization Act of 2007 established a sentencing commission as an independent agency of the judiciary. The commission makes separate sentencing guidelines offense by offense. As of 2022, sentencing guidelines have been created for 44 categories of offences. The period from 2007 to the present can be called the "cruising democratic period." During this period, more protection has been provided for the procedural rights of suspects and defendants, parties have gained more opportunities to speak directly before judges, the court has become the core of factual findings, and the democratic oversight of the citizens on trials has become even stronger.

Roughly speaking, from 1945 onward, the Korean criminal justice system witnessed the transition from authoritarian to democratic, from social order to human rights, and from crime control to due process.[2] In addition, there was a recent reform in 2020 that mainly targeted the prosecution. It repealed the supervisory authority of prosecutors over police investigation, restricted the investigation initiated by prosecutors, and established a new investigatory agency for the crimes of high-ranking officials. However, this reform is controversial in terms of whether it follows the direction thus far.[3]

2. Court and Parties

(1) Court

1) Jurisdiction

The Korean judiciary has a dual supreme court system: the Constitutional Court and the Supreme Court. Despite a few problems, such as possible conflicts coming from different decisions on the same issue, the dual system has contributed substantially to the improvement of human rights. The Constitutional Court has jurisdiction over cases listed in the constitution,[4] while all the other cases fall under the jurisdiction of the Supreme Court. Any person whose fundamental rights are infringed by the government can file a constitutional complaint to the Constitutional Court; however, this does not hold for court decisions, for which the Supreme Court is the last resort. The Supreme Court does not review the decisions of the Constitutional Court either. Korea has two supreme courts. As special courts, military courts have jurisdiction over military offences; however, the Supreme Court has the final jurisdiction over these courts as well.

Courts of first instance are single judge courts or collegiate panel courts composed of three judges belonging to district courts or branch

2 The crime control and due process models were proposed by Herbert L. Packer, *Two Models of the Criminal Procedure*, 113 UNIVERSITY OF PENNSYLVANIA LAW REVIEW 1 (1964).

3 For more details, see Sang Won Lee, *The Backward Reform of the Criminal Justice System in Korea*, 19 JOURNAL OF KOREAN LAW 119 (2020).

4 Article 111: Constitutionality of statutes, constitutional complaint, etc.

courts. In principle, panel courts hear cases punishable by imprisonment of at least one year or more. For these cases, high courts serve as appellate courts. Cases punishable by penalties less than the above are to be heard by single judge courts in the first instance and by panels of district courts in the second instance. Regardless of the court of first instance, the Supreme Court is the court of last resort. Its proceedings are *en banc* or conducted by panels of four justices. Panel judgment must be unanimous, but the *en banc* court decisions are rendered on a majority basis. When a panel fails to reach a unanimous agreement, the case is referred to the *en banc* court. Further, when rules at issue—except statutes legislated by the Congress, which are under the jurisdiction of the Constitutional Court—contradict higher laws or when the Supreme Court changes its precedents, then the *en banc* court hears the case.

2) Exclusion of Judges

(a) Debarment. A judge shall be barred from exercising his/her judicial office in the following conditions: if he/she himself/herself was aggrieved by the offence; if he/she is or was a relative of the accused or the victim; if he/she acted in the case as a prosecutor, a police officer, a defense council, or a lawyer for the victim; or if he/she was involved in reaching the decision contested by way of appellate remedy, etc. (b) Challenge of judge. A judge may be challenged on grounds of debarment or for fear of bias. (c) Recusal. A judge can recuse himself/herself if he/she has a ground for challenge.

(2) Prosecutor and Police Officer

1) Prosecutor

Corresponding to the court organization, the prosecutors' office consists of the Supreme Prosecutors' Office, high prosecutors' offices, district prosecutors' offices, and branch offices. Prosecutors have the authority of investigation, prosecution, and sentence enforcement. Although prosecutors can initiate an investigation, the target offences are limited by law: important crimes prescribed by a presidential decree from among corruption crimes, economic crimes, etc.

The newly created Investigation Office for the Crimes of High-ranking Officials has prosecutors as well. The prosecutors have the authority to investigate the crimes of high-ranking officials related to their duties prescribed in law. While these prosecutors can investigate all those crimes, they can prosecute only judges, prosecutors, and high-ranking police officers; these are criminal justice agencies. Cases against other high-ranking officials are referred to the above-mentioned prosecutors' offices after investigation. For these cases, prosecutors' offices have the authority of prosecution.

2) Police Officer

The police has the authority to investigate any crime. After investigation, if guilty, the police refer the case to the prosecutors' office, and if not guilty, then the police closes the case. For the former, the prosecutor can demand the police for further investigation. In the latter case, the police shall send the investigatory documents and evidence to the prosecutors' office and the prosecutor can request the police to investigate again if closing the case is not adequate.

There are also special police officers in charge of investigating specifically designated crimes related to forests, marine affairs, tax, etc. These police officers conduct their duties under the direction of prosecutors.

(3) Defense

1) Suspect and Defendant

A suspect is a person that a police officer or a prosecutor believes has committed a crime. This person is usually under investigation and subject to interrogation or compulsory measures. When a suspect is brought to trial for his/her criminal conduct, he/she becomes a defendant. Suspects and defendants enjoy procedural rights at both the constitutional and statutory levels: presumption of innocence, right to counsel, privilege against self-incrimination, etc.

2) Defense Lawyer

Suspects and defendants are constitutionally entitled to employ counsels. Defendants who are unable to employ their counsels are constitutionally entitled to public defenders and the CPC expands the range of protection. The court is required to appoint a defense counsel *ex officio* when the defendant is (i) under detention, (ii) a minor, (iii) 70 years or older, (iv) deaf and dumb, (v) likely to have a mental disorder, or (vi) prosecuted for a crime with imprisonment for at least three years. For indigent defendants, counsels are appointed at the request of the defendants. Even without these reasons, the court may appoint counsel at its discretion when needed. When arrested, a public defender is appointed even before a suspect is prosecuted. In addition, public defenders are appointed for certain proceedings such as jury trials. Further, counsels and would-be counsels have the right to communicate with their clients, to participate in the interrogation, to read and copy the investigatory documents, etc.

(4) Victim

A victim is not a party of the criminal procedure. Private prosecution is not allowed. However, victims have various constitutional and statutory rights. The constitution guarantees that victims have the right to make statements in pertinent trials. Victims of crimes such as sexual assault and child abuse may have counsels appointed for legal assistance in the process. When no counsel is available, the prosecutor may appoint a counsel for the victim.

3. Investigation

(1) Overview

1) Requirement for Investigation

Agencies may initiate an investigation when they have a suspicion that an offense has been committed. The suspicion does not have to be objective. Subjective suspicion is sufficient, but it should not be a willful suspicion.

Certain offences are to be prosecuted only upon accusation by the victim or his/her guardian. In such cases, an investigation is not permitted when there is little possibility for an accusation. In addition, certain offences are not allowed to be prosecuted against the victim's will. In such cases, agencies can investigate until the victim raises an objection.

Excessive investigation is not allowed. Only investigation that is necessary to find the offender and evidence is permitted. Proportionality is required for investigation. The measures of investigation must be reasonable. Entrapment (agent provocateur) is illegal when the offence is solicited by agencies.

2) Clues of Investigation

Agencies begin investigation when they have clues to crimes. They can find various clues through various ways. Clues like autopsy in the case of an unnatural death, stop and question, arrest of a flagrant offender, and finding additional crime during an ongoing investigation allow agencies to investigate through their own experience, while clues like accusation (or complaint),[5] self-denunciation, and report of offense allow agencies to investigate through the experiences of other people.

With regard to offenses subject to accusation, a victim should file an accusation to an investigative agency within six months after he/she becomes aware of the criminal. He/she can withdraw the complaint, but not after the decision is rendered by the court in the first instance. Moreover, an individual who has withdrawn a complaint cannot file the same complaint again.

3) Conducting an Investigation: Compulsory and Non-compulsory

Once an investigation is initiated, agencies conduct the investigation as they believe appropriate. Agencies may take various measures as they deem fit for the investigation. However, compulsory measures are prescribed in statutes, and agencies cannot resort to new measures if they are compulsory but not prescribed.

Request for documents, inquiry of fact, interrogation, and expert opinion are typically classified as non-compulsory measures. Arrest, detention, and search and seizure are traditional compulsory measures. Commentators disagree with regard to the criterion for distinguishing between compulsory and non-compulsory measures. The Constitutional Court holds that investigation with physical force is compulsory. However, as new measures are emerging with the development of science and technology, physical force does not serve as a good criterion any more in numerous cases. A majority of commentators distinguish between the two according to whether or not the measure is against the will of the investigated.

Among many measures of investigation, we will see interrogation as a form of non-compulsory investigation (see (2) below), and then will see arrest·detention (see (3) below) and search·seizure (see (4) below) as compulsory

5 Accusation and complaint are distinguished in that an accusation is made by a victim or his/her guardian while a complaint is filed by a third person other than the victim.

investigation. The constitution demands a judicial warrant for arrest, detention, and search or seizure (Articles 12 and 16). In addition, the constitution bestows the authority to apply for such warrants solely upon prosecutors. The police cannot directly apply to a judge. In practice, courts designate certain judges in charge of warrant affairs and those judges are usually senior judges with much experience. This shows that the Korean Judiciary recognizes how important warrant decisions are for the protection of human rights. Warrants are to be issued *ex ante* in principle, with some exceptions of *ex post facto* warrants. The CPC specifically provides the contents of the warrant system. Arrest and detention are measures *in personam* and search and seizure are measures *in rem*. These are typical measures of a compulsory investigation.

4) Conclusion of Investigation

After conducting an investigation, the agency concludes it. Before the 2020 amendment, only prosecutors had the authority to conclude an investigation, and the police would refer the case to a prosecutor once they finished their investigation. The prosecutor would then make a conclusion and terminate the case. Now, the police also have the authority to terminate the case.

(2) Interrogation

Agencies may interrogate suspects or witnesses. Not only witnesses but even suspects have no obligation to answer questions regardless of whether or not the statement is incriminating. Before the interrogation of suspects, the agency is required to give a Miranda warning. The interrogation must be documented, which becomes a "suspect record" or a "witness record." The agency may record the interrogation on videotape. For witnesses, the agency must obtain their consents; for suspects, notice is sufficient. When interrogating suspects, the agency must record not only the statements but also the entire process from arrival at the station to departure. This is a scheme to ensure the legality of the interrogation process.

During the interrogation of suspects, another agent other than the interrogator must be present. A suspect has the right to ask for his/her counsel to be present, and the counsel also has the right to be present at the interrogation.

(3) Arrest and Detention

Arrest and detention constitute the two phases of the custody system.

1) Arrest

Originally, arrest is defined as the "action" of seizing the body of a person. Such seizure does not have to continue. However, in order to meet the purpose of the arrest, arrest for a short duration of time is inevitable to a certain extent. An arrested person can be in custody only for the time being. Nonetheless, arrest cannot justify the long custody of a person. The need for long custody is served by detention. Arrest might last, but only for a short period of time.

A warrant is required to arrest a person. A prosecutor may request a judge to issue an arrest warrant in cases where (i) probable cause exists to have a suspicion that the person has committed a crime and (ii) he/she fails or is likely to fail to appear for interrogation without reason (CPC Article 200-2). A police officer may ask a prosecutor to make a request for an arrest warrant. Where the requirements are met, the competent judge issues an arrest warrant, based on documents. At the time of arrest, the agent must present the warrant to the arrestee, inform him/her of the gist of the suspected crime, the reasons for the arrest and the right to counsel, and give him/her the opportunity to defend himself/herself.

Although a warrant is required in principle (warrant requirement), there are two exceptions where arrests without warrants are allowed: arrest in *flagrante delicto* and arrest in exigent circumstances. Anybody can arrest a flagrant offender (CPC Article 212). A flagrant offender is a person who is in the act of committing a crime or has just committed it. A person is regarded as a flagrant offender (i) when he/she is pursued by hue and cry as an offender; (ii) where he/she is seemingly in possession of stolen goods, weapons, etc. related to a crime; (iii) where his/her body or clothes carry apparent traces of criminal evidence; (iv) where he/she attempts to flee when asked about his/her identity. A prosecutor or a police officer may arrest a suspect without a warrant in exigent circumstances, such as when there is no time to obtain a warrant, upon probable cause of a suspicion that he/she has committed a crime punishable by death, life imprisonment, or imprisonment for not less than three years; where he/she has fled, or is likely to flee or destroy evidence (CPC Article 200-3).

After arresting a suspect, the agent is required to notify the suspect's counsel or family about the arrest. If the arrestee is to be detained, an application for a detention warrant must be made without any delay within 48 hours from the time of arrest. Otherwise, the arrestee shall be released.

2) Detention

A detention warrant is required to detain a person. A prosecutor may request a judge to issue a detention warrant in cases where (i) probable cause exists to have a suspicion that the person has committed a crime and (ii) falls under any of the following categories: (a) that he/she has no fixed abode, (b) that he/she is likely to destroy evidence, or (c) that he/she has fled or is likely to flee (CPC Article 201). A police officer may ask a prosecutor to make a request for a detention warrant. A detention warrant can be sought not only for an arrested suspect but also for a non-arrested suspect.

In either case, the judge must conduct a warrant hearing. The establishment of the current warrant system has come a long way since the colonial period. The police and prosecutors in the colonial period were allowed to arrest and detain suspects without judicial warrants. Repealing the colonial system, the provisional government introduced the judicial warrant system through government ordinances in 1948. However, the reality was somewhat distorted. The police sought warrants when they arrested suspects, but most warrants were *ex post facto* warrants. They usually applied for warrants after the suspects were already suspected without judicial warrants. To improve the practice, the CPC of 1954 demanded the submission of supporting evidence when applying for a warrant, and the prosecutors instructed the police to seek *ex ante* warrants. Nevertheless, the police attempted to find an expedient means, which is 'voluntary accompaniment.' According to this, suspects were asked to consent to accompany the policemen to the police station, where they were interrogated. Then, the police sought warrants with the records of the interrogation (ironically, these were *ex ante* warrants). Despite the term 'voluntary,' the accompaniment was, in fact, rather involuntary because it was not easy for suspects to say "No" when they were asked to consent by the police, where they felt a substantial pressure and were actually taken to the police station by force in many cases. Voluntary accompaniment was in fact an involuntary arrest. The Supreme Court challenged this practice and ruled that voluntary accompaniment is illegal,[6] that *ex ante* warrant after actual arrest is illegal,[7] and violent resistance to a policeman forcing a suspect to the station does not constitute a crime.[8]

The introduction of warrant hearings in 1995 uplifted the system to the next level. Until then, warrants had been issued based on documents provided mainly by the prosecutors. Initially, it was at the discretion of judges whether or not to hold a hearing, but it was revised to let suspects choose in 1997 and then revised again to be mandatory in 2007. Currently, warrant hearings are mandatory. After a warrant hearing, a competent judge issues a detention warrant that meets all the requirements. The detention warrant is executed by a police officer under the direction of a prosecutor. During the execution, the agent must present the warrant, inform the detainee of the gist of the crime, etc., and then the agent must notify the counsel or family of the detainee about the arrest.

Further, there is a time limit for the detention. The police must transfer its case to the prosecutor within 10 days after the arrest or detention without arrest (CPC Article 202). Otherwise, the suspect must be released. The prosecutor must prosecute the suspect within 10 days after the arrest or detention without arrest, or the extradition of the suspect from the police (CPC Article 203). Otherwise, the prosecutor is required to release the suspect. The prosecutor may request the judge to extend the time limit by another 10 days, which, however, is allowed just once more.

3) Pretrial Release

Arrestees or detainees may be released before trial under several circumstances.

The first circumstance is in the case of a legality review of arrest or detention. A suspect who is arrested or detained may request the court to review the legality of his/her arrest or detention (CPC Article 214-2). The defense counsel or the family of the arrestee or the detainee may also do this. The judge will order the release not only if the arrest or the detention was originally illegal but also if it turns out to be inappropriate at the time of the decision, even though it was not originally illegal. The court may release

6 Supreme Court Decision 85Mo16, July 29, 1985.

7 Supreme Court Decisions 93Da35155, November 23, 1993; 93Do958, March 11, 1994.

8 Supreme Court Decision 91Do453, May 10, 1991.

the suspect with or without conditions. The main condition is to deposit a certain sum of money. This is a kind of bail for a suspect before prosecution, which was introduced in 1995. Before this, the pretrial release decision was a binary choice: either release or deny. The judge now has a third option. A bail bond or personal security is also admissible instead of bail money. Other appropriate conditions such as residential restrictions may also be added to the bail.

The second circumstance is provisional release. When appropriate, the court, the prosecutor, or the police may release the defendant (suspect) *ex officio* for a period of time, putting him/her under the supervision of relatives or institutions with or without residential restrictions (CPC Articles 101, 209). In practice, this release is usually used in urgent cases such as serious illness, childbirth, and funerals for those deceased in the family.

The third circumstance is revoking detention. Where the grounds to justify the detention are found to be originally absent or do not exist anymore, the court, the prosecutor, or the police may revoke the detention *ex officio* or upon request (CPC Articles 93, 209). The decision has an *ex nunc* effect of releasing the defendant (suspect).

4) Detention and Release of Defendants during Court Proceedings[9]

The court may summon the defendant by issuing a summons during court proceedings—for example, during a trial (CPC Articles 68 and 73). If the defendant does not appear at the designated place (courtroom), the court can issue a detention warrant. With or without prior summons, the court in charge of a pending case may issue a detention warrant for the defendant. The substantial requirements for judicial detention are the same as those for investigatory detention (CPC Article 70). A detention warrant authorizes either apprehension or confinement. A detention warrant for confinement authorizes apprehension as well. However, a detention warrant for apprehension does not authorize detention for over 24 hours (CPC Article 71).

Further, a detainee can be in custody for no more than two months after the judicial detention. When he/she is detained by investigatory agencies before prosecution, the two-month period starts from the time of

9 For convenience of understanding, we include judicial detention after prosecution here, although it belongs to the court procedure rather than the investigation.

the prosecution (CPC Article 92). This two-month period can be renewed up to twice by the trial court and up to three times by appellate courts (Article 92). This implies that no defendant can be in jail based on the same detention warrant for longer than 18 months throughout the entire process, all the way to the Supreme Court level, awaiting final conviction.[10] If the court exceeds the time limit, the defendant is set free even if his/her case is pending in court. This fosters an expeditious judicial process.

During a court procedure, defendants in custody can be released in several ways. For example, as suspects before prosecution, defendants after prosecution can be released by provisional release or revoking of detention before the court renders a judgment on the merits of the case (CPC Articles 93 and 101).

Bail is a typical means of releasing a defendant. The defendant, his/her counsel, and family members may file a motion for release on bail. The court shall accept the motion unless it falls under the following stipulated exceptions: (i) the defendant committed a crime punishable by capital punishment, life imprisonment, or imprisonment exceeding 10 years; (ii) the defendant is a repeat or habitual offender; (iii) there are conditions for detention, such as no fixed dwelling, destruction of evidence or its likelihood, and flight or its likelihood; or (iv) the defendant did or may do harm to life, body or property of the victim, witnesses or their families (CPC Article 95). Even where it falls under the exceptions, the court has the discretion to grant bail (CPC Article 96). Release is mandatory in principle, but discretionary in exceptional cases. Further, release may be on recognition or with conditions such as bail money, bond, residence restriction, prohibition of approaching or harming the victim or witnesses, etc. (CPC Article 98). Bail can be revoked if the defendant flees, fails to appear in court, does not stick to the conditions, etc. When bail is revoked, the defendant returns to jail and bail money is forfeited.

10 Trial court {two months (original)–two months (first renewal)–two months (second renewal)}. Appellate court {two months (first renewal)–two months (second renewal)–two months (third renewal)}. Highest court {two months (first renewal)–two months (second renewal)–two months (third renewal)}.

(4) Search and Seizure

1) Object of Search and Seizure

The object of seizure is what is to be evidence or forfeit. Physical objects such as effects and papers are typical examples. Posts and telecommunications are also such objects, for which the Communication Protection Act provides details. Financial information and DNA can also be seized, for which the Act on Real Name Financial Transactions and Confidentiality and the Act on Use and Protection of DNA ID Information provide details, respectively. In addition, there are certain restrictions on seizure of secretes of government, military, doctors, lawyers, etc.

With the growing popularity of electronic devices, electronic or digital information has emerged as a hot target. In line with preceding recording tapes and video tapes, judicial decisions have allowed the search for and seizing of digital information even without clear provision. The CPC was revised in 2011 to provide explicit clauses regulating digital information (CPC Article 106).

Search is conducted to find seizable objects or persons. The objects of search include bodies, chattels, houses, places, etc.

2) Conditions of Search and Seizure

Lawful search and seizure should meet three requirements: (i) circumstances of criminal suspicion, (ii) need for investigation, and (iii) relevancy of the object and the crime.

First, the threshold for criminal suspicion here is deemed to be lower than that of arrest or detention, according to the majority of commentators.

Second, need here implies not merely necessity but also subsidiarity and proportionality. Accordingly, search and seizure are not allowed if other less infringing measures are sufficient for the investigation, and restriction of human rights should be proportionate to the justice the investigation attempts to achieve.

Thirdly, relevancy means relation in general but it varies in details according to the area. It is means, product or fruit of the crime in seizure for forfeiture; while it is probative value in seizure for evidence. Relevancy in search is possibility of existence of the target. Although relevancy has long been required, it is getting even more important with digital evidence emerging, which is because of its massiveness. The Supreme Court elaborates evidentiary relevancy with the concepts of objective relevancy and subjective relevancy: the former includes not only direct evidence related to the criminal conduct itself but also indirect evidence related to motive, circumstances, time or place, but not evidence related to similar crimes; the latter includes not only the suspect himself but also his/her accomplices.

3) Warrant in Principle

It is a constitutional demand that a warrant is required for search and seizure. The constitution overtly asks at least an *ex post facto* warrant (Article 12(3)). According to the constitution, the CPC stipulates an *ex ante* warrant as a principle and an *ex post facto* one as an exception. The latter allows warrantless search and seizure at the time of the initial investigative conduct. Thus, search and seizure with a warrant is the principle, and search and seizure without a warrant is an exception.

First, a warrant is required for investigative search and seizure (CPC Article 215). A prosecutor may request a judge to issue a search and seizure warrant and a police officer may ask a prosecutor to make a request for such a warrant (CPC Article 215). However, this request is only allowed before the prosecutor brings the case to the court because the authority for compulsory measures belongs solely to the court after prosecution.[11] The court may issue an *ex officio* warrant during court proceedings (CPC Article 106). The requirements for this are not different from those for investigative search and seizure. The court may order the owner, possessor, or custodian to produce the object to be seized (CPC Article 106(2)). This order of production is available only for courts and not for investigative agencies. Persons against whom search and seizure is ordered are obliged to accept compulsory governmental actions, which implies passive obligation. In contrast, persons who receive an order of production have an active obligation. However, it does not imply an obligation to produce information inside their brains such as passwords, or other obligations to cooperate actively with agencies such as decoding or removal of passwords.[12] Search and seizure warrants should particularly describe the place, the body or the things to be searched for

11 Supreme Court Decision 2009Do10412, April 28, 2011.

12 A few commentators contend that these obligations should be introduced, but the majority (and court decisions) do not have such an understanding, at least under the current law (*de lege lata*).

and the things to be seized (CPC Article 114). This particularity requirement is especially emphasized in practice with regard to financial information. Courts usually allow search and seizure only of the accounts immediately before and after the account that is the original subject of search and seizure.

Second, the CPC allows several exceptions to *ex ante* warrant requirement. ① A police officer or a prosecutor may search houses, buildings, airplanes, or cars in order to arrest or detain a suspect or a defendant, if it is exigent (CPC Article 216(1)(i)). ② A police officer or a prosecutor may search or seize at the locus of arrest (CPC Article 216(1)(ii), (2)). Commentators have several different views regarding the meaning of the term "locus of arrest," and the majority require that the agents at least started to arrest the suspect. The same opinion is held in judicial practice. Therefore, search and seizure in the absence of a suspect from the beginning is not allowed, but those right after the suspect fled is lawful. ③ Search and seizure at the crime scene is allowed while a crime is being committed or right after that, if it is exigent (CPC Article 216(3)). ④ If it is necessary to urgently seize an article owned, possessed, or kept by the person arrested pursuant to CPC Article 200-3 (exigent arrest), a police officer or a prosecutor may search for or seize such an article within 24 hours from the time of arrest (CPC Article 217(1)). ⑤ A police officer or a prosecutor may seize articles that have been discarded by a criminal suspect or any other person or those which have been voluntarily produced by their owner, possessor, or custodian (CPC Article 218). In the above aspects, ②, ③, ④, *ex post facto* warrants must be obtained without delay, otherwise the seized articles must be returned (CPC Articles 216(3), 217(2), (3)).

Third, search and seizure of communications are regulated further by other statutes. ① Interception of communications: Interception includes wiretapping of telecommunication and censorship of mail. Lawful interception is only allowed in relation to certain crimes prescribed in the Communication Protection Act, to prevent such crimes, arrest the criminals and collect evidences (Article 5). This is based on the court's permission. The permission is a kind of warrant but not the same as a search and seizure warrant. The objects of interception are real-time communications, while those of search and seizure are retained communication data already received. This is why the written permission specifies the period of interception, which cannot exceed two months; moreover, once the target information is obtained, the interception shall be immediately discontinued even before the expiration of the said period (Article 6). In exigent circumstances, where there is no time to obtain judicial permission, a police officer or a prosecutor may intercept without permission. In such a case, the agent gets *ex post* permission. ② Verification of communication: A police officer or a prosecutor may ask a telecommunication service provider to provide data to verify telecommunications, which include the dates of communications by a user, their start and end times, telephone numbers, incoming and outgoing phone numbers, location of outgoing calls, etc. To ask for such data, the agencies need to obtain judicial permission *ex ante* in principle, but exceptionally *ex post* in exigent circumstances (Communication Protection Act Article 13). ③ User data: Agencies may request a telecommunication service provider to provide information about its user, which includes the user's name, ID, address, phone number, dates of subscription or termination etc. (Telecommunications Business Act Article 83). The provider does not have any obligation to comply with the request, as it is non-compulsory.

4) Digital Information

The weightage given to digital information in modern criminal procedure is increasing. Basically, general regulations of search and seizure are applied to digital information, too. However, there are several issues to consider.

The first is objects. There has been a debate regarding whether the object of seizure is storage media or data information, but now most commentators and the judicial practice regard data information as the object and no meaningful objection thereto is found. The second is relevancy. Irrelevant data are not to be seized and only relevant data are allowed to be seized. This is why the CPC provides that seizure of digital evidence must be conducted by printing out or duplicating only the relevant data within a specified scope, and not the entire storage media, the seizure of which is allowed only when the retrieval of relevant data on the spot is impossible or impractical (CPC Article 106). In the latter case, the agent continues to search for and retrieve the relevant data in an office, where he/she can resort to more thorough digital forensics. The third is the right to participate. The suspect/defendant or his counsel has the right to attend the conduct of search and seizure, thereby enabling him/her to monitor which data are searched and seized. He/she has the right to remain in place until the searching and seizing activity is concluded. Because the object of seizure is not media but the data stored therein, seizing ends when the agent finally retrieves relevant data. The fourth is evidence of other crimes. While conducting search or seizure, if an agent finds data that are not relevant to the target crime but relevant to other crimes, he/she shall stop there and obtain a judicial warrant for further search and seizure. Korean law does not have a plain view doctrine. The fifth is remote search and seizure. Investigative agents with lawful warrants can extend search and seizure to a physically separate storage media or system, if they have lawful access to the initial and extended media or system. For example, if the agent lawfully has the ID and password of an email address, he/she can connect to the email server and retrieve emails, which, however, is lawful only when a judicial warrant specifically allows it. If the above requirements are met, the conclusion remains the same, even when the remote media (server) is located overseas.[13] The sixth is voluntary production. Even though agencies may seize data storage media voluntarily produced by the owner, etc., only relevant data must be seized, unless the producer clearly expresses the intention to produce the entire data therein. For example, if a suspect voluntarily hands in his cellular phone as it is, the agent may seize only relevant data from it, unless the suspect clearly says that he/she is submitting all the data on the phone. If the producer is a third party, such as a victim, who is in possession of a suspect's phone, then the relevancy shall be more strictly restricted and the suspect who has substantial interest has the right to attend the searching and seizing procedure.[14]

(5) Closing an Investigation

1) Conclusion of a Police Investigation

After an investigation has been conducted, a police officer decides on the case. If he/she finds that a crime has occurred and the suspect has committed the crime, he/she forwards the case to a prosecutor. Otherwise, he/she closes the case and sends the investigative documents and evidence collected with a written decision not to forward the case. The reason for sending the documents and evidence is to let a prosecutor review the legality and validity of the police decision.

13 Supreme Court Decision 2017Do9747, November 29, 2017.
14 Supreme Court Decision 2016Do348, November 18, 2021.

Although prosecution is originally a prosecutor's job, there are cases where the police may file a complaint for a trial with the court (Summary Trial Act). In a summary trial, the judge may impose a fine not exceeding KRW 200,000, penal detention (one day or more but less than 30 days in jail), or minor fine (KRW 2,000 or more but less than KRW 50,000) to the defendant.

Juveniles younger than 14 years old are criminal minors and are not subject to criminal punishment. Juvenile delinquents between the age of 10 and 18 years may be subject to juvenile protective measures, such as probation. The police may directly forward to the court the juvenile cases not to be subject to criminal penalty but to protective measures, which is a kind of filing a case (Juvenile Act).

2) Conclusion of Prosecutorial Investigation

A prosecutor makes final decisions on both cases of his/her own investigation and cases forwarded by the police. If he/she finds that the suspect committed a crime, he/she decides to prosecute and files an information with the court. Otherwise, he/she decides not to prosecute. Decisions not to prosecute include several subcategories: (i) no commission when the suspect is innocent or lacks evidence; (ii) not guilty when the suspect's commission does not constitute a crime because of self-defense, insanity, etc.; (iii) bar to prosecution, when there is a ban to prosecute the suspect because of the statute of limitations, double jeopardy, etc.; and (iv) suspension of prosecution, where it is appropriate not to prosecute considering extenuating circumstances, although there is sufficient evidence. The decision not to prosecute is not an acquittal and the principle of double jeopardy does not apply. In juvenile cases, a prosecutor may request juvenile courts to pursue protective dispositions.

Prosecutors of the Investigative Office for the Crimes of High-ranking Officials have the same authority as ordinary prosecutors for cases related to judges, prosecutors, and high-ranking police officers. However, with regard to the cases where they do not have the authority to prosecute, they forward the cases—after conducting an investigation—to the Seoul Central Prosecutors' Office.

3) Challenge to Investigatory Decision

In cases in which a police officer decides not to forward the case to a prosecutor, the accuser or the victim may challenge the decision by filing an objection with the police. Upon receiving an objection, the police forward the case to a prosecutor along with the investigative documents and evidence (CPC Article 245-7).

In cases in which a prosecutor decides not to prosecute, the accuser or the complainant may file an appeal with the high prosecutors' office by submitting a written appeal to the district prosecutors' office to which the prosecutor belongs (Prosecutors' Office Act Article 10). Against the decision to dismiss his/her appeal, the appellant may file a re-appeal to the Prosecutor General by submitting a written re-appeal to the high prosecutors' office (Prosecutors' Office Act Article 10).

A person who has accused or complained against a suspect to an investigative agency, upon receiving a notice of a decision not to prosecute, may file a motion to obtain an order to prosecute with a competent high court (CPC Article 260). While both accusers and complainants can do this, the scope differs between the two. As for accusers, the motion is allowed for all accusers who are victims or their guardians; as for complainants, only for those who has complained about the crimes stipulated in the CPC, such as abuse of power, unlawful arrest or confinement, assault, or cruel treatment committed by public servants. In order to file the motion, the accuser or complainant resorts to the prosecutorial appeal procedure first, as described above. However, re-appeals to the Prosecutor General are not allowed for those who can file the motion with the court, and they can resort to the prosecutorial appeal procedure only once.

Any person whose fundamental rights are infringed upon may file a constitutional complaint with the Constitutional Court (Constitution Article 111, Constitutional Court Act Article 68). A crime victim may have his/her rights infringed by the decision not to prosecute and can file a constitutional complaint. However, in reality, most victims cannot make use of the complaint, as it can only be filed after exhausting all other available remedies, if any, and victims can resort to prosecutorial appeal and judicial motion, while constitutional complaints against judicial decisions are not allowed. The reason why judicial decisions are not subject to constitutional complaints is that Korea has adopted a dual judicial system with the Supreme Court and the Constitutional Court functioning as independent bodies. In contrast, suspects who receive a prosecutorial decision of suspended prosecution may file a constitutional complaint because they cannot resort to the aforementioned judicial motion.

4. Adjudication

(1) Prosecution

Korea does not have any private prosecution, and only public prosecutors have the authority to prosecute. With no grand jury system, a prosecutor files an information[15] with the court on his/her own authority. To prosecute, a prosecutor shall submit a written information, which specifies the defendant, the crime he/she is charged with, the factual grounds for it, and the violated statute. A non-specified information shall be dismissed as it is. At the time of filing, evidentiary documents are not allowed to be submitted so that these documents do not prejudice the judge before trial.

Most crimes have statutory limitations: 25 years for crimes punishable with the death penalty, 15 years for crimes punishable with life imprisonment, etc. (CPC Article 249). However, there are no statutory limitations for crimes such as homicide punishable with death penalty, sexual assault against minors less than 13 years of age or disabled persons, crime of genocide, etc.

Despite prosecutorial discretion, it is important that this not be abused. If a prosecutor arbitrarily exercises her prosecutorial authority and causes substantial harm to the defendant, the prosecution is deemed abusive. An abusive prosecution is invalid and shall be dismissed.

An information has an effect on the person who the prosecutor designates as the defendant. If the true criminal, A, was investigated and prosecuted under the name of B, the prosecution has the effect on A not B, because the prosecutor intended A as the defendant. A charge against a part of one offence is applicable to the full extent of the offence. The full extent of one offence is a kind of procedural unit that has oneness and sameness. However, the actual subject of the trial is what is stated in the written information. For example, when the fact charged is that the defendant swindled 7,000 dollars out of the victim, the court cannot render a decision that he swindled 10,000 dollars, even if that latter is true. Nevertheless, the judgment of 7,000 dollars has the effect of the full extent of the fraud of 10,000 dollars, and the additional prosecution against 3,000 dollars would

15 Here, an information corresponds to an indictment in the indictment jurisdiction.

place the defendant in double jeopardy. If the prosecutor changes the information from 7,000 dollars to 10,000 dollars, then the court can decide on the 10,000-dollar fraud.

For a prosecutor to change or amend the information, he/she needs to obtain permission from the court. He/she can change the information within the scope of sameness, which implies that the changed fact remains as part of the same one offence as the fact originally charged. If the change of information is about trifle matters and does not cause any further procedural burden to the defendant, the court may recognize a different fact without a change in information. For example, the court can decide the 7,000-dollar fraud *ex officio* even when the defendant is charged with a 10,000-dollar fraud.

Further, the prosecutor may even withdraw a file. In this case, the prosecution shall be dismissed.

(2) Trial

1) Overview

When a defendant is prosecuted, the court hears the case and renders a judgment. If we examine this more specifically, there are several forms of trials or procedures.

The first is a regular trial. The CPC provides a trial by a judge as a formal, regular, ordinary, and basic form of a trial. In principle, a charge filed by a prosecutor is examined on such a trial. Most provisions of the CPC are provided on the basis of regular trials.

The second is a simple trial procedure. Where the defendant makes a confession to the charge in the trial court, the court may try the case by a simple trial procedure (CPC Article 286-2). In the procedure, the trial follows simple proceedings: a few evidentiary rules such as the hearsay rule does not apply; the court is not required to strictly adhere to the methods stipulated in the CPC for examining evidence, instead, it may adopt any approach it deems appropriate.

The third is jury trial. Although bench trials are mainstream in Korean trials, it also has a kind of jury trial. The jury trial was introduced by the Act on Citizen Participation in Criminal Trials of 2007. A jury trial includes two stages: proceedings for juror selection and proceedings on the merits.

The fourth is a brief procedure. A prosecutor may file a case with the court in seeking punishment by fine (CPC Article 448). In a brief procedure, the court reviews the case based on documents and renders a decision without holding an oral trial (courtroom hearing). If the court considers the case inappropriate for a brief procedure, he/she refers it to a regular trial. When served with a copy of the written decision, the defendant or the prosecutor may request a regular trial within seven days, and the court renders a judgment through a regular trial. Otherwise, the decision by a brief procedure becomes final and has the same force as a regular judgment.

The fifth is a summary trial. In such a trial, the police file a complaint for a summary trial, and a judge of a district court promptly adjudicates the case trough this expedited procedure (Summary Trial Act). The trial is held in a courtroom. In this procedure, the judge may find the defendant guilty even when his/her confession is the only evidence. The judge renders an immediate decision. If the defendant or the police request a regular trial within seven days, the judge refers the case to the competent court via the police and the prosecutors' office. Otherwise, the decision by summary trial becomes final and has the same force as a regular judgment.

2) Pretrial Procedure

Upon prosecution, the court shall serve the defendant or his/her counsel with a copy of the written information without delay (CPC Article 266). The defendant or her counsel shall submit a written opinion—that is, an answer to the information (CPC Article 266-2). Of course, the defendant has the right not to answer.

The defendant or his/her counsel may request the prosecutor to disclose the documents, witnesses, etc. that the prosecutor is going to provide as evidence. If the prosecutor refuses to disclose them, the defendant may file a motion to discover. If the prosecutor does not comply with the order of the court to discover, he/she may not present the documents or witnesses as evidence in the trial (CPC Articles 266-3, 266-4). The prosecutor can also request the defendant's disclosure of related information if the defendant makes a legal or factual argument at trial, such as insanity or alibi defense (CPC Article 266-11).

The presiding judge may put a case to preparatory proceedings for the efficiency and concentration of a trial (CPC Articles 266-5 to 266-17). Preparatory proceedings may go with or without a pretrial conference. During this conference, the court clarifies the factual and legal basis of the counts, determines the admissibility of evidence, and sets trial schedules. Once the conference ends, the parties are generally not permitted to introduce evidence at trial that they did not offer during the conference, with a few exceptions such as instances without serious fault or substantial delay. Proceedings for which no conference is held are conducted by documents. Parties can submit documents for the preparation of trial. The court may, if necessary, examine witnesses and other evidences even before trial.

The court, on its own or on a party's motion, may ask public or private organizations for reports on a particular matter or for documents they possess (CPC Article 272). The presiding judge sets the trial date and issues a subpoena to order to be present at the set trial (CPC Article 267-2). The subpoena is served at least five days before the trial date.

3) Regular Trial

A trial or a trial hearing is held in a courtroom. A trial begins with calling the case number out loud in the courtroom. No trial is held without the presence of the defendant. However, there are a few exceptions. ① If the defendant is an incompetent or a corporate body, his/her legal representative shall attend on behalf of him/her, and the defendant does not need to be present at the trial (CPC Articles 26, 27). ② The court may hold a trial too, where the charges are minor crimes or the information is to be dismissed (CPC Articles 277, 306) or where the defendant in custody refuses to attend the trial without cause and it is impossible or impracticable for guards to bring him/her to the court (CPC Article 277-2). ③ If a witness cannot make a free statement in the presence of the defendant, the presiding judge may order him/her to withdraw from the courtroom and hear the testimony (CPC Article 297). After the testimony, the court shall inform the defendant of the gist of the testimony. ④ When the defendant's whereabouts are unknown for more than six months, the court may hold a trial without the defendant, except in the case where the defendant is charged with a crime punishable by imprisonment of over 10 years (Expedition of Procedure Act Article 23). If the defendant has been found guilty in his/her absence but the absence was due to reasons unattributable to him/her, he/she may file a motion for retrial within 14 days after he/she recognizes it (Expedition of Procedure Act Article 23-2). ⑤ The appeals court may proceed to hear that case in the absence of the defendant, if he/she fails to appear on two consecutive dates of hearing (CPC Article 365). The Supreme Court may hear the case in the absence of the defendant at any time (CPC Article 389-2).

At trial, the presiding judge informs the defendant of the right to remain silent (CPC Article 283-2), and confirms the identity of the defendant by asking name, age, address, etc. (CPC Article 284). The prosecutor makes an opening statement by reading the written information and then the defendant makes one by stating whether she admits to the facts charged (CPC Articles 285 and 286). If the defendant confesses to the crime, the court may put the case to the simple trial procedure (CPC Article 286-2), where lenient evidence rules apply. Otherwise, the adjudication follows the regular procedure. After opening statements, the presiding judge asks questions to identify the issues and let both sides present arguments and a plan to prove. The next step is the examination of evidence. The court examines the evidence of prosecution's side first and then that of the defendant. Thereafter, the court examines *ex officio* if necessary. When the examination of evidence is complete, the prosecutor and the defense counsel may ask the defendant questions concerning the charge, which is called defendant questioning. Before the 2007 amendment, the questioning of the defendant came first before the examination of evidence that included witnesses. This actually had the risk of forcing the defendant to make a statement even before the evidentiary stage, but the amendment changed the order—evidence first and then the subsidiary questioning of defendant. The statements the defendant makes while questioned can be incriminating evidence, and it can also be called an examination of the defendant. Witnesses have the right to refuse testimony when such testimony might incriminate himself/herself or his/her family (CPC Article 148). In addition, lawyers, doctors, priests, etc. may refuse to testify if such testimony is about secretive aspects of their duty (CPC Article 149). A witness takes an oath before testifying, except when she is under 16 years old or she is unable to understand the meaning of an oath (CPC Articles 156, 159). When there is a worry that face-to-face testimony could make the witness feel nervous, the court may let the witness testify through video or from behind a screen fence (CPC Article 165-2). In addition, a criminal victim has the constitutional right to speak at trial (Constitution Article 27) and the court will take her as a witness on his/her request (CPC Article 294-2).

When the examination of evidence and defendant is finished, the prosecutor shall state her opinion on the case including sentencing (CPC Article 302), and then the defense counsel and the defendant are afforded to make their final plea (CPC Article 303). After the final statements of the defendant, the court closes the hearing

4) Jury Trial

The following are the key characteristics of the Korean jury trial. (i) The defendant does not have a constitutional right to jury, and it is only statutory. Jury is not for indictment but hearing and decision—that is, only petit jury. (ii) Jury trials are allowed for cases under the jurisdiction of a panel court. However, if the defendant does not want a jury trial or the court decides not to proceed to a jury trial, the case is heard in a bench trial. (iii) The number of jurors on a jury vary from five to nine depending on the severity of the crime and whether the defendant confesses to the crime. Jurors are randomly selected from among lay citizens who are over 20 years old and without disqualification. (iv) Jurors have power not only to find facts but also to present opinions about law and sentencing. When the jurors reach a unanimous opinion, the jury delivers the unanimous verdict directly; when they disagree, it delivers a majority verdict after having heard the judge's opinion. (v) Upon a guilty verdict, jurors debate on sentencing with judges and give their opinions. (vi) The verdict and opinion of the jury have no binding force; they only have advisory force, and the judge makes the final decision. However, judges generally defer to the jury's verdict, and when they a make different decision from the jury, they explain the reason for the difference to the defendant and record it in the written judgment.

Korean jury trial is somewhat distinctive and different from the US jury trial and German lay judge system (*Schöffengericht*). However, it has similarities as well: it is similar to the US system in that the jury reaches a verdict independently from judges on the one hand and similar to the German system in that the jury hears the opinions of judges in the case of a split verdict and sentencing debate.

5) Judgment

Whether the trial is by the jury or by the court, the judgment is rendered by the court. In principle, the court renders the judgment on the very day of closing the hearing. However, courts usually take another day for judgment because of deliberation and making a copy of the written judgment. The date for the judgment is usually within 14 days from the closing of the hearing (CPC Article 318-4).

There are several types of judgments. The first is conviction. If the charges are sufficiently proved and the defendant is found to be guilty, the court convicts him/her and pronounces a sentence. Trial proceedings for fact-finding and sentencing proceedings for punishment determination are not separate. The court is in charge of these two phases, and conviction and sentencing are conducted together. Further, the written judgment includes the criminal act, list of evidence, application of law, and decision on the defendant's legal arguments (CPC Article 323). The second is acquittal. If the defendant is found to be not guilty or the prosecutor fails to prove the charge, the court acquits him/her (CPC Article 325). The third is the exemption of prosecution. The court exempts the defendant from prosecution when (i) he/she was already judged on the matter (double jeopardy), (ii) he/she was pardoned for the offence, (iii) the statute of limitations ran out, or (iv) the law was amended not to punish the act any more (CPC Article 326). The fourth is dismissal. Dismissal may be rendered in the form of either a judgment or a decision.[16] Oral arguments in a courtroom are necessary for a judgment but not for a decision. The court renders a dismissal decision, where (i) the prosecution is withdrawn, (ii) the defendant dies, (iii) the charge does not include a criminal act, etc. (CPC Article 328). The court renders a dismissal judgment, when (i) the court has no jurisdiction over the defendant, (ii) the process of prosecution is illegal, (iii) the case is already pending in court, (iv) the case was filed again without any new important evidence after already being dismissed owing to the prosecutor's withdrawal, (v) the victim's accusation is withdrawn in a case in which the accusation is necessary for prosecution, or (vi) the prosecution goes against the victim's will in a case where the prosecution is not allowed to go against the victim's will (CPC Article 327).

(3) Evidence Law

1) Overview

Korean law has separate evidence laws for civil and criminal cases. Pursuing not only substantive truth but also human rights, criminal evidence law has a mission as a bill of rights in the process of fact-finding.

The CPC clearly pronounces basic principles of evidence law: fact-finding shall be based on evidence and criminal facts shall be proved beyond

16 The term 'decision' here refers to the narrow sense of decision. The broad sense of decision includes judgments.

reasonable doubt (CPC Article 307). Evidence to prove facts shall be admissible by law and examined by the methods prescribed in law, which is called 'strict proof.' However, not every fact must follow the rule. Most procedural facts may be exempt from certain evidentiary rules, such as hearsay, and the court may examine evidence in a reasonable manner not bound by stipulated methods, which is called "free proof." The facts related to the admissibility are procedural and usually follow the free-proof rule.

The burden of proof lies on the prosecution, encompassing not only *actus reus* and *mens rea* of an offence but also facts such as those that negate self-defense or insanity. In order to successfully prove the facts charged, the evidence that the prosecution presents shall be admissible and have probative value. Admissibility and probative value are two pillars in evidence law.

The CPC stipulates several rules regarding admissibility: exclusion of illegally obtained evidence (Article 308-2), exclusion of confession (Article 309), hearsay rules (Articles 310-2 to 316), and voluntariness of the statement (Article 317). Certain inadmissible evidence may be recovered if the defendant consents (Article 318) or if used for impeachment (Article 318-2). Judicial decisions and commentators ask further requirements for admissibility: relevancy, authentication, and originality of documents.

The evaluation of probative value of admitted evidence is at the discretion of the court (CPC Article 307). However, the discretion is not arbitrary, rather it abides by logical and empirical rules. Although the court evaluates probative value on its own free discretion, there are a few provisions limiting it: the *corpus delicti* rule (CPC Article 310), exclusiveness of trial records (CPC Article 56), and impeachment (CPC Article 318-2).

2) Relevancy, Authentication, and Originality

Relevancy is in itself a presupposition of admissibility. The CPC does not have a provision to ask for relevancy as a general requirement, but it is implied in the court's discretion to determine admissibility (CPC Article 295) and in the requirements of search and seizure (CPC Article 106). Specifically, relevancy has increasing practical importance in terms of digital evidence. Court decisions exclude irrelevant evidence based on the exclusionary rule with the logic that search and seizure of such evidence is illegal because it violates Article 106 of the CPC.

Authentication is also a requirement, although not clearly stipulated as a general rule in the CPC. Article 318 of the CPC may be interpreted as an implying provision, which asks genuineness of evidence. Originality is treated in two ways. The case law places oral statements before records thereof and original documents before reproduced copies. Courts consider the former as a matter of probative value, while the latter as that of admissibility. For digital evidence, originality is not so important and identity or sameness has emerged as a key issue. It is because the electronically reproduced copy precisely shows the original and this is good enough as long as the copy is identical to the original. Prosecutors usually prove identity with hash values but not limited thereto. When the prosecutor fails to prove the identity of an offered piece of evidence, it is not admissible. Identity requirement in digital evidence substantially implies authentication and originality. In confirming identity, such issues as integrity, reliability, chain of custody etc. are being reviewed, as they are ultimately elements that constitute identity.

3) Exclusionary Rule

The exclusionary rule includes several rules.

First, exclusion of confession. If the court has reason to suspect that a confession of a defendant is made involuntarily due to torture, violence, threat, prolonged custody, deceit, etc., the confession is inadmissible (CPC Article 309). This rule is grounded in the constitution (Article 12(7)). The rationale of the rule is to avoid the risk of false confession substantively and to procedurally protect the defendant's human rights. According to precedents, a causal relationship is required between the confession and its underlying motive for the confession, such as torture, but the causation is presumed to exist.

Second, voluntariness of statement. A statement made by a defendant or anyone else shall not be admissible unless the statement is proved to be made voluntarily (CPC Article 317). This rule applies to any statement: defendant or not, hearsay or firsthand, oral or written.

Third, exclusion of illegally obtained evidence. Evidence obtained in violation of due process is excluded (CPC Article 308-2). This rule includes the abovementioned two rules, in that compelling or extracting involuntary statements is illegal, but the focus of each is different: confession, statements, and physical evidence, respectively. The CPC provided for the inclusion of involuntary confession and statements from the outset but had no clear provision regarding physical evidence that is illegally obtained. In addition, the courts had a rule that the nature and attributes of physical evidence are immutable even when illegally obtained, and the evidence is not excluded. However, in 2007, the Supreme Court adopted the exclusionary rule in search and seizure, ruling that illegally obtained physical evidence be excluded in principle.[17] The Supreme Court admitted exceptions where the illegality is sufficiently trifle not to violate the substance of due process of law and the exclusion of the evidence would be against justice. The decision also adopted the "fruit of the poisonous tree" doctrine there. Meanwhile, the CPC introduced the rule in the 2007 amendment and it went into effect in 2008, immediately after the decision. The decision's ruling is effective in the amended the CPC as well, which is current law. With the exclusionary rule, provisions on search and seizure have actual and practical meaning, because the evidence is excluded if the agents did not follow the provisions during search or seizure. With the increasing proportion of digital evidence in investigation, the focus of the exclusionary rule moves to such evidence. Examples of the most commonly summoned cases include violations of warrant clause, improper search and seizure of irrelevant information, and the infringement upon the right to participate. Once illegally seized, the fact that a warrant is issued *ex post facto* does not fix the flaw. When only part of the search and seizure process is illegal, the judge determines the illegality of the entire process, where the criterion for judgment is whether or not the illegality is sufficiently serious to make the entire process illegal.[18] The exclusionary rule applies to the evidence collected illegally by a private person, too. However, the test is somewhat more lenient than that conducted by investigative agencies—comparing the infringed rights such as privacy and the public interest in finding criminal facts.[19]

4) Hearsay Rule

Hearsay is not admissible unless otherwise provided (CPC Article 308-2).

A court record containing the statements of the defendant or others is admissible as it is (CPC Article 311). Public documents issued by government officials certifying facts within their authority such as certificates of family

17 Supreme Court Decision 2007Do3061, November 15, 2007.
18 Supreme Court Decision 2011Mo1839, July 16, 2015.
19 Supreme Court Decision 2020Do3972, October 29, 2020.

relations, records of regular business such as commercial books, and other similar documents made with circumstantial guarantees of trustworthiness are also admissible as they are (CPC Article 315).

An interrogation record of a suspect written by an investigative agent is admissible when it is made in compliance with the law and the suspect and defendant or his/her counsel acknowledges the truth of the contents of the record in the trial (CPC Article 312(1), (3)). A record of a witness statements written by an investigative agent can be admissible when (i) it was made in compliance with the law, (ii) it is proven by the witness at trial or by objective media such as a video recording that what is written matches what she said to the agent, (iii) the defendant or his/her counsel has the opportunity to cross-examine the witness at trial, and (iv) it is proven that the statement was made with circumstantial guarantees of trustworthiness (CPC Article 312(4)).

Other documents containing statements of a person are admissible when (i) the document was written in the handwriting of the declarant (the person who made the statement) or the document has his/her signature or seal, unless it is on a digital medium, (ii) it is proven by the declarant's statement at trial, or by an objective method such as digital forensic that the document presented is the very document of his/her statement and what is written matches what he/she stated (CPC Article 313). In addition, a document of the defendant's statement written by a third person may be approved by the third person even when the defendant denies the genuineness, if the statement was made with circumstantial guarantees of trustworthiness. The defendant or his/her counsel shall be given the opportunity to cross-examine against a document containing the third person's statement.

In cases where the person who shall make an approving statement at trial according to the Articles 312, 313 of the CPC is not available due to death, disease, living abroad, unknown whereabouts, and other equivalent reasons, then the above statements may be admitted if it is proven that the statement was made with circumstantial guarantees of trustworthiness (CPC Article 314).

Further, a court statement of a third person that includes a statement of the defendant is admissible when the latter statement was made with circumstantial guarantees of trustworthiness (CPC Article 316(1)). Where such a court statement includes a statement of another person other than the defendant, an additional requirement must be met: the declarant is unavailable due to death, disease, living abroad, unknown whereabouts, and other equivalent reasons (CPC Article 316(2)). According to case law, hearsay within hearsay is inadmissible as it is, even if each part of the combined meets the above requirements, because the CPC has no provision that allows for such an exception. However, if a document containing hearsay statements conforms with both requirements of the written (CPC Articles 311 to 315) and oral statements (CPC Article 316), it is admissible.

5) Restoration of Admissibility

In cases where both parties agree, documents and physical evidence may be admitted as evidence if the court confirms they are genuine (CPC Article 318(1)). Thus, consent restores the admissibility of the evidence that is otherwise deemed inadmissible. Nevertheless, evidence obtained illegally is not admissible even if the parties agree. When the defendant is not present at trial in cases where the defendant's presence is not necessary, he/she is deemed to agree to the admission (CPC Article 318(2)).

Hearsay evidence, otherwise inadmissible, is admissible to impeach the statements of the defendant or a witness at trial (CPC Article 318-2(1)). However, courts and commentators generally hold the opinion that a video recording shall not be used as impeachment evidence. This understanding stems from the recognition that the CPC prohibits the use of video recordings of statements made during investigations from being admitted as evidence to establish the facts on the merits, including for impeachment purposes. Such a video recording may be employed to assist the defendant or a witness in recollecting the facts of which he/she has a vague memory while making statements at trial (CPC Article 318-2(2)).

6) Evaluation of Probative Value

It is left to the court's discretion to evaluate how much probative value a piece of evidence has to prove facts. The court may take one of the two contradictory pieces of evidence and find a fact based on one piece of evidence at its discretion. However, the discretion has to be rational, not arbitrary. (i) The inference of facts from evidence must be logical and correspond with our experience. (ii) It is not permitted to infer guilt from the fact that the defendant exercises the right to silence or that a witness exercises the right to refuse to testify. In addition, exercising such rights is not considered as an aggravating sentencing factor either, unless the defendant attempts to mislead the court.

In addition to the theoretical limitations, there are a few statutory restrictions as well. (iii) Where the confession of a defendant is the only evidence against him/her, he/she shall not be found guilty based on the evidence, and additional supplementary evidence is needed to convict him/her (CPC Article 310, Constitution Article 12(7)). According to the court ruling, the confession here means the defendant's own confession and the confession of his/her accomplice does not need to be supplemented. Supplementary evidence must be independent from the confession. A confession during investigatory interrogation or a testimony that a witness who heard the confession cannot serve as a supplement to a confession made at trial. According to the court ruling, supplement implies whether the additional evidence makes the confession credible—it does not necessarily prove *corpus delicti* (the body of the crime). (iv) Proceedings of hearings written in court records can be proved only by such records (CPC Article 56). (v) Impeachment, counterevidence, and cross-examination are methods to weaken the weight of an evidence. Hearsay may be introduced for impeachment (CPC Article 318-2). An out-of-court statement contradictory to courtroom testimony can be offered as impeachment evidence, but statements in a record of examination made by an investigative agency to rebut the testimony after that are not admissible as impeachment evidence.

(4) Appeals

1) Overview

A defendant and a prosecutor may file an appeal against the decisions of a trial court and an appellate court to the appellate court and the Supreme Court, respectively. The counsel who defended during the proceeding that is to be challenged, the legal representative, and the defendant's family may appeal on behalf of the defendant.

An appeal against a judgment must be filed within seven days from the date the judgment is rendered. The appellant may waive his/her right to appeal or may withdraw her appeal. A decision (judgment) is finalized when the parties cannot appeal any more, which is the result of exceeding the seven-day appeal period, waiver, withdrawal, or final decision of the Supreme Court. The final decision has an internal and external force: the power to execute the decision of the case, and the power to bind other courts later trying cases of the same crime, respectively. Double jeopardy is interpreted as a revelation of external force of a finalized judgment. This is why the prosecutor may appeal against the judgment of acquittal because double jeopardy is not yet effective while the case is pending on appeal.

The purpose of an appeal is to change the lower court's decision into a more favorable one for the appellant. If the decision is already sufficiently favorable and no room is left to obtain a more favorable decision through appeal, the appeal shall be dismissed. The possibility of obtaining a more favorable decision is called benefit of appeal, which is a prerequisite for appeal. The defendant may appeal against a judgment of conviction seeking for acquittal or a more lenient punishment, but not for a more severe one because he/she has no benefit from an appeal. Moreover, a "favorable" decision means "legally favorable." The defendant may not appeal against a judgment of acquittal seeking dismissal, because acquittal is the most favorable decision. An appeal against a dismissal in order to seek an acquittal is not allowed either, because the defendant does not have the right to request a verdict on the merits. However, it is allowed if the dismissal is illegal—for example, if the applied provision is declared unconstitutional. In contrast, the prosecutor may appeal not only for the government but also for the sake of the defendant as a public servant. He/she can appeal against an acquittal and seek a conviction, and vice versa.

When the defendant appeals or the prosecutor appeals for the defendant, the appellate court cannot impose a more severe punishment than the lower court, even if new evidence emerges or the appellate court disagrees with the lower court (CPC Article 368). The trial court that reviews a decision by brief procedure can increase the amount of fine imposed by brief procedure even when the defendant requested a regular trial, but cannot escalate the type of punishment—for example, from a fine to imprisonment (CPC Article 457-2). In contrast, the appellate court can change at the disadvantage of the prosecution *ex officio*. For example, the court may impose milder punishment at its own discretion even when only the prosecutor appealed.

2) Proceedings of Appellate Court

To file an appeal with the appellate court, the appellant submits a written appeal to the original trial court (CPC Article 359). The original court dismisses the appeal if it is illegal—for example, appeal after the expiration of the appeal period (CPC Article 360), otherwise the court sends the trial records and evidence to the appellate court within 14 days (CPC Article 361). When the appellate court receives them, it notifies the appellant and the appellee thereof (CPC Article 361-2(1)). If the defendant is in custody, the prosecutor who receives the notice transfers him/her to a jail in the location of the appellate court within 14 days (CPC Article 361-2(2)). The appellant or his/her counsel is required to submit an appellate brief within 20 days from the receipt of the notice (CPC Article 361-3(1)). If it is not submitted within the deadline, the appeal shall be dismissed (CPC Article 361-4). The court shall serve the copy of the brief on the appellee and he/she shall submit a written response to the court within 10 days (CPC Article 361-3(2), (3)).

The following grounds of appeal are stipulated in the law: (i) errors of law or fact which affected the judgment, (ii) breach of jurisdiction, (iii) abolition, change, pardon of punishment after the judgment, (iv) illegal composition of the court, (v) engagement of a judge who is to be debarred, (vi) violation of the rule of open court, (vii) no reasoning or contradictory reasoning in the written judgment, (viii) grounds for re-adjudication, and (ix) unjust sentencing (CPC Article 361-5). The court reviews the grounds included in the appellate brief, but it may review *ex officio* additional grounds that affected the lower court's judgment even if they are not explicitly mentioned in the brief.

The appellate court takes over the lower court's proceedings and continues adjudication, including hearings. Regulations regarding trial of first instance apply *mutatis mutandis* to appellate proceedings. If agreeing with the lower court's judgment, the appellate court affirms it. If disagreeing, it reverses the judgment or remands the case to a lower court. The remanding judgment has a binding effect on the lower court. However, the appellate court defers to the trial court's factual findings and sentencing, unless it is substantially erroneous or unjust.

3) Proceedings of the Supreme Court

An appeal against the judgment of the appellate court (the second appeal) may be filed with the Supreme Court (CPC Article 371). Exceptionally, an appeal against the trial court's judgment directly to the Supreme Court is allowed in cases where the judgment did not apply the law or applied it erroneously, or where the punishment is abolished, changed or pardoned after the judgment (CPC Article 372). This is called extraordinary appeal. This appeal focuses on unified legal interpretation rather than relief of individual rights, whereas normal appeals focus on the latter along with the former.

Grounds of the second appeal include: (i) errors of law which affected the judgment; (ii) abolishment, change, pardon of punishment after judgment; (iii) grounds for re-adjudication; (iv) substantial error of fact which affected the judgment or unjust sentencing, in cases where the death penalty or imprisonment of 10 years or more was imposed (CPC Article 383).

The standards of review for the second appeal is "on the record" and "at the time of the appellate judgment." In contrast to appellate courts, the Supreme Court primarily reviews errors of law. The Court does not have to hold an oral hearing and may review based on documents only (CPC Article 390). Regulations regarding appellate proceedings apply *mutatis mutandis* to the proceedings.

The Supreme Court renders a judgment, affirming or reversing the lower court's judgment. When it disagrees with the lower court, the Supreme Court usually remands the case. The remanding judgment has a binding effect on the lower court in the case.

(5) Re-adjudication

Once finalized, a judgment cannot be changed. However, upon stipulated grounds, a case can be re-adjudicated exceptionally. Re-adjudication is a procedure against a finalized judgment for the benefit of the person convicted (CPC Article 420). A judgment of an acquittal or dismissal is not a subject.

The following are the grounds for re-adjudication: (i) the evidence of the original judgment is found to have been forged or altered by another finalized judgment; (ii) the testimony, expert opinion, interpretation, or translation of the original judgment is found to be false by such a judgment; (iii) the accusation against the defendant is found to be false by such a judgment; (iv) the judgment on which the original judgment based is altered by another finalized judgment; (v) a clear evidence to acquit the defendant, to exempt the prosecution or the sentenced punishment, or to lessen such punishment is newly discovered; (vi) the original judgment convicted the defendant on charges of infringing intellectual property and the property right is found to be void by a finalized administrative review or judicial judgment; or (vii) judges, prosecutors, or police officers who engaged in the case of the original judgment or its investigation are found to have committed a crime while carrying out their official duties (CPC Article 420). With regard to the fifth ground above, the discovery of clear and new evidence, the case law says that "new" implies that the evidence did not exist or could not be discovered at the time of the original trial or it could not be presented without fault attributable to the defendant, and that "clear" implies that there is a high probability for the original judgment to be overturned considering the new evidence and other closely related evidence. Additional grounds are provided by statutes other than the CPC: (i) where the defendant was convicted by a finalized judgment and the Constitutional Court declared unconstitutional the provision on which the conviction is based (Constitutional Court Act Article 47), and (ii) where the defendant was convicted at a trial in absentia by a finalized judgment (Expedition of Procedure Act Article 23-2). In the latter case, the claimant may request re-adjudication within 14 days from the date when he/she learned about it.

A request for re-adjudication can be filed by a defendant, his/her representative, or a prosecutor. A prosecutor files the request for the benefit of the defendant, as a representative of public interest. If the court, finding a ground for re-adjudication, accepts the request, it decides to commence re-adjudication. When the decision is finalized, the court shall hold an adjudication again at the same level of court as the original adjudication (CPC Article 438). In re-adjudication, a heavier sentence than the original cannot be imposed on the defendant (CPC Article 439).

5. Execution and Others

(1) Execution of Judgment

A judicial decision is executed under the direction of a prosecutor after it is finalized, except otherwise provided (CPC Articles 459, 460).

The death penalty is executed by an order of the Minster of Justice (CPC Article 463). Even though Korea retains the death penalty in its legal system and courts continue to impose this penalty, it has not been executed since 1997. Korea is now categorized as a country that has effectively abolished the death penalty.

Imprisonment or penal detention is executed by confining the offender in a correctional facility (Criminal Act Articles 67, 68). A prosecutor may postpone the execution when the offender is incompetent, when his/her health is likely to be endangered by the execution, when he/she is over 70 years old, etc. (CPC Articles 470, 471). If the offender is not in custody, the prosecutor summons him/her for execution, and if he/she fails to appear, the prosecutor issues an order of execution to arrest him/her. The order has the same force as a detention warrant issued by a judge (CPC Articles 473, 474).

Financial penalty or asset forfeiture shall be executed by a prosecutor's order to which the Civil Execution Act or National Tax Collection Act applies (CPC Article 477).

A convicted person who is doubtful about the interpretation of a judgment can make a request for an interpretation to the court that rendered the judgment (CPC Article 488). In addition, a person who has undergone the execution of the judgment can file an objection to the court that rendered it on the ground that the prosecutor's disposition regarding the execution is unjust (CPC Article 489).

(2) Compensation

The constitution grants the right to compensation for miscarriage of justice to a suspect or a defendant who was in custody but is subsequently not prosecuted or acquitted (Constitution Article 28). The Act on Criminal Compensation and Restoration of Impaired Reputation stipulates the details of this right. A claim for compensation can be filed within three years from the day when the suspect was notified of the decision not to forward or prosecute (the above Article 28) or when the defendant was acquitted through a finalized judgment, or within five years from the day when the acquittal judgment was finalized (the above Article 8). When the claim is accepted and the compensation decision is finalized, the court announces the essence of the decision in an official gazette and, on application, in two or more newspapers (the above Article 25).

(3) Proceedings to Support Victims

The status of crime victims in criminal proceedings has been increasingly strengthened.

A victim has a constitutional right to make statements in the pertinent adjudication (Constitution Article 27(5)). The court shall examine the victim as a witness if he/she requests (CPC Article 294-2). While examining a victim, the court or agents may allow a person who has a relationship of trust with the victim to accompany her (CPC Articles 163-2, 221).

A victim has a right to be informed about the procedure. The prosecutor is required to notify the victim about the conclusion of the investigation and the trial, etc. (CPC Article 259-2). A victim can file a motion to access and copy trial records (CPC Article 294-4).

Victims of crimes such as sexual assault, child abuse, crime against the disabled have the right to appoint their own counsels or be provided with public defenders, as stipulated in the Act on the Punishment of Sexual Crimes, etc. If they encounter communication challenges while giving statements during investigative or court proceedings, they can be assigned a person to assist them in effective communication.

Further, victims of crimes such as assault, injury, sexual assault, theft, robbery, fraud may file a motion for a damages order, which is a court's order against the defendant in a criminal proceeding to compensate for damages caused by the crime he/she committed (Expedition of Procedure Act Articles 25, 26). This legal framework aims to facilitate swift and efficient compensation for victims, eliminating the need for a separate civil lawsuit.

The constitution grants the constitutional right for victims of crimes who have suffered harm to their life or body to obtain protection from the government, as prescribed by the relevant statutes (Constitution Article 30). The Crime Victims Protection Act and the Crime Victims Fund Act provides several legal institutions to protect and aid victims. The government's Crime Victims Protection Fund is one among such institutions.

Chapter 8

Administrative Law*

Seongwook Heo**

1. Legislative Background

Like many other legal fields, the system of administrative law can be divided into civil law and common law systems. Since the end of Chosun dynasty and the colonial period of Japanese occupation, Korean administrative law has been heavily influenced by civil law traditions. However, a separate administrative law tribunal outside the judiciary, like the Conseil d'État in France, has not yet been established. After decolonization began in 1945, treating administrative law cases in the general courts was introduced under the US military regime and has been maintained through the present day. While there is a separate administrative law court in Seoul, it is still inside the judiciary. In this sense, the administrative law system is based upon a mixture of civil law and common law systems.[1]

* The purpose of this chapter is mainly to introduce the background and contents of Korean administrative law. In that context, I hereby acknowledge that some sections were drawn from my previous writings in other papers and books and modified to fit this chapter.

** Professor, Seoul National University School of Law.

1 Yoo-Hwan Kim, MODERN ADMINISTRATIVE LAW (현대행정법), Pakyoungsa 15 (2021) (in Korean).

2. Separation of Powers and Administrative Power

Like many other democratically advanced countries, the fundamental idea of Korean administrative law is based on the constitutional value of the separation of powers. In this vein, the power of the administrative branch is based on the principles of the rule of law and the non-delegation doctrine. Historically, the former has been differently understood: "the rule of law" found in common law jurisdictions and Germany's "principle of administration by legislation."

The rule of law in common law realms was systemically explained by Albert V. Dicey. He counted three factors as fundamental to the rule of law: (i) the absolute predominance of regular law; (ii) equality before the law, guaranteeing the application of common law at court; and (iii) the Constitution and fundamental rights as outcomes of precedents.

By contrast, the German-style principle of administration by legislation was explained by Otto Mayer as having the following three key factors: (i) the principle of priority of legislation, (ii) the principle of delegation by legislation, and (iii) the principle of norm creation by legislation. This approach was overly reliant on the formalistic requirement of legislation enacted by the legislator and contributed to the failings of the Third Reich. After World War II, the German approach became less formalistic and more substantive, particularly in the following three ways: (i) the principle of priority of constitutional legislation, (ii) the extension of the principle of delegation by legislation, and (iii) the principle of norm creation by legislation, general principles, and common law.[2]

In its earliest days, Korean administrative law was heavily influenced by the German notion of the principle of administration by legislation. However, as time has passed, notable changes have been witnessed in both academia and the judiciary.

2 Yoo-Hwan Kim, *supra* note 1, 17-23; Nam-Cheol Kim, THE ADMINISTRATIVE LAW INTRODUCTION (행정법입문), Deep Reading 19-21 (2021) (in Korean).

3. Overview of Korean Administrative Law

(1) General Act on Public Administration (GAPA)

The General Act on Public Administration (GAPA) is relatively new, having come into effect on March 23, 2021. It mainly prescribes the basic concepts and principles of administrative action that were previously discussed only in academic contexts and cases without codified legislation. GAPA consists of four: Chapter I, General provisions; Chapter II, Legal principles of administration; Chapter III, Administrative action; and Chapter IV, Legislative activities of administration.

It is notable that Chapter II enumerates the legal principles of administrative action. The rule of law, equality, proportionality, the duty of good faith, a prohibition on abuse of authority, the protection of trust, and substantial relations between ends and means are the principles enumerated. Given that the principles of law are not friendly to codification, how these principles are interpreted and applied in real cases needs to be monitored to identify differences with the pre-GAPA period, when those principles were constructed by precedents and academic interactions.

(2) Framework Act on Administrative Regulation (FAAR)

The Framework Act on Administrative Regulation (FAAR) has been in force since March 1, 1987. It largely prescribes basic matters concerning administrative regulations; it aims to contribute to improving the quality of life of citizens and to enhance national competitiveness in a sustained manner by facilitating self-regulation and creative initiative in social and economic activities through the repeal of unnecessary administrative regulations and the avoidance of inefficient administrative regulations.

The FAAR is composed of five chapters: Chapter I, General provisions; Chapter II, Principles and examination of establishment and reinforcement of regulations; Chapter III, Revision of existing regulations; Chapter IV, Regulatory reform committee; and Chapter V, Supplementary provisions. It should be noted that Article 7 of Chapter II requires regulatory impact assessments, including cost-benefit analyses.

Given that other regulatory legislation in Korea, such as the National Environmental Policy Framework Act, prescribes the precautionary principle, how these two competing principles can be harmonized in real-world regulation is an important point in both academic research and practical effects.

(3) Administrative Procedures Act (APA)

The Administrative Procedures Act (APA) has been in force since January 1, 1988. It deals primarily with prescribing administrative procedures, and its purpose is to ensure fairness, transparency, and credibility in administrative operations and to protect the rights and interests of citizens by providing for common matters regarding administrative procedures and thus allowing citizens better access to administrative procedures.

The APA is composed of eight chapters: Chapter I, General provisions; Chapter II, Dispositions; Chapter III, Reports; Chapter IV, Administrative preannouncement of legislation; Chapter V, Pre-announcement of administration; Chapter VI, Administrative guidance; Chapter VII, Strengthening citizen participation; and Chapter VIII, Supplementary provisions.

Korea's APA is noteworthy in the sense that it governs only administrative procedures and not administrative litigation; in this sense, it differs from the its counterpart in the United States. It is academically interesting to examine how any violations of the procedures prescribed in the APA affect the validity of final administrative measures, including dispositions.

(4) Administrative Litigation Act (ALA)

The Administrative Litigation Act (ALA) has been in force since January 1, 1988. It focuses on administrative litigation procedures, and its purpose is to protect citizens from having their rights or interests infringed by illegal dispositions of administrative agencies and the exercise or non-exercise of public authority and to ensure the proper resolution, through administrative litigation procedures, of disputes over rights based on public law or the application of law.

The ALA comprises five chapters: Chapter I, General provisions; Chapter II, Revocation litigation; Chapter III, Appeal litigation other than revocation suits; Chapter IV, Party litigation; and Chapter V, Lawsuits against public bodies and agencies.

The areas of standing and disposition play a meaningful role in determining the border between politics and the judiciary from the perspective of the separation of powers. There have been extensive academic discussions and debates about these threshold issues in Korean public law; it is now time to move on to the issues of merits.

(5) Administrative Law in Each Regulated Field

Other than the major basic framework acts on administrative law noted above, there are many regulatory acts that govern administrative law issues in specific fields. I will skip this part for the purpose of efficiency and focus.

4. Administrative Law Principles

In the past, no codified administrative law principle could be found in Korean statutes. Administrative law principles were discussed academically and theoretically, commentated on by scholars, and affirmed by court decisions. However, since the enactment of the GAPA, major principles have been codified in the statutes. It is still too early to evaluate how GAPA will affect the interpretation and application of these principles in actual cases and what differences from the period before the codification of principles might arise.

(1) Principle of Rule of Law in Administration

Any administrative action shall not contravene a statute, and if it restricts the rights of citizens, imposes obligations on citizens, or has material impacts on the lives of citizens, it shall have a statutory basis. (GAPA Article 8)

(2) Principle of Equality

Administrative authorities shall not discriminate against citizens without reasonable grounds (GAPA Article 9).

(3) Principle of Proportionality

Any administrative action shall comply with the following principles:

(i) It shall be effective and appropriate to achieve administrative purposes;
(ii) It shall be taken to the minimum extent necessary to achieve those administrative purposes;
(iii) The infringement of citizens' interests due to an administrative action shall not be greater than the public interest it is intended to uphold (GAPA Article 10).

(4) Duty of Good Faith and Principle of Prohibition of Abuse of Authority

(i) Each administrative authority shall perform its duties in good faith under statutes, regulations, and the like.
(ii) No administrative authority shall abuse its power or exceed the scope of its authority (GAPA Article 11).

(5) Principle of Protection of Trust

(i) An administrative agency shall protect a citizen's legitimate and reasonable trust in administration, except where the public interest or a third party's interest is likely to be significantly undermined.
(ii) An administrative authority shall not exercise an authority if citizens had good cause to believe that the authority would not be exercised because the agency had not exercised that authority for a long time, despite the opportunity to do so. However, this shall not apply where the public interest or a third party's interest is likely to be significantly undermined (GAPA Article 12).

(6) Principle of Substantial Relations between Ends and Means

In taking an administrative action, an administrative authority shall not impose on a party obligations unrelated in effect to the administrative action (GAPA Article 13).

5. Administrative Actions

(1) Disposition

Disposition is the most common form of agency actions in administrative regulations. In the academic tradition, the concept of 'administrative action' was created to capture the legal identity of agency action in parallel with private persons' legal actions.

However, in 1984, with the enactment of the ALA and its definition of the concept of 'disposition' as the main way for agencies to act, academic debates arose as to whether dispositions and administrative actions were identical or not. The majority opinion is that a disposition differs from an administrative action in that it encompasses a wider scope of agency actions, but there are not many significant differences in actual cases.

By the characteristics of their effects on another party, dispositions can be classified into beneficial, intrusive, and double effect dispositions. They can be also divided into against-person dispositions, against-thing dispositions, and mixed dispositions, based on the object of agency action. Finally, they can also be divided into binding and discretionary dispositions, depending on whether an agency has discretion in the final decision-making process.

One of the key questions in academic discussions surrounding dispositions is the division between binding and discretionary dispositions and how to control and review agencies' discretionary decision both inside the administrative branch and in the judicial review process.

(2) Rulemaking

Another key form of agency action is through rulemaking by the government. Under the umbrella of the rule of law or the principle of administration by legislation, agencies can carry out their own normative rulemaking such as enforcement ordinances or department ordinances.

An important issue in this section is the distinction between legal orders and administrative rules. The former involves administrative rulemaking that can affect the rights and obligations of citizens. For that reason, a strict rule of delegation from the National Assembly applies to both the procedure and content of legal orders. On the other hand, administrative rules are internal rules created by agencies that should be followed by government officials in their daily work and do not directly affect the rights or obligations of citizens.

Unlike this textbook way of explaining the difference between legal orders and administrative rules, the real world of agency rulemaking is not that simple, which has led to a number of academically important issues.

Certain kinds of administrative rules can have the effect of legal orders regardless of their formal designation, while some kinds of legal orders have no legal effects on citizens' rights and obligations. How to deal with this discrepancy between form and reality is an important topic.[3]

Another key issue in administrative rulemaking is how to control and review it, both within the administration and using judicial review. A related legal topic is determining the effect of agency dispositions based on administrative rulemaking that is later declared illegal or unconstitutional during the judicial review process.[4]

(3) Planning

Agency actions can be executed by more than dispositions and rulemaking. When there is a necessity for long-term planning and consideration, agency actions can be designed by planning.

Administrative planning is a relatively new phenomenon that arose in response to the modern demand for long-term, multi-agency actions. There has been debate over whether administrative planning is a kind of disposition or a different form of rulemaking. Court decisions have acknowledged the complex and multifaceted nature of administrative planning, according to which certain kinds of planning can be the target of direct administrative litigation and others cannot.[5]

(4) *De Facto* Administrative Action

De facto administrative action is an action by an agency that does not entail legal effect; it brings about only factual outcomes. Examples include

3 Yoo-Hwan Kim, *supra* note 1, 113.
4 Yoo-Hwan Kim, *supra* note 1, 106.
5 Yoo-Hwan Kim, *supra* note 1, 218-219.

building a bridge or other structure, and providing services like cleaning or legal counseling to private entities.

There is a question as to whether *de facto* administrative action is governed by the delegation principle when it has *de facto* legal effect. This is especially the case when a *de facto* administrative action has an aspect of coercive power exercised by the agency; in those instances, delegation from legislation enacted by the National Assembly is required.

There is also an academic debate over whether *de facto* administrative action can be the target of administrative litigation under which a plaintiff's claim to reverse or annul an action can be maintained. Different opinions exist among commentators, but the Supreme Court of Korea has acknowledged the dispositional nature of some *de facto* administrative actions of agencies when they have coercive power over citizens' property and rights.

6. Judicial Review of Administrative Actions

(1) Administrative Law Court

As has been noted above, administrative law cases in the Korean capital city of Seoul are dealt with by the Seoul Administrative Law Court which is separately established inside the judiciary. Outside that court, administrative law cases are dealt with by specialized tribunals in each court. This is because specialized experience and knowledge are required to effectively review administrative law cases.

(2) Types of Administrative Litigation

First, administrative litigation can be divided into two categories based on the relationship between plaintiff and defendant.

There are types of administrative litigation in which a citizen as the plaintiff is bringing a claim claiming against an agency action when a coercive position is involved. This type of litigation can be called appeal litigation and be divided into three types: requests to cancel an agency action, requests to confirm the invalidity of an agency action, and requests to confirm the illegality of agency inaction.

The other type is administrative litigation occurs when the plaintiff makes a claim against an agency as an equal party in a legal relationship. For example, plaintiffs can seek monetary payments from a government agency on the basis of public law relations, like claims in the public takings process or wage payment claims that have arisen in the context of public service employment.

(3) Standing

One of the issues in Korean public law most deeply contested by academics is the range and scope of standing in appeals seeking the cancellation or reversal of an agency action. Unlike general civil litigation, in which anybody with a claim against a defendant has standing, standing in administrative litigation involving the cancellation of reversal of an agency action is strictly prescribed by Article 12 of the ALA.

That article limits standing in cancellation litigation to the person with a legal interest in that cancellation. There have been different opinions and long-running academic debates in Korean administrative law circles about this clause. Among those opinions, the "the theory of legal interest protected by legislation" is held by a majority of scholars; the Supreme Court also takes that position. Against this perspective, the "the theory of legal interest that deserves to be protected" has been forwarded by some scholars, and there have been efforts to modify Article 12 of the ALA to reflect that view. However, these efforts have been all unsuccessful for political and economic reasons.

Compared to the majority opinion and the court rulings, the dissenting view would widen the range and scope of persons who could be granted standing. Scholars who support this opinion claim that broadening standing would more vigorously protect citizens' rights. However, this issue is much more intimately related to the fundamental constitutional value of the principle of separation of powers. According to the majority opinion and court rulings, the scope and range of person who are admitted standing and having chances to argue in front of judge on merit are decided by the legislators. On the other hand, according to the competing opinion, this scope and range are determined by the judiciary because the issue of who deserves the protection of legal right cannot be determined at the legislating stage. In this context, it is yet to early or inappropriate to accept the competing opinion.

(4) Judicial Reviewability of Agency Actions

The next key issue is the scope of agency action against which an appeal litigation can be raised. Article 19 of the ALA holds that dispositions and the like are targets of appeal litigation regarding cancellation or reversal of agency actions. This brings up the academic debate on the scope of reviewability.

Before the complete revision of the ALA in 1984, the concept of disposition in the act was understood as no different from the academic conception of administrative agency action, against which cancellation litigation could be brought. But, with the 1984 revision of ALA article 19, not just the disposition itself, but also 'other agency actions which can be understood same as disposition' was added to the scope of agency reviewability.

Under this background, the opinion that article 19 of ALA is meaning the same thing of administrative agency action and the other opinion that those two are meaning different things are competing. The court ruling is yet unclear on which position it is standing.

(5) Mootness

Even after the standing and reviewability requirements are fulfilled, cancellation litigation cannot be pursued if the plaintiff cannot acquire adequate redress of damages due to an agency action.

(6) Merits

When all the requirements noted above are fulfilled, the plaintiff can then argue his or her claims in a courtroom and obtain a final ruling on the merits of the case. I elaborate on this topic in the later sections.

7. The Codification of Korean Administrative Law[6]

(1) Background of Codification

As Korea's legal system was heavily influenced by European civil law systems when it was founded during the period of modernization, codification is a very familiar concept, and the area of Korean administrative law is no exception. Compared to other developed countries, Korea has a relatively systemically codified form of administrative law.

Korean administrative law is composed of several basic acts. These are the major pieces of legislation: the APA, the Administrative Litigation Act (ALA), the Administrative Adjudication Act (AAA), the Framing Act on Administrative Regulation (FAAR), and the Personal Information Protection Act (PIPA). In addition, there are many regulatory acts in a wide range of economic spheres, such as environmental, broadcasting and telecommunication, energy industry, and fair-trading and anti-monopoly regulations.

The general rules of administrative law in Korea developed under the influence of several sources of law. There can thus be differences of opinion over the exact concepts and precise scope of the general rules; however, the following points are commonly understood as the general rules of administrative law in Korea.

The principle of the rule of law, the principle of non-delegation, the principle of proportionality, the principle of equality, the principle of unreasonable correlation, and the principle of protection of trust are all acknowledged as integral to Korean administrative law. The most influential source of law affecting those general rules is the Korean Constitution, and most of the general rules enumerated above are based on concepts enshrined in the constitution. However, like the constitutions of many other developed countries, the clauses in the Korean constitution are often quite abstract and vague. Therefore, the contents of the general rules are not defined by the constitution itself and need to be reinforced and completed by legislative

6 The contents of this section were drawn primarily from Seong-Wook Heo, *The Codification of Administrative Law in South Korea*, CODIFICATION IN EAST ASIA – SELECTED PAPERS FROM THE 2ND IACL THEMATIC CONFERENCE (W. Y. Wang ed.), Springer 161-165 (2014).

enactments, judicial judgments, and academic opinions. Even though the National Assembly passes many administrative measures, it is not common for the general principles of administrative law to be prescribed in such enactments. Much of the content of the general principles of administrative law is formed by judicial decisions and academic opinions. Several among these general principles have been codified at GAPA as explained above.

The essential notion in systematizing administrative law as a whole in Korea is the administrative law or act. As noted above, Korean administrative law is composed of several basic acts and a wide range of other acts dealing with different economic sectors. The general principles established by the constitution, the basic acts, judicial decisions, and academic opinions are applied to these specific regulatory fields.

(2) The Situation of Codification Concerning General Rules of Administrative Law

The general principles of administrative law have been declared very abstractly in Korea's Constitution before the GAPA legislation; it was not also easy to find cases where general principles are specifically codified in administrative enactments. Exceptions could be found in the APA, Article 4 of which deals with good faith and protection of belief as follows:

> (i) Administrative agencies must follow the duty of good faith in doing their jobs.
> (ii) When the manner of an administrative action has been accepted as an established custom by the people affected, administrative agencies should not betray the reasonable reliance of the people by acting differently unless the public interest or a just interest of a third party is injured by that custom.

Even though the definition, form, procedure, and substantive rules for administrative activities like rulemaking, administrative acts, administrative contracts, planning, and administrative guidance are all essential concepts in Korean administrative law, they were not codified to a significant degree.

Administrative law in Korea has all the concepts of administrative activities exemplified above (rulemaking, administrative act, administrative contract, planning, administrative guidance), but those concepts were academically defined and then refined by judicial decisions before GAPA.

Korea does have a basic framing act on administrative enforcement that codifies the basic rules and procedures of public enforcement of administrative duty. It does not cover financial sanctions. Korean administrative law uses several types of monetary sanctions as means of public enforcement, but it does not have a single basic framing act that applies to all those sanctions. Regulatory statutes in different fields have their own clauses covering monetary sanctions. Similarly, each regulatory statute has its own clauses on the matter of inspections.

The Korean parliament passed a basic framing act on the protection of private information in which the scope and process of the openness of information and the protection of personal data are prescribed. That act came into force in September 2011.

Korea has a long history of codifying the procedures of judicial review of administrative actions. The ALA was first enacted in 1951; that act simply followed Japan's administrative litigation procedure act and comprised only 14 articles, with no substantive contents on judicial review of administrative actions. It was not until the mid-1980s that the ALA was transformed into a substantial procedural act on administrative review. Before then, Korea was ruled, often with great severity, by a military dictatorship, and it was not easy for average people to bring suits against administrative agencies. Therefore, social pressures to systemize administrative litigation were not great. With the trend toward democratization in politics and society, the need to restructure the administrative litigation system became more pressing. Even though most of the 1980s were during the period of military rule in Korea, things began to change.

After many discussions among scholars and lawyers, the Korean parliament passed a new ALA in 1984, which came into force in 1985. After efforts at judicial reform in the early 1990s, the ALA underwent another revision that saw the establishment of a new administrative court. This ALA came into force in 1998. Despite these two major revisions of the ALA, the many scholars believe that it is still not adequate to cope with the legal issues that arise in the modern administrative context. Against this background, efforts to revise the ALA have been undertaken by both the Supreme Court and the Ministry of Justice since 2000; however, no significant results have yet emerged.

The ALA is composed of five chapters. The first chapter contains general provisions like the purpose of the act, definitions, classification of administrative litigation, and so on. The second chapter is the main part of the ALA and covers the general prescriptions regarding revocation suits. The scope of standing, procedural requirements needed to bring a revocation suit, the object of revocation suits, the procedural rules of trials and rulings, complementary clauses, and so on are all prescribed in that chapter. Chapters 3, 4, and 5 are composed of clauses on the various categories of administrative litigation, other than revocation suits.

To deal with administrative organization and relations between administrative organs with one another, Korea has the Government Organization Act, which prescribes the establishment, structure, and scope of power of administrative organizations. Korea also has the Basic Framing Act on Local Government (BFALG) which prescribes the basic rules of local government organization and function. However, the national general administrative law codes also apply to local governments.

(3) Codification in Each Branch of the Public Administration

Korea has very complicated branches of administrative law in diverse areas like land use law, environmental law, social security, and economic regulation. As these branches were created at different times to address a range of legal and policy issues, they are enumerative rather than systemically organized. Many efforts have been undertaken inside government to systemize these enumerative statutes, but there is still much work to be done.

(4) Theory of Codification

As noted at the beginning of this chapter, the Korean legal system is based on the civil law tradition and is thus quite familiar with codification. Many legal scholars had academic backgrounds in European countries like Germany and France, so it was considered natural to have codification in the general administrative law when necessary.

However, as the language used in codification cannot avoid being abstract and vague at last to some extent, it is always necessary to complement codified language with statutory interpretation, and judicial decisions and academic opinion play important roles in that process.

One issue on the topic of codification that merits particular notice is the relationship between democracy and judicial authority. Compared to situations when the general principles of administrative law are largely formed by the constitution and judicial interpretation, having most of those general principles codified can be understood as being more heavily influenced by democratic processes, as codification is taken care of by the National Assembly and its democratic procedures. In this sense, we can perceive that the level of codification of administrative law in each country depends on the decisions made regarding the balance between democratic checks and judicial authority.

What is the situation in Korea? Even though there were several cases of poor judicial judgments under the military regime, the overall trust of the Korean people in the judiciary is quite high. This is especially true when compared with the high levels of mistrust of politics and politicians among the Korean people. Moreover, before President Roh Moo-hyun's term (2003-2008), politically significant issues like moving the capital city from Seoul or impeaching the incumbent president were rarely taken to court. Therefore, popular demands to subject the judiciary to democratic control were not urgent. However, since that period, there has been significant democratization in many areas, and more people have become interested in the role of judiciary.

It is worth observing how this trend toward democratization in Korean society has affected discussions about revising the ALA, including the issue of codification of the general principles of administrative law.

(5) Discussions on ALA Revision in 2012

After a couple of failed efforts at ALA revision, Korea's Ministry of Justice commissioned a TF team to undertake a full revision of ALA in 2011. The Committee for ALA Revision, which was composed of legal scholars and practitioners, first met on November 15, 2011, and had 10 sets of meetings through April 2012.

The major issues faced by the revision committee were as follows: (1) modifying the administrative lawsuit structure, which was composed of two somewhat restrictive categories; (2) the introduction of preventive injunction lawsuits; (3) modifying the qualifications for suspension of enforcement; (4) introducing injunctive relief in administrative procedures; (5) enlarging the scope of public law litigation against the government; and (6) introducing recommendations for compromise to rulings in administrative trials.

As of March 11, 2013, the final contents of the ALA revision had not yet been confirmed, even inside the government. Therefore, it was expected many more discussions and that a much longer time will be required for Korean government to decide on the final terms of the ALA revision and enact it through legislation passed by the National Assembly. After that, up until the year of 2022, no significant achievement has been made on this task.

8. Principle of Proportionality and Democratic Accountability[7]

The merits of most administrative law cases are centered on the issue of balancing competing interests. Sometimes this means balancing public and private interests; at other times, it is a matter of balancing two public interests. In administrative law in the civil law realm, the principle of proportionality has traditionally been used as a tool to find the right answer in cases involving competing interests. The principle of proportionality has the following requirements.

(1) Principle of Suitability

This means that administrative measures should be chosen from among measures that are suitable for achieving the administrative goal.

(2) Principle of Necessity

This means that administrative measures should not exceed the boundary necessary to achieve the administrative goal; the administrative agency has

7 The contents of this section were drawn primarily from Seong-Wook Heo, *The Judicial Review Criteria in Korean Administrative Litigation: The Proportionality Principle in Korean Administrative Law and Democratic Accountability*, THE FUNCTIONAL TRANSFORMATION OF COURTS: TAIWAN AND KOREA IN COMPARISON (Jiunn-rong Yeh ed.), V&R Unipress 93–102 (2015).

to choose the least infringing measure among all policy options to achieve the public interest goal.

(3) Principle of Proportionality

This is the narrow meaning of the principle of proportionality; it requires that the administrative agency should not implement a certain administrative measure—even if that measure is necessary for the achievement of a legitimate administrative goal—when the cost of implementing that policy measure is greater than the benefits derived from it.

The way the proportionality principle is applied in the judicial review of administrative action is quite comparable to the Chevron deference doctrine in US administrative law. While that doctrine deals with how much deference a court should give to the statutory interpretation of an administrative agency, the context is not identical to the proportionality principle. However, if we understand that an agency's discretionary power under the proportionality principle essentially comes from statutes enacted by the legislature, judicial review of discretionary administrative power can be also understood from the perspective of statutory interpretation, and what matters in the proportionality principle is also how much deference should be given by the courts to an agency's statutory interpretation. As we see below, the major difference between the proportionality principle and the Chevron deference is that in the former, it is judges who decide, on the merits, on the most appropriate administrative measure in a given case.

The Chevron deference principle involves two steps.[8]

> First is the question whether Congress has directly spoken to the precise question at issue. If the intent of Congress is clear, that is the end of the matter. In this case, the court must give effect to the unambiguously expressed intent of Congress.
>
> If, however, the court determines that Congress has not directly addressed the precise question at issue, the court does not simply impose its own construction on the statute, as would be necessary in

8 *Chevron, Inc. v. Natural Resources Defense Council*, 467 U.S. 837 (1984).

> the absence of an administrative interpretation. Rather, if the statute is silent or ambiguous with respect to the specific issue, the question for the court is whether the agency's answer is based on a permissible construction of the statute.[9]

The first step is about the typical issue of the interpretation of the intent of Congress in a statute. If the intent of Congress found in the first step is obvious or unambiguous, then there is nothing for the court to do beyond reviewing whether the agency has faithfully executed the intent of Congress as expressed in the statutory language. That is all.

However, in the real world of statutory interpretation, both agencies and courts are almost always faced with ambiguity in the statutory language. That can happen inadvertently or intentionally for many reasons, which can be scientifically analyzed using public choice theory. In situations of ambiguity, the Chevron deference principle requires the court to review only whether the statutory interpretation taken by the agency is permissible or reasonable. When that interpretation is permissible, even if the court does not fully agree with the agency's application of that interpretation, the court should not substitute its own preference for the agency's conclusion. Rather, it must defer to the agency's decision.

In this regard, the Chevron deference principle directs the court to address the issue of judicial review very differently from the proportionality principle, which raises the issue of democratic accountability.

According to the detailed version of the proportionality principle, the court makes the final decision on the legality of an administrative discretionary decision. After passing the stages of the principle of suitability and the principle of necessity, at the stage of the narrow meaning of the principle of proportionality, the court balances between public interest and private interest, the benefits and costs of the regulation, and the private interest of one group and the private interest of the other group influenced by the administrative action.

As noted above, the proportionality principle originally comes from German legal theory and arose under a police state. In such a context, the

9 Stephen G. Breyer, Richard B. Stewart, Cass R. Sunstein, and Adrian Vermeule, ADMINISTRATIVE LAW AND REGULATORY POLICY - PROBLEMS, TEXT, AND CASES, 6th ed., Aspen Publishers 242-246 (2006).

people had fairly simple expectations regarding the role of the state. It was functioning well if it maintained the basic social order and defended the country from foreign enemies. In that situation, the proportionality decision was also quite simple, and it was reasonable to expect that judges would do that job quite well. Naturally, the issue of democratic accountability could be hidden under the veil of the protection of private rights from state power.

However, in the modern world, the people's expectations of the state are much more complex and multi-dimensional. Most modern administrative actions are carried out in situations of scientific uncertainty: climate change, food safety, bird flu, nuclear energy, COVID 19, and so on.

Given this uncertainty, there is no guarantee that a court will make an appropriate decision on a complex issue. Of course, there is also no guarantee that an administrative agency will always do better in decision making than a court. However, it is true that an agency is generally supported by many more resources and professional staff than a court. Moreover, the administrative agency generally has much more democratic accountability in the sense that it is composed of public officers who are nominated and dismissed by the president, who is elected by the people. Finally, administrative agencies are all subject to oversight by the National Assembly.

For the proportionality principle to be justifiable in modern administrative state, it should be able to provide much more sophisticated criteria to decide the legality of administrative actions carried out under scientific uncertainty. It is not enough to let courts choose the best way by considering all the relevant factors.

In this regard, we can see many reference points from the Chevron deference principle that can offer valuable lessons to the proportionality principle. Of course, it is true that active discussion is continuing on in US administrative law scholarship surrounding the exact meaning and scope of the Chevron deference principle. However, after sometimes fierce discussions among judges and scholars on the meaning and scope of the Chevron deference during the nearly four decades since its appearance in 1984, it is now safe to say that it has become the basic foundational tool in judicial review of administrative actions and that the Chevron decision has become the most cited decision in US jurisprudence.

There is one more thing to check. By requiring the courts to find the best way to resolve an issue through consideration of all relevant factors in a proportionality test, are we not implicitly letting courts behave much like the court in the context of the Chevron deference doctrine? If that is true in today's world, we need to try to fill the gap between the normative principle and the real world as soon as possible. In analyzing this point, insights from public choice theory can provide useful tools to better understand the real world of interest group activity and the incentive structure of many players in regulatory regimes.

9. Rational Choice in Modern Administrative Law in Korea[10]

(1) Introduction

In the modern administrative state, determining the proper role of the state is not as simple as it used to be in the police state. In the police state era, the proper role of government was relatively simple. Governments generally were regarded as doing well if kept the peace. Public administrative goals were largely clear and simple. The government was required to arrest criminals and protect the territory of the state from foreign invasion. Of course, due to the scarcity of resources, governments could not fulfill every requirement of the people, but the administrative goals and the means to achieve them were generally obvious and correlated well with each other.

Compared to that time, the proper role of the modern administrative state is much more complex, making it much more difficult to find the right answer in modern administrative actions. One major cause is that modern administrative states have to deal with issues of risk; governments have to make choices under conditions of uncertainty.[11]

What is important is that—however uncertain the world may be—governments cannot simply run away from making decisions on risk-laden issues. Moreover, governments have to do their best to make rational choices in making policy decisions.

10 The content of this section was largely drawn from Seong-Wook Heo, *Rational Choice in Modern Administrative Law: With the Behavioral Economics Approach to the Two Major Cases in Korea*, 12(2) JOURNAL OF KOREAN LAW 219-239 (2013).

11 For a brief overview of risk in modern society, see Cass R. Sunstein, RISK AND REASON: SAFETY, LAW, AND THE ENVIRONMENT, Cambridge University Press (2002).

(2) Rational Choice Theory in Public Law

The analysis of rational choice in a market economy is simpler than that in the area of public law.[12] People generally have no difficulty in assuming that market players are seeking to maximize their self-interest in market decisions like consumption and production.

It is, however, difficult to apply this utility or welfare maximization assumption to public law decisions. Many people who happily accept the self-interest maximization assumption in market decisions hesitate to accept the assumption that public agents would also try to maximize their self-interest in public decisions.[13]

Indeed, a large number people believe or expect that public agents are focused on the public interest rather than being private-interest seekers. This difference in perspectives on people behaving in the public sphere leads to two categorical theories regarding public law. One is the public interest theory of public law, and the other is the public choice theory of public law.

The former holds that the reason we need public law in the form of regulation is to correct market failures, whereas the public choice theory of public law criticizes public interest theory for lacking a logical underpinning for its claim that the existence of market failures naturally brings about government regulations to address those failures.[14]

(3) Social Preference Function

As we have seen above, it is not easy to determine rational choice of public policy in the area of public law. This is largely because modern societies are composed of large numbers people with a vast number of often diverse preferences. To find the rational public choice outcome in this context, it is

12 On the issue of rationality in public law, see Jerry L. Mashaw, GREED, CHAOS, AND GOVERNANCE – USING PUBLIC CHOICE TO IMPROVE PUBLIC LAW, Yale University Press, Chapter 3: Public Choice and Rationality Review 50-80 (1997).

13 On the reasoning of the validity of self-interest-seeking agent assumptions in the public area, see Geoffrey Brennan and James M. Buchanan, THE REASON OF RULES – CONSTITUTIONAL POLITICAL ECONOMY, Cambridge University Press (1985).

14 On the critical understanding of public law from the public choice theory perspective, see Daniel A. Farber and Philip P. Frickey, LAW AND PUBLIC CHOICE – A CRITICAL INTRODUCTION, The University of Chicago Press (1991).

necessary to have a social preference function with which to correlate each set of people's preferences into a single communal preference.[15]

As a given society's total amount of resources can be technically calculated (even if it may require immensely complex processes and a vast amount of time), once a coherent and consistent social preference function is found, then the rational public choice outcome can theoretically be found.

The democratic process, which is based on majority rule, is also an example of a social preference function most commonly followed in modern democratic societies. It is a way to make communal decisions based on each person's different preferences. To develop a more sophisticated way of communal decision making, human beings have historically tried to develop better political and democratic processes.[16]

However, the Nobel laureate Kenneth Arrow has mathematically proven that no social preference function can be established without a dictator once the other minimum requirements have been met (rationality, pareto principle, independence from irrelevant factors, universal applicability); this is known as Arrow's Impossibility Theorem.[17] This means that there is no

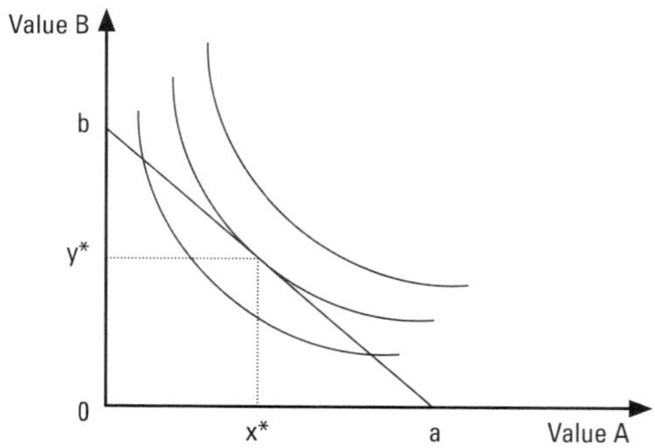

Figure 1[18]

15 On the issue of finding the social preference function by collecting social choice from individual values, see Kenneth J. Arrow, SOCIAL CHOICE AND INDIVIDUAL VALUES, Yale University Press (1951).

16 On the issue of understanding democracy from the perspective of economics, see Anthony Downs, AN ECONOMIC THEORY OF DEMOCRACY, Addison-Wesley (1957), and Mancur Olson, THE LOGIC OF COLLECTIVE ACTION – PUBLIC GOODS AND THE THEORY OF GROUPS, Harvard University Press (1965).

17 Kenneth J. Arrow, *supra* note 15.

18 This figure and related explanations are from Seong-Wook Heo, *Public Law Theory and Public Policy (I) – A Theoretical Foundation of Public Choice Theory as an Analytical Tool for Public Law Theory* (공법이론과 공공정책 (I)-공법이론 연구방법론으로서 공공선택이론), 6(2) KOREAN JOURNAL OF LAW AND ECONOMICS (법경제학연구) 139 (2009) (in Korean).

coherent and consistent social preference function with which to draw a society's preference from all its members' different sets of preferences.

This is quite a disappointing result. After Arrow's Impossibility Theorem made its debut in the academic world, many social scientists tried to prove it wrong. However, the more they tried to demonstrate its flaws, the more its logical soundness was confirmed. This leaves us little choice but to try to build up the second best type of social preference function by sacrificing one or two of the conditions provided above for the social preference function to be consistent and coherent.

(4) Cost Benefit Analysis vs. Precautionary Principle[19]

As we have discussed above, unlike market equilibrium analysis in consumer choice theory, it is not easy to define what rational choice means in administrative law. We turn now to the question of cost-benefit analysis (CBA).

In market analysis, the assumption of the self-interest maximization of market players is widely, if not universally, accepted. On the other hand, in analyzing public law topics, people are often hesitant to accept the presumption of self-interest among public players. Many people try to establish something other merely monetary value as a public goal that should be the target of efforts in the public arena.

However, it cannot be denied that many of the public goals in modern society are susceptible to calculation and comparison in terms of utility or welfare. Indeed, in today's administrative state, CBA is an increasingly common tool for evaluating the validity of government regulations. In Korea, the Framework Act on Administrative Regulation (FAAR) requires every administrative agency to conduct a Regulation Impact Assessment, including a CBA, when introducing new or stricter regulations.

But the story in real life is not as simple as that statutory provision. Let us return to the two Korean cases presented in the introduction. In both cases, the CBA results and public responses diverged.

In the US beef case, the government's CBA analysis showed that

19 For a description of the debate between the precautionary principle and CBA and efforts to develop a more sophisticated understanding of the precautionary principle in modern risk-laden societies, see Cass R. Sunstein, *supra* note 11.

importing inexpensive beef from the United States would increase the overall welfare level of the Korean people. In that sense, the government thought it was making a rational public policy choice by allowing the importation of US beef. But people who participated in protests against the government felt very differently. Of course, the politics of mad cow disease protests in 2008 are far more complex than just the CBA issue, but those dramatic events are somewhat more easily understood through the frame of 'CBA vs. Precautionary principle' in risk issues.

In the Cheon-seong Mountain tunneling case too, the government's CBA results showed that tunneling through the mountain was the most efficient KTX route. But the monk Jiyul and environmental groups had different ideas.

The arguments of people who did not agree with the government's CBA analysis in the mad cow case and the Cheon-seong Mountain tunneling case can be understood as motivated by two reasons. The first is that the risk of humans contracting mad cow disease is so dangerous that its cost side should have been counted more intensively. In that case, there was no guarantee that benefits would exceed costs. The second reason is that because the value of the cost side, like protecting vulnerable species in nature, is incalculable and incommensurable with the monetary benefit side, CBAs simply should not be applied to that kind of policy decision.

Under this view, people argue that in dealing with risk issues, governments should not simply follow CBAs in their decision making; rather, the state is required to undertake whatever measures it can to mitigate risk. This tension between CBAs and the precautionary principle is another front in the conflict between different views of rational choice in the public sphere.

(5) Rational Choice in Democratic Processes

As Francis Fukuyama once pointed out, liberal democracy can be regarded as the most fully developed social preference function to date, even though we may not actually have reached the end of history.[20]

Even with the many variations in forms of voting, majority vote is still

20 Francis Fukuyama, THE END OF HISTORY AND THE LAST MAN, Avon Books (1992).

the most commonly used form of collective decision-making. However, as Condorcet showed over two centuries ago, the majority voting system is far from perfect. When more than one voting participant has a multi-peaked preference, cycling of voting outcomes occur, and no final decision would be made.

What, then, is the rational choice in terms of democratic process? Broadly speaking, there are two views on this topic: pluralism and republicanism. Pluralists claim that because individuals are as rational in their public decisions as in their market decisions, there is no need for the state to intervene in people's decision-making processes. The sum of each individual's rational choice can be regarded as the rational choice of the community.

On the other hand, republicans note the possibility that each individual's political decisions could be hampered by irrationality and the possibility that summing each individual's rational choice might not necessarily lead to the rational choice for the public. In this sense, they argue that the rational choice of a society comes not from a pluralistic process but from a deliberative process undertaken by the representatives of the society who have the virtue of being sincerely concerned about a better future for the community.

This difference of views on democracy also affects how to cope with issues of uncertainty in modern administrative law. Pluralists would argue that regardless of what it might turn out to be, what the public desires, as expressed through the democratic political process, should be respected as the rational choice of that community. By contrast, republicans would argue that because respect for democracy political processes does not mean respect for the blunders of the public but respect for sincere wishes for the prosperity of the community, the government should not just follow public opinion, whether presented through majority voting or protest.

It is not easy to directly link this difference in views on democracy to the differences in attitude toward the 2008 mad cow disease protests and the Cheon-seong Mountain hunger strike, but the lenses of pluralism and republicanism can help us better understand the structure of tensions between groups with different ideas about a society's rational choice.

(6) Behavioral Biases in People's Choices

We have thus far discussed the connection between rational choice and modern administrative law from several angles. Those discussions implicitly supposed that all people make rational choices, at least as individuals. What was at issue is whether each individual's rational choice could be summed to determine rational choice of an entire community.

Would that be true in real life? As Cass Sunstein has noted in many books and papers, the results of some empirical studies show that people tend to behave differently from the results predicted by classical rational choice theory.[21, 22]

1) The Availability Heuristic

People tend to be affected much more powerfully by things with which they are in the closest contact. For example, when a person is constantly exposed to media reports about bird flu, he or she may think that the risk of bird flu is much greater than other risks that receive less attention. In thinking about risks, people rely on certain heuristics, or rules of thumb, that help them simplify their inquiries.[23] In thinking about what to do in risky situations, people commonly use the availability heuristic. People assess risk magnitude by asking themselves whether examples of those risks come readily to mind.[24]

The first factor affecting the availability heuristic is familiarity. For example, "a class whose instances are easily retrieved will appear more numerous than a class of equal frequency whose instances are less retrievable."[25] According to a simple but elegant study by Daniel Kahneman, Paul Slovic, and Amos Tversky, people identified more male than female

21 A basic introduction to those behavioral biases and their application to legal analysis can be found in Cass R. Sunstein, WHY SOCIETIES NEED DISSENT, Harvard University Press (2003). The behavioral economics approach to risk is also applied in the second chapter of his later book, THE LAWS OF FEAR.

22 The original research on this topic was carried out by Daniel Kahneman, Paul Slovic, and Amos Tversky and reported in JUDGMENT UNDER UNCERTAINTY: HEURISTIC AND BIASES, Cambridge University Press (1982).

23 Cass R. Sunstein, *supra* note 11, 37.

24 *Id.*

25 Daniel Kahneman, Paul Slovic, and Amos Tversky, *supra* note 22, 11, cited in Cass R. Sunstein, *supra* note 11, 36.

names on a list as well known, even when the list was composed of equal numbers of male and female celebrities.[26] This result demonstrates how familiarity can affect the availability of instances. Familiar risks, like those associated with smoking, will be seen as more serious than risks that are less familiar, like those associated with sunbathing.[27]

In addition to familiarity, salience also affects the availability heuristic. In an example offered by Kahneman, Slovic, and Tversky, the impact of a burning house on people is likely to be greater when they can see the fire with their own eyes than when they only read about the same fire in a newspaper. Under the same logic, recent events will have a greater impact than earlier ones.[28]

The 2008 mad cow disease protest is a nearly textbook example of the availability heuristic. Many Korean people became very upset about the possibility of being infected by mad cow disease right after the MBC program aired. When they were exposed to salient images of mad cow disease, like a sick cow that could not stand up or an interview with a dying girl supposedly suffering from human mad cow disease, they came to think that eating beef imported from the United States was very dangerous. The familiar and salient images of mad cow disease led many Korean people to rely on the availability heuristic in their decision making.

2) The Cascading Effect and Group Polarization

Human beings are of course not simply sheep.[29] In everyday life, however, they do have a tendency to follow other people's opinions, often to an extent that many might find surprising. This tendency becomes stronger when people are faced with difficult rather than easy questions.

Moreover, in situations of uncertainty, when a large number of people have already shared their views in some form, it becomes very easy for a newcomer to simply follow their lead. Cascading is a real phenomenon, and there are innumerable examples of cascading events in human history. Some were beneficial, while others were tragic in their consequences.

26 Cass R. Sunstein, *supra* note 11, 36-37.

27 *Id.* 37.

28 *Id.*

29 Cass R. Sunstein, WHY SOCIETIES NEED DISSENT, Oliver Wendell Holmes Lectures 54 (2003).

Cascades can involve judgment about either facts or values. They happen within legislatures, political parties, religious organizations, the judicial system, and among diverse groups of citizens in any society.[30]

Cascades are neither good nor bad *per se*. History offers cases of cascades in which people came to a sound collective conclusion. Part of the reason why the apartheid regime in South Africa fell was a cascade. The downfall of communism and the US civil rights movement showed similar dynamics.[31] These are good examples of cascades. The problem is that people can converge on erroneous or insufficiently justified outcomes through exactly the same process as occurs when reaching desirable conclusions.[32] This problem can be quite serious.

Many of the risk issues in modern administrative law are related to the effects of cascading in public decision-making processes. With mad cow disease, as scientific evidence for human mad cow disease was still uncertain at best, people had no objective criteria to help them decide on the issue. In that situation, once a large enough number of people got together to share the idea that eating US beef might put people at risk of contracting the human form of mad cow disease, many other people naturally joined the stream that cascaded into protests against the government.

Cascading has both informational and reputational aspects. When people lack the precise information needed to make thoughtful decisions under conditions of uncertainty, they consider it quite rational to simply follow whatever majority opinion has already coalesced. From the perspective of collective wisdom, if each individual in a group made the effort to make a rational choice based on all available information, then the collective outcome might be close to the best outcome. However, participants in a cascade might fail to see that the blind are really leading the blind—that the decisions of most of their predecessors, many of whom were already simply following others, offer little independent information.[33]

The key thing is how to reduce the risk of bad cascades. It has been suggested that the more people with professional knowledge on an issue are included in a group and the more a social culture allowing dissenting

30 *Id.*
31 *Id.* 55.
32 *Id.*
33 *Id.* 60.

opinions to be freely expressed is cultivated, the lower the risk of negative cascading.

In Korea, whether the mad cow disease episode was an example of bad cascading remains a matter of debate is still going on. As is well known to Korean people, the producers of the MBC program were ultimately found not guilty by the Supreme Court, which ruled that even if some factual content of the program proved to be false, it was not a defamation of the public officers negotiating with United States on beef imports, because the program was about an issue with public and social meaning, and as journalists, the producers had a greater range of freedom of speech.[34]

However, that does not automatically mean that the mad cow disease episode was a good cascade or that the import of US beef was a bad idea that should have been stopped by the brave dissenting opinions of PD sucheop.

Group polarization is another kind of human bias often found in processes of group thinking. It refers to the fact that people tend to reach more polarized conclusions when they deliberate in groups than on their own. This tendency becomes stronger when a group is composed of people with similar political preferences but is weakened when one or more people in a group have scientifically precise answers on the issues being discussed or can freely express their ideas.

A person who simply did not like the idea of imported beef could quickly become an extreme opponent of importing US beef after participating in protests with people who were highly polarized in that direction.

3) Probability Neglect

As Sunstein notes, the availability heuristic and the social cascading can produce inaccurate assessments of probability. However, people will sometimes make little effort to assess probability at all, especially when powerful emotions are involved.[35] In such cases, large-scale variations in probability matter little, even when those variations should matter a great deal. This happens on both the hope and fear sides. The behavior of people buying lottery tickets is an example of probability neglect on the hope side. However, it is probability neglect on the fear side that is most relevant to risk

34 Supreme Court Decision 2010Do17237, September 2, 2011.

35 Cass R. Sunstein, *supra* note 11, 39.

issues.[36]

Probability neglect can easily be connected to the precautionary principle in risk management. When people fall into the probability neglect trap in assessing salient risks, they focus on one emotionally gripping outcome among a large set of possibilities; this can bring about excessive public concern about certain very low-probability risks.[37]

A number of examples of probability neglect have been observed when dealing with modern risk issues: in areas ranging from dying in an airplane crash through genetically modified food to climate change, people can easily ignore the actual probability of a risk being realized. In both the mad cow disease and Cheon-seong Mountain cases, people in Korea showed a tendency to neglect probability. Even though the scientific probability of human being mad cow disease was very low—indeed, close to zero—the people in the protest were categorically opposed to all attempts to import US beef. They were not rationally calculating the probability of mad cow disease or conducting a rational CBA on importing US beef; they were simply and emotionally rejecting the small possibility of the risk of illness, no matter how small it might be. The citizen group in the Cheon-seong Mountain case acted in largely the same way. They were not rationally calculating the probability of the effect of tunneling on wildlife in that area; they did not even accept the results of the environmental impact assessment.

If enough people have attitudes that involve probability neglect, they can exert a significant influence on public decision making through a range of political activities. One core issue in modern administrative law is how to deal with probability neglect, given its capacity to affect the political will of the people.

4) Framing Effects

Framing effects occur when people cannot escape the frame through which a problem has been presented. The existence of the tendency for framing effects to emerge was first tested by psychologists Amos Tversky and Daniel Kahneman in 1981.[38] Their experiment involved asking a large group of

36 *Id.*

37 *Id.*

38 For a more detailed academic explanation of framing effects in jury decision making, see Edward J. McCaffery, Daniel J. Kahneman, and Matthew L.

people questions about a particular disease prevention strategy. The first question asked respondents to decide between two options involving 600 people affected by a hypothetical deadly disease.

- Option A will save 200 people's lives.
- Option B has a 33% chance of saving all 600 people and a 66% chance of saving no one.

Obviously, these two options have the same expected value of saving 200 people, but option B carries more risk. Almost three quarters (72%) of participants chose option A, with only 28% selecting option B. The other question was the same as the first one but was framed somewhat differently and asked to another group of people.

- If option C is taken, 400 people will die.
- If option D is taken, there is a 33% chance that no people will die and a 66% chance that all 600 people will die.

In this case, 78% chose option D (which is logically equivalent to option B), whereas only 22% chose option C, which is equivalent to option A. This experiment shows that depending on how questions are framed, people's choices can differ quite dramatically. If this is true in real life, we cannot help but raise serious questions about the effectiveness of rational choice approaches in public choice contexts. If people's choices or preferences are at least partly determined by the frame in which an issue is raised, then it may be impossible—or at best very difficult—to determine the rational choice for a society by basing that decision on the sum of individuals' preferences.

More empirical research is needed to determine how the framing effect may have influenced the processes of creating social consensus in the two Korean cases. However, it is reasonable to suspect that if people in the mad cow disease protest were asked about the risks of eating US beef or the benefits of importing US beef in different contexts or frames, their answers might have been very different from what was visible in the streets.

Spitzer, *Framing the Jury: Cognitive Perspective on Pain and Suffering Awards*, BEHAVIORAL LAW & ECONOMICS (Cass R. Sunstein ed.), Cambridge University Press, Chapter 10 (2000).

5) Hindsight Bias

Hindsight bias is the psychological inclination to think events that have already occurred as being more predictable than they were before they took place.[39] It can affect both risk measurement and risk policy. In evaluating a certain policy proposal related to risk, it is important to measure the probabilities of risky events. Because risks are all around us in many different shapes, and it is impossible to take precautionary measures against all those risks, we need to decide which risks should be dealt with first and which risks can be addressed later, if at all. In making that decision, it is crucial to consider the probability of each risk's occurrence.

However, if the probability of a given risk's occurrence is calculated differently before and after that risk materializes, there would be problems in reliably evaluating the soundness of a risk management policy. The Great East Japan Earthquake and the tsunami-driven Fukushima nuclear power plant accident in 2011 offer an example of hindsight bias. Before those events transpired, few people expected that such a powerful tsunami would hit the Fukushima area and allow seawater to pour into the power plant. The view of experts was that the height and strength and of the plant's walls' would be sufficient to protect it against whatever natural disaster might strike. However, once a tsunami strong enough to damage the plant occurred and caused the nuclear accident, many people—not only in Japan but also around the world—reacted strongly and blamed the Japanese government and the Tokyo Electric Power Company for not taking adequate precautions. In that situation, because people had already witnessed a nuclear accident, they tended to regard the probability of such an accident as greater than they did before it took place.

As we have seen above, hindsight bias is a real factor that can affect people's decision-making processes, which is another reason why classical rational choice theory cannot fully explain people's real-world behavior. For modern administrative law to be more sophisticated, it should be able to account for these kinds of newly researched topics.

39 For a more detailed academic explanation of hindsight bias, see Jeffrey J. Rachlinski, *A Positive Psychological Theory of Judging in Hindsight*, BEHAVIORAL LAW & ECONOMICS (Cass R. Sunstein ed.), Cambridge University Press, Chapter 3 (2000).

10. Administrative Law in the Age of Artificial Intelligence

Artificial intelligence (AI) technology is developing at a breathtaking pace and changing virtually every aspect of our lives. One of the most notable changes is that human decision making is being replaced by AI in many areas of life. This trend will affect government decision-making processes in a wide range of ways.

In traditional democratic administrations, government agencies try their best to establish the legitimacy of administrative decisions based on the will of the people as delegated to the legislature and, through that body, to administrative agencies. However, in the near future, government decision making will be based on big data and AI algorithms, whether or not that is beneficial for citizens. For example, government officials could try to defend illegal or inadequate decisions by asserting that they were relying on unverifiable datasets and algorithms.

There is not yet a clear solution to this issue, but these kinds of questions are sure to arise in the near future. Developing new logics and systems to cope with this kind of question is one of the most challenging tasks that administrative law must undertake in the years to come.

11. Conclusion

Compared to other democratically advanced countries, the Republic of Korea has a very short history of administrative law. Notwithstanding that limited experience, Korea has developed a highly sophisticated administrative law system, as I have summarized in this chapter.

Now that it has developed an administrative law regime that is nearly complete, Korea needs to turn its attention to the remaining tasks in that area. One is crafting a pragmatic and sophisticated legal doctrine to solve merit issues at trial. The other is preparing for radical changes in the future due to rapid technological developments like AI and new risks like climate change.

Chapter 9

Intellectual Property Law

Sang Jo Jong*

1. Introduction: Dramatic Changes and Their Implications

From a historical perspective, the intellectual property ("IP") system, one of the most brilliant European inventions, was first exported to America and then to Asia and other parts of the world. In the second half of the 20th century, Asian countries like Korea imported the Western concept of IP. In the 70 years since the founding of the Republic of Korea,[1] the role of IP laws has undergone dramatic changes. Until the mid-1980s, although IP laws existed, they were not widely used; indeed, they were often ignored. The number of patent applications was relatively small, and unauthorized copying was taken for granted.

In 1986, all the relevant statutes were amended to significantly strengthen the protection of IP. These amendments were made partly due to pressure from the Europe and the United States and partly due to domestic demands. During the course of trade negotiations in the mid-1980s, the United States and Europe insisted on stronger patent protection and on the protection of foreign copyright works in Korea. At the same time, Korea was experiencing so many labor disputes and such rapid wage increases that its economic structure shifted from labor- to technology-intensive

* Professor, Seoul National University School of Law.

1 Korea was subject to Japanese colonialism for most of the first half of the 20th century.

industries; thus, protecting IP became much more important.[2] Rapid economic developments in Korea[3] have caused substantial changes in both the country's general economic structure and the role of IP laws.

Since that protection was strengthened in the mid-1980s, awareness of IP among companies and individuals has increased, as have their IP activities. While only 10,587 patent applications were filed in 1985, 226,756 were filed in 2020, a more than 20-fold increase.[4] According to IP indicators for 2020, the number of patent applications filed in Korea ranks fourth in the world.[5] By contrast, utility model applications during the same period fell sharply from 18,548 to 4,981. In contrast to patent applications, the number of utility model applications decreased by approximately three quarters during the same period. These dramatic changes occurred because Korean companies and individual inventors increasingly recognized that the protection afforded by US-style patent law was more important than the protection of small inventions. The number of trademark applications also increased tenfold, from 26,069 to 257,933.[6]

As patent and trademark applications increased at a rapid pace, disputes and litigation related to them also grew. The Patent Court of Korea was established on March 1, 1998, to create more efficient and uniform trials in patent and trademark disputes. Although the court was modeled after the US Court of Appeals for the Federal Circuit, the patent validity rate in Korean courts did not increase the way it did in the United States. In calculating the amount of damages for patent infringements, Korean judges have taken a very strict attitude in accepting proof for damages and thus awarded relatively small amounts of damages. For example, while Apple was awarded US$539 million in a US patent case against Samsung, Apple and Samsung each claimed less than $100,000 in Korea[7] because both

2 Sang-Hyun Song and Seong-Ki Kim, *The Impact of Multilateral Trade Negotiations on Intellectual Property Laws in Korea*, 13 UCLA PACIFIC BASIN LAW JOURNAL 118 (1994).

3 The GDP per capita of Korea increased from US$158 in 1960 to US$2,834 in 1986, when intellectual property laws were amended at https://data.worldbank.org/indicator/NY.GDP.PCAP.CD?locations=KR.

4 Intellectual Property Statistics Service, Korea Intellectual Property Office: https://www.kipo.go.kr/en/HtmlApp?c=97000&catmenu=ek07_03_01.

5 World Intellectual Property Indicators 2021 at https://www.wipo.int/publications/en/details.jsp?id=4571&plang=EN.

6 https://www.kipo.go.kr/en/HtmlApp?c=97000&catmenu=ek07_03_01.

7 Seoul Central District Court Decisions 2011Gahap39552, August 24, 2012;

companies were aware that large amounts of compensation simply could not be awarded in that country.

It is a notable irony that, despite Korea strengthening its IP protection, illegal copying and counterfeit goods did not suffer a significant decline in prevalence. Some Western scholars have pointed out that the rampant infringements in Korea were due to its Confucian culture. Stealing a book was not regarded as a crime until the 19th century in the Chosun Dynasty, the predecessor of the Republic of Korea. Confucianism dominated the Chosun Dynasty, taught people to value knowledge and wisdom over property ownership, and encouraged them to share and spread knowledge and wisdom as widely as possible.

However, 21st-century infringements of intellectual property rights are completely different from Confucian practices. Given that property ownership has become well established in Korea, new ideas and creations are now all regarded as subject to property ownership. At the same time, young students have relatively limited resources to buy content or have difficulty gaining easy access to their favorite content on the internet. For the past three decades or so, infringements have declined considerably as average income has increased and more distribution channels developed in Korea.

What really matters in today's Korea is the civil law tradition that has largely replaced its former Confucian culture. Lawyers trained in civil law tend to be bound by statutory provisions. Accordingly, public prosecutors in Korea often prosecute young people who download small amounts of content, and judges are not especially troubled by punishing creative entrepreneurs whose product or service inadvertently violates patent. There is still no judicial precedent allowing for parodies or fair use of trademarks in Korea.

2011Gahap63647, August 24, 2012.

2. Patent

(1) Subject Matter

An invention is "a highly inventive creation of a technical idea using the laws of nature" under the Patent Act of Korea (Article 2(1)). Since patent law aims to contribute to industrial development by promoting technological innovations, the concept of invention is also crucial to realizing this goal. With the development of industrial technologies, the concept of an invention protected by patent law has been expanded. For example, the Statute of Monopolies, a modern form of patent law in the United Kingdom, started with inventions related to machines such as steam engines. Prior to the 1986 revision, the Korean Patent Act protected only inventions related to machines, manufactures, or methods; today, however, inventions related to chemical substances, genes, business methods, and medical uses are also protected.

New plant varieties can theoretically be protected by patent law. In reality, a breeder who has developed or cultivated a new plant variety is protected by a separate law called the Act on the Protection of New Varieties of Plants. The breeder applies for registration of his or her plant variety protection rights. If the new plant variety meets the four requirements of novelty, distinctiveness, uniformity, and stability, its breeder is granted a variety protection right through this registration process (The New Plant Variety Protection Act Article 16).

1) Gene Sequences

If information about a gene that exists in nature is simply discovered, it is not patentable. However, patentability may not be denied with respect to "genes artificially isolated and confirmed from living organisms and whose functions and usefulness have been revealed" (XXXXXX). The Korean Intellectual Property Office recognizes patentability when expressed sequence tags are artificially isolated and proved useful for diagnosing specific diseases.[8]

8 Patent Examination Guidelines (Korea Intellectual Property Office, 2021), p.234 at https://www.kipo.go.kr/upload/en/download/Patent_Examination_Guidelines_2021.pdf.

By contrast, in *Association for Molecular Pathology v. Myriad Genetics, Inc.*,[9] the US Supreme Court has ruled that a naturally occurring DNA segment is a product of nature and not eligible for a patent merely because it has been isolated. That court has also ruled that an artificially synthesized complementary DNA (cDNA) created by manipulating genes is eligible for a patent because it does not occur naturally. It remains to be seen whether the Korean Intellectual Property Office will continue to allow patent registration for gene fragments as gene isolation becomes more common and it becomes easier to use computers to compare them with other genes and confirm specific gene functions.

2) Medical Treatment

The question of whether a patentable subject matter includes inventions related to medical treatment by patent law is a difficult issue that requires striking a balance between incentives for technological innovations and the importance of public health. The Supreme Court of Korea has held that inventions of methods for operating on, treating, or diagnosing humans—that is, medical treatment—may not be eligible for patent registration.[10] In particular, according to the Patent Act, the effect of a patent right on an inventive method of mixing two or more drugs or an invention of a drug itself does not affect any prescription or preparation of a drug or drugs under the Pharmaceutical Affairs Act (Article 96). Finding a new use for a drug and applying it to a patient may also amount to a medical treatment, and a new medical use may also give a new effect to the drug by expressing the properties of the drug. If it falls under the invention of a product that can be made, an invention for medical use can also be protected as an invention of the product itself.[11] Likewise, the method of administration or delivery of a drug can be patented as a new pharmaceutical use of that drug. This is because the administration method and delivery of a drug are not the medical treatment itself but can rather be a component that gives a new character to the drug by expressing its advanced properties or efficacy.[12] If an administration method or delivery of a drug shows its advanced efficacy and use, it can be

9 569 U.S. 576 (2013).
10 Supreme Court Decision 90Hu250, March 12, 1991.
11 Supreme Court Decision 2006Hu3564, January 30, 2009.
12 Supreme Court Decision 2014Hu768, May 21, 2015.

protected as an invention of a product but still may not meet the requirement of patentability as an invention of a medical treatment or a method of using the drug. For example, in an American case, *Mayo v. Prometheus*,[13] the US Supreme Court ruled that the patent claims made about a method of giving a drug to a patient—measuring metabolites of that drug within the patient's blood and deciding whether to increase or decrease the dosage of the drug—were not patentable. In this case, the court ruled that the correlation between the level of metabolites and the efficacy of the drug is merely a "natural law" that is neither patentable nor to be monopolized.

3) Industrial Designs

Industrial designs are protected by several methods: design rights under the Design Protection Act, utility models under the Utility Model Act, copyright under the Copyright Act (CA), and tort liability under the Unfair Competition Prevention and Trade Secret Protection Act (UCPA).

Unlike in the United States, where designs are eligible for patent registration, design registration is available for new designs under Korea's Design Protection Act, which is separate from its Patent Act. The Design Protection Act grants the design right to the person who creates a design. Creators who apply for a design registration and are granted a design right have the exclusive right to use the registered design, or any similar design, commercially for 20 years after the date of application (Design Protection Act Articles 91, 92). The Korean Design Protection Act has a similar structure to the Patent Act in terms of registration requirements, examination, effect and duration of rights, and invalidation trials. Since there were more than 50 lawsuits between Samsung and Apple in 10 jurisdictions,[14] Korea realized the importance of design patents in the United States and design rights in Korea and has accordingly amended its Design Protection Act several times. A design under the law means "a shape, pattern, color, or a combination thereof of an article (including parts of an article and fonts), which invokes a sense of aesthetics through visual perception."[15] While an article usually means movable property, during the course of amendments to the law, its

13 Mayo Collaborative Services v. Prometheus Laboratories, 566 U.S. 66 (2012).

14 Samsung Elecs. Co., Ltd. v. Apple Inc., 137 S. Ct. 429 (2016); Seoul Central District Court Decision 2011Gahap39552, August 24, 2012.

15 Design Protection Act Article 2.

concept has expanded to include "part of the article" in 2001, "fonts" in 2004, and "a virtual device" in 2021. A virtual device—a newly adopted concept of an article—means a figure or symbol that is expressed by digital technology or electronic method and used for operation of a machine or to perform a specific function.[16]

In the past, a design for a virtual device meant the design of icons and the like displayed on the liquid crystal screen of devices like mobile phones. Under the amended act, a design for a virtual device expressed either in the air or on the ground may be totally separated from physical objects or movable property. The expansion of the concept of design to include a design for a virtual device was largely a response to the development of technologies related to augmented reality and virtual reality. The right to a design for a virtual device allows the holder to prohibit any copying, use, or transmission of the design and the transfer, rental, import, or export of any media storing the design.

Unlike ornamental designs, utility designs—those without any aesthetic value—may also be protected under the Utility Model Act of Korea. While that law began by protecting utility designs, the current act covers a much broader concept of utility models that encompasses technical ideas using natural laws regarding the shape or structure of an article or combination of articles. Since technical ideas using natural laws are also entitled to patent protection, the current Utility Model Act has several similarities with the Patent Act.

The utility model system is viewed as a second patent system that protects small inventions quickly and efficiently. For example, an abstract type of technical idea like an electric circuit may be protected as a utility model by considering the structure of the article. In addition, if a visually identical article can perform a new function through its physical or chemical properties, it is construed as falling under a utility model related to the structural characteristics of that article. For example, a magnetic razor blade may not look different from a non-magnetic blade but may still embody a technical idea worthy of utility model registration.

However, in a utility model, manufacturing methods are not subject to utility model protection because the technical idea must be embodied

16 Design Protection Act Article 2.

in the shape or structure of an article or combination of articles. While utility model registration is very similar to patent registration in that the requirement of an inventive step or non-obviousness is required for successful registration, the inventive step involved is relatively modest. If a person having ordinary skill in the art (PHOSITA) to which the utility model belongs can devise a utility model extremely easily based on prior art, that model may not be registered.[17] However, it is difficult to provide a clear theoretical or practical explanation of how and to what extent the degree of the inventive step of a utility model is lower than that of a patented invention.

Compared to patents, utility model rights have limited duration because registration requirements such as an inventive step are more relaxed. While a patent right lasts from the date of patent registration until 20 years after the filing date, the utility model right lasts just for 10 years after the filing date (Article 22).

In addition to registered design rights and utility models, copyright protection is also available for some industrial designs, but only when the design can be distinguished and is separable from the article used.[18] In the specific case of typeface designs, court decisions are very confusing. The Supreme Court once held that it was difficult to recognize typeface copyrightability on the grounds that the aesthetic elements and originality of typeface designs were neither separable from nor independent of the original function of the typefaces themselves and that typeface designs thus could not be protected under copyright.[19] In particular, the Supreme Court is concerned that, if protection under the Design Protection Act and the CA overlaps with respect to industrial designs, the policy goal of the Design Protection Act could be severely harmed. On the other hand, the Supreme Court later ruled that a font program was protected as a program work because it was designed to direct the computer to produce a typeface design on a computer screen or printed page.[20]

17 Utility Model Act Article 4(2).
18 Supreme Court Decision 2003Do7572, July 22, 2004.
19 Supreme Court Decision 94Nu5632, August 23, 1996.
20 Supreme Court Decisions 98Do732, May 15, 2001; 99Da23246, June 29, 2001.

(2) Patent Registration

1) Requirements for Registration

Patent rights are granted by registration, which requires novelty and an inventive step. If an invention exactly overlaps a single prior art, the invention is regarded as lacking novelty. When an invention is novel, the next question would be about its inventive step: whether a PHOSITA to which the invention pertains could have easily made the invention. When comparing a filed invention to a prior art, if the PHOSITA finds difficulty in making its structure of the invention elements as a whole, remarkability in its effect, and uniqueness in its purpose, the inventive step requirement is satisfied.[21]

2) Invalidation of Registration

The elements of an inventive step are central to both infringement and invalidation actions, which are separated in a two-tier system in Korea. While infringement actions are brought to judicial courts, invalidation actions first must go through the Intellectual Property Tribunal. The Patent Act of Korea only negates the effects of a patent right through a patent invalidation trial at the Intellectual Property Tribunal. An appeal against the trial decision of the tribunal can be filed with the Patent Court of Korea; since that is a court of appeals, it takes appeals not only from the Intellectual Property Tribunal but also from judicial courts on patent infringement.

The two-tier system has often led to time-consuming and expensive dispute resolution processes.[22] Thus, the courts have allowed the "publicly known or worked invention" defense—in which a defendant argues that the allegedly infringing product derives from a publicly known or worked invention—to prove that their invention does not fall under the scope of the plaintiff's patent rights.[23]

Even before a patent invalidity trial is finalized, the court may determine whether an invalidating factor clearly exists, and filing a motion seeking an injunction or damages when a patent right is clearly invalid is

21 Supreme Court Decision 2019Hu10609, April 8, 2021.
22 Supreme Court Decision 99Hu2150, April 12, 2002.
23 Supreme Court Decision 2002Hu2037, April 27, 2004.

construed as an abuse of rights.[24] Based on the same theoretical background in a recent case relating to a printer's photo-sensitive drum, the Seoul High Court dismissed claims for injunction and damages given that when the patent or invention in question is clearly invalid due to its lack of an inventive step, requesting an injunction and damages is an abuse of rights.[25]

(3) Remedies

1) Injunctions

A patentee may bring a lawsuit in court to seek an injunction against infringement of his or her patent rights. Whereas injunctions are an equitable remedy in the United States, injunctions are automatically granted by courts in Korea when patent infringements have been found. As an exception to the remedy, the court may reject injunction motions when the patentee is found to have abused his or her patent rights. For example, when a patented invention clearly lacks novelty or an inventive step, the courts can find a patentee bringing a lawsuit to seek an injunction to be abusing his or her patent right and thus deny injunctive relief.

There has been a question as to whether a motion for injunction against infringement by the holder of a standard essential patent (SEP) is an abuse of the patent right. In 2012, a lower court decision recognized the theoretical possibility that a patentee's exercise of the right to injunctive relief in certain cases despite the fair, reasonable, and non-discriminatory (FRAND) commitment could constitute an abuse of the patent right. In the patent litigation between Samsung and Apple, the Seoul Central District Court deviated from the purpose or function of the standard patent system by filing a patent infringement request without sincere negotiation for a license in spite of the FRAND commitment by the patentee holding the SEP. If it is recognized that there is no valid legal protection, such as disturbing a fair competition and trading order and violating the principle of good faith in the relationship with the consumer or other party, the exercise of the patent right took the form of exercise of the right.[26] However, it was eventually held that there was no actual evidence for an abuse of the rights related to

24 Supreme Court Decision 2000Da69194, October 28, 2004.
25 Seoul High Court Decision 2003Na8802, January 25, 2005.
26 Seoul Central District Court Decision 2011Gahap39552, August 24, 2012.

the SEP in the Samsung–Apple dispute. Given the specific facts relating to the negotiations between the two firms, it was held that Samsung's actions did not deviate from the purpose or function of the standard patent system and that it did not violate the principle of good faith negotiation with the other party for FRAND licenses. Although the court rejected an injunction motion in *Samsung v. Apple*, the court acknowledged a theoretical possibility that, in the case of a SEP with a FRAND commitment to a standardization organization, the exercise of patent rights such as injunctions may be restricted in light of the policy goal of the patent law and SEPs. As the Supreme Court of Korea has not yet made a decision on this matter, it is difficult to tell whether the patent abuse theory will be extended to a breach of FRAND commitment and, in particular, whether there will be a major change in granting injunctions due to the FRAND commitment.

2) Damages

The Patent Act suggests several methods of calculating damages: "damage based on the amount of sales," "damage based on the infringer's profit," "damage equivalent to royalties," "amount of damage subject to the discretion of the court," and so on (The Patent Act Article 128). However, judicial decisions made by the court of first instance indicate that the plaintiff claimed "damage based on the infringer's profit" in 66% of cases and, unlike in the United States, only 12.9% claimed "damage equivalent to the royalties." Despite the plaintiff's preference for "amount of damage based on the infringer's profit," the largest proportion (61.3%) of judicial decisions were made on the basis of the "amount of damage subject to the discretion of the court."[27] In relying on its discretion to calculate the amount of damages, courts have to take into account the infringer's sales, the infringer's profit, reasonable royalties, and any other available factors. The court's preference for its discretion method is understood as a heuristic judgment that recognizes the most appropriate level of damages.

The amount of damages not only becomes an important variable in the

27 Jisun Choi, *Statistical Analysis and its Implications on the Relative Rate of Utilization of Influencing Factors for Each Provision of Article 128 of the Patent Act When Calculating the Amount of Damages for Patent Infringement* (특허침해 손해액 산정시 특허법 제128조의 조항별 활용도, 인용규모 및 영향요인 간 관계에 관한 통계분석과 시사), 13(2) REVIEW OF LAW AND ECONOMICS (법경제학연구) 248 (2016) (in Korean).

value of patent rights but also significantly affects technological innovation in the long run. The level of damages awarded in courts of Korea is so low that there concerns have been expressed that Korean patent rights may be undervalued. On the other hand, it is a general trend in foreign case law that the amount of damage awarded to the SEP holder is called a 'FRAND royalty,' which is much lower than the normal reasonable royalty. Given the fact that SEP rights are often licensed under FRAND conditions by multiple licensees, we will have to wait to see how Korean judges rely on their discretion in calculating appropriate damages amounts for SEPs.

3. Copyright

(1) Dramatic Changes in the Copyright Act

Artists rely on freedom of expression and copyright for their works. However, just as the Constitution of the Republic of Korea did not literally give artists freedom by itself, its copyright statute did not fully guarantee artists a copyright. Thus, Korean artists, who achieved artistic freedom through protests and litigation in the early 1990s, may have to fight again in the 21st century to secure copyright law.

Looking back over the past 60 years of Korean copyright law history, copyright statutes have been amended several times to strengthen copyright protection. While the cultural industry has benefited from these enhancements, the status of average authors has become relatively weaker. While the first CA of Korea was enacted in 1957, copyrights were of no use to authors amid postwar ruin.[28] In the 1960s and 1970s, recording and purchasing records was a luxury to Koreans. In the mid-1980s, as Korea's trade surplus increased dramatically, there was increasing trade pressure from Europe and the United States to protect foreign copyrights in Korea. In response to this foreign push to protect copyright, several cultural organizations, including the Korean Publishers Association, took to the streets and set fire to books to protest against copyright protection of foreign

28 The Korean War, which started on June 25, 1950, and ended on July 27, 1953, was among the most destructive conflicts of the modern era: more than three million people died, and all of Korea's major cities and industrial facilities were ravaged.

works.[29] When the entire CA was amended to protect authors and artists in 1986,[30] there was widespread concern that American music and Japanese cartoons would flood the country.

As Korea's international trade increased, the CA was frequently revised beginning in the mid-1990s, with most amendments directed toward expansion of copyright scope and term. For example, in order to prevent the distribution of unauthorized record albums, the CA as amended in 1994 granted the copyright holder a new right to lend albums for sale for commercial purposes.[31] A 1995 amendment made it clear that, even in the case of copyrighted works published or commercialized before the effective date of the relevant treaty, the rights of foreign authors were retroactively protected.[32] With the rapid development of internet technology, the CA as amended in 2000 added a new right—the "transmission right"—to the list of available copyrights,[33] and the CA as amended in 2003 granted a certain range of rights to database producers to extend some protection even to uncopyrightable compilation of data.[34] In order to strengthen the protection of artists on the internet, a 2004 amendment granted singers, other performers, and record producers the right to transmit their performances and records.[35] In 2006, the CA was amended to grant singers and other performers the right to the attribution and integrity of their performances.[36] Finally, in response to developments in free trade agreements with Europe and the United States, the CA was amended in 2011 to extend the term of copyright from 50 years after the author's death to 70 years after the author's death.[37]

29 *1986*, NamuWiki at https://namu.wiki/w/1986%EB%85%84 (last visited January 11, 2021).

30 Copyright Act of 1986 [1986년 저작권법] Article 9.

31 Copyright Act of 1986 [1986년 저작권법], as amended by Act No. 4917, January 7, 1994.

32 *Id.*, as amended by Act No. 5015, December 6, 1995.

33 *Id.*, as amended by Act No. 6134, January 12, 2000.

34 *Id.*, as amended by Act No. 6881, May 27, 2003. This is a legislative response to the gap in copyright protection for compilation of data which was shown in the US decision, Feist Publications, Inc., v. Rural Telephone Service Co., 499 U.S. 340 (1991).

35 *Id.*, as amended by Act No. 7233, October 16, 2004.

36 Copyright Act, amended by Act No. 15823, October 16, 2018, translated in Korea Legislation Research Institute's online database at https://elaw.klri.re.kr/eng_service/main.do.

37 *Id.*, as amended by Act No. 10807, June 30, 2011.

While the copyright granted to authors was strengthened and its term extended under the CA, the status of authors and artists did not improve in reality. Although strengthening of copyright has enabled the cultural industry to reap more profits, most authors and artists are now in a relatively weaker position, and there is a poorer environment for creative activities. The energy and passion needed for creation come from the artists, but the profits generated from their efforts are often taken by corporate entities like entertainment companies. Since most authors and artists are of limited financial means and have difficulties in obtaining legal help, they are often excluded from a fair distribution of profits in their contracts.[38]

(2) Moral v. Economic Rights

1) Moral Rights

Modeled after the French dualist theory, the CA of Korea not only splits copyright into moral and economic elements but also treats the two totally differently. Moral rights in Korea include an author's right to make his or her works public, the right of paternity, and the right of integrity (Articles 11 to 13). Unlike French law, however, Korea's CA does not provide enough special rules for the protection of authors in case of copyright assignment and licensing. Since there is no substantial amount of limit on copyright assignment or licensing, the moral rights of authors turn out to be empty in reality.

The moral rights accorded to authors remain with the author and are thus inalienable (CA Article 14). Even after copyright, authors can still claim their moral rights. As is the case with motion pictures, even if all or part of a copyright is transferred by contract or statute, the author may still prevent anybody, including the copyright transferee, from making any changes to the copyrighted work on the basis of the right of integrity, one of an author's moral rights. Authors and artists often realize the weakness of their status when the transfer includes their right to make derivative works.

2) Economic Rights

Economic rights give the copyright owner the opportunity to make

38 Ministry of Culture, Sports, and Tourism, *Survey on the Actual Condition of Artists* 86 (2006).

commercial gains from the exploitation of his or her work. Copyright owners are entitled to a bundle of economic rights: rights to reproduction, public performance, public transmission, exhibition, distribution, rental, and production of derivative work (Articles 16 to 22). Each of the different categories of economic rights may be subdivided, owned, and enforced separately and is independent and capable of being separately infringed.

Reproduction refers to the fixation of the works or the reproduction of works in tangible media of expression by means of printing, photocopying, copying, sound or visual recording, or other means. The right to reproduction is an author's most traditional and fundamental right.[39] As digital technologies have evolved, however, the concept of reproduction has changed to accommodate temporary reproduction like copies in a computer's random access memory (RAM). Accordingly, making temporary copies in RAM without authorization of the copyright owner may qualify as copyright infringement, albeit with some exceptions; for example, digital copies may be temporarily reproduced during the course of computer processing to the extent deemed necessary for efficient usage in a computer (CA Article 35-2).

Distribution refers to renting or transferring the original or copies of a copyrighted work in a tangible form to the public. Since distribution in tangible form under the CA is different from public transmission in digital form by wired or wireless communication, the concept of distribution in Korea is defined much more narrowly than in the United States. The right of distribution of a copyrighted work in tangible form is usually subject to the doctrine of exhaustion or the first sale doctrine, meaning that the right to distribution is exhausted after selling an original or copy of a copyrighted work in tangible form; thus, the buyer has the right to dispose of the original or copy without needing any further permission by the copyright owner (CA Article 20). It is understood, however, that the first sale doctrine is not applicable to the right of public transmission. There is a further exception to the first sale doctrine: copyright owners, performers, and phonogram producers are granted a right to rental of their phonograms and computer programs regardless of the first sale doctrine (CA Article 21). The right to

39 An Act for the Encouragement of Learning, by Vesting the Copies of Printed Books in the Authors or Purchasers of such Copies, during the Times therein mentioned, 8 Anne, ch. 19 (1710).

rental was introduced to reflect technological advancements that made it easy and inexpensive for rental shops and consumers to copy phonograms and computer programs.

The right to public performance includes not only live performances such as a play in a theatre or an orchestral performance in a concert hall but also performances by means of sound recording or phonogram played over amplifying equipment at public places like nightclubs, hotels, and so on. As technology develops in the field of wired and wireless transmission, it is becoming increasingly difficult and complex to distinguish the rights of public performance from those of public transmission.

3) Neighboring Rights

Neighboring rights are granted by the CA of Korea to performers, phonogram producers, and broadcasters who make creative contributions or investments to bring the intellectual creations of others to the public in the form of performances, phonograms, and broadcasts. Performers, phonogram producers, and broadcasters may or may not make creative works that satisfy the originality requirement under the CA. Performers, phonogram producers, and broadcasters are granted certain exclusive rights and remuneration rights no matter regardless of whether their works are original. Their rights are called "neighboring rights" because they include the right of reproduction and some other exclusive rights which are similar to—but not identical with—the author's economic rights. In addition to economic rights, performers are granted moral rights such as the right of paternity and integrity.

(3) Copyright Contracts

While moral rights are inalienable, economic rights may be transferred to others. In extreme cases of copyright assignments, authors or artists can be unfairly excluded from profit distribution. Approximately 30 years ago, the then-unknown composer and singer Y.P. Cho signed a record production contract with Earth Records for 31 songs and unwittingly assigned all his rights to reproduction and distribution to the record company. His songs were an enormous success, and Earth Records has reaped vast profits over the past 30 years. Unfortunately, due to his contract with the record company, Y.P. Cho could not share in those profits. No matter how successful a song was, the contract between the artist and the record company, made 30 years ago, did not allow Y.P. Cho any share of the profits.[40]

Copyright assignments are often exploited not only by record companies but also by book publishers. Since large book publishers have much more bargaining power than authors, designers, and other artists, they can easily be tempted to impose contractual terms that are unfair to those parties. For example, when a picture book for children entitled *Cloud Bread* was successful, with total sales exceeding US$400 million, the book's publisher pointed to the contractual terms assigning all rights from Baek, the designer–author, to the company. Before the book's commercial success, the company paid Baek US$7,000 plus US$9,000.[41] Baek won the 2020 Astrid Lindgren Memorial Award for *Cloud Bread*, which is the sector's equivalent to an Academy Award. When the author brought a lawsuit, however, the Seoul High Court held that given the business risk relating to marketing an unknown author's work, contractual assignment of all rights for future works need not be regarded as either invalid or unfair.[42]

The harm caused by assignment contracts may be more devastating to artists in the case of long-term contracts. Unlike in the United States, most entertainment agencies in Korea play the roles of both agents and managers, often conclude long-term contracts with artists, and exploit their rights of publicity and copyright.[43] Whereas agents and managers in the United States treat artists as clients, Korean entertainment companies consider celebrities to be assets.[44] Celebrities are the most important assets for entertainment companies because the companies make upfront investments to select and train artists and earn profits through their exclusive use of the artists'

40 *Recovering the rights of Cho Yong-pil*, Herald Economy (February 13, 2014) (in Korean) at http://news.heraldcorp.com/view.php?ud=20140213000342&md=20140216004546_BL.

41 *Hwang Bo-Ram and Pai Jae-Jeong's copyright law amendment to the 'Cloud Bread Protection Act'*, JOONGANG ILBO (May 8, 2015) at https://news.joins.com/article/17708494.

42 Seoul High Court Decision 2019Na2007820, January 21, 2020.

43 Boeun Jang, *A Study on Exclusive Contracts for Entertainers* (연예인 전속계약에 관한 연구), 84 JOURNAL OF CIVIL LAW STUDIES (민사법학) 69-82 (2018) (in Korean).

44 Choi Hyun-sook, *A Review on the Typographicalization of Exclusive Management Contracts According to the Legal Character* (전속매니지먼트계약의 법적 성격에 따른 유형화에 관한 소고), 34 THE JOURNAL OF PROPERTY LAW (재산법연구) 227 (2018) (in Korean).

rights. Therefore, most of the exclusive management contracts signed with a trainee or artist stipulate that the copyright for songs and videos produced and recorded by the trainee or artist during the contract period belongs in its entirety to the company. In addition, the company typically receives the right to use the artist's name, stage name, signature, and publicity. Therefore, the company is not an agent of the artist but can exercise the copyright by itself and exploit the artist's publicity rights while distributing a certain percentage of the profits to the artist.

Complaints grew among member artists of one of the largest entertainment agencies, SM Entertainment, when long-term exclusive contracts restricted their freedom despite their soaring popularity. Since SM initially invested a great deal of time and money in auditioning, training, and marketing new celebrities, it argued that it was necessary to set the term of the exclusive contract to 10 years or more to recover the investment and prevent free riding from competitors. However, in a lawsuit filed by an SM member artist claiming the invalidity of the exclusive contract, the court found that SM used its dominant position to place an excessive burden on the artist, who was involved in too many entertainment activities, and made it difficult even to terminate a contract because doing so would incur an excessive penalty. The court held that the contract so excessively restricted the artist's economic freedom that it was invalid.[45]

(4) Artists and Consumers

1) Internet Connecting Artists with Consumers

With the development of the internet, there are many opportunities for artists to communicate directly with consumers. In the distribution of music, the role of record companies has decreased substantially. Music-producing artists can connect directly with fans who consume their music without any involvement by a record company. It is extremely difficult for Korean artists to be recognized by major US record companies and release records on the world stage. At the same time, 'Gangnam Style' received over two billion views on YouTube eight years ago without the help of an American record company, creating a considerable fandom around the world with its horse

45 Seoul Central District Court Order 2009Kahap2869, October 27, 2009.

dance.[46]

Fans in the internet era are not simply consumers of music but can actively support artists—and sometimes make trouble—through a number of internet activities. Behind the success of BTS, the wildly popular Korean boy band, lies the passionate support of its fans, called "ARMY."[47] ARMY helped BTS win a Billboard award with 300 million online votes, surprisingly ending a six-year winning streak by Justin Bieber.[48] The 40 million members of ARMY are so active that they are heavily involved in developing their own platforms like Weverse.[49]

With numerous websites and social networks around the world, fans spend hours posting content, sending messages, and sharing their devotion to their celebrity heroes. While most of their activities on the internet may help artists, some may not. During the course of their online activities, fans often use all or part of copyrighted or trademarked work of their heroes. What happens if there are copyright infringements by fans? What is the best approach for artists to take about such possible copyright infringement?

2) Fan-generated Content

Fans in the internet age are 'prosumers' in the sense that they consume content and produce something new at the same time. Fans who have been inspired by songs, films, or novels make their own creative products and sell them through online marketplaces like Etsy.[50] Authors and artists may be happy with fan-generated content or products. Sometimes, however, they are not, especially when the content or products seriously infringe on copyrighted or trademarked work.

46 Sookeung Jung and Hongmei Li, *Global Production, Circulation, and Consumption of Gangnam Style*, 8 INTERNATIONAL JOURNAL OF COMMUNICATION 2790 (2014).

47 ARMY (or A.R.M.Y.) is BTS's official fandom name; it stands for "Adorable Representative M.C. for Youth" and carries a significant meaning. BTS Wiki, ARMY, FANDOM at https://bts.fandom.com/wiki/ARMY (last visited January 11, 2021).

48 Kat Moon, *Inside the BTS ARMY, the Devoted Fandom With an Unrivaled Level of Organization*, Time (November 18, 2020) at https://time.com/5912998/bts-army.

49 Weverse is a web platform hosting a variety of free and subscription content and artist-to-fan and fan-to-fan communications. WEVERSE at https://www.weverse.io/ (last visited January 11, 2010).

50 Madhavi Sunder, *When Fandom Clashes with IP Law*, HARVARD BUSINESS REVIEW (July 23, 2019) at https://hbr.org/2019/07/when-fandom-clashes-with-ip-law.

In 2009, an internet user named Yang uploaded user-generated content in the form of a video file, in which his five-year-old daughter was dancing on a chair and singing the copyrighted song 'Must Have Been Crazy.'[51] The video, which included the chorus of the song lyrics, was uploaded to his internet blog on one of Korea's most popular internet portals.[52] The copyright owner of the song sent a takedown notice to the internet service provider, which immediately removed the video file. Yang asked the internet service provider to repost the video, but his efforts were in vain. Yang was able to get his video back on the internet only when a court held that his video made use of a small quantity of the song for a non-commercial purpose, meaning it fell into the category of fair use.[53] The challenges Yang faced are just one example of the potential disputes that could have a chilling effect on fans' passion and supportive activities.

The episode involving Yang shows that copyright law and policy must change. Korea's current copyright law is entirely in favor of the copyright owner and disregards both authors and internet users. While there is a notice-and-takedown procedure for the benefit of the copyright owner, it is extremely difficult for an internet user to repost his or her own video once it is taken down. Even from the perspective of the copyright holder, it is questionable whether it is desirable to delete all user-generated content on the internet on the grounds of copyright infringement. Content, including parodies, created by fans promote artists on the internet, and excessive copyright enforcement could cause a fan backlash. That is why the copyright holder of 'Gangnam Style' did not request the deletion of any fan-created content on YouTube. As a result of widespread fan-generated videos, 'Gangnam Style' had become the most watched video on YouTube. A copyright holder's wise application of copyright can make both artists and fans happy. Behind the choice of a wise approach by copyright holders, internet service providers like YouTube must adopt and implement flexible copyright policies.

51 The facts are quite similar to an American episode in Lenz v. Universal Music Corp., 572 Federal Supplement 2d, 1150 (N.D. Cal. 2008).

52 The video lasts approximately 53 seconds; the URL of the video file on the plaintiff's blog is http://blog.naver.com/yang456/140062293006.

53 Seoul High Court Decision 2010Na35260, October 13, 2010.

3) Copyright Trolls Threatening Consumers

As internet users shared contents like music or images and downloaded them without permission at the beginning of the 21st century, copyright holders increasingly filed copyright infringement lawsuits against both users and internet service providers. Copyright infringement lawsuits against internet users led to a serious problem: turning fans into enemies through copyright enforcement.[54]

In addition, notorious copyright trolls have harmed the general awareness of copyright in Korea; they are also one reason why a consumer backlash against copyright protection in Korea persists. When consumers download music, images, or photos without permission or upload their own content, it is often unclear whether copyright has been infringed or the action is legitimate fair use. Without regard to whether an unauthorized download or upload is copyright infringement, a lawyer representing the copyright holder often asks for an excessive settlement as compensation for allegedly unauthorized internet activity.

The Korean CA defines all copyright infringement as a crime, regardless of amount (Article 136).[55] If consumers, especially young students, are threatened with criminal charges if they do not pay settlement money for unauthorized downloads or uploads, then their parents are usually forced to pay excessive settlements to protect their children. It is this threat of criminal punishment that makes copyright trolls so active in Korea. Because they can make a lot of money by threatening young students, the perception of copyright is deteriorating among music fans and cultural consumers.[56]

Criminal punishment for copyright infringement undermines not only the creativity of artists and their fans but also the innovative activities of internet companies. This is because individuals and companies have to invest time and capital to try to avoid creation or innovation that might

54 Racquel C. Callender, *Harmonizing Interests on the Internet: Online Users and the Music Industry*, 48 Howard Law Journal 787, 812 (2005); Stacey M. Lantagne, *The Morality of MP3s: The Failure of the Recording Industry's Plan of Attack*, 18 HARVARD JOURNAL OF LAW & TECHNOLOGY 269 (2004).

55 Translated at the Korea Legislation Research Institute's online database at https://elaw.klri.re.kr/eng_service/main.do (search required).

56 Daehee Lee, *A Study Analysing the Copyright Environment Through Big Data Analysis and Recommendations for Improving Policy and the Legal System* (빅데이터 분석을 통한 저작권 환경 분석과 정책 및 법제도 개선 제언에 관한 연구), Research Paper, Korea Copyright Commission (한국저작권위원회) 162 (2016) (in Korean).

be regarded as constituting copyright infringement. In the first decade of the 21st century, the operator of Soribada, who succeeded in developing a website for its members to share MP3 files, was held liable not only for damages but also for criminal penalties for aiding copyright infringement.[57] By contrast, the operator of the American company Napster, which provided the same internet service as Soribada, was not subject to criminal penalties.

4. Trademark

(1) Registered Marks

According to the Trademark Act, a trademark is "a mark used to distinguish one's own product from another's product." Here, mark means "all marks used to indicate the origin of goods, such as signs, characters, figures, sounds, smells, three-dimensional shapes, holograms, movements, or colors, regardless of their composition or expression method" (Article 2). With the revision of the Trademark Act, the concept of a trademark has been expanded, and colors, sounds, and smells can now be protected as independent trademarks. Trademarks also include three- and two-dimensional marks. In addition, the Supreme Court recognized location trademarks as eligible for registration when a combination of symbols, characters, or figures forms a certain shape, the location of which makes the designated goods distinguishable from other goods.[58]

In order to register a trademark under the Trademark Act, it is necessary to actually use the trademark or intend to use it in the future (Article 3). However, since the intention to use a trademark is internal to the holder's mind, it can be difficult to examine the intention to use a trademark at the registration stage. In reality, there are many cases where trademarks are registered without any serious intention to use them. To respond to these expedient registrations, the Trademark Act provides for cancellation of trademark registration by a trial for revocation for trademarks that have not been used for more than three years (Article 119(1)(iii)).

57 Supreme Court Decisions 2005Do872, December 14, 2017; 2005Da11626, January 25, 2007.

58 Supreme Court Decision 2010Hu2339, December 20, 2012.

The Trademark Act does not require the applicant to be using the trademark at the time of filing an application for registration. It is sufficient to have the intention to use the trademark as a condition for registration of a trademark. However, in order for a descriptive mark or geographical name to be effectively registered as a trademark, the secondary meaning as an indication of source, needs to be remarkably recognized among consumers by the use of the mark or name. Therefore, in the case of a descriptive mark or a geographical name, actual use *is* required for registration (Article 33(2)).

(2) Well-known Marks

Under the Trademark Act, trademark rights arise only when a trademark is registered. Accordingly, no matter how well known a trademark may be, it cannot be protected under the Trademark Act unless it is registered. On the other hand, well-known marks can be protected under the UCPA, regardless of whether the trademark is registered. A business activity that confuses the source of a product or business by using a well-known mark commits an act of unfair competition under the UCPA (Article 2(i)(a),(b)). Confusion of sources in the UCPA often overlaps with trademark infringement in the Trademark Act. The UCPA also protects trade names, characters, and domain names if they fall under the well-known source indication. However, no matter how well known a character is, unlike protection under the CA, protection under the UCPA emphasizes use as a source indication. In a case of selling toys with well-known characters from a famous cartoon, the Supreme Court of Korea ruled that it was not enough for a character to be widely known in Korea for protection to be granted. The Court required the character to be recognized as a source of the toys to consumers through continuous publicity, advertisement, and quality control.[59]

The UCPA protects well-known marks regardless of whether the trademark is registered. A well-known mark is defined as one that is objectively widely known in terms of period of use, method, type, amount of use, scope of transaction, and so on. The brand's publicity means that it is widely recognized by domestic consumers, but it does not require that it be known to everyone throughout the country. It is sufficient to be known

59 Supreme Court Decision 2005Do70, April 29, 2005.

among consumers or business entities within a certain area of the country. There may also be protection from anti-competition laws.[60]

Under the Trademark Act, if a trademark identical with or similar to a registered trademark is used on goods identical with or similar to the designated goods without permission, an infringement of trademark rights has occurred. On the other hand, unfair competition due to the unauthorized use of well-known marks takes place only when there is confusion as to source among consumers. In determining unfair competition due to consumer confusion about sources, the courts often look to consumers' knowledge of the mark, the degree of the mark's distinctiveness, the degree of similarity between the well-known mark and the allegedly infringing mark, the existence of a competitive relationship due to overlapping consumer groups, malicious intent, and so on.[61] It is common for source confusion to occur at the time of sale. Sometimes, "initial interest confusion" or "post-sale confusion" lead to unfair competition.[62]

(3) Unfair Competition

As the demand to strengthen the protection of well-known trademarks increased both in Korea and abroad, the amendment of the UCPA in 2001 made trademark dilution an act of unfair competition.[63] In other words, even if there is no source confusion due to unauthorized use of a well-known mark, a person or entity that blurs its distinctiveness or tarnishes its reputation is liable for unfair competition. The prohibition of dilution is not designed to prevent source confusion or to protect consumers but to protect the property value of the well-known mark itself.

The UCPA stipulates an exception to dilution: unauthorized use of a well-known mark for non-commercial purposes or for other justifiable reasons is not an act of unfair competition. For example, there is a justifiable reason for unauthorized use when a well-known mark is used for news reporting or when the use is not contrary to fair trade practices. This

60 Supreme Court Decisions 2000Da4487, April 10, 2001; 2011Do10469, April 26, 2012.

61 Supreme Court Decision 2011Da64102, May 9, 2013.

62 Supreme Court Decision 2014Da24440, January 28, 2016.

63 The UCPA was amended by Law No. 6421 on February 3, 2001.

exception to dilution appears to be equivalent to the fair use exception in the United States. When a parody of a well-known mark conforms to fair trade practices, it does not constitute an act of unfair competition in Korea. There has as yet been no case where the parody of a well-known mark was allowed as an exception to dilution in Korea.[64]

In addition to well-known marks, the UCPA protects trade secrets and new ideas. A person who causes losses to or inflicts injuries on another person by an unlawful act, whether intentionally or negligently, shall be bound to make compensation for damages arising therefrom under the Civil Code (Article 750). However, what is unlawful or illegal is unclear in a rapidly changing market. The UCPA is designed to make it explicit that taking another party's trade secret is unlawful and subject to liability. Furthermore, the UCPA added the act of free-riding on the ideas of others as an act of unfair competition.[65] In other words, the act of infringing on the economic interests of others by the unauthorized use of the results of other people's significant investments or efforts for one's own business in a way that contravenes fair trade practices or a competitive order is an act of unfair competition. Recently, the UCPA was amended again to add another category of unfair competition: the act of acquiring an idea with economic value through trade consultation, bidding, or competition and commercializing it without any compensation to obtain enormous economic profit is also an act of unfair competition.[66] This recent addition is designed to protect SMEs and venture companies that actively provide their own valuable ideas to large established companies during the course of negotiations or consultations.

There have been several cases where remedies have been granted against unfair business practices like free-riding. For example, when a defendant game company was alleged to have imitated certain game rules of the plaintiff's game, the Seoul Central District Court upheld the plaintiff's unfair competition claim.[67] The court found that during the course of developing its own unique set of game rules, the plaintiff had

64 Seoul Central District Court Decision 2016Gahap36473, October 4, 2018.

65 The UCPA was amended by Law No. 11963 on July 30, 2013.

66 The UCPA was amended by Law No. 15580 on April 17, 2018.

67 http://www.kimchang.com/newsletter/201604/en/newsletter_ip_en_spring2016_Section08.html.

invested substantial effort and resources, including money, technology, and expertise. It was clear in this case that the characters, colors, and game effects in the defendant's game were totally different from those in the plaintiff's game and, thus, far from copyright infringement. While the game rules in question were not subject to copyright protection, the court noted that misappropriation of those rules *was* subject to liability under the UCPA. There remains a serious question, however, about how to strike an appropriate balance between the protection of economic freedom and the fruits of investment and effort.

5. Impact of Artificial Intelligence on IP

Advances in the development and deployment of artificial intelligence ('AI') will have an enormous impact on IP systems. First, there is a question about the patentability or copyrightability of products created by AI. While the current IP system assumes that patentable inventions or copyrightable works are all invented or created by human beings, we will soon have to answer the very difficult question of whether an invention or work created by a machine consisting of or heavily using AI is also eligible for patent or copyright protection. If ideas or expressions created by AI are new and impress our heads or hearts, there is no obvious reason not to protect those ideas and expressions.[68]

Second, there is also a question about the non-obviousness or originality of inventions or content created by AI, which depends on an algorithm that mechanically creates an invention or content. Obviously, AI is different from a human inventor or author in its process of invention or creation. If AI only applies mechanical changes to existing technologies or contents, it may be difficult to recognize any non-obviousness or originality. As the sophistication of AI increases, however, it will soon create inventions or expressions that meet a prima facie core requirement of patent or copyright protection.

If inventions or content created by AI are protected by patent or copyright law, the next question involves identifying the inventor or

68 Annemarie Bridy, *Coding Creativity: Copyright and the Artificially Intelligent Author*, STANFORD TECHNOLOGY LAW REVIEW 5 (2012).

author and the owner of the patent or copyright: (1) the programmer who developed the algorithm for AI, (2) the user who made a series of choices or issued instructions about deploying AI, (3) the person who made AI learn and trained it, or (4) the AI or robots themselves. This problem poses highly complex issues of patent and copyright legislation and interpretation.

From a utilitarian point of view, to facilitate creation of products by AI, copyright may be awarded to the programmer or users. It may also be necessary to acknowledge the authorship of AI and, yet, grant copyright to programmers or users. As long as an AI is viewed as a mere machine, it requires only energy such as electricity, not copyright.[69]

Th third impact of AI will involve data ownership. Data are protected in various forms, such as personal information, copyright works, databases, and trade secrets. In addition, misappropriation of data may constitute a violation of unfair competition prevention laws. The legal protection of data in Korea is the strongest on earth, whereas the scope of the fair use of data is rather limited, unclear, and uncertain. While Korea's copyright law has adopted an American style of general provision on fair use, lawyers still rely on only a limited number of civil law-based copyright restrictions. This is simply because judges in Korea are not used to balancing the social benefits of fair use and the economic interests of copyright holders. Given that fair use is a critical issue that can even lead to criminal punishment, the limited interpretation and uncertainty of fair use could be a serious obstacle to the use of data by robots and AI.

In response to the increasing importance of data and the uncertainties relating to fair use, several legislators have proposed a legislative bill to amend the CA. According to the amendment bill, the reproduction and transmission of data are allowed as fair use to the extent necessary to generate additional value by analyzing large amounts of data, including a large number of copyright works. In the amendment bill, the fair use of data analysis is distinguished from enjoying the thoughts or feelings expressed in the work. That distinction is reminiscent of the approach taken by the Japanese Copyright Act. Still, the reproduction and transmission of data would be limited to cases in which the data can be accessed legally. There are thus still questions as to whether and to what extent spiders and crawlers

69 *Id.* 51.

are free to have access to data over the internet.

6. Conclusion

Over the past 70 years, Korea has experienced, along with rapid economic growth, dramatic changes in its IP rights system. In the first 35 years of that growth, foreign technologies and work were literally copied and learned. In the last 35 years, however, through dramatic institutional changes, IP rights were protected at the same level as in Europe and the United States. It is worth noting that, 180 years ago, the United States simply did not honor the copyrights of foreign authors.[70] While it took roughly two centuries for the United States to change from a pirate country to one that respects IP rights, it took just 35 years for Korea to make that transition. The United States is now a leading advocate for IP protection at the international level, and Korean law now protects IP rights as thoroughly as, and sometimes more vigorously than, the United States.

In the last 35 years, the protection of IP rights has been strengthened, eventually promoting innovation and creation by Korean companies and individuals. Although the protection of IP rights has been strengthened through several revisions of relevant statutes, the actual results are sometimes contrary to the statutory goals.

First, the possibility of excessively broad criminal sanctions may endanger corporate investment and product development and harm the general public's perception of IP rights. For example, a newly established company could face both criminal penalties and civil damages for patent infringement. Furthermore, since even minor copyright infringements are subject to criminal punishment, youngsters run the risk of criminal punishment while enjoying content on the Internet.

Second, although IP rights have been strengthened due to the amendment of the law, the damages awarded for infringements are not enough for compensation in many actual cases. Although copyright has been strengthened, the courts often overlook the unfair terms and conditions of copyright contracts. Accordingly, corporate copyrights are

70 https://creativelawcenter.com/dickens-american-copyright.

protected, but the economic status of individual creators is becoming weaker.

Third, as the use of AI increased, a number of statutes were enacted or amended to protect data assets. For example, the recently revised UCPA lists the illegal use of data assets as a new type of unfair competition. The recently enacted Industrial Digital Transformation Promotion Act grants industrial data producers the right to use and profit from industrial data (Article 9).[71] In order to clarify that AI-driven data analysis falls under fair use, revisions of the CA are also under way. In the 21st century, as AI is becoming more and more popular and powerful, it is expected that Korea's IP laws will strike a balance to effectively protect inventions and creations while promoting fair use.

71 Statute No. 18692, enacted on January 4, 2022.

Chapter 10

Private International Law and International Civil Procedure Law

Kwang Hyun Suk*

1. Introduction

(1) Concept of Private International Law

As long as countries have distinctive legal orders, dealing with a case with foreign elements requires a solution different from that used for pure domestic cases. Private international law, also known as conflict of laws, reconciles conflicts between different legal orders, and its importance has grown in today's highly mobile, globalized context. The main topics of private international law are international jurisdiction to adjudicate, determination of the law applicable to certain legal relationship or issues – this topic is also referred to as private international law in its narrow sense – and recognition and enforcement of foreign judgments. In addition, international civil judicial cooperation (or assistance), international insolvency (or cross-border insolvency) and international commercial arbitration are dealt with in this chapter as matters of international civil procedure law, which is closely related to private international law.

* Former Professor in Private International Law and Internationl Business Transactions Law, Seoul National University School of Law.

(2) Structure of This Part and Sources of Law

This Part is intended to help readers understand Korean law: more specifically, Korea's private international and international civil procedure law. This area of law, which deals with international civil and commercial matters, is of great importance for international relations involving natural or legal persons, and this is especially true regarding Korea, with its open economy and high reliance on trade.

The order of discussion is as follows: introduction (Section 1), international jurisdiction to adjudicate (Section 2), choice of law rules (Section 3), international judicial cooperation (Section 4), recognition and enforcement of foreign judgments (Section 5), international insolvency (Section 6), and international commercial arbitration (Section 7).

The single most important piece of Korean legislation on private international law is the Act on Private International Law of Korea (APIL), which consists mainly of provisions on applicable law and international jurisdiction in civil and commercial matters.[1] Under the Constitution (Article 6(1)), treaties concluded and officially published in accordance with the constitution and generally accepted international rules of law have the same force as Korean law. Korea became a Member State of the Hague Conference on Private International Law (Hague Conference) in 1997. As of June 1, 2021, Korea is a contracting State to the following four Hague Conventions: the 1961 Convention Abolishing the Requirement of Legalization for Foreign Public Documents (*Apostille* Convention), the 1965 Convention on the Service Abroad of Judicial and Extrajudicial Documents in Civil or Commercial Matters (Service Convention), the 1970 Convention on the Taking of Evidence Abroad in Civil or Commercial Matters (Evidence Convention), and the 1980 Convention on the Civil Aspects of International Child Abduction (Abduction Convention).

1 An unofficial English translation of the prior APIL by Kwang Hyun Suk is available in the YEARBOOK OF PRIVATE INTERNATIONAL LAW V, 315-336 (2003), ENCYCLOPEDIA OF PRIVATE INTERNATIONAL LAW 4, 3810-3821 (2017), and the website of The Korean Law Information Center (https://law.go.kr/LSW/lsInfoP.do?lsiSeq=179501&viewCls=engLsInfoR&urlMode=engLsInfoR#0000). An unofficial English translation of the jurisdiction provisions of the new APIL by Junhyok Jang is available in the XXVII(2) KOREA PRIVATE INTERNATIONAL LAW JOURNAL 443-463 (2022).

The main sources of law for other areas are noted in the relevant passages below.

(3) Characteristics of the APIL

Unlike some countries that include private international law in the civil code, Korea adopted an independent act, first through the initial APIL (*Seoboesabeop*), which was promulgated in 1962. A revised APIL (Act No. 6465 of 2001; *Gukjesabeop*) was promulgated in April 2001 and took effect on July 1, 2001. The 1951 APIL had been modeled on the private international law chapter of the *Einführungsgesetz zum Bürgerlichen Gesetzbuch (EGBGB)* of the Federal Republic of Germany, which entered into force on January 1, 1900 (German PIL) and the Japanese Private International Law (Japanese PIL). While the 1962 APIL had been silent on the issue, the 2001 act introduced rules on international jurisdiction and reflected the ideas of diversification of connecting factors, expansion of the party autonomy principle, consideration of the contents of substantive law protecting socio-economically weaker parties, and methodological pluralism for the choice of law. The legislators considered the efforts consistently made by the Hague Conference toward progressive unification of choice of law rules, especially in the areas of family law and succession law.

As Korea uses a civil law system, the APIL naturally follows the approach of the traditional private international law statutes in continental Europe. The APIL is the product of efforts to eliminate problems under the earlier APIL and to modernize by adopting the standards laid down in international conventions and national laws considered to have made considerable progress in terms of private international law. The Korean legislature indeed took account of the Rome Convention, the 1987 Swiss Private International Law Act, the German PIL, and various Hague Conventions, thus giving the APIL greater universal validity.

It is particularly noteworthy that while the APIL consists almost exclusively of choice of law rules, with the promulgation in January 2022 of a revised APIL (referred to as the new APIL below) containing 34 new articles setting forth detailed rules of international jurisdiction, Korea is now equipped with two major elements related to private international law matters: rules of governing law and rules of international jurisdiction. Since the new APIL has come into effect on July 5, 2022, it is discussed together with the 2001 APIL (referred to as the prior APIL) below.

2. International Jurisdiction to Adjudicate

(1) Introduction

In international litigation, geographic distance and language differences can make it more or less difficult for the parties, especially the plaintiff, to bring a claim before a given forum and may incite them to have recourse to forum shopping. The following differences are also worth noting. First, due to the *lex fori* principle, the rules of procedure applied to litigation can differ. Second, the substantive norms applied to the substance in dispute may vary because each State applies its own choice of law rules. Third, the plaintiff can also be affected by whether the court is likely to render a favorable judgment that is enforceable where the defendant's property is located. When assessing the legal risks of international transactions, the decision of the forum is an important factor for the parties.

In Korea, private international law matters come under the jurisdiction of ordinary courts dealing with civil and commercial matters. However, in order to strengthen the expertise of judges dealing with international commercial transactions, several Korean courts, including the Seoul Central District Court of first instance and the Seoul High Court of second instance, designated some of their panels as Special Panels in Charge of International Cases.

Korean law distinguishes *facultas iurisdictionis* (*jaepankwon*) from international jurisdiction. *Facultas iurisdictionis* is raised as a matter of sovereign (or State) immunity or the immunity of diplomatic missions only when the State or diplomatic mission is the defendant. It differs from international jurisdiction in that the latter becomes an issue in ordinary international cases. Exemption from *facultas iurisdictionis* is a matter of public international law, but the issue of international jurisdiction—that is, whether the courts of a specific country as a whole (in the United States, the unit is the state) should judge legal disputes—is understood, except for treaties, to be a matter of domestic law: in other words, private international law.

In international jurisdiction, direct and indirect jurisdiction must be distinguished. When a lawsuit is filed before a Korean court, the issue of whether that court can decide on the case is an issue of direct jurisdiction. When the recognition and enforcement of a judgment rendered by a foreign court are discussed before a Korean court, the issue of whether that foreign court had jurisdiction to hear the case is an issue of indirect jurisdiction. As mentioned above, 34 new articles setting forth elaborate rules of direct jurisdiction are part of the new APIL.

(2) Basic Jurisdictional Rules

The prior APIL introduced three articles on international jurisdiction. Article 2 lays down general rules, while Articles 27 and 28 describe special rules to protect socio-economically weaker parties. Article 2 states that detailed and refined rules on international jurisdiction should be developed by consulting, but without being bound by, the venue provisions of the Civil Procedure Code (CPC venue provisions and CPC, respectively) in civil or commercial matters. The special characteristics of international jurisdiction, as opposed to domestic territorial jurisdiction, must also be considered. The underlying idea of Article 2 is to require judges to establish more detailed and refined rules on international jurisdiction after considering the special characteristics of international jurisdiction, instead of mechanically assuming that the "rules on international jurisdiction" are identical with the CPC venue provisions. Accordingly, the CPC venue provisions could be used as a reference for Korean courts in developing detailed and refined international jurisdictional rules. Article 2 is retained in the new APIL, since the latter's rules of international jurisdiction are not yet complete. However, considering the fact that detailed rules of international jurisdiction can be found in the new APIL, the language of Article 2 has been slightly revised.

The specific criteria that Korean courts will apply in determining the question of jurisdiction are listed below. Where relevant, provisions of both the prior and new versions of the APIL are mentioned.

1) General Jurisdiction: Defendant's Domicile

CPC Articles 2, 3, and 5 provide that an action is subject to the jurisdiction of the court of the place of the defendant's domicile (natural person) or principal place of business (legal person). It is generally recognized that this rule (*actor sequitur forum rei*) applies to international jurisdiction. Therefore, the new APIL has a similar provision in Article 4(1), albeit with slight modifications. Under the new APIL, Korea has general jurisdiction if a natural person has his or her habitual residence in Korea. In the case of associations or legal persons, the new APIL confers general jurisdiction on Korean courts if the legal person has its principal place of business, statutory seat, or central administration in Korea or was incorporated or formed under Korean law (Article 4(3)).

2) Corporations

Actions against a person or a legal person maintaining an office or a business office (營業所) can be brought before the courts located in Korea if they concern the business affairs of that office or business office (CPC Article 12). This rule is generally considered to apply to international jurisdiction, and Article 4 of the new APIL makes that explicit. In addition, Art 4(2) of the new APIL expressly provides actions against a person or a legal person engaging in a continuous and organized business activity in or as directed to Korea can be brought before the courts in Korea if they concern that business activity.

3) Presence of Property

Actions concerning property rights against a person without a domicile in Korea may be brought before the court of the location of the subject matter of the claim, the subject matter for security, or any attachable property of the defendant (CPC Article 11). This appears to confer jurisdiction merely on the grounds of the location of any specified subject matter or property. The Supreme Court of Korea ruled 1988 that Article 11 may be applied to international jurisdiction. In a July 2019 case, while acknowledging the jurisdiction of the location of the property, the Supreme Court held that if a plaintiff's claim is not directly related to the defendant's property, international jurisdiction should be determined in light of the circumstances in which the property came to be in Korea, the value of the property, the need for remedies for the plaintiff's rights, and the effectiveness of the judgment, because admitting international jurisdiction unconditionally where the property is accidentally located in Korea may cause significant disadvantages to the defendant.

Under Article 5 of the new APIL, the presence of property belonging to the defendant could constitute a ground for jurisdiction for a pecuniary action (i.e., an action related to property rights in general) if the property can be subject to arrest or seizure. However, this rule does not apply when (i) the case in dispute has only a slight connection or no connection at all with Korea, or (ii) the value of the property is substantially small.

4) Intellectual Property

The most problematic disputes concerning intellectual property are those involving registration or validity of patents or other similar rights requiring registration. It should be noted that in a 2011 patent case, the Supreme Court distinguished between proceedings dealing with the validity or existence of patents from those dealing with the interpretation and effects of the contractual obligations between the parties and held that only the former proceedings fall under the exclusive jurisdiction of the state of registration.

Three articles have been inserted in the new APIL. First, an action relating to the validity and extinction of intellectual property rights created by registration may be filed before Korean courts only when they are registered in Korea; however, the foregoing shall not apply when those matters arise as incidental questions (Article 10(1)). In addition, the foregoing shall not apply when the transfer or registration that is the subject matter of the proceedings is performed pursuant to a contract between the parties. Second, an action relating to contractual matters such as license of intellectual property rights may be filed before Korean courts if such rights are protected, exploited, or registered in Korea (Article 38). Third, an action relating to the infringement of intellectual property rights may be filed before Korean courts if the infringement (whether the infringing act or a result thereof) took place in Korea or the infringement was directed toward Korea (Article 39), in which case the jurisdiction of Korea is limited to the result that occurred in Korea, unless Korea is the location of the principal infringing act.

5) Contractual Obligations: Place of Performance

Actions concerning contractual obligations may be brought before the court of the place of performance of the obligations (CPC Article 8). While the Supreme Court held in 1972 that Article 8 could be the basis of international jurisdiction, it did not follow this approach in a 2006 case on a contractual dispute, casting doubt on whether it still applies. To clarify the jurisdiction for actions concerning contractual obligations, concrete criteria have been introduced in the new APIL; they are described below.

Under Article 41 of the new APIL, an action relating to contracts may be filed before Korean courts under one of the following conditions: (a) in matters relating to the supply of goods, the goods were supplied in Korea; (b) in matters relating to the provision of services, the services were provided in Korea; or (c) in matters relating both to the supply of goods and the provisions of services, performance of the principal obligation took place in Korea. This means that the place of performance of a contractual obligation can be a ground for jurisdiction in relatively limited situations. An action relating to contracts other than those listed above may be filed before Korean courts if the place where the obligation constituting the ground of the claim was actually performed is in Korea or the place where the obligation constituting the ground of the claim was agreed to be performed is in Korea. In other words, in the absence of the parties' agreement on a place of performance of obligation, the place where the obligation is to be performed under the law applicable to the contract cannot be a ground for jurisdiction. The reason for this limitation is that the factual situations of contracts were so diverse that jurisdiction based on the place of performance of a contractual obligation could not always be justified.

In addition, the new APIL sets forth special rules on international jurisdiction in respect of passive consumer contracts and individual employment contracts to protect socio-economically weaker parties (Articles 47 to 48, modeled on the Brussels Convention and the Brussels I Regulation, with certain modifications to reflect internet transactions in the case of Article 47). Whereas the consumer's habitual residence is relevant in consumer contracts, the place where the employee habitually works is relevant in individual employment contracts. Accordingly, Korean consumers, many of whom make direct online purchases from foreign businesses such as Alibaba, could be protected by Article 47 in terms of international jurisdiction and applicable law, even in the presence of any provisions designating foreign law as applicable law and granting international jurisdiction to foreign courts in the terms and conditions. These protective jurisdiction rules remain largely unchanged except that the scope of consumer has been slightly expanded to offer consumers stronger protection.

6) Place of Tort

Actions in tort may be brought before the court of the place where the tortious act occurred (CPC Article 18). It is generally recognized that Article 18 applies to determine international jurisdiction. When the tortious act and the consequence of the injury occurred in different places, each could be a ground for international jurisdiction. The majority view maintains that the places should be determined rationally from the viewpoint of international jurisdiction and that, in the case of product liability in particular, regard must be paid to whether either the place of acting or the place of injury were reasonably foreseeable for the defendant. The Supreme Court endorsed this view in a 1995 product liability case. This judgment was influenced by the ideas of "reasonable foreseeability" and "purposeful availment" appearing in the decisions of the United States Supreme Court (Volkswagen Corp. case of 1980 and the Asahi Metal case of 1987).

Under the new APIL, a lawsuit relating to tort may be brought before a Korean court if the tortious act is committed in or directed toward Korea, or if a result thereof occurs in Korea, except where it could not have been foreseen that said result would occur in Korea (Article 44).

7) Family Matters

According to a leading Supreme Court case from 1975, Korean courts' jurisdiction is subject to the location of the defendant's domicile in Korea, because the *forum rei* principle is also valid for family matters, including divorce cases. However, by way of exception, Korean courts may still have jurisdiction when that condition is not met if a refusal to entertain the action could constitute denial of justice. As situations amounting to denial of justice, the Supreme Court mentioned cases where the defendant is missing or in a similar situation or actively responds to the action. It has long been underlined that more concrete criteria needed to be established in the APIL, and the new APIL does introduce detailed rules of international jurisdiction for cases related to marriage, paternity, maintenance, and adult guardianship (Chapter 7), as described below.

In marriage-related cases, Korean courts have special jurisdiction (i) if the couple's last common habitual residence was in Korea and one of the spouses still has a habitual residence in Korea, or (ii) if both spouses are Korean (Article 56). In paternity-related cases, Korean courts have special jurisdiction (i) if the child's habitual residence is in Korea, or (ii) if the child and either of the sued parents are Korean (Article 57). The Korean courts have special jurisdiction over cases on the legal relationship between parents and children—that is, parental responsibility, custody, and rights of visitation or guardianship of a minor child—if the child's habitual residence is in Korea (Article 59). In maintenance cases, Korean courts have jurisdiction (i) if the maintenance creditor has his or her habitual residence in Korea, (Article 60; the purpose is apparently to protect the maintenance creditor), or (ii) if the habitual residence of the defendant is in Korea (Article 3). Furthermore, the new APIL (Article 60) allows jurisdictional agreements to be concluded that treat maintenance cases as having a property law nature.

8) Succession

Actions concerning successions, bequests, or other acts becoming effective by death may be brought before the court of the location of the deceased's general forum at the time of the commencement of the succession (CPC Article 22). In addition, actions concerning a succession claim and the liability of an estate that does not fall under Article 22 may be brought before such court if the estate in whole or part is located in the jurisdiction area of the court under Article 22. It is generally recognized that these rules apply to international jurisdiction. The new APIL expressly sets forth these rules, in addition to allowing for jurisdictional agreements to a limited extent (Article 76).

9) Jurisdiction Agreement and Appearance

Parties' agreements on jurisdiction in a cross-border action, generally accepted in Korea, play a very important role in practice. The Supreme Court held in 1997 that the validity of a jurisdiction clause conferring exclusive jurisdiction on a foreign court is subject to the following conditions: (i) the case does not fall under the exclusive jurisdiction of Korea, (ii) the foreign court has valid jurisdiction under its law, (iii) the case has a reasonable relationship with the chosen foreign court, and (iv) the agreement is not egregiously unreasonable or unfair.

Even a person who is not otherwise subject to Korean courts' international jurisdiction who appears before the Korean court and responds to the merits without objecting to the jurisdiction can be deemed to have consented to it, and the Korean court will have jurisdiction.

The new APIL expressly provides for jurisdiction agreement (Article

8) and appearance (Article 9). The much-criticized third condition of jurisdiction was not included in the new APIL. Regarding the law applicable to the validity of the jurisdiction agreement, the new APIL provides that the law of the State to which jurisdiction is granted (including its private international law) shall be applied, thus adopting a position consistent with that of the 2005 Hague Choice of Court Convention.

10) Exclusive International Jurisdiction

Although the CPC is silent on Korean courts' exclusive international jurisdiction, the majority of commentators consider Korean courts to have exclusive international jurisdiction in proceedings concerning (i) rights *in rem* in immovable property situated in Korea; (ii) the validity of the constitution, the nullity or dissolution of companies, or the validity of the decisions of their organs, if the company was established under Korean law; (iii) the validity of entries in public registers kept in Korea; and (iv) the registration or validity of patents, trademarks, or other similar rights required to be registered, if the registration was applied for or took place in Korea. The new APIL expressly enumerates exclusive jurisdictional rules similar to those suggested by the majority of commentators, although with slight modifications to reflect the position of the Supreme Court (Article 12).

11) Forum non Conveniens

Korean legal commentators' opinions diverge as to whether the doctrine of *forum non conveniens*, under which Korean courts may refuse to exercise international jurisdiction even if Korean courts have international jurisdiction according to the standard established by the APIL, is allowed under the APIL. While there is no judicial precedent directly on point, the *forum non conveniens* doctrine is expressly included in the new APIL (Article 12).

3. Choice of Law Rules

(1) Introduction

As noted above, the single most important Korean legislation on choice of law rules is the new APIL. By way of analogy of Article 1 of the Civil Code (CC), customary laws apply in the absence of applicable statutes, and, jori (條

理 i.e., the nature of things) applies in the absence of statute and customary law. There is no customary law in the area of private international law in Korea. Case law is not a source of law in Korea, but it plays a complementary role that is particularly important regarding choice of law rules because the new APIL has many gaps.[2] As to doctrinal writings, they have only persuasive authority. Choice of law rules under the prior APIL remain mostly unchanged in the new APIL, explanations of the prior APIL are still valid under the new APIL.

(2) Basic Choice of Law Rules[3]

1) Structure and General Provisions of the New APIL

The following ten chapters of the new APIL deal with choice of law rules: general provisions (Chapter 1), person (Chapter 2), juridical act (Chapter 3), rights *in rem* (Chapter 4), intellectual property (Chapter 5), obligations (Chapter 6), family (Chapter 7), succession (Chapter 8), bills of exchange, promissory notes, and checks (Chapter 9), and maritime matters (Chapter 10).

Section 1 includes provisions on issues of a general nature that arise when applying choice of law rules. Article 7 (new APIL Article 20) sets forth the application of internationally mandatory rules of Korean law if it is clear from their legislative purpose that they must be applied irrespective of the governing law. Article 8 (new APIL Article 21) introduces the escape clause (or exception clause) in order to achieve the principle of the closest connection, which is modeled on Switzerland's 1987 Private International Law Act (Article 15). The Supreme Court applied the escape clause in connection with Article 60 of the APIL (corresponding to new APIL Article 94) for the first time in a maritime law case that is discussed below.

Although there is no express provision in the new APIL, the courts must apply the choice of law rules of the new APIL *ex officio* if they find that the case involves a foreign element. Further, the new APIL expressly

2 For example, case law has been determinative in filling gaps on issues such as the *lex fori* principle for procedural matters, hidden renvoi, and the law applicable to distance torts (*Distanzdelikte*).

3 For developments on choice of law rules under the APIL, see Kwang Hyun Suk, ENCYCLOPEDIA OF PRIVATE INTERNATIONAL LAW 3, 2243-2252 (2017); Hongsik Chung, *Private International Law*, INTRODUCTION TO KOREAN LAW (Korea Legislation Research Institute eds.), Springer, 271 et seq. (2013).

provides that the courts shall examine and apply *ex officio* the contents of the foreign law designated as the governing law under the new APIL and may request the parties' cooperation for that purpose (Article 18 of the new APIL). If foreign law is not proven to the satisfaction of the courts even after the courts have exerted reasonable efforts to identify the contents of the foreign law, the court may apply a law that is similar to the applicable foreign law. The primary form of evidence to prove foreign law in practice consists of the opinions, submitted by the parties, of experts qualified in the relevant jurisdiction. Judicial cooperation on provision of information on foreign law contemplated by several bilateral treaties concluded between Korea, Australia, China, Mongolia, Uzbekistan, and Thailand may be useful for that purpose.

The new APIL does not permit transmission, except under Article 51(1). However, the new APIL permits direct *renvoi* (remission) to Korean law. There are cases where direct *renvoi* is not permitted (listed in Article 22 of the new APIL), as when the parties chose the governing law, when the law governing a contract is designated by the new APIL, or when *renvoi* would be contrary to the purpose of designating the governing law by the new APIL. In a 2006 divorce case between US citizens, the Supreme Court permitted hidden *renvoi* and applied Korean law instead of the law of the State of Missouri originally designated by Article 39 of the prior APIL. Foreign law shall not be applied where its application is manifestly incompatible with the good morals and other social order of Korea (Article 23 of the new Article), which is understood as meaning international public policy.

Where the national law designated by the new APIL is the law of a country with internally varied local laws, the law designated by the relevant choice of law rules of that country governs; if there are no such rules, the law of the local district with which the person in question is most closely connected applies (new APIL Article 16(3)). There is no provision on characterization, incidental question, *fraus legis*, or adaptation, which are resolved by court precedents. Although there is no provision on point, procedural matters are governed by *lex fori*.

Below, we review the choice of law rules applicable to principal legal relationships provided by the new APIL.

2) Legal Persons and Corporations

In order to respect the parties' interests more appropriately and promote legal certainty, the first sentence of Article 16 (new APIL Article 30) adopts the theory of incorporation. As an exception to this principle, the second sentence provides that Korean law applies if the head office of the legal person or association is located in Korea or its principal activities are conducted in Korea, in order to protect third parties engaging in business transactions with such legal persons and associations in Korea.

3) Juridical Act

Although it is not common to have choice of law rules on juridical acts, separate choice of law rules on the formal validity and agency of juridical acts are inserted in Chapter 3 of the new APIL since a juridical act that includes both unilateral acts and contracts is an important concept under the Civil Code. Article 31 of the new APIL adopts the *favor negotii* principle by subjecting the formal validity of a juridical act to either the law governing its substance or the law of the place where it is effected (the *locus regit actum* principle). As regards the law applicable to voluntary agency, the internal relationship between principal and agent is subject to the law governing the legal relationship between the parties, whereas the external relationship is governed by the law of the country of the agent's place of business or, if there is none or the agent's place of business is not ascertainable by the third party, by the law of the country where the agent acted in the particular case (new APIL Article 32).

4) Property (Real Rights)

The new APIL sets forth general rules applicable to immovables and movables and special rules on certain types of property such as means of transportation, bearer securities, *res in transitu*, and contractual security interests over claims (債權), shares, and other rights (new APIL Articles 33 to 37). The new APIL contains no separate provision on the law governing trusts. Real rights concerning immovables and movables and other rights subject to registration are governed by the *lex situs* of the subject matter, whereas acquisition, loss, or change of real rights is governed by the *lex situs* of the subject matter at the time of the completion of the causal action or event. Bearer securities are treated as movables and thus subject to the *lex cartae sitae*. The law applicable to the disposition of the intermediated securities is not clear, although there is an influential view supporting the "place of the relevant intermediary approach" (PRIMA).

A minority view argues that the law of the country of origin should be applied in the case of cultural properties where the protection of the true owner is important. However, in a September 2018 case involving a stolen Royal Seal of the Joseon Dynasty, the Seoul High Court followed the majority view and rejected the *bona fide* acquisition by applying the law of the State of Virginia to the plaintiff's claim that he had validly acquired a stolen Royal Seal located in that state from an internet auction site; this was because the Virginia law does not recognize the *bona fide* acquisition of stolen goods.

5) Intellectual Property

According to Article 40 of the new APIL, protection of intellectual property rights is subject to the law where the right was infringed, which is interpreted broadly as designating the law of the protecting country in matters relating to intellectual property rights in general, embodying the *lex protectionis* principle.[4] However, contractual matters such as disputes on license agreements are governed by the provisions on the law applicable to contract (Articles 45, 46, and 49 of the new APIL). If the relevant international treaties on specific intellectual property rights such as the Paris Convention[5] and the Berne Convention[6] are interpreted to include choice of law rules, such rules override Article 44 of the new APIL.

6) Obligations

Chapter 6 of the new APIL consists of choice of law rules on (i) contractual obligations modeled on the Rome Convention[7] with some modifications (Articles 45 to 49), (ii) non-contractual obligations (Articles 50 to 53), and (iii) the assignment of both contractual and non-contractual claims, the

4 For developments on the law applicable to infringement of intellectual property under the APIL, see Kwang Hyun Suk, *Law Applicable to Infringement of Foreign Copyright under the Berne Convention and the Korean Act on Private International Law*, ANNOTATED LEADING COPYRIGHT CASES IN MAJOR ASIAN JURISDICTIONS (Liu Kung-Chung eds.), City University of Hong Kong Press 481-493 (2019).

5 Paris Convention for the Protection of Industrial Property (1883).

6 Berne Convention for the Protection of Literary and Artistic Works (1886).

7 EC Convention on the Law Applicable to Contractual Obligations (1980).

assumption of obligations, and the transfer of a claim by operation of law which are applicable to both contractual and non-contractual obligations (Articles 54 to 55).

❶ Contractual Obligations[8]

New APIL Article 45 declares the party autonomy principle and permits *dépeçage* and a subsequent change of the law applicable to the contract. Under the "English governing law clause" of the Institute of London Underwriters Cargo Clauses (ICC) used by Korean insurance companies, it is generally understood that the formation of the contract is governed by Korean law if the clause subjects to English law "only the liability for and settlement of any and all claims." According to the prevailing view, express or tacit choice of a non-State law is not allowed.

In the absence of choice of law, a given contract is governed by the law most closely connected to it. Article 46 of the new APIL introduces a rebuttable presumption based on the characteristic performance, an illustrative list of which is contained therein. As regards contracts with passive consumers and individual employment contracts, Articles 47 and 48 of the new APIL restrict party autonomy and modify the general rules on the objective governing law in order to protect socio-economically weaker parties. Originally modeled on Article 5(2) of the Rome Convention, the scope of consumer contracts has been modified to also cover consumer contracts concluded via the internet.

❷ Non-contractual Obligations

Articles 50 to 53 of the new APIL deal with non-contractual obligations arising from *negotiorum gestio*, unjust enrichment, and tort. First, regarding non-contractual obligations in general, Article 53 of the new APIL permits ex post party autonomy in favor of Korean law, provided that the rights of third parties are not prejudiced by such agreement. In the absence of a choice of Korean law, the rules below apply.

8 For developments on the law applicable to contract under Korean law, see Kwang Hyun Suk, *South Korea*, CHOICE OF LAW IN INTERNATIONAL COMMERCIAL CONTRACTS: GLOBAL PERSPECTIVES ON THE HAGUE PRINCIPLES (Daniel Girsberger et al. eds.), Oxford University Press 662-677 (2021).

Unjust enrichment is governed by the laws of the country in which the enrichment took place (new APIL Article 51). This connecting principle could be displaced by the law governing the legal relationship between the parties if the unjust enrichment resulted from an act based on the existing legal relationship.

Article 52(1) of the new APIL provides for the *lex loci delicti* principle. The connection under Article 52(1) of the new APIL could be displaced by the law of the country of common habitual residence if the tortfeasor and injured party had their habitual residences in the same country at the time of the tort. Moreover, the connecting principles under Articles 52(1) and 52(2) could be displaced by the law governing the legal relationship between the parties if the tort violates an existing legal relationship between the tortfeasor and the injured party (the accessory connecting principle). Where a tort is governed by foreign law, damages arising from the tort shall not be awarded if the nature of the loss is clearly inappropriate so as to merit compensation to the injured party or if the damages so awarded would substantially exceed the amount of compensation deemed appropriate in the particular case (new APIL Article 52(4)). Punitive damages and 'grossly excessive damages' are examples of the former and the latter, respectively.

The new APIL does not include choice of law rules for special types of torts such as product liability or defamation. However, there are unilateral choice of law rules in other statutes, such as the Monopoly Control and Fair Trade Act (Article 2bis) and the Capital Market and Financial Investment Business Act (Article 2), both of which embody the 'effects doctrine.'

7) Family Matters

The choice of law rules of the new APIL on international family relations pertain to (i) marriages (Article 63 to 66), (ii) parent-child relationships (Article 67 to 72), (iii) maintenance (Article 73), and (iv) guardianship (Article 75).

❶ Law of International Marriage

The substantive requirements for the formation of marriage are governed by each party's national law. The formal validity of a marriage is in principle governed by the law of the place of ceremony or the national law of either party. As regards the general effects of marriage, Article 64 of the new APIL adopted the 'cascade connecting principle' by subjecting them first to the common national law of the spouses, second to the law of their common habitual residence, and third to the law of the place with which the spouses are most closely connected. The matrimonial property regime is governed by the law applicable to the general effects of marriage; however, party autonomy is permitted under certain restrictions. Divorce is subject to the law governing the general effects of marriage (new APIL Article 66). In order to relieve Korean family registration officers of the practical burden of determining which law applies, the new APIL introduced the 'Korean clause,' which subjects divorce to Korean law if one of the spouses is a Korean national with habitual residence in Korea.

❷ Law of International Parent-Child Relationships

The new APIL distinguishes between the formation of a parent-child relationship and the rights and obligations arising therefrom.

Articles 67 to 69 provide different connecting factors for the parent-child relationship depending on whether the child is legitimate or illegitimate. Article 69(1) facilitates the legitimation of illegitimate children by subjecting them to the national law of the father or the mother or to the law of the child's habitual residence at the time of completion of the event constituting legitimation. The requirements for the formation and effects and dissolution of an adoption are governed by the national law of the adoptive parent at the time of adoption. The child's or a third party's consent to the formation of the parent-child relationship is necessary if required by the child's national law. Korea has yet to ratify the Hague Adoption Convention,[9] which was signed in 2013. Currently, outbound adoption of Korean children is governed by Korea's Special Adoption Act (several provisions of which concerning eligible child and adoptive parents are regarded as internationally mandatory rules) and the adoptive parents' national law. Fortunately, the Act on International Adoption, which serves as the implementing legislation for the Hague Adoption Convention, has been promulgated in July 2023 and will enter into force in July 2025. Ratification of the Hague Adoption Convention is also expected to take place around that date. Once the Act on International Adoption enters into force, future international adoptions will be governed by the Hague Adoption Convention and the Act on International Adoption. Until recently, there

9 Convention on Protection of Children and Co-operation in Respect of Intercountry Adoption (1993).

was no reported international surrogacy case in Korea directly dealing with whether a surrogate mother could be regarded as the legal mother of a child.[10]

The rights and obligations arising from a parent-child relationship that was established by one of the governing laws described above are determined by the law of the child's habitual residence (new APIL Article 72). However, if the child's national law is also the national law of both the father and mother, then that law applies.

As a special rule to new APIL Article 72, the Abduction Convention, which is designed to protect children's fundamental rights under the 1989 UN Convention on the Rights of the Child, took effect in Korea in 2013. As opposed to a classic kidnapping conducted by a person unrelated to the child, kidnapping by a parent or close relative is called 'child abduction.' To combat such abductions, the Hague Conference adopted the Abduction Convention, which provides for a system of cooperation between central authorities of the Contracting States and a speedy procedure for the return of the child to its country of habitual residence. The Abduction Convention seeks to secure the prompt return of children wrongfully removed to or retained in any Contracting State and to ensure that the rights of custody and of access under the law of a Contracting State are effectively respected in other Contracting States. Korea has enacted an implementation act and designated the Ministry of Justice as the central authority in this regard.

❸ Law of International Maintenance

Article 73 of the new APIL reflects the choice of law rules of the Hague Maintenance Convention,[11] even though Korea is not a party to it, by subjecting maintenance obligations to a uniform connecting factor. Maintenance obligations are governed by the law of the maintenance creditor's habitual residence. However, if the maintenance creditor is unable to obtain maintenance from the debtor under that law, the law of their common nationality applies. Maintenance obligations between divorced spouses are governed by the law that applied to the divorce if the divorce

10 For developments on surrogacy under the APIL, see Kwang Hyun Suk, *Private International Law Issues on Cross-border Surrogacy Agreement under Korean Law*, NOMOS, Kansai University 83-106 (2018).

11 Convention on the Law Applicable to Maintenance Obligations (1973).

was granted or recognized in Korea.

❹ Law of International Guardianship

Matters relating to international guardianship are governed by the ward's national law, irrespective of whether the ward is a minor or an adult (new APIL Article 75).

8) Succession Matters

Matters of succession, testate and intestate, are governed by the national law of the deceased at the time of death (new APIL Article 77(1)). The new APIL adopts the principle of unity. Influenced by the Hague Succession Convention,[12] the new APIL introduces party autonomy to a limited extent (new APIL Article 77(2)). Issues relating to a will are governed by the testator's national law at the time the will was made, while an amendment or withdrawal of a will is governed by the testator's national law when the will was amended or withdrawn (new APIL Article 78). As to the form of a will, the APIL mentions the law of the testator's habitual residence at either the time the will was made or the time of death, the law of the testator's nationality at either the time the will was made or the time of death, and the law of the place where the testator made the will. Although Korea is not a party to the Hague Testamentary Dispositions Convention,[13] the new APIL was modeled on a rule from that convention to facilitate the satisfaction of the form of testamentary disposition.

9) Maritime Matters

New APIL Chapter 10 consists of special choice of law rules for maritime commerce. Article 94 of the new APIL subjects the following matters to the law of the country of the ship's flag (understood as the ship's country of registration): (i) ownership, mortgage, maritime lien, and other real rights (rights *in rem*) in a ship; (ii) priority of the security interests in a ship; (iii) whether the shipowner, charterer, manager, operator, or other users of the ship can invoke limitation of liability and the scope of such limitation of

12 Convention on the Law Applicable to Succession to the Estates of Deceased Persons (1989).

13 Convention on the Conflicts of Laws Relating to the Form of Testamentary Dispositions (1961).

liability; (iv) general average; and (v) the power of agency of a shipmaster.

Although the Supreme Court applied Article 60 of the prior APIL (corresponding to new APIL Article 94) to ships with a flag of convenience, in a July 2014 case it applied the escape clause (APIL Article 8 corresponding to new APIL Article 21) to decide whether the plaintiffs had acquired a maritime lien on a Panamanian-flagged ship. Based on the escape clause, the Supreme Court applied the Korean Commercial Code to the issues of the existence of the maritime lien and the priority of the plaintiffs' maritime lien and the defendant's ship mortgage.

Chapter 10 of the new APIL also includes separate choice of law rules on ship collisions (Article 95) and salvage (Article 96). Article 95 of the new APIL is a special rule having priority over Article 52 of the new APIL on tort, while new APIL Article 96 is a special rule that has priority over Article 50 of the new APIL on *negotiorum gestio*.

4. International Judicial Assistance (Cooperation)

(1) Introduction

While the phrase 'international judicial assistance' has various meanings, in Korea it generally refers to international judicial assistance related to service and taking evidence on an international level. In the civil law system, service of documents and taking of evidence are exercises of sovereignty, so a court of one country cannot directly conduct such an act in another country; the cooperation of foreign judicial institutions is required. To this end, the Hague Conference adopted the Service Convention and the Evidence Convention. Service of documents is used much more frequently than taking of evidence.

The main Korean legislation in this area is the International Civil Judicial Assistance Act, which contains rules on civil and commercial judicial assistance when such assistance is required from or provided to a foreign country. Korea has been a party to the Service and Evidence Conventions since 2000 and 2010, respectively, and has also signed bilateral treaties on international civil judicial assistance with Australia, China, Mongolia, Uzbekistan, and Thailand. International judicial assistance in the context of insolvency is regulated by the Insolvency Act, which is discussed below.

(2) Service under the Service Convention

The Service Convention provides for services involving or excluding the central authority.

1) Service through the Central Authority

Service through the central authority is the primary method. Each Contracting State shall designate a central authority to receive and process requests for service from other Contracting States (Article 2). The central authority is not the forwarding authority. Where a request for service complies with the terms of the Service Convention, the requested State may refuse to comply therewith only if it deems that compliance would infringe on its sovereignty or security. The Korean government designated the Office of Court Administration of the Supreme Court as the central authority and made a declaration pursuant to Articles 8, 10, and 15(2) of the Service Convention.

2) Service Excluding the Central Authority

The Service Convention allows direct service by a diplomat or consular officer, indirect service by a consular officer to a designated authority in the destination country, service by mail (or by postal channel), direct service between judicial officials, and the like. However, through declarations, the Korean government has objected to direct service by diplomats or consular officers to persons other than their own nationals and to all convenient methods of service. As Korea did not have extensive experience in international judicial assistance when it joined the Service Convention in 2000, such objections may be understood as reflecting Korea's conservative attitude. However, since Korea has gained more experience in this area, it needs to consider withdrawing its objections and revisiting its rigid position in the framework of the Service Convention or at least in the bilateral treaties.

(3) Taking of Evidence under the Evidence Convention

In common law countries, the taking of evidence without compulsion is the duty of the parties and the lawyers and is therefore not a violation of foreign sovereignty; in civil law countries, however, it is a sovereign activity led by the court, which explains why courts are not permitted to take evidence in foreign countries. The Evidence Convention is intended to overcome this conflict. The main methods of taking evidence under the Evidence Convention include (i) taking evidence through the central authority and (ii) taking evidence by diplomats, consular officers, and delegates.

1) Taking of Evidence through the Central Authority

The Evidence Convention provides for the taking of evidence by letter of request and involves the central authority designated by each Contracting State. The Government of Korea has designated the Office of Court Administration in this regard. The State receiving the letter of request shall promptly execute it in accordance with its laws. In addition, in accordance with the Evidence Convention (Article 8), the Korean government permits judges of requesting authorities of other Contracting States to be present at the execution of a letter of request with prior authorization by the Office of Court Administration.

A Contracting State may at the time of signature, ratification, or accession declare that it will not execute letters of request issued for the purpose of obtaining pre-trial discovery of documents, as is done in common law countries (Article 23). The Korean government made a British-style limited reservation. As a result, even a request from a US court for pre-trial discovery of documents may not be unconditionally refused, and if the request relates to particular documents specified in the letter of request, it must be executed. Under the Korea–US Consular Convention (Article 4(c)), which took force in 1963, US consuls may take depositions under oath from Koreans in Korea.

2) Taking of Evidence by Diplomats, Consular Officers, and Commissioners

A diplomatic officer or consular agent may take evidence, without compulsion, against nationals of a given State in aid of proceedings commenced in the courts of the State they represent. In addition, they may, in certain cases and subject to the permission of the competent authorities of the receiving State, take evidence, without compulsion, against nationals of the receiving State or third States within the territory of the receiving State. Moreover, since the Evidence Convention introduced the Anglo-American commissioner system, the commissioner can in certain cases take evidence without compulsion in aid of the proceedings commenced in the courts of the State he or she represents within the territory of the receiving State. By declaring the exclusion of Articles 16 and 17 of Chapter II of the Evidence Convention, the Government of Korea has completely disallowed the taking of evidence against nationals of Korea and third States by diplomats, consular officers, and commissioners.

5. Recognition and Enforcement of Foreign Judgments[14]

(1) Introduction

According to the territoriality principle and the idea that judgments are the result of the exercise of sovereignty by the courts, the effect of court judgments is limited to the country of the court rendering the judgment. However, insisting on these principles undermines the stability of legal relations with foreign elements and hinders the prompt resolution of disputes in international civil and commercial cases. Therefore, many countries, including Korea, recognize and enforce foreign judgments, subject to certain conditions.

General provisions on recognition and enforcement of judgments are included in CPC Articles 217 and 217-2 and Articles 26 and 27 of the Civil Execution Act (CEA), which were largely modeled on the German Code of Civil Procedure. Korea is not a party to any treaty or international agreement on the matter in general. The CPC does not apply to the recognition and enforcement of foreign arbitral awards, which is governed by the United Nations Convention on the Recognition and Enforcement of Foreign Arbitral Awards of 1958 (New York Convention) and/or the Arbitration Act, which is discussed below.

14 For developments on the recognition and enforcement of foreign judgments under Korean law, see Kwang Hyun Suk, *Recognition and Enforcement of Foreign Judgments in the Republic of Korea*, YEARBOOK OF PRIVATE INTERNATIONAL LAW 15, 421-437 (2013/2014); Kwang Hyun Suk, *South Korea*, RECOGNITION AND ENFORCEMENT OF FOREIGN JUDGMENTS IN ASIA (Adeline Chong ed.), Asian Business Law Institute 179-201 (2017).

(2) Conditions for Recognition and Enforcement of Foreign Judgments

In order for foreign judgments to be enforced in Korea, an enforcement judgment (*exequatur*) pursuant to CEA Articles 26 and 27 is required. A prerequisite for obtaining *exequatur* is the satisfaction of the conditions for recognition specified in CPC Article 217, pertaining to (i) eligible judgment, (ii) international jurisdiction, (iii) due process, (iv) public policy, and (v) reciprocity.

In determining whether those conditions are satisfied, Korean courts are not to reexamine the merits of a case; that is, *révision au fond* is prohibited. However, Korean courts may review the merits of foreign judgments insofar as such review is necessary to determine whether the conditions are satisfied.

1) Judgments Entitled to Recognition

Foreign judgments that may be recognized in Korea are those rendered by foreign courts or other foreign juridical organs to determine legal rights or relations of a private law nature, including not only judgments per se but also decrees or decisions rendered by foreign courts. It is not material whether the foreign judgment deals with property rights, contractual claims, or personal relations. To be entitled to recognition in Korea, a foreign judgment must be final, conclusive, and no longer subject to ordinary review.

2) International Jurisdiction

The jurisdiction requirement is specified in Article 217, para 1(1): "the foreign court should have had international jurisdiction under the principles of international jurisdiction laid down in Korean law or international treaties." This means that Korean courts recognize foreign judgments only when the international jurisdiction of the court having rendered the judgment (i.e., indirect jurisdiction) is established on the basis of the criteria that the Korean court would apply in determining jurisdiction in a similar case (i.e., direct jurisdiction). Accordingly, the criteria that Korean courts may apply in determining the question of jurisdiction when presented with cross-border actions are generally same as those reviewed in the context of direct jurisdiction (see Section 2 above).

Although not expressly stated in Article 217, the foreign court must have had *facultas iurisdictionis* (*jaepankwon*); that is, the defendant State must not have been entitled to sovereign immunity in the foreign State in which the judgment was rendered. In January 2021, the Seoul Central District Court considered international human rights law following a lawsuit brought by plaintiffs who had been forced into military sex slavery during the Japanese occupation of Korea and were seeking damages against the Japanese government. Addressing whether Japan was entitled to sovereign immunity after having violated international law, especially *jus cogens*, the Court held that sovereign immunity cannot be recognized. The Court referred to a 2004 judgment by the Italian Supreme Court in the Ferrini case, where Germany's sovereign immunity was denied, and an October 2014 ruling by the Italian Constitutional Court that a law enacted by the Italian Congress to embrace the judgment of the International Court of Justice (ICJ) in February 2012 that recognized Germany's sovereign immunity[15] violated the Italian Constitution.

However, in April 2021, in a similar case concerning victims forced into military sex slavery for Japanese soldiers, the Seoul Central District Court took a different view by recognizing Japan's sovereign immunity based primarily on the recognition of Germany's sovereign immunity by the ICJ in the Ferrini case, which it held to be current international customary law. The Court added that a cautious approach is necessary when creating new exceptions that have not been recognized in current international customary law. An appeal against this second judgment is pending before the appellate court, and the Supreme Court is expected to make a final decision in the future.

3) Service of Process

As one of the conditions for recognizing foreign judgments, the CPC provides that "the defendant who has lost the case should have been served with the complaint (or equivalent document) and the summons or any orders in a lawful manner (other than public notice or similar methods) in advance so as to allow sufficient time for preparation of his defense, or the defendant should have responded to the suit without having been served" (Article 217,

15 Jurisdictional Immunities of the State, Germany v. Italy: Greece intervening.

para 1(2)). Even where a Korean defendant was not served with process, the CPC condition would be satisfied if the defendant voluntarily responded to the action.

In order to satisfy this condition, the service of process should be lawful under the laws of the rendering jurisdiction, provided that if the service is made in the State of enforcement, it should also be lawful under the laws of that State. Accordingly, if a US court serves a defendant in Korea by mail, a method to which Korea has objected under the Service Convention, it is not lawful under Korean law and a US judgment based thereon would not be recognized. At the time of its accession, Korea objected to the use of the methods of service cited in Articles 8 and 10 of the Service Convention. As mentioned above, Korea also concluded bilateral treaties with five countries, including Australia and China, on judicial assistance in civil and commercial matters.

4) Public Policy

CPC Article 217, para 1(3) reads that "the recognition of the foreign judgment should not be contrary to the good morals or other social order of Korea." The public policy here includes both substantive and procedural aspects. With regard to substantive public policy, the most problematic issue is the question of foreign judgments (particularly those of US courts) awarding punitive damages, treble damages, or excessive damages. In the past, Korean law did not recognize punitive damages or multiple damage unrelated to the actual damage suffered by the victim. Thus, the majority view takes the position that recognition of foreign judgments awarding such damages would be denied.

CPC Article 217-2(1), introduced in 2014, adopted this view by providing that where a final judgment concerning damage compensation gives rise to an outcome that is clearly contrary to the general order under Korean laws or the international treaties to which Korea is a party, it shall not be recognized in whole or in part by Korean courts. However, because the concept of treble damages was introduced in 2011 by the Act on Fairness of Subcontracting Transactions (Article 35(2)) and other codifications, it remains to be seen how Korean courts will react to this change. In this regard, it is noteworthy that on March 11, 2022 the Supreme Court rendered a judgment directly dealing with the recognition and enforcement of a foreign judgment ordering the payment of treble damages. In this case, the plaintiffs received from the court of the U.S. State of Hawaii a favourable judgment ordering the defendant to pay treble damages for the harm suffered by the plaintiffs, on the ground that the defendant violated Section 480-2(a) of the Hawaii Revised Statutes by unfair competition methods and unfair deception through the interference with the exclusive import and sales contracts of foodstuffs. The plaintiffs filed a suit in Korea seeking for an enforcement judgment. The Seoul High Court dismissed the part of the judgment awarding treble damages. The reason was that the effect of the recognition of the part ordering the payment of treble damages would be against the public policy of Korea because there is no individual Korean law allowing treble damages for the type of illegal act which constituted the cause of damage of the judgment of the State of Hawaii. However, the Supreme Court reversed the judgment of the Seoul High Court by holding that recognizing the judgment of the State of Hawaii ordering the payment of treble damages is not unacceptable in light of the principles, ideology, and system of the Korean damage compensation system. As a result, recognition and enforcement of foreign judgments ordering the payment of treble damages is now possible in Korea if the foreign law on which the treble damages were based falls within the area of individual laws of Korea setting forth treble damages.

As regards excessive damages, it was believed that the recognition of foreign judgments awarding damages for an amount far greater than what could be awarded by Korean courts in a similar case would be contrary to Korean public policy. As a result, several Korean lower courts confronted with this question reduced the amount of compensation that could be enforceable to 50% of the original amount. However, after Article 217-2 was introduced in 2014, the Supreme Court held that Article 217-2(1) was adopted to limit to an appropriate degree the recognition of foreign judgments awarding punitive damages and that if the final judgment of a foreign court only ordered damages that cover the costs actually incurred by the party to be compensated, the recognition of that judgment should not be limited by Article 217-2(1). There is a debate over whether the Supreme Court's position can be justified.

It is also noteworthy that in the two May 2012 judgments (one against Mitsubishi and the other against Nippon Steel Corporation of Japan), the Supreme Court refused to recognize the Japanese judgments that dismissed the compensation claims by victims of forced labor. The Supreme Court held that the Japanese rule of the Korean peninsula from 1910 to 1945 was an illegal occupation from a normative viewpoint and that neither Korea's diplomatic protection of the plaintiffs nor the plaintiffs' individual rights were extinguished by a 1965 bilateral treaty between Korea and Japan. Recognition of the Japanese judgments was regarded as violating Korean public policy because forced labor based on Japanese law during the colonial era constituted a tort under Korean law, and recognition of the Japanese judgments would contravene the fundamental principles of Korean law.

5) Reciprocity

One of the conditions for recognition of foreign judgments is the existence of reciprocity between Korea and the relevant foreign country (Article 217, para 1(4)). The expectation of receiving reciprocal treatment is sufficient, even if there are no actual cases extending reciprocity to Korean judgments. Although the reciprocity requirement has been criticized by some legal commentators on the grounds that it has a retaliatory element and is not conducive to the protection of justified claims, it should be respected under the current law. This is also the case with family matters, including divorce and adoption.

It is sufficient that the foreign courts concerned recognize Korean judgments under conditions that are not substantially different from those of the CPC in any material respect. The extent of reciprocity should be determined for the same kinds of judgments, such as monetary and non-monetary judgments.

It has been held that reciprocity exists between Korea and Germany, Japan, England and Wales, the Canadian province of Ontario, Argentina, Hong Kong, and it is also well established that reciprocity exists between Korea and those US states that have adopted the Uniform Foreign (or Foreign-Country) Money Judgment Recognition Act, at least insofar as monetary judgments are concerned. The existence of reciprocity between Korea and China was a controversial point in the past,[16] because Chinese courts did not recognize foreign judgments absent a treaty, and Chinese

16 For developments on the reciprocity issue between Korean and China, see Kwang Hyun Suk, *Recognition and Enforcement of Judgments between China, Japan, South Korea in the New Era: South Korean Law Perspective*, 13 FRONTIERS OF LAW IN CHINA 190 et seq. (2018).

courts refused to recognize Korean courts' judgments in several cases, despite Korean courts having recognized Chinese judgments on multiple occasions. Recently, however, Chinese decisions recognizing the existence of reciprocity between two countries were rendered in two cases by the Intermediate People's Courts in Qingdao and Shanghai. In addition, Chinese courts in recent cases recognized foreign judgments (e.g., from the United States) in the absence of a treaty. Since Korean courts have consistently affirmed the existence of reciprocity, Chinese courts are expected to continue to affirm the existence of reciprocity between the two.

(3) Effects of Recognition of Foreign Judgments

Foreign judgments complying with the CPC requirements for recognition are automatically recognized and have the same effects in Korea as in the rendering jurisdiction, except that their enforcement is subject to an enforcement judgment from a Korean court (CEC Articles 26 to 27). This is because enforcement of foreign judgments has a greater impact on the legal status quo in Korea than simple recognition. To obtain an enforcement judgment, establishment of the satisfaction of the CPC conditions for recognition is required. Reviewing the merits of the case is prohibited under the CEA.

(4) Korea's Accession to the Hague Conventions

The number of cases where recognition and enforcement of foreign judgments are sought in Korea is expected to increase in the future, and Korean law concerning these matters will have to evolve to meet the needs of an international community seeking the efficient, economical, and consistent adjudication of cross-border actions. Given the current diversity of the conditions, effects, and procedures of the recognition and enforcement of foreign judgments in different countries, it is desirable to conclude an international convention on the subject. Accordingly, Korea should consider becoming a party to the 2005 Convention on Choice of Court Agreements and the 2019 Convention on the Recognition and Enforcement of Foreign Judgments in Civil or Commercial Matters.

(5) Family Matters

Scholar views' differ as to whether CPC Article 217 also applies to family law judgments of foreign courts. However, in light of precedent and the practice of family registration, the provision has been held to apply to foreign judgments in family matters; thus, the existence of reciprocity is also required in family matters.

6. International Insolvency

The main Korean legislation in this area is Part 5 of the Debtor Rehabilitation and Bankruptcy Act (InsolA), which is modeled after the 1997 UNCITRAL Model Law on Cross-Border Insolvency (MLCBI).

(1) Introduction

Issues of cross-border insolvency law arise when bankruptcy, rehabilitation, and similar proceedings (insolvency proceedings) are commenced in a country against a debtor with assets in multiple countries or conducting business internationally. According to Korea's former insolvency law, which was based on the territoriality principle, the effect of insolvency proceedings commenced in Korea was limited to Korea, while the effect of insolvency proceedings commenced in foreign countries did not extend to property in Korea. This hindered the justice of insolvency law based on creditor equality and the achievement of the purpose of insolvency proceedings. To remedy this situation, Korea used the MLCBI in drafting the InsolA, which adopted a moderate universality principle and came into force in 2006. The various issues arising in international insolvency are discussed below.

(2) Insolvency Proceedings of and International Jurisdiction for Foreigners

The InsolA did not introduce the concepts of main and non-main proceedings, which are the core concepts of the MLCBI. A main proceeding is one initiated in the country where the debtor's center of main interests is located, and a non-main proceeding is one initiated in any other country.

If a foreign corporation with its principal place of business in a foreign country has a subordinate place of business in Korea, that foreign country may initiate the main proceeding, while Korea may initiate a non-main proceeding.

(3) Recognition of Foreign Insolvency Proceedings

1) Objects of and Requirements for Recognition

Under the MLCBI, the effects of recognition differ depending upon whether the insolvency proceeding is a main or non-main proceeding. In order for a foreign insolvency proceeding to be recognized in Korea, the representative of that proceeding must submit various documents, including an application. If there is a legitimate reason for refusal (including violation of public policy), the court must reject the application. Recognition and enforcement of an insolvency-related judgment are controversial; in an interesting case, the question arose as to whether the recognition of the discharge effect resulting from the US bankruptcy court's approval of a reorganization plan of a natural person results from CPC Article 217 or InsolA Article 632. The Supreme Court held that the discharge effect could be recognized via the CPC rather than the InsolA. Legal uncertainty had also resulted from the MLCBI, which led to the adoption of the Model Law on Recognition and Enforcement of Insolvency-Related Judgments by the UNCITRAL in 2018. Korea has not yet received it.

2) Procedures of Recognition

Under Korean law, foreign judgments and foreign arbitration awards are automatically recognized when the requirements are satisfied. However, under the InsolA, foreign insolvency proceedings can be recognized by a Korean court's decision (*exequatur*) because recognition of foreign insolvency proceedings has a greater effect than recognition of foreign judgments.

3) Effect of Recognition

Regarding the effect of recognition of foreign insolvency proceedings (especially main proceedings), several models exist: (i) the extension model, in which the effect of the decision commencing insolvency proceedings under the law of the State commencing the proceedings extends to the recognizing State; (ii) the assimilation model, in which the effect of the recognizing

State under existing insolvency law is recognized; and (iii) the ML model, in which the effect of the recognizing State under a domestic law that has enacted the MLCBI is recognized. Under the MLCBI, when a foreign main proceeding is recognized, the effect under Article 20 is given automatically, while the effect under Article 21 is given at the discretion of the recognizing court. On the other hand, only the effect under Article 21 is given at the discretion of the recognizing court when a non-main foreign proceeding is recognized.

According to the InsolA, even if Korean courts render a recognition decision, the effect of foreign proceedings does not automatically extend to Korea; it merely allows Korean courts to make individual assistance decisions at their discretion. This is more passive than the ML model. In other words, recognition of foreign insolvency proceedings under the InsolA merely confirms that foreign insolvency proceedings may receive assistance from Korean courts, however, that assistance is not guaranteed. It is desirable that Korea faithfully follows the MLCBI.

(4) External Effect of Domestic Insolvency Proceedings

Insolvency representatives in domestic insolvency proceedings have the authority to act in a foreign country as permitted by that country's law. In this respect, the InsolA aims to be universal. Because Korea accepted the MLCBI, in the case of Hanjin Shipping—which was then the largest shipping company in Korea—that began in September 2016, the insolvency representative of Hanjin Shipping was able to obtain both a recognition order and a stay order for the Korean rehabilitation proceeding from ten countries, including the United States.

(5) Coordination of Parallel Insolvency Proceedings

Concurrent insolvency proceedings brought against the same debtor in multiple countries inevitably require coordination, and in this respect, the MLCBI gives priority to domestic insolvency proceedings, then the foreign main proceeding, and finally foreign non-main proceedings. The InsolA generally follows the MLCBI but is simpler. Most notable is the hotchpot rule of fair distribution between creditors. A creditor who has received partial payment in respect of its claim in a foreign insolvency proceeding or from the debtor's foreign assets may not receive a distribution or payment for the same claim in a domestic insolvency proceeding of the same debtor, so long as the payment to the other creditors of the same class is proportionately less than the distribution or payment that the first creditor has already received (Article 642).

(6) Cooperation with Foreign Courts and Foreign Representatives

Cooperation with foreign courts and representatives in foreign insolvency proceedings is the most realistic way to efficiently carry out international insolvency by preventing the dissipation of debtor assets and maximizing their value. Cooperation includes cooperation between insolvency courts and between insolvency representatives. Unlike the international judicial assistance under the Service Convention and Evidence Convention, which require the intervention of central authorities, international judicial cooperation under the InsolA is carried out directly between the relevant courts. An insolvency representative in domestic proceedings can conclude a coordination agreement called a protocol with a foreign court or a foreign representative.

(7) Choice of Law Rules in Insolvency

In international insolvency, the scope of the estate, the effect of the insolvency proceeding on executory contracts, and the law applicable to avoidance of detrimental acts are all important issues left unaddressed in the InsolA. Procedural aspects of insolvency are subject to the *lex fori concursus* (i.e., the law of the country where the insolvency proceedings commenced), while on substantive aspects of insolvency, there is a persuasive view that only 'substantive legal effects typical of insolvency' or 'substantive effects specific to the insolvency law' should be governed by the *lex fori concursus*. This view was adopted by the Supreme Court in May 2015. However, the scope of any exceptions to the principle has yet to be clarified.

7. International Commercial Arbitration

(1) Introduction

The main Korean legislation in this area is the Arbitration Act (ArbA), which is modeled after the 1985 UNCITRAL Model Law on International Commercial Arbitration and the New York Convention. Korea has also reflected in the ArbA the 2006 Amendments to the UNCITRAL Model Law on International Commercial Arbitration.

Under Korean law, the widely known alternative dispute resolution method of arbitration is a procedure for resolving disputes over property rights and non-property disputes that can be resolved by settlement between the parties through an arbitrator's decision rather than court proceedings. Korea has a permanent arbitration institution, the Korean Commercial Arbitration Board, which established in the International Arbitration Center in April 2018 to deal with international arbitration. Korea also established the Seoul International Dispute Resolution Center (SIDRC), an independent legal entity providing venues and facilities for arbitration hearings. Furthermore, to promote the arbitration industry, the Act on the Promotion of the Arbitration Industry was enacted in 2016 and took effect in 2017. Korea has signed but not yet ratified the United Nations Convention on International Settlement Agreements Resulting from Mediation (Singapore Convention on Mediation), which came into effect in September 2020.

(2) Key Concepts in International Commercial Arbitration

1) Place of Arbitration

The place of arbitration is the legal environment of the arbitration. The parties are free to choose the place of arbitration. In principle, the ArbA applies to cases where the place of arbitration is in Korea. The place of arbitration also determines the nationality of the arbitral award.

2) Arbitration Agreement

Arbitration proceedings are based on an arbitration agreement between the parties. There are two types of arbitration agreements: a submission agreement, which is an independent agreement, and an arbitration clause that is included in a main contract such as a sales contract. Following the principle of separability or independence, the validity of the other terms of the main contract shall not affect the validity of the arbitration clause.

The New York Convention requires a written arbitration agreement; the ArbA requires the same, but under it the writing requirement is deemed to have been met when the contents of the arbitration agreement are recorded, whether it is made orally, by conduct, or by any other means.

If a lawsuit is filed with respect to a dispute that is the subject of an arbitration agreement, the court must dismiss the lawsuit when the defendant cites the existence of an arbitration agreement, unless it finds that the arbitration agreement is null and void, inoperative, or incapable of being performed.

3) Arbitrability of the Subject of Dispute

Unlike litigation, not all disputes can be resolved by arbitration; that is, a dispute must have arbitrability. In its absence, the arbitration agreement may become invalid, preventing the arbitrator from rendering an award. Even if an arbitral award is made, that award can be set aside and its recognition or enforcement refused on this ground. Under the ArbA, disputes over property rights and non-property disputes that can be resolved by the parties' settlement can be subject to arbitration, but it remains unclear whether such disputes include public law disputes.

(3) Arbitral Proceedings and Arbitration Awards

The ArbA does not specify the arbitration proceeding in detail, because the parties may agree on any arrangement that does not violate the mandatory provisions of the ArbA; if no agreement can be reached, the arbitral tribunal may proceed with the arbitration proceeding in an appropriate manner. In the case of institutional arbitration, the arbitration rules of the institution selected by the parties and the arbitration law of the place of arbitration govern the proceeding. All parties should be treated equally in arbitration proceedings and have sufficient opportunity to present their case (Article 19). This is a key element of the 'Magna Carta of Arbitral Procedure' or the principle of due process in arbitration.

For the parties, an arbitral award has the same effect as a final judgment of the court. While appeals against arbitral awards are not permitted under the ArbA, a court may in exceptional circumstances set aside an award; this is the only way to challenge arbitral awards. The ArbA limits the grounds for setting aside and the period for filing an application to have an award set aside. If an arbitral award is set aside, it loses its effect.

(4) Recognition and Enforcement of Arbitral Awards

Since arbitration is a private dispute resolution method, arbitral awards as such cannot be enforceable. Therefore, if the party losing the arbitration does not voluntarily comply with the arbitration award, the state's help is needed to enforce it.

The ArbA distinguishes between domestic and foreign arbitral awards. The former are to be recognized and enforced unless there is a reason to set aside an award, while the latter are classified according to whether the New York Convention applies. That convention lists seven grounds for refusal of recognition of foreign arbitral awards. The five grounds specified in Article 5(1) are those that the parties must present, and the two grounds specified in Article 5(2) are those that the court can judge *ex officio*.

If certain documents are submitted to a Korean court and there is no ground for refusal of recognition as set forth by the New York Convention, a foreign arbitral award has effect in Korea. If the applicant who won the arbitration wishes to enforce the foreign arbitral award in Korea, he or she must obtain approval from a Korean court. Until the 2010 ArbA, an enforcement judgment (*Jiphaengpankyeol*) was required, but the 2016 ArbA replaced that requirement with an enforcement decision (*Jiphaengkyeoljeong*), which is less burdensome in many respects, to expedite the process. Overall, Korean courts are regarded as adopting a favorable attitude toward the recognition and enforcement of foreign arbitral awards.

8. Conclusion

In this Part, the author has dealt with the main subjects of private international law: international adjudicatory jurisdiction, determination of applicable law to a particular legal relationship or issue, and the recognition and enforcement of foreign judgments. The author has also reviewed procedural matters closely related to private international law such as international civil judicial assistance (or cooperation), international insolvency law, and international commercial arbitration law. In this area, Korea has a well-established legal system in general, and a fair evaluation would conclude that Korean courts faithfully follow these laws. It is noteworthy that legal models provided by the United Nations were adopted in the area of international insolvency law and international commercial arbitration law. Since detailed rules of international adjudicatory jurisdiction were introduced in 2022, it is expected that an abundance of precedents and academic discussions on the rules of international adjudicatory jurisdiction will follow. In the legal field addressed here, Korea's future priorities include ratifying the Hague Adoption Convention, deciding whether to accede to the 2005 Choice of Court Convention and the 2019 Judgments Convention adopted by the Hague Conference, and deciding whether to adopt the 2018 UN Model Law on recognition and enforcement of insolvency-related judgments. We must also continue to push for the gradual revision of the choice of law rules of the new APIL, which still has room for improvement. In addition, continued efforts should be made to address the problem of surrogacy and the various issues raised by the development of new technologies and the digital transformation.

Chapter 11

Corporate Law and Governance*

Kyung-Hoon Chun**

1. Introduction

Corporations are the main actors in the modern economy. Large businesses are rarely organized as sole proprietorships or partnerships but usually take the form of incorporated entities (i.e., corporations). Corporations in various jurisdictions manufacture, sell, buy, export, and import goods; develop, provide, and buy services; lend and borrow money; hire and pay employees; and finance local, national, and international governments and foundations by paying taxes and making donations. It is difficult to imagine modern society without corporations. Thus, to fully understand how the modern economy and society work, one needs to understand how corporations are organized and operated. Because a corporation is an artificial entity created by law, its organization and operation are stipulated in and governed by the law of the relevant jurisdiction. Understanding the Korean economy and

* Part of this chapter is based on the author's previous publications. "3. Duties and Liabilities of Directors" was developed from paragraphs from Kyung-Hoon Chun, *Corporate Opportunity Doctrine as a Basis for Directors' Liability: A New Statutory Experiment in Korea*, GERMAN AND ASIAN PERSPECTIVES ON COMPANY LAW (Holger Fleischer et al. eds.), Mohr Siebeck 63-81 (in particular, 66-70) (2016), "4. Shareholders' Rights and Power" was developed from paragraphs from Kyung-Hoon Chun, *Shareholder Activism in Korea: The Cases of PSPD and NPS*, GERMAN AND EAST ASIAN PERSPECTIVES ON CORPORATE AND CAPITAL MARKET LAW: INVESTORS VERSUS COMPANIES (Holger Fleischer et al. eds.), Mohr Siebeck 65-85 (in particular, 66-71) (2019).

** Professor, Seoul National University School of Law.

society thus requires a basic understanding of Korean corporations and Korean corporate law.

Where can we find and recognize Korea's corporate law? More technically, what are the *sources* of Korean corporate law? The most important source of laws governing corporations in Korea is Chapter 3 (titled "Corporations") of the Korean Commercial Code (*Sang-beob* in Korean and also known as KCC; referred to as ComC in this book).[1] It was heavily influenced by and very similar to Japan's Commercial Act (*shoho*) when it was first enacted in 1962, but multiple amendments of the relevant laws in both countries since the 1960s resulted in a significant divergence between them.[2] Other statutes, such as the Financial Investment and Capital Markets Act (CMA),[3] Acts on External Audit of Stock Corporations (AEA),[4] and Monopoly Regulations and Fair Trade Act (MRFTA),[5] are also important sources of corporate law in Korea. In addition, judicial precedents are now accorded almost as much respect as in common-law countries by Korean practitioners and academics, although they do not have binding effects in a strict legal sense and thus cannot be legitimately called sources of law under the Korean

1 ComC was first promulgated on January 20, 1962 (Act No. 1000), took effect on January 1, 1963, and has been amended more than 25 times thus far.

2 In particular, the Asian financial crisis and the International Monetary Fund's bail-out program in Korea in the late 1990s prompted Korea to institute significant reforms in corporate governance by adopting new devices, such as audit committees and independent directors. For more details, see Kon-Sik Kim, *Transplanting Audit Committees to Korean Soil: A Window into the Evolution of Korean Corporate Governance*, 9 ASIAN-PACIFIC LAW & POLICY JOURNAL 163 (2007).

3 CMA regulates, among others, public offerings of securities, public disclosures of listed corporations (both periodic and ad hoc disclosures), and unfair dealings on capital markets (such as short swing, use of non-public material information, and stock price manipulation). It also regulates tender offer, reporting of substantial shareholdings, proxy solicitation, and certain corporate finance matters of listed corporations.

4 AEA requires corporations above certain thresholds (in terms of revenue, total assets, number of employees, and others) to be subject to an external audit by an accounting firm or a team of certified public accountants. In 2022, 37,519 corporations (including 2,542 listed ones) were subject to the mandatory external audit requirement. AEA also regulates the internal control system of corporations.

5 MRFTA is the basic antitrust statute that regulates, among others, anti-competitive mergers and acquisitions, collaboration among competitors (including price fixing), retail price maintenance, and other unfair trading practices (including price discrimination, exclusive dealing, and refusal to deal). MRFTA has relevance to corporate law because it also regulates various corporate governance issues of the large business groups in Korea, also known as *chaebols*.

legal system.

ComC identifies five forms of incorporated entities: general-partnership company (*hapmyeong hoesa*), limited-partnership company (*hapja hoesa*), stock corporation (*jusik hoesa*), limited company (*yuhan hoesa*), and limited-liability company (*yuhan chaegim hoesa*). By far, prevalent among these are stock corporations, in which the shareholders are not personally responsible for the corporation's liability. Around 95% of all for-profit incorporated entities in Korea are stock corporations. A stock corporation is the only type of incorporated entity whose shares are eligible to be listed and traded on the stock exchange. Thus, "corporations" or "companies" in this chapter refer to stock corporations, unless otherwise indicated.

This chapter aims to shed light on how Korean corporations are organized and operated under the relevant law. Toward this end, we first review the basic governance structure of Korean corporations, including the roles and authorities of the general meeting of shareholders, the board of directors, and management (2). We then analyze the duties and liabilities of directors (3) and the rights of shareholders (4) and address a few issues concerning large business groups (5). Finally, we conclude the chapter with a brief outlook (6).

2. Basic Governance Structure of Korean Corporations

(1) Overview

ComC provides that certain fundamental matters of a stock corporation must be resolved at the general meeting of shareholders (GMS), and less fundamental but still important business affairs must be decided by the board of directors. The representative director (RD), who is a member of the board of directors and usually plays the role of chief executive officer (CEO), acts on behalf of the corporation, subject to the resolutions of the GMS and the board of directors. As the RD has the authority to act on behalf of the corporation, the corporation is, in principle, legally bound by the RD's acts.

(2) General Meeting of Shareholders

1) Convening a Meeting

Every Korean corporation must hold a GMS once a year pursuant to a resolution of the board of directors (ComC Article 365(1)). This GMS is called an ordinary or annual GMS. In addition, the board may convene a GMS at any time whenever necessary. This GMS is usually called an extraordinary GMS (ComC Article 365(3)). Written notices stating the time, place, and agenda items of the GMS must be sent out to each shareholder at least two weeks before the date of an ordinary or extraordinary GMS (ComC Article 363(1)).[6]

It is the board of directors that convenes both the ordinary GMS and the extraordinary GMS and sets their time, place, and agenda items (ComC Article 362). In other words, although shareholders have the power to decide on fundamental matters concerning the corporation in a GMS, in principle, they cannot exercise this power without the board of directors taking the initiative. There are exceptions to this, however. In some cases, shareholders can convene a GMS or propose agenda items, as discussed later in this chapter.[7]

2) Voting

At a GMS, holders of voting stocks have the right to vote. It is noteworthy that Korean law maintains a strict "one share, one vote" rule (ComC Article 369(1)). The creation of shares with multiple or fractional votes is not allowed by the law, even if it is allowed under the articles of incorporation. On the contrary, shares with no voting right or with limited voting rights (i.e., voting is allowed only for certain agenda items) can be created as a different class of shares, if allowed under the articles of incorporation (ComC Article 344-3(1)). Non-voting or limited-voting shares, however, cannot exceed a quarter of the total issued shares of the corporation (ComC Article 344-3(2)).

6 A less strict rule applies to a small corporation with a legal capital of less than KRW1 billion (ComC Article 363(3)). In listed corporations, with regard to the shareholders holding not more than 1% of the total issued shares, the notice requirement may be satisfied by publishing the notice twice in a daily newspaper or posting it on the electronic disclosure system of the Financial Supervisory Service or the Korea Exchange (ComC Article 542-4(1)).

7 See *infra* 4. (2).

A shareholder may cast a vote either personally or by proxy (ComC Article 368(2)). For listed corporations, those who wish to solicit proxy voting must (i) file a report with the regulator and (ii) make public disclosures regarding the details of the soliciting party and the target corporation (CMA Article 152). This special rule intends to protect investors from fraud and help them make proper decisions on whether and whom to appoint as a proxy for voting purposes by providing the public with sufficient information on the soliciting parties and the target corporation.

Shareholders are allowed to vote in writing if such is allowed under the articles of incorporation (ComC Article 368-3). Electronic voting, which is becoming increasingly common, is allowed if authorized by the board of directors (ComC Article 368-4). The increasing use of proxy and electronic voting means that a substantial portion of the votes are already cast prior to the date of the GMS, and that the results of the GMS are often determined even before the actual meeting takes place.

3) Resolutions

Shareholders exercise their authority by passing a resolution at a GMS. However, the GMS's authority to pass a resolution is limited to the matters prescribed in ComC or in the articles of incorporation (ComC Article 361). In other words, although GMS is the most powerful organ within a corporation which decides on fundamental issues, matters not enumerated in the law or in the articles of incorporation are beyond its authority.

To pass a resolution at a GMS, either the ordinary or special resolution requirements must be satisfied, depending on the agenda item. Unless otherwise provided for in ComC or in the articles of incorporation, the passing of a resolution at a GMS requires a majority of the votes present at the meeting, which must also represent at least one-fourth of the total number of shares (ComC Article 368(1)). A resolution passed in this way is called an ordinary resolution and applies to, among others, the election of directors and statutory auditors, the approval of financial statements, the declaration of dividends, and stock repurchase.

For certain matters, an ordinary resolution does not suffice, and a special resolution is required. A special resolution is passed by at least two-thirds of the votes present at the meeting, which must also represent at least one-third of the total number of voting shares (ComC Article 434(1)). Agenda items that require a special resolution include removal of directors, granting of stock options, reduction of legal capital, merger, corporate division (also known as spin-off), business transfer, dissolution, conversion of the corporation into a different corporate type, comprehensive stock swap,[8] and amendment of the articles of incorporation.

4) Lawsuits Concerning GMS Resolutions

If the resolution passed at a GMS is defective, a shareholder, director, or statutory auditor may file a lawsuit to challenge the validity of the resolution. If the defect lies with the procedure of convening a meeting or passing a resolution (e.g., the notice period was shorter than two weeks, there were incorrect statements in the meeting notice, the meeting notice failed to be delivered, or there were errors in counting the votes) or if the substance of the resolution violates the articles of incorporation, a lawsuit can be filed to cancel the resolution within two months from the date on which it was passed (ComC Article 376). When such prescribed period expires without any challenge to the resolution being made, the resolution will no longer be challengeable on the aforementioned grounds. However, if the substance of the resolution violates the law or if the procedural defects are so serious as to render the resolution non-existent in effect, a lawsuit can be filed, without a statute of limitation, to seek confirmation that the resolution is null and void (ComC Article 380). Not surprisingly, there have been many disputes regarding whether a defective resolution can be challenged under Article 376 (when the defects are procedural and not very serious) or Article 380 (when the defects are substantive or very serious).

The aforementioned lawsuits are quite common in Korea and often become the main battleground amid hostile takeovers or management disputes. For example, the offense side often tries to challenge the validity of the important GMS resolutions passed under the leadership of the incumbent board and the controlling shareholder by highlighting the defectiveness of such resolutions. By winning these lawsuits, the plaintiffs may nullify important resolutions, such as the election or removal of directors, which will have serious impacts on the progress of the hostile takeovers or other similar disputes.[9]

8 This is a transaction by which one corporation becomes a parent and the other becomes a wholly owned subsidiary (ComC Article 360-2).

9 For more details on this topic, see Kon-Sik Kim and Moon-Hee Choi, *Declining*

(3) Board of Directors

1) Powers and Functions

The board of directors, composed of the directors elected at a GMS, has the power to determine corporate affairs, such as the transfer of major assets and the borrowing of large amounts of assets (ComC Article 393(1)). The term 'corporate affairs' may be interpreted so broadly as to include potentially almost all decisions of the corporation. It is generally accepted, however, that the non-daily, more important affairs of the corporation must be decided on by the board of directors while the day-to-day operation of the corporate business may be delegated to the RD. In practice, it is unclear to what extent the board is allowed to delegate its power to the RD and to what extent the board has to decide by itself without delegation. Such delegation is commonly described in the internal regulations of the board,[10] but the court is not bound by such regulations when it decides *ex post* whether the delegation was legitimate.[11]

Aside from determining major corporate affairs (ComC Article 393(1)), the board of directors is also required to "supervise the execution of duties of directors" (ComC Article 393(2)). The board of directors, therefore, is expected to perform both an executive function (Article 393(1)) and a supervisory or monitoring function (Article 393(2)). This reflects a change in the notion of directors under corporate governance theory and practice: directors were seen more as executives in the past but are now seen more as monitors. Put roughly, the executive function is important in a small close corporation, where ownership and management are not separated, while the monitoring function is highlighted in a large listed corporation, where ownership and management are separated.

Relevance of Lawsuits on the Validity of Shareholder Resolution in Korea – A Comparative Essay, GERMAN AND ASIAN PERSPECTIVES ON COMPANY LAW (Holger Fleischer et al. eds.), Mohr Siebeck 217-242 (2016).

10 The regulation usually provides a list of transactions that must be reviewed and approved by the board of directors. Each item in the list is usually defined by using a threshold money amount, such as "sale or purchase of assets exceeding [x] won" and "borrowing or incurring debt in an amount exceeding [y] won."

11 Supreme Court Decision 2005Da3649, July 28, 2005.

2) Independent Directors

In the 'monitor' model, the directors need to be independent from the management. This has led to the formation of the concept of 'independent directors': non-executive directors who are independent from the management and the major shareholders.[12]

ComC neither positively defines the concept of 'independence' nor provides specific criteria for it. Instead, ComC provides a lengthy list of reasons for disqualification from independence (i.e., lack of independence). The list is very complicated,[13] but in short, independent directors must be independent from the corporation in all respects, including ownership, kinship, employment, and business relations. Generally, the disqualification criteria are similar to those found in the listing rules of other jurisdictions but are notably wider than those in the United States as ComC clearly excludes the major shareholders[14] (or those related to the major shareholders) from being independent.

For an unlisted corporation, if it decides to establish an audit committee as its internal supervisory organ instead of appointing a statutory auditor, then at least two-thirds of the audit committee members must be independent directors (ComC Article 415-2(2)). It is only to this extent that unlisted corporations are required to have independent directors. On the contrary, listed corporations must have independent directors on their boards. With certain narrow exceptions, at least one-quarter of the total number of directors of a listed corporation must be independent directors (ComC Article 542-8(1)). Moreover, a 'large listed corporation' (one with a total asset of KRW2 trillion or more) must have at least three independent directors constituting the majority of the board of directors (ComC Article 542-8(1)).

12 The direct translation of the Korean term *sawae-isa* is 'outside director.' However, as ComC requires the *sawae-isa* to be independent from the management and the major shareholders, 'independent director' may be another proper translation.

13 For unlisted companies, the disqualification criteria include (ComC Article 382(3)) (i) directors, executives, and employees engaged in the regular business of the relevant company, or those who were in such positions within the last two years; (ii) the largest shareholder and his/her spouse and lineal ascendants/descendants; (iii) in cases where the largest shareholder is a company, its directors, statutory auditors, executives, and employees; and many others. There are additional criteria for listed corporations (ComC Article 542-8(2)).

14 A major shareholder is a holder of 10% or more of the total issued shares of the corporation or a person who has *de facto* influence on the major management affairs of the corporation (ComC Article 542-8(2)(vi)).

This scheme of mandatory independent directors is unique to Korean law.[15]

(4) Representative Directors

The board of directors, which performs its functions through meetings, is incapable of executing its own decisions. Thus, the board of directors appoints one (or more) of its members as an RD (or RDs), authorizing him/her (or them) to carry out the decisions of the board of directors.[16] In most Korean corporations, one person concurrently holds both the positions of CEO and RD, creating a general perception that RD is a synonym for CEO. Conceptually, however, they are not the same. The CEO is the head of the executives and does not need to be a board member while the RD must be a board member by definition.

The RD is authorized to represent the corporation with respect to its business "within or out of the court" (ComC Articles 389(3) and 209(1)). For example, the RD is authorized to file a complaint and sign a contract, an official letter, and a settlement to end a lawsuit on behalf of the corporation. The authority of the RD is subject to the authority of the board of directors, but externally (i.e., against a third party), the RD has full authority to represent and legally bind the corporation in any and all of its business activities. Any limitation on an RD's power of representation imposed by the board of directors or the articles of incorporation may not be asserted against innocent third parties (ComC Articles 389(3) and 209(2)). Thus, when an RD signs a contract on behalf of the corporation without obtaining the board's approval, which is necessary under the law or the articles of incorporation, the contract is valid and enforceable despite the absence of board approval. To avoid the binding effect of such a contract, the corporation must prove that the counterparty to the contract knew or was grossly negligent in not knowing the absence of the necessary board approval.[17]

The RD is often assisted by some senior executives who are usually

15 For more details, see Kyung-Hoon Chun, *Korea's Mandatory Independent Directors: Expected and Unexpected Roles*, INDEPENDENT DIRECTORS IN ASIA: A HISTORICAL, CONTEXTUAL AND COMPARATIVE APPROACH (Dan W. Puchniak et al. eds.), Cambridge University Press, 176 ff. (2017).

16 The power to appoint and dismiss an RD belongs to the board of directors, unless the articles of incorporation grant such power to the GMS (ComC Article 389(1)).

17 Supreme Court Decision 2015Da45451, February 18, 2021.

not board members but carry such titles as 'president' (*sajang*), 'vice president' (*busajang*), and 'managing director' (*jeonmu* or *sangmu*). These senior executives, together with the RD, are usually called the management. Especially in large listed corporations, the RD and the senior executives make substantive business decisions while the board of directors, where the independent directors comprise the majority, is periodically convened to hear the reports of the management and to make decisions on a limited number of matters reserved for the board's decision by the statutes or articles of incorporation.

Another matter to note in relation to the RD's authority is the existence of controlling shareholders. In Korea, even giant corporations are often led by a controlling shareholder, who dominates the corporate decision-making process either directly, in the capacity of an RD, or indirectly, by appointing a trusted associate or subordinate as an RD. The indirect method is more common in Korean business groups. In such a case, the RD is usually under the close direction and supervision of the controlling shareholder, who is often called the *hoejang* (chairman) or *chongsu* (leader) of the business group. ComC stipulates the roles, powers, duties, and liabilities of the directors, including the RDs, but does not clearly regulate those of the controlling shareholders who are not board members but are exercising *de facto* control over the corporation. This is a serious gap in Korean corporate law. Article 401-2 of ComC, discussed in a later section of this chapter, is a statutory attempt to fill such gap.[18]

(5) Statutory Auditors and the Audit Committee

Korean corporations must have an internal supervisory organ, either a statutory auditor or an audit committee.

A statutory auditor is a natural person elected at a GMS who supervises and audits the business and accounting affairs of the corporation (ComC Article 409). ComC provides a few measures to secure the independence of the statutory auditor from the management. First, a statutory auditor cannot serve concurrently as a director, a general manager, or any other employee of the corporation or its subsidiaries (ComC Article 411). Second, when electing

18 See *infra* 3. (2) 3).

a statutory auditor at a GMS, each shareholder is allowed to vote only up to 3% of the total outstanding voting shares (Article 409(2)). This '3% rule' intends to restrict the influence of large shareholders on the appointment of a statutory auditor.

Instead of a statutory auditor, a corporation may choose to have an audit committee, which is a subcommittee of the board of directors in charge of supervising and auditing the business and accounting affairs of the corporation (ComC Article 415-2(1)). Two-thirds of the members of the audit committee must be independent directors (ComC Article 415-2(2)). Under ComC, an audit committee can be either 'normal' or 'qualified,' with the most significant distinction between these pertaining to how the members are elected. The members of a 'normal' audit committee are elected by the board of directors among its members (ComC Articles 415-2(1) and 393-2) while the members of a 'qualified' audit committee are elected by the shareholders at a GMS (ComC Article 542-12(1)).[19] In addition, at least one member of a 'qualified' audit committee must be an expert in accounting or finance, and its chair must be an independent director (ComC Article 542-11(2)). Large listed corporations (corporations with a total asset of KRW 2 trillion or more) must establish a 'qualified' audit committee (ComC Article 542-11(1)).

Both a statutory auditor and an audit committee have the duty to supervise the operation and accounting of the relevant corporation. If they find out that a director has violated a law or the articles of incorporation, they must report such matter to the board of directors (ComC Article 391-2(2)). They must examine the GMS agenda items and related materials before each GMS and express their opinions about these at the GMS (ComC Article 413). In performing their supervisory role, they are authorized to investigate the business affairs and financial status of the corporation (ComC Article 412(2)) and those of its subsidiaries (ComC Article 412-5).

Aside from appointing a statutory auditor or establishing an audit committee, corporations beyond a certain size also have to hire an accounting firm or a team of certified public accountants as external auditors (AEA Article 4). It is the external auditor appointed pursuant to AEA rather than the statutory auditor or audit committee that performs

19 With regard to the election of a member of the qualified audit committee at a GMS, each shareholder is allowed to vote only up to 3% of the total outstanding voting shares (ComC Article 542-12(4)).

the actual work of auditing the corporation's accounts. Hence, continuous cooperation and communication between the internal supervisory organs and the external auditors is important to enhance the quality of supervision.

3. Duties and Liabilities of Directors

(1) Directors' Duties

1) Overview

A director of a Korean corporation has fiduciary duties toward the corporation (ComC Article 382(2)). Notably, ComC states that directors have fiduciary duties toward the corporation rather than toward the shareholders. In principle, however, the ratable interest of the shareholders as a whole is mostly identical to the interest of the corporation unless the corporation is insolvent. Directors' fiduciary duties are usually categorized as duty of care and duty of loyalty.

2) Duty of Care

❶ Degree of Care

Directors' duty of care requires directors to use the same degree of care that an ordinarily prudent man or woman is generally and objectively expected to provide in performing their duties. This duty applies to all types of board members, whether executive or independent directors. However, the required degree of care is unclear in practice. In a case in which a director is accused of breaching his/her duty of care, his/her primary defense may be to assert that he/she made the decision in good faith for the best interest of the corporation, and on the basis of a review of the relevant information and the reasonable business judgment in such case.

❷ Business Judgment Rule

Although its legal implication is not exactly the same as that of its US equivalent, Korean courts have recognized the *business judgment rule* as a defense in duty-of-care cases. If a director is able to show that "a business decision was made in good faith for the best interest of the corporation, on the basis of a sufficient review of the necessary information reasonably available," then he/she will be deemed to have acted within "a permissible range of discretion," and the reviewing court will not find breach of fiduciary duty "unless the substance of such judgment is egregiously irrational."[20] In other words, the failure of directors' business decisions should not be challenged on a hindsight basis unless there is a lack of "sufficient review of the necessary information" or a lack of "good faith for the best interest of the corporation." The Supreme Court has consistently held, however, that the business judgment rule does not apply to illegal misconduct. For example, the use of corporate funds for bribery, window dressing, and other types of violations of law cannot be justified under this rule even if the misconduct might have brought more benefit than harm to the corporation.[21]

Unlike the courts in many other jurisdictions, the Korean courts have not clearly declared that the business judgment rule does not apply to conflict-of-interest situations.[22] In reality, however, the Korean courts tend to hold directors liable when a corporation allegedly incurred a loss in a transaction with parties related to it.[23] Most of the major Korean corporations belong to a business group composed of dozens of affiliate companies that often have vertical or horizontal business relations. Thus, related-party transactions are inevitable and ubiquitous in Korea, and there have been increasing attempts to hold directors liable for allegedly unfair related-party transactions. In such cases, the business judgment rule is not entirely non-applicable per se, but it does not provide a complete defense.

❸ Oversight Duty

As a ramification of the duty of care, a director is obliged to oversee the

20 For example, Supreme Court Decisions 2001Da52407, June 14, 2002; 2003 Da69638, October 28, 2005; and 2006Da33333, October 11, 2007.

21 Supreme Court Decisions 2003Da69638, October 28, 2005 (bribery); 2006 Da33333, October 11, 2007 (violation of antitrust law); 2007Da60080, December 13, 2007 (illegal accounting); and 2006Da19603, November 30, 2007 (illegal accounting).

22 The Delaware court, for example, applies the business judgment rule only to cases where the defendant's interest is not in conflict with the corporation's interest. A stricter standard, such as the entire fairness rule or the intrinsic fairness rule, is applied when there is a conflict of interest between the defendant and the corporation.

23 For example, Supreme Court Decisions 2003Da69638, October 28, 2005; 2006 Da33333, October 11, 2007; 2008Da14633, April 14, 2011; 2007Do8373, April 11, 2008; and 99Do1141, June 25, 1999.

conduct of the management and peer directors. The Supreme Court held that the oversight duty also applies to non-standing directors and covers matters not included in the agenda of board meetings.[24] In a case involving illegal accounting (also known as 'window dressing'), the directors who were not directly involved in and were even ignorant of the misconduct were also held liable for it on the grounds that they had breached their duty to monitor their peer directors' conduct to prevent them from engaging in any misconduct. The Supreme Court stated that ignorance of misconduct would not exempt directors from liability if they had not made any effort at all to establish "a reasonable information and reporting system" and if the misconduct had resulted from "a sustained and systematic failure to exercise oversight,"[25] using phrases apparently influenced by the *Caremark* case of the Delaware court.[26] This ruling drew greater attention to a "reasonable information and reporting system" or a compliance system as a method of fulfilling the oversight duty.

In a more recent case in which the executives of a steel manufacturing corporation committed continuous price fixing in collusion with its competitors and in which the corporation eventually had to pay a large penalty to the competition authority, the court pointed out the lack of an internal compliance system to deter such misconduct and held that the RD breached his oversight duty.[27] Because of these court precedents, the oversight duty and the internal compliance system are attracting increasing attention and causing concerns among Korean corporations. Building and operating a reliable and efficient compliance system within a firm is an important task of the in-house lawyers, compliance officers, and board members.

3) Duty of Loyalty

Directors must avoid conflicts of interest with the corporation in performing their duties. This duty is often called the duty of loyalty. Three provisions of ComC may be cited as statutory examples. First, directors may not

24 Supreme Court Decision 84Daka1954, June 25, 1985.

25 Supreme Court Decision 2006Da68636, Septembr 11, 2008.

26 *In re Caremark International Inc. Derivative Litigation*, 698 A.2d 959 (Del. Ch. 1996).

27 Supreme Court Decision 2017Da222368, November 11, 2021.

compete with the corporation in the same area of business without prior approval from the board of directors (ComC Article 397). Second, directors may not engage in self-dealing transactions with the corporation without prior approval from the board of directors (ComC Article 398). Third, directors may not appropriate a "corporate opportunity" without prior approval from the board of directors (ComC Article 397-2).[28] A corporate opportunity is a business opportunity currently or potentially profitable to the corporation, which is either (i) learned about through the use of corporate information or in the course of performing the directors' duties or (ii) closely related to the corporation's current or planned business.

It is noteworthy that in the aforementioned three provisions, the relevant acts (i.e., competition with the corporation, self-dealing, and use of corporate opportunity) are not prohibited per se but may be justified by obtaining prior board approval. Board approval, however, does not necessarily exempt the involved directors from liability in such cases. If the board of directors had approved a director's competing business with the corporation, self-dealing transaction, or appropriation of a corporate opportunity but such approved act turned out to be harmful to the corporation, then the issue would be whether the approving directors had performed their fiduciary duties in the course of reviewing and approving the act. If it turned out that the directors had breached their fiduciary duties at the time of their review and approval of the relevant act, they could be subject to liability, as discussed below.[29]

Article 398 on self-dealing, the most frequently invoked provision among the three mentioned above, warrants a few further notes. First, it regulates a corporation's transaction not only with its directors but also with a wide range of related parties. Prior board approval is required for a corporation's transactions with its directors, major shareholders, or persons specially related to them.[30] Second, a self-dealing transaction entered into

28 It is unique that Korean law stipulates the corporate opportunity doctrine and even dares to define "corporate opportunity" in the statute. For more details, see Hwa-jin Kim et al., *Favoritism and Corporate Law: The Confused Corporate Opportunity Doctrine in the Hyundai Motor Case,* 3 MICHIGAN BUSINESS & ENTREPRENEURIAL LAW REVIEW 41 (2013); Kyung-Hoon Chun, *Corporate Opportunity Doctrine as a Basis for Directors' Liability: A New Statutory Experiment in Korea*, GERMAN AND ASIAN PERSPECTIVES ON COMPANY LAW (Holger Fleischer et al. eds.), Mohr Siebeck (2016).

29 See *infra* 3. (2) 1).

30 More specifically, the following persons must obtain board approval before

without the necessary board approval is null and void between the parties but is valid vis-à-vis an innocent third party. For example, if a director purchased a building from the corporation without board approval, the corporation may nullify the transaction and demand that the director return the building (in exchange for the money the corporation was paid). The corporation, however, cannot resort to such a remedy vis-à-vis a third-party purchaser of the building unless the corporation successfully proves that the third-party purchaser knew or was grossly negligent in not knowing the absence of the necessary board approval.[31]

(2) Directors' Liabilities

1) Civil Liabilities to the Corporation

If a director breaches the law or the articles of incorporation or fails to perform his/her duties, he/she is liable to the corporation for the loss caused by his/her breach (ComC Article 399(1)). If more than one director is involved, the directors are jointly and severally liable. Note that under Article 399, the directors are liable to the 'corporation' instead of the 'shareholders.' Holding directors directly liable to the shareholders requires other legal grounds, such as Article 401 of ComC (discussed below) or the provisions of CMA on false disclosures.[32]

In a case in which a director's act in question is based on a resolution of the board of directors, the directors who voted for the resolution are also liable to the corporation (ComC Article 399(2)). If a director's opposition to the resolution is not recorded in the minutes, the director is presumed to have voted in favor of the resolution in question (ComC Article 399(3)).

Directors may be sued either by the corporation, through a direct ac-

entering into a transaction with the corporation: (i) directors or major shareholders (shareholders holding 10% or more of the total issued shares of the corporation or have *de facto* control over the corporation); (ii) their spouses and lineal ascendants/descendants; (iii) their spouses' lineal ascendants/descendants; (iv) a corporation in which (i)–(iii) hold 50% or more of the total issued shares or its subsidiary; and (v) a corporation in which (i)–(iv) hold 50% or more of the total issued shares (ComC Article 398).

31 Supreme Court Decision 2011Da67651, December 27, 2012.

32 For more details regarding liability for false disclosures, see Kyung-Hoon Chun, *Investor Protection in the Korean Capital Market through Disclosures and Litigation*, 16 JOURNAL OF KOREAN LAW 193, 210-222 (2016).

tion, or by the corporation's shareholders, through a derivative action. When the corporation brings a direct action against its directors, the statutory auditor (not the RD, to guarantee a fair and independent handling of the lawsuit) must represent the corporation (ComC Article 394(1)). Typical examples of cases in which directors were held liable under Article 399 of ComC include those involving (i) sale of a corporation's asset at a considerably low price,[33] (ii) embezzlement of the corporation's funds or assets,[34] (iii) provision of a loan to a financially distressed company without taking proper measures to secure repayment,[35] (iv) violation of a law resulting in the corporation's payment of a fine or monetary penalty,[36] and (v) commission of accounting fraud resulting in inflated profits and overpayment of dividends and corporate income tax.[37]

2) Civil Liabilities to Third Parties

A director is held liable to a third party who suffers a loss caused by the director's intentional or grossly negligent failure to perform his/her duty (ComC Article 401(1)). For example, if a director manipulated the financial statements of the corporation and a creditor provided a loan to the corporation relying on such false financial statements, the creditor may bring an action against the director on the basis of Article 401.[38] The article does not state that a director has a direct duty to a third party. Rather, a third party who suffered harm due to the director's breach of his/her duty to the corporation may sue such director. What has been breached here is the director's duty to the corporation and not to a third party, such as a creditor.

As in the case of liability to the corporation, if more than one director is involved, the directors are jointly and severally liable (ComC Article 401(1)). The third-party plaintiff, however, has a higher burden of proof than the corporation has under Article 399 because he/she has to prove at least gross negligence on the part of defendant directors.

There is a dispute as to whether the aforementioned liability extends to 'indirect' damage. Indirect damage refers to damage incurred by a third

33 Supreme Court Decision 2003Da69638, October 28, 2005.
34 Supreme Court Decision 91Da36093, January 26, 1993.
35 Supreme Court Decision 2012Da98850, October 29, 2015.
36 Supreme Court Decision 2006Da33333, October 11, 2007.
37 Supreme Court Decision 2007Da60080, December 13, 2007.
38 Supreme Court Decision 2007Da31518, September 11, 2008.

party as a consequence of damage inflicted on the corporation. For example, if the corporation's value decreases due to a director's misconduct, the shareholders will suffer indirect damage as a result of the declining share price. The Supreme Court held that shareholders cannot claim indirect damage against an erring director under Article 401.[39] In such cases, a shareholder will have to rely on a derivative action (ComC Article 403) to recover the damage inflicted on the company.[40]

3) Extension of Civil Liabilities to *De Facto* Directors

Articles 399 and 401 of ComC address the liability of "directors" to the corporation and a third party. ComC also adopted a concept similar to a "*de facto* director" or a "shadow director" and extends the liabilities under Articles 399 and 401 to such persons. More specifically, the following persons can also be held liable under Article 399 or 401 even if they do not formally hold the position of a director: (i) a person who, by taking advantage of his/her influence on the corporation, directed a director to execute the business of the corporation in a particular manner; (ii) a person who executed the business of the corporation in the name of a director; and (iii) a person who executed the business of the corporation using a title regarded as granting him/her the authority to execute the corporation's business (e.g., 'honorary chairperson,' 'chairperson,' 'president,' 'vice president,' 'executive director,' and 'director') (ComC Article 401-2).

'Influence' is the key element in item (i) above while 'title' is the key element in item (iii).[41] Thus, a controlling shareholder who exercised influence over the management and caused harm to the corporation can be held liable under item (i). An officer who carries the title of 'president' can be held liable under item (iii) for the corporation's loss caused by his/her breach of duty of care even if he/she is not a member of the board of directors.

4) Criminal Liabilities

One distinctive feature of Korean law with regard to corporate governance is the frequent use of criminal charges. Pursuant to the Criminal Act and

39 Supreme Court Decisions 91Da36093, January 26, 1993; 2010Da77743, December 13, 2012.

40 See *infra* 4. (3).

41 Supreme Court Decision 2011Da6120, June 10, 2011.

other statutes, if a person taking care of another person's affairs breaches his/her duties and causes harm to such person by obtaining or causing a third party to obtain unlawful profits (*baeim* or 'criminal breach of trust'), he/she is subject to criminal fine or imprisonment, which may be extended to lifetime imprisonment depending on the amount of unlawful profit made.[42] The elements of criminal breach of trust are (i) breach of duty (ii) by a person who is taking care of another person's affairs, (iii) loss to the principal, and (iv) profit to the actor or a third party.

In Korea, civil actions have not been very effective in preventing director and manager misconduct. The absence of punitive damages, discovery systems, and class action at least partially explains the weakness of the civil remedies. However, prosecutors have played an important role by applying criminal breach of trust to various types of misconduct of directors, officers, and controlling shareholders. The Supreme Court has held directors and controlling shareholders criminally liable for such types of misconduct as (i) acquisition of shares of an affiliate company at par value even though their fair value was zero,[43] (ii) provision of a loan or guarantee to a financially distressed affiliate company without taking proper measures to secure repayment,[44] and (iii) sale of assets to an affiliate company at a considerably low price.[45] Civil actions against directors and officers are often preceded by their criminal convictions.

4. Shareholders' Rights and Power

(1) Right to Vote

At a GMS, holders of voting stocks have the right to vote in favor of or against a resolution. Below are some important matters requiring the shareholders' passage of a resolution at a GMS.

42 Articles 355(2) and 356 of the Criminal Act and Article 3 of the Act on Aggravated Penalties on Specific Economic Crimes.

43 Supreme Court Decisions 2012Do1283, June 14, 2012; 2004Do520, June 24, 2004.

44 Supreme Court Decisions 2013Do10516, July 10, 2014; 2013Do5214, September 26, 2013; 2009Do7435, July 12, 2012; and 2007Do541, July 23, 2009.

45 Supreme Court Decision 2013Do5214, September 26, 2013.

1) Election and Removal of Directors

Directors are elected at an ordinary or extraordinary GMS. The names of the directors nominated by the current board of directors[46] are usually indicated in the GMS notice, and the shareholders vote for or against each candidate. If the number of affirmative votes for a candidate satisfies the ordinary resolution requirement (i.e., a majority of the votes present at the meeting and at least a quarter of the total issued shares), the candidate is declared a director. This may be referred to as 'majority rule,' as opposed to 'plurality rule,' in the sense that the candidate must acquire affirmative votes from the majority of the shareholders with voting shares present at the meeting. Under this scheme, majority shareholders, in effect, have absolute power to appoint all board members.

To curtail majority shareholders' power and protect minority shareholders, ComC has adopted a cumulative voting system. When two or more directors are to be elected at a GMS, shareholders holding at least 3% (1% in the case of large listed firms) of the total issued voting shares of the corporation may request that the resolution be passed through cumulative voting (ComC Article 382-2(1)). However, the corporation may opt out of cumulative voting in its articles of incorporation (ComC Article 382-2(1)). More than 90% of the listed firms in Korea have opted out of cumulative voting through their articles of incorporation.

It is noteworthy that shareholders may remove directors through a special resolution passed at a GMS without cause and at any time (ComC Article 385(1)). If a director is removed during his/her term of office without just cause, the removed director is entitled only to monetary compensation from the corporation (ComC Article 385(1)), which generally corresponds to the remuneration he/she could have earned during the remainder of his/her term of office had he/she not been removed. Such potential for unilateral removal shows the great power granted to shareholders by Korean law.

2) Approval of Fundamental Changes

As discussed earlier in this chapter, the implementation of fundamental changes to a corporation requires a special resolution to be passed at a

46 Independent directors of large listed corporations and financial institutions are nominated by the Independent Director Candidate Nomination Committee, a subcommittee of the board of directors (ComC Article 542-8(4)).

GMS. In other words, the board of directors or the RD may initiate the process for the implementation of such fundamental changes, but it is the shareholders who have the final authority to decide on the matter. The matters that require the passage of a special resolution at a GMS include removal of directors, granting of stock options, reduction of legal capital, merger, corporate division, transfer or acquisition of business, dissolution, conversion into a different corporate type, comprehensive stock swap, and amendment of the articles of incorporation.[47]

In the case of merger, comprehensive stock swap, and transfer or acquisition of business, the dissenting shareholders are given appraisal rights (ComC Articles 360-5, 374-2, and 522-3). Once these dissenting shareholders exercise their appraisal rights, the corporation must buy back their shares. The price is to be determined by the corporation and shareholders through consultations and agreements. In unlisted corporations, if the corporation and shareholders fail to agree on the price, the court determines a "fair" price upon either party's application for such. In listed corporations, if the corporation and shareholders fail to agree on the price, a hypothetical price calculated using a formula prescribed by CMA will apply,[48] but if either party does not accept such hypothetical price, it may ask the court to determine a fair price (CMA Article 165-5).

3) Directors' Remuneration

Any type of director remuneration, including salary, bonus, incentive, and severance pay, must be (i) stated in the articles of incorporation *or* (ii) determined at a GMS (ComC Article 388). Without such a basis in the articles of incorporation or a shareholder resolution, the directors cannot claim such remuneration from the corporation even if they have a written contract with the corporation stipulating it. This is a powerful form of shareholder involvement in the directors' salary, stronger, for example, than any radical proposal in the United States for 'say on pay,' because the shareholders of

47 See *supra* 2. (2) 3).

48 The hypothetical price, in essence, is an arithmetic average of (i) the volume-weighted average of the daily closing prices in the two months before the date of the board resolution, (ii) the volume-weighted average of the daily closing prices in the month before the date of the board resolution, and (iii) the volume-weighted average of the daily closing prices in the week before the date of the board resolution (CMA Enforcement Decree Article 176-7(3)).

Korean corporations not just 'say' but 'determine' the directors' pay.

In practice, however, the actual power of shareholders on the directors' pay is not as formidable as it seems. Many Korean corporations approve an annual firm-wide ceiling for the aggregate amount of director remuneration at an ordinary GMS, rather than determining each director's salary. Each director's salary is determined within such a ceiling, without the further involvement of the shareholders. Such ceiling applies to the directors (i.e., board members), but not to the other members of the management.

Granting stock options requires (i) a special resolution at a GMS *and* (ii) a relevant provision in the articles of incorporation (ComC Article 340-2). It applies regardless of who holds the stock option; not only the directors or statutory auditors but also the employees and executives at every rank need both requirements to receive stock options.

(2) Right to Initiate Corporate Decision Making

Even though the shareholders' voting power is important in corporate governance, it can be exercised only when a GMS is convened and only with respect to the agenda items presented at the GMS. The incumbent directors are the ones who determine whether to convene a GMS, and set the date, location, and agenda items for the GMS. In other words, the shareholders exercise their voting power within the framework set by the board. ComC provides two powerful weapons as exceptions to this passive aspect of shareholder power: the right to call an extraordinary GMS and the right to make a proposal for the GMS.

Shareholders holding at least 3% of the total issued shares of the corporation may request the board to convene an extraordinary GMS (ComC Article 366(1)). In a listed firm, shareholders who have held at least 1% of the total issued shares of the corporation for at least six months have the same right (ComC Article 542-6(1)). The shareholders must submit to the board a written statement of the agenda item they desire to address and the reasons for their request to convene a GMS. If the board fails to take immediate steps to convene a GMS, the shareholders may convene one themselves with the approval of the court (ComC Article 366(2)).

Shareholders holding 3% of the total issued and outstanding voting shares of the corporation can submit a proposal to be resolved at a GMS (ComC Article 363-2(1)(2)). In a listed firm, shareholders who have held at least 1% (0.5% in the case of a larger firm) of the total issued and outstanding voting shares of the corporation for at least six months have the same right (ComC Article 542-6(2)). The board of directors must include the proposed item in the GMS agenda, which the shareholders will be notified of unless there exist narrow exceptions, such as that the substance of the proposal is against the law (ComC Article 363-2(3)). The removal of a director can also be initiated through a shareholder proposal, but the board of directors of listed corporations may legitimately reject a proposal for removing a director (ComC Enforcement Decree Article 12(iv)) while the board of directors of unlisted corporations must accept such a proposal and include it in the GMS agenda. Changing the articles of incorporation is also a legitimate item for a shareholder proposal; thus, the board of directors must include it in the GMS agenda if it is duly proposed by the shareholders.

(3) Right to Pursue Directors' Liabilities: Derivative Actions

1) Overview

Korean law allows shareholders to bring a derivative action against erring directors on behalf of the corporation. Derivative action was introduced to Korean law when ComC was enacted in 1962, under the heavy influence of US law. It was hardly used in the past, but the number of derivative actions is now increasing, albeit slowly.

A few features of the derivative actions in Korea are noteworthy. First, non-governmental organizations, such as the People's Solidarity for Participatory Democracy and the Solidarity for Economic Reform, have played important roles in organizing and initiating actions against the directors of Korean conglomerates, especially in the late 1990s and early 2000s. Their main goal is to improve the allegedly rigged governance of Korean corporations as a part of social reform, rather than maximizing shareholder value. Such sociopolitical motives have made them bring a number of derivative actions against the directors of a few large and famous firms in Korea, even if they have little economic incentive to do so. Second, the derivative actions in Korea frequently follow criminal prosecutions or administrative inspection proceedings on the basis of the facts found in such proceedings. For example, after a director is found guilty of embezzlement or criminal breach of trust, the shareholders tend to bring a derivative action against him/her. In the absence of a US-style discovery process, this is the most convenient and only practical way to collect evidence for a derivative action.

2) Requirements for Plaintiffs

Under ComC, shareholders holding at least 1% of the total issued shares of the corporation can bring a derivative action against an erring director on behalf of the corporation (ComC Article 403(1)). In a listed firm, shareholders who have held at least 0.01% of the total issued shares of the corporation for at least six months have the same right (ComC Article 542-6(6)). Although the 1% or 0.01% ratio can be satisfied in aggregate by multiple shareholders, this requirement is probably one of the main barriers to bringing derivative actions against erring directors in Korea.

However, ComC also has some rules rendering the aforementioned requirement not as strict as it seems. Once the plaintiff meets the minimum shareholding ratio at the time of filing of the lawsuit, any reduction in such plaintiff's shareholding ratio will not affect his/her standing as long as he/she holds at least one share (ComC Article 403(5)). Moreover, unlike the relevant US law,[49] ComC does not have a *contemporaneous* share ownership requirement; that is, the plaintiff need not have been a shareholder at the time that the challenged misconduct was committed. The rationale for this is that the plaintiff shareholder is enforcing the corporation's cause of action as an agent and not as a principal, with the legal effects of the lawsuit vested with the corporation. Thus, it does not matter whether the plaintiff him/herself suffered any damage from the challenged misconduct at the time it was committed.

Under Korean law, the corporation itself is neither a plaintiff nor a defendant in a derivative action. Only the shareholders can be plaintiffs,[50] and the persons liable to the corporation (usually the directors who breached their fiduciary duties) are the defendants. The corporation is merely allowed

49 US Federal Rule 23.1(b) requires the verified complaint of a derivative action to allege that the plaintiff was a shareholder at the time of the transaction complained of.

50 To meet the minimum shareholding ratio requirement, multiple shareholders usually form a group of plaintiffs, often through online media. However, it is not a class action per se. Only those shareholders who are specifically named as plaintiffs in the complaint and who themselves signed or affixed their seals on the complaint or did so through their attorneys become the plaintiffs of a derivative action.

to participate in the proceedings on the plaintiff's side, and only if it wants to do so (ComC Article 404(1)). The plaintiff must notify the corporation of the action without delay so that the corporation may participate in the proceedings if it wants to (ComC Article 404(2)). This is strikingly different from the practice in the United States, where the corporation is usually named one of the defendants.[51]

Also, ComC clearly allows "multiple derivative actions" (ComC Article 406-2). Under this scheme, which was introduced in the 2020 amendment of ComC, the shareholders of a parent company can bring an action against the directors of a subsidiary of the company who have caused harm to the subsidiary.[52]

3) Demand Requirement

Before filing a derivative action, the shareholder must demand that the corporation file a lawsuit against the relevant director (ComC Article 403(1)). If the corporation fails to file such a lawsuit within 30 days from the date of demand, the shareholder may immediately bring a derivative action on behalf of the corporation. If any irreparable damage is likely to arise, the shareholder may immediately bring a derivative action without making such a demand (ComC Article 403(3)).

The demand requirement under Korean law is different from the 'demand-on-board requirement' under many US state laws. Under the laws of the states of Delaware and New York, for example, a written demand must be submitted to the board of directors unless the case meets the 'demand futility test.' The board of directors has broad discretion in determining whether to file a lawsuit. Unlike US law, Korean law does not recognize the board's or any special committee's discretion not to file or terminate a lawsuit. Once the 30-day demand period lapses, regardless of the board's decision, the plaintiff shareholder may legitimately bring a derivative action (ComC Article 403(3)). Therefore, this requirement is not a significant barrier

51 The custom of making the corporation a nominal defendant in a derivative action demonstrates the survival of the historical conception that a derivative suit is two suits in one: a suit against the corporation and a suit against the wrongdoer. Robert C. Clark, CORPORATE LAW, Aspen, 639 (1986).

52 For more details, see Kyung-Hoon Chun, *Multiple Derivative Actions: Debates in Korea and the Implication for a Comparative Study*, 15 BERKELEY BUSINESS LAW JOURNAL 306–336 (2019).

to bringing a derivative action in Korea.

4) Underlying Claim

A derivative remedy is available only when the corporation suffered harm from the defendant's misconduct. In other words, for a valid derivative action to be brought against a director, the corporation must have a substantive claim against the latter. Such a claim typically arises when a director causes harm to the corporation by breach of his/her fiduciary duty or violation of the law (ComC Article 399).

5) Ancillary Remedies

ComC allows injunctive remedies by shareholders. When a director is likely to breach the law or the articles of incorporation and the corporation may incur irreparable damage as a result of such breach, shareholders holding at least 1% of the total issued shares (in listed firms, including shareholders who have held at least 0.05% or 0.025% of the total issued shares of the corporation, depending on the size of the corporation, for at least six months) or a statutory auditor may seek injunctive relief prohibiting the relevant director from undertaking the act in question (ComC Article 402).

To facilitate derivative actions or injunctive relief, ComC allows shareholders to access corporate books and records. Each shareholder may inspect or copy the financial statements and audit reports kept at the corporation's main or branch office (ComC Article 448(2)). In addition, shareholders holding at least 3% of the total issued shares (in listed firms, including shareholders who have held at least 0.1% or 0.05% of the total issued shares of the corporation, depending on the size of the corporation, for at least six months) may gain access to the accounting books and records (ComC Article 466(1)). To deny such access to the shareholder, directors must prove the unreasonableness of the shareholder's demand (ComC Article 466(2)).

(4) Preemptive Rights

Issuance of new shares may have negative impacts on the existing shareholders. If such shareholders cannot participate in the purchase of new shares on a pro rata basis, their shareholding ratio will decrease, and depending on the issue price, the value of their shares may be diluted. To protect the existing shareholders from such risks, ComC gives them preemptive rights. That is, unless otherwise provided for in the articles of incorporation, shareholders have a right to subscribe to new shares in proportion to their shareholding ratio (ComC Article 418(1)).

As an exception to the aforementioned rule, new shares can be issued to a third party if the corporation has corresponding provisions in its articles of incorporation and a proper business purpose for such third-party allotment (ComC Article 418(2)). Most listed corporations have provisions in their articles of incorporation authorizing third-party allotment, but 'a proper business purpose' is not always acknowledged by the court. For instance, the Supreme Court held that defense against hostile takeovers did not constitute a proper business purpose for issuing new shares to a third party that was friendly to the incumbent board.[53]

(5) Remarks

As shown above, at least as a matter of blackletter law, shareholders have a strong set of rights under Korean law. They may convene an extraordinary GMS, may initiate an amendment to the articles of incorporation by way of a shareholder proposal to such effect, may remove directors without cause and at any time through a special resolution to such effect, and even enjoy the preemptive right to subscribe to new shares on a pro rata basis. These are representative characteristics of the UK model of strong shareholders, as opposed to the US model of weak shareholders.[54] At least in these respects, Korean law resembles UK law rather than US law, and may be evaluated as pro-shareholder rather than pro-management.

In reality, however, there are significant hurdles that need to be overcome. First, the shareholding thresholds for exercising certain rights are restrictive and sometimes prohibitively high. For example, bringing a derivative action requires holding 1% of the total issued shares for unlisted corporations and 0.01% of the total issued shares for listed corporations. For large listed corporations, 0.01% of the total issued shares may be

53 Supreme Court Decision 2008Da50776, January 30, 2009. See also Sang Gon Kim, *Issuance of New Shares as a Takeover Defense and Countermeasures*, 8 JOURNAL OF KOREAN LAW 325 (2009).

54 C. Bruner, CORPORATE GOVERNANCE IN THE COMMON-LAW WORLD – THE POLITICAL FOUNDATIONS OF SHAREHOLDER POWER, Cambridge University Press 37-40 (2013).

equivalent to millions of US dollars, depending on the prevailing stock price, which makes derivative action virtually unavailable for most minority shareholders. Second, the Korean judicial system and its practices are generally not very friendly to plaintiffs. Korean law does not have a US-style discovery system and does not allow class actions, except for certain types of securities litigation.[55] Also, as punitive damages are not recognized, the amount of monetary compensation is limited to the actual loss suffered by the plaintiff, and the plaintiff generally has the burden of proof. Thus, in Korea, civil actions and the possibility of civil liability generally pose less threat than criminal charges or administrative penalties do.

5. A Few Notes on Large Business Groups

(1) Overview

In Korea, some large business groups (LBGs), commonly known as chaebols, dominate the corporate scene. Chaebol refers to a large group of related corporations engaged in diverse lines of business under highly concentrated family or individual control. LBGs such as Samsung, Hyundai Motors, SK, LG, Lotte, Hanwha, GS, Hyundai Heavy Industry, Shinsegae, CJ, Hanjin, and Doosan have played a crucial role in Korea's economic development and still account for a critical portion of the Korean economy in terms of revenues, exports, hiring, research and development, and others.

There have been long-time debates on the positive and negative contributions of LBGs. Undoubtedly, the success of the Korean economy is largely due to the LBGs' outstanding performance and to the inspired entrepreneurship of their founders. On the other hand, the LBGs have been criticized for some alleged problems, including (i) excessive concentration of economic power (which may lead to the concentration of social, political, and cultural power), (ii) monopolization of certain product and service markets (which may lead to suboptimal consumer welfare), and (iii) corporate governance problems such as tunneling[56] by the controlling shareholders (which may lead

55 Securities Related Class Action Act (enacted in 2003 and effective as of 2005).

56 Tunneling means the transfer or diversion of wealth from a corporation to the controlling shareholders or managers at the expense of the non-controlling

to the undervaluation of the Korean capital market). Of these problems, the third is a typical corporate law issue and is briefly discussed below.

(2) Governance

LBGs' governance styles are diverse. Some LBGs have a holding company structure, in which a holding company located at the top of the entire group owns and controls dozens of subsidiaries.[57] Others have a more complicated (and traditional) structure, such as a circular holding structure, where no single holding company can be identified. In either case, a few large corporations within the group are usually listed on the stock market, but many other affiliates remain unlisted. Furthermore, the controlling family members' shareholding ratio in the listed flagship corporations of each group is usually far less than 50% (and sometimes as low as 5-10%),[58] which creates the typical problem of 'controlling-minority shareholders.'[59]

In most cases, the controlling shareholder of an LBG holds a title such as 'chair' or 'honorary chair' and exercises control over the management of the entire group, either as a board member (and CEO) of the flagship company or as the *de facto* or shadow director, who is not officially a member of the board elected at a GMS. In other words, the controlling shareholders of LBGs are mostly not just passive investors but the heads of the company management, with the ultimate power to make important business decisions and to hire and fire senior members of the management.

shareholders. For a further explanation, see Simon Johnson et al., *Tunneling*, 90 AMERICAN ECONOMIC REVIEW 22 (2000).

57 Note that in Korea, many subsidiaries are also listed on the stock exchange. The presence of minority shareholders both at the holding company level and the subsidiary level (and the different cash-flow rights of the controlling shareholders over the holding company and subsidiaries) may create conflict-of-interest problems.

58 It is challenging for the controlling family members to maintain *de facto* control over the group in spite of their low shareholding ratio. To do this, they often resort to such methods as adopting a pyramid structure (which leverages the ownership by way of multi-layered partially owned subsidiaries), circular ownership, collaboration among the affiliate companies, and cooperation with other LBGs.

59 For an analysis of the problems caused by the controlling minority shareholders in Korea, see Ok-Rial Song, *The Legacy of Controlling Minority Structure: A Kaleidoscope of Corporate Governance Reform in Korean Chaebol*, 34 LAW & POLICY IN INTERNATIONAL BUSINESS 183 (2002).

(3) Alleged Tunneling

In LBGs, the controlling-minority shareholder structure creates a gap between the control and the cash-flow right. For example, if X owns 30% of the shares of Company A and takes 30% of its dividends (this being the cash-flow right) but somehow has complete control over Company A, then X may engage in various transactions benefiting him/her at the cost of the other shareholders of Company A. Let us assume that Company A (in which X owns 30% of the shares) is the flagship corporation of the group listed on the stock exchange, and that X's son, Y, is the sole shareholder of Company B. Below are some examples of related illicit practices that have frequently been found in Korea.[60]

One example is the use of underpriced new shares. X causes Company A to issue new shares at a price lower than the fair market price to Y or Company B.[61] This benefits Y but at the expense of the other shareholders of Company A. Alternatively, when Company A has shares of Company C, Company C issues new shares to each shareholder at a low price. If Company A voluntarily gives up its preemptive right, and Company C allocates the new shares to Company B or to Y, then Y will benefit at the expense of the other shareholders of Company A.[62]

Another example is the use of related-party transactions. If Company A and Company B enter into a transaction (e.g., sale of assets) under terms advantageous for Company B, then the wealth is transferred from Company A to Company B, ultimately from the non-controlling shareholders of Company A to Y. Such a transaction may constitute a self-dealing transaction and thus requires prior board approval from Company A (ComC Article 398),[63] but the management may come up with justifications that the

60 For a further analysis of tunneling in LBGs and the reaction of the Korean judiciary and legislature to it, see Kyung-Hoon Chun, *Management Succession in Korea: Tunneling, Semi-Tunneling, and the Reaction of Corporate Law*, 53 VANDERBILT JOURNAL OF TRANSNATIONAL LAW 753 (2020).

61 Because the default rule under ComC is that every shareholder has a preemptive right to buy new shares on a pro rata basis, Company A must prove a proper business purpose to avoid such rule. See *supra* 4. (4).

62 A similar fact pattern was at issue in Supreme Court Decision 2011Da57869, September 12, 2013, but no one was held liable because the decision of Company A's board not to purchase new Company C shares was found to have been a rational business decision.

63 See *supra* 3. (1) 3).

board cannot easily deny.[64]

A third example is the so-called funneling of businesses. To illustrate, Company B provides logistics services to the affiliate companies within the group and makes most of its revenue from such intragroup transactions. The price and other terms of each contract may be arm's length, but the large volume of business stably coming from the affiliate companies serves as a great advantage to Company B that its competitors cannot have.

On the aforementioned occasions, the corporate law regime of fiduciary duty and shareholder rights has not been very successful. The non-controlling shareholders who were allegedly harmed have little incentive to take any action, given the absence of punitive damages and of a class action system. Also, because the transactions are usually structured in such a way as to circumvent the restrictive rules, and as the directors and managers try to justify the transactions on the basis of the business judgment rule, it is very hard to prove violation of the law or breach of fiduciary duty. Indeed, the Korean courts have not actively interpreted and enforced the fiduciary duties of directors and controlling shareholders. Such weak enforcement of corporate law has prompted the frequent use of criminal penalties in corporate matters[65] and the competition authority's intervention in corporate governance issues, both of which are unique to Korean law.

(4) Regulations under FTA

The Korea Fair Trade Commission (KFTC), the main competition authority of Korea, enforces various rules in FTA, including those on LBGs. Every year, KFTC designates LBGs (Types I and II) on the basis of the amount of total assets,[66] and announces the list of designated groups, the member corporations of each group, a diagram of the shareholding structure of each group, and other related information.

64 There have been a number of court cases where the involved directors were held liable for related-party transactions within LBGs. Two examples are Supreme Court Decisions 2003Da69638, October 28, 2005 (civil liability for Samsung Group) and 2013Do5214, September 26, 2013 (criminal liability for Hanhwa Group).

65 See *supra* 3. (2) 4).

66 In terms of the total assets, the thresholds for Types I and II are KRW5 trillion and KRW10 trillion, respectively. The latter will soon be changed to 0.5% of the gross domestic product.

Corporations belonging to a Type I business group are subject to certain restrictions: prohibition of cross-holdings between the affiliates (MRFTA Article 21), prohibition of circular holdings among the affiliates (MRFTA Article 22), and prohibition of cross-guarantees between the affiliates (MRFTA Article 24), to name a few. Corporations belonging to Type I and II business groups are also required to make various public disclosures on the intragroup transactions and the group's ownership structure even if the member corporations are unlisted and close ones (MRFTA Articles 26, 27, and 28).

MRFTA also prohibits "undue support" between affiliate companies (MRFTA Article 45(1)(ix)). More specifically, it prohibits "unduly supporting a specially related party or another company through . . . providing advanced payments, loans, manpower, real estate, commercial notes, goods, services, intangible property, etc., to a specially related party or another company, or transacting on terms considerably advantageous for them." The scope of this article is not limited to LBGs, but in practice, the article has primarily been enforced against tunneling in LBGs. Thus, roughly speaking, any intragroup transaction within LBGs that is not on arms-length terms may constitute undue support. Violation of this provision is subject to a cease and desist order, an administrative fine of up to 5% of the related revenue, and/or criminal penalty of up to three-year imprisonment. KFTC has been active in enforcing the undue support clause, adjudicating many related cases over the last two decades.[67]

6. Conclusion

This chapter reviewed and analyzed the corporate law of Korea, focusing on the following aspects: (i) the internal governance structure consisting of the GMS, board of directors, statutory auditors, and RD; (ii) the duties

67 In addition to the undue support clause, the MRFTA also regulates "taking private benefits" (MRFTA Article 46). It prohibits the provision of benefits from "a company within an LBG" to "a member of the controlling family and the companies owned by them." For a more detailed analysis, see Yong Lim and Geeyoung Min, *Competition and Corporate Governance: Teaming up to Police Tunneling*, 36 NORTHWESTERN JOURNAL OF INTERNATIONAL LAW AND BUSINESS 267 (2016).

and liabilities of directors; (iii) the rights and powers of shareholders; and (iv) some issues concerning LBGs. Overall, Korean law provides a relatively good set of rules and principles for regulating the management and directors and a system of checks and balances between the shareholders acting through the GMS and the board of directors. Korean law also grants various rights to shareholders to protect them against director and manager misconduct.

In practice, however, the aforementioned rights granted to shareholders have not been actively exercised, presumably because there is little incentive on the part of each shareholder to exercise them and because of the insufficient litigation system in the country. Recently, however, an increasing number of institutional investors have been actively engaging with the management of their portfolio companies and invoking their rights as shareholders. In particular, the National Pension Service (NPS) of Korea, the third largest pension fund in the world, is taking a more aggressive approach to settling disputes or addressing scandals in its portfolio corporations. NPS justifies its activism as a way to maximize the value of its portfolio shares. However, there is also strong criticism against NPS's activism, based on the concern that it may be used by the government as a tool to intervene in the private market, given that NPS is under government control. The Korean Stewardship Code adopted in 2016, a soft law that addresses institutional investors' engagement with portfolio companies, is also galvanizing institutional shareholders' activism.[68] The rising trend of ESG (environmental, social, and governance) investment may also affect such shareholders' behaviors.

The activism of institutional investors may gradually cause changes in Korean corporations, where the controlling shareholders and the management have enjoyed relatively comfortable relationships with the passive non-controlling shareholders. For the next decade, regardless of whether the blackletter rules of Korean corporate law will be further changed, the rise of institutional investors' activism and such investors' interactions with LBGs will be interesting points to observe.

68 For more details regarding the Korean Stewardship Code, see Sang Yop Kang and Kyung-Hoon Chun, *Korea's Stewardship Code and the Rise of Shareholder Activism*, GLOBAL SHAREHOLDER STEWARDSHIP, Cambridge University Press (2022).

Chapter 12

Competition Law

Yong Lim*

1. Introduction: Birth of Modern Competition Law in Korea

(1) Korea's Legacy of Combating Monopolies

1) The Rise of State Sanctioned Monopolies (*Gum-nan-jun-kwon*)

There is a perception in Korea and abroad that the country's competition law regime is a foreign construct rooted in the U.S. and German legal traditions that was implanted in 1980 when the Monopoly Regulation and Fair Trade Act (MRFTA) was enacted. In reality, however, Korea has a rich history of both regulating and promoting competition as part of economic policy. A prominent example is the enactment and abolishment of *gum-nan-jun-kwon*. The Kingdom of Chosun had enlisted certain merchants (*shee-jun-sang-in*) with the task of procuring certain staple goods for the king and his court (and the capital more broadly), which was an attempt to stabilize the supply and thus prices of such goods. The merchants in turn were provided with the exclusive privilege of selling those goods in and around the capital. The power of these merchants grew as a result of the state's patronage during the latter part of the dynasty, and around the 17th century they gained the authority to regulate and discipline merchants who infringed on their privilege by selling such goods in the capital's

* Associate Professor, Seoul National University School of Law.

marketplaces. This authority was called *gum-nan-jun-kwon*. However, as is often the case with government-endowed monopoly power, the merchants acting in conjunction with those in power abused their authority, stifling the livelihoods of other merchants and creating market distortions. Recognizing the problems arising from this monopoly power, King Jungjo abolished the merchants' authority to regulate and limited their privileges, leading to a blossoming of market activity and economic growth. This reform is known as *shin-hae-tong-gong* and remains a cautionary tale of the unintended and in some cases corrupting consequences of state intervention in the market.

(2) The "Three Powder" Scandal and the Introduction of the Price Management Act

Chaebols, large conglomerates controlled by a family, were instrumental in implementing industrial policy during Korea's postwar development, particularly from the 1960s onward.[1] In this capacity, they were also the beneficiaries of government aid and preferential regulatory treatment which allowed and in some cases actively facilitated the acquisition of significant market power in the sectors where they were active. Then, in 1963, the "Three Powder" (*sambun*) case scandalized the Korean public's perception of the *chaebols*. The case involved several *chaebols* that produced the staples of wheat flour, sugar, and cement colluding with one another to raise prices to the detriment of Korean consumers; in some cases, their artificial creation of supply shortages led to prices that were three or four times the listed amount. This led to a public consensus behind the need to prevent abuses by large companies and regulate monopoly power. Legislation that would have been the country's first competition law was repeatedly drafted and subsequently scuttled, often in the face of opposition from the government bureaucracy and legislators who prioritized economic development over excesses of market power. Instead, legislation that purported to regulate high prices and thus limit the exploitation of consumers was introduced and eventually passed in the form of the Price Stabilization and Fair Trade Act of

1 See Michael A. Witt, *South Korea: Plutocratic State-led Capitalism Reconfiguring*, THE OXFORD HANDBOOK OF ASIAN BUSINESS SYSTEMS 2 (Michael A. Witt & Gordon Redding, eds., 2014).

1975.

(3) The Enactment of the Monopoly Regulation and Fair Trade Act

By 1980, the share of the top 30 *chaebols* amounted to 36% of the national economy as measured by their portion of revenues in the manufacturing and mining sector. Perhaps unsurprisingly, a significant portion of the nation's economy at the time operated in markets controlled by monopolies or oligopolies. The military government that had come into power the previous year undertook various economic reforms, one of which was the enactment of the MRFTA in 1980, which came into effect the following year. This was a significant milestone in Korea's development of a robust competition law regime, which continued through amendments that were intended to strengthen the law's reach in the market.

For example, in 1986, several regulations aimed at curbing economic concentration were incorporated into the MRFTA because the concentration of economic power in the hands of the *chaebols* was perceived as a threat to the sustainable and balanced development of the nation's market economy. These included targeted restrictions against *chaebols* regarding the establishment of holding companies, direct cross-shareholdings, ceilings on the total possible amount of investment, and the exercise of voting rights by affiliates in the financial and insurance sectors. Despite these attempts to stem the tide of economic concentration in the hands of the *chaebols*, their economic power and influence continued to grow throughout the subsequent decade. By 1995, the top five *chaebols* accounted for more than 25% of Korea's total economic activity, while the top 30 *chaebols*' share of activity increased to 40.7%. During this period, the *chaebols* also expanded their reach into additional markets through the acquisition or establishment of affiliated companies. In 1987, the total number of companies affiliated with the top 30 *chaebols* was 493. A decade later, that number had increased to 819. The concentration of economic power was further reflected in the *chaebols*' market power. As of 1997, one of the top 30 *chaebols* was among the top three competitors in 83.4% of the product markets in which the *chaebols* were active, and *chaebols* were the leading firms in 41% of such markets. The undue support clause, which is a peculiar feature of Korean competition law, was introduced into the MRFTA against this backdrop. The law has been frequently amended to reflect changes in jurisprudence and to meet the evolving challenges of the market. Most recently, the law was comprehensively revamped in late 2021 as part of Korea's modernization of its competition regime and to better account for the digital age.

2. Korea's Current Competition Law Regime

(1) Goals of Korean Competition Law

Debates over the goals of competition law are generally contentious, and Korea is no exception. While the MRFTA specifies a number of goals, including economic development, its three main aims are generally understood as (i) facilitating competition, (ii) protecting consumers, and (iii) ensuring fairness and economic opportunity.

As noted in the title of Korea's primary competition law statute, the concept of "fairness" is a prominent goal of Korean competition law. It undergirds different acts like the subcontracting law and has provided the conceptual foundation for *gab-eul* legislation, which purports to correct imbalances in economic and bargaining power. It also features prominently in the unfair trade practices clause of the MRFTA.

(2) The Main Pillars of Korean Competition Law

1) Prohibition of Abuse of Dominance

The prohibition of abuse of dominance is of particular importance given the continuing problems with *chaebols* in the Korean economy. Following the Posco case, which strengthened the legal standards for finding a violation (including intent to distort competition), many commentators have lamented the lack of enforcement and often found fault with the jurisprudence that sprung from the case. However, enforcement has continued under the relevant provisions, most recently culminating in the Naver shopping case, which took issue with exclusionary behavior that involved algorithms.

2) Prohibition of Anticompetitive Mergers and Business Combinations

Merger reviews are a staple of competition law practice. Korea has established and enforced a robust review process for mergers and has taken action against those deemed anticompetitive. Recently, the Korea Fair

Trade Commission (KFTC) took action against a proposed merger between Delivery Hero Korea and Woowa Brothers by ordering the acquiring company to essentially divest its current business. The COVID pandemic has also tested the KFTC by presenting it with mergers that argue the failing company defense, based on the dire economic effects of the pandemic.

3) Prohibition of Cartels

As noted above, popular support for Korea's competition law regime has long been rooted in the prohibition of collusion among businesses. Cartel enforcement has recently focused on information exchange between businesses, with a new comprehensive amendment specifying information exchange as a possible act of collusion. Unlike US antitrust law or EU competition law, both of which use broad language that could incorporate virtually any type of agreement or coordinated action, the MRFTA exclusively provides for specific types of agreements that are prohibited. This has led some to argue that Korea should also adopt broad statutory language like that in the US and EU laws. However, that position was not adopted in the recent amendment.

4) Prohibition of Unfair Trade Practices

The MRFTA prohibits unfair trade practices. Despite being viewed by some as a non-traditional competition law, the prohibition against unfair trade practices has consistently comprised a large portion of KFTC enforcement actions, showing its importance to competition policy in Korea. The regulation prohibits a wide range of activities that qualify as abuses of market power, use methods of competition deemed unfair and outside of normal market practice, or result in trading terms that are regarded as unfair. In particular, the regulation of abuses of a superior bargaining position features prominently in enforcement actions, which are intended to correct unfair terms and conditions that result from imbalances in bargaining power.

5) Others

❶ Remedying Corporate Governance Violations: Regulating undue Support and Tunneling

At the time of the enactment of the clause prohibiting undue support among affiliates, inter-group (affiliated) dealings among the large *chaebols* constituted nearly 25% of their total revenues. There were concerns that the significant volume of affiliated transactions supported the expansion and consolidation of the *chaebols*' economic power. These affiliated transactions are often perceived as intended to maximize the socioeconomic prestige and influence wielded by a *chaebol*-owning family rather maximizing shareholder value and efficiency. Thus, the stated primary legislative goal of the Undue Support Clause was to control economic concentration. While the perceived problems of affiliated dealings likely reflected a breakdown in corporate governance, such concerns—like harm to creditors and minority shareholders—were not explicitly discussed or even mentioned in the legislative documents. However, due to the nature of the targeted activities, the regulation of undue support had ramifications for corporate governance. This was particularly evident in cases where undue support appeared more oriented toward expanding the size and scope of a *chaebol* (thus boosting the prestige of the prestige of the family that controlled it) rather than the interests of shareholders. That left the door open for possible future injections of corporate governance considerations into the statute, which is precisely what happened in the wake of the 1997 Asian financial crisis. That crisis exposed a slew of problems with the management and corporate governance of *chaebols*. In response, the authorities increasingly began to view the Undue Support Clause as part of their corporate governance toolkit. The KFTC's regulation of undue support among *chaebol* affiliates became an integral part of the Korean government's post-crisis corporate restructuring and reform program. This shift in the underlying perception of the role and purpose of the Undue Support Clause culminated in a 2003 Korean Constitutional Court decision stating that one of the statute's goals was to prevent activity that "degraded corporate transparency and harmed the interests of shareholders (particularly minority shareholders) and creditors." While the court's statement has been the subject of much criticism, it at least seems clear that the Undue Support Clause was enacted to intervene into the affairs of the *chaebols*, including their corporate governance. Determining the proper extent and scope of such intervention has been a core issue in the enforcement of the statute.

Article 23(1)(vii)(a) of the MRFTA prohibits a firm from harming fair trade by providing support to another party (where a person or company, affiliated or non-affiliated) through the transfer of resources or transacting such resources on terms that are considerably favorable to the other party. On its face, the scope of the statute is not limited to tunneling activities, since its reach extends to transfers of wealth not only to the controllers of a firm or affiliates but also to non-affiliated third parties. However, the statute has primarily been enforced against tunneling occurring at *chaebols*. Article 23(1)(vii)(b) prohibits a specific type of tunneling called "tolling," where a party (usually affiliated with the controllers) is inserted into the transaction chain without a proper business reason, resulting in its extraction of part of the value generated by the transaction. Both sections 23(1)(vii)(b) and 23(2) were added to Article 23 through an amendment of the MRFTA in 2013. The amendment also added Article 23(2), which prohibits the provision of certain improper benefits to specially related parties.

❷ Correcting Economic Imbalances: Regulating *Gab-eul* Relationships

Korean competition law encompasses special legislation that is intended to correct economic imbalances in Korean society. These generally take the form of industry- or sector-specific legislation, mainly in big box retailing, franchising, and the logistics sector.

(3) Enforcement of Korean Competition Law

1) Administrative Enforcement

❶ Korea Fair Trade Commission

Currently, the primary form of competition law enforcement is administrative enforcement by the KFTC, which enjoys broad investigative powers like conducting dawn raids, often coordinated with foreign authorities. The KFTC has seven commissioners, some standing and some non-standing. While it is an agency of the government, the KFTC is an independent administrative agency that has the authority to promulgate regulations and guidelines that regulate market competition.

With regard to remedies, the core remedial measure for the KFTC is the cease-and-desist order. That being said, as seen in the final phrase of Articles 5 and 24 ("other corrective measures as necessary"), the MRFTA has been interpreted as granting discretionary power to the KFTC to impose measures that go beyond a simple cease-and-desist order, commonly referred to as "fencing" measures.[2] There are, however, limits to such discretion. Most commentators doubt that the KFTC could break up a firm based on the above phrase,[3] and it has not yet been formally tested by the KFTC in this manner. It is also understood that the KFTC does not have the authority to issue corrective orders that essentially promulgate a particular market outcome, such as ordering a dominant firm to charge a specific price.[4] On the other hand, the KFTC enjoys broad discretion in fashioning the particulars of a remedy that it deems necessary to rectify problematic conduct.[5] Corrective measures such as providing access to a firm's facilities or assets, (re-)commencing dealings with third parties, rescinding or revising contract terms and conditions, unbundling products, disclosing information, and negotiating with counterparties in good faith have all been ordered as remedies against MRFTA violations.

The primary guiding principles for remedies are proportionality and that a corrective order be clear and specific in what it requires of offending firms. Both principles effectively tether the corrective order to the underlying liability theory and related factual findings by the KFTC. The remedy ordered must be proportionate to the substance and level of the violation.[6] And while ensuring that a corrective order is effective means that

2 The provision that stipulates remedies for cartels under the MRFTA includes the same phrase (Article 21). The Korean Supreme Court ruled in a decision concerning collusion among flour manufacturers that the phrase allowed for measures necessary to correct illegality in addition to ordering firms to cease and desist from colluding. In that case, the firms had exchanged information to carry out collusion, and thus the KFTC's order prohibiting such information exchange was upheld as within the bounds of the provision (Supreme Court Decision 2007Du24616, May 28, 2009). See also Supreme Court Decision 2001Du5347, February 20, 2003.

3 Hyeung-Bae Kim, THEORY AND PRACTICE OF THE FAIR TRADE ACT (공정거래법의 이론과 실제), Samil 815-816 (2019) (in Korean); Chul-Soo Han, FAIR TRADE ACT: MARKET AND LEGAL PRINCIPLES (공정거래법: 시장과 법원리), Korea Fair Competition Federation 651 (2016). By contrast, the MRFTA explicitly allows for the dissolution of a consummated business combination (e.g., by ordering the transfer of shares or businesses and suing to nullify mergers; Articles 16(1) and (2)).

4 Ohseung Kwon and Jeong Seo, MONOPOLY REGULATION ACT: THEORY AND PRACTICE (독점규제법-이론과 실무) (3rd ed.), Bubmoonsa 727 (2018).

5 In a case where a private schooling service provider had illegally bundled its online and offline lectures, the court upheld the KFTC's remedy, which ordered the firm to post a message on its website for two (2) years, alerting consumers that they were free to decide whether or not to subscribe to its online classes (Seoul High Court Decision 2009Nu5635, November 12, 2009).

6 Supreme Court Decision 2007Du24616, May 28, 2009. Unlike Article 7(1) of Regulation (EC) No 1/2003 (OJ L1/1), the MRFTA and the relevant regulations do

it may inevitably be somewhat "wide-ranging" and "abstract," the offending firm must at a minimum be capable of understanding specifically what is prohibited and/or required of it based on the findings and reasoning within the decision itself.[7] The KFTC's own Guidelines on the Administering of Corrective Orders also cite effectiveness, tailoring, and practicability as additional principles for corrective orders in general.[8] The principle of effectiveness requires that the corrective order be suitable for rectifying the illegal conduct. The principle of tailoring requires that the corrective order must be fashioned in a manner that closely reflects the finding of illegality. The principle of practicability requires that the order can legally and actually be carried out by the offending firm.

Firms may challenge the legality of a corrective order, separate from the liability theory and findings of the KFTC.[9]

2) Private Enforcement

A recent amendment to the MRFTA is intended to expand the reach

not limit structural remedies to cases where equally effective behavioral remedies are not available or would be more burdensome to the firm. However, it seems likely that a structural remedy would be subject to similar scrutiny by the courts under the principle of proportionality.

7 For example, in a case where the KFTC had ordered a big box retailer to refrain from returning products to a supplier unless the supplier was at fault or had consented to such return, the Korean Supreme Court found the order illegal since the reasoning in the KFTC's decision did not specify which suppliers had been subject to the problematic practice and when such practice had occurred, rendering it impossible for the firm to determine what specific conduct was prohibited (Supreme Court Decision 2004Du7146, January 12, 2007); see also Seoul High Court Decision 2012Nu27994, June 13, 2014.

8 KFTC, Guidelines on the Administering of Corrective Orders, V.1. The guidelines, however, do not bind the courts because the MRFTA and the relevant presidential decree do not delegate the power to enact such guidelines concerning corrective orders to the KFTC. The guidelines themselves make clear that the KFTC staff may deviate from the guidelines if that is necessary to correct the conduct (III.2).

9 Under the MRFTA, the KFTC is also authorized to conduct market investigations that are not tied to a particular infringement, in cases where the market structure has been monopolistic or oligopolistic for an extended period of time (Article 3(1)). The KFTC should establish and implement policies to facilitate competition in such markets and can also present opinions to other relevant government authorities if necessary to pursue such policies (Article 3(2)). However, unlike the UK's Competition and Markets Authority, the KFTC does not have the authority to issue and enforce remedies targeting specific firms without an infringement finding. Market investigations can, of course, lead to follow-on investigations targeting specific conduct by individual firms.

of private enforcement, which has traditionally focused on damage actions. Private parties do not have to wait for the KFTC to undertake an investigation or decision to lodge their own actions. The amendment has introduced injunctive relief for private plaintiffs for abuses of dominance, unfair trade practices, and the like, which has the effect of greatly broadening the possible pool of judges who will hear and decide competition law cases.

3) Criminal Enforcement

Criminal enforcement has picked up in the last decade. The primary driving force has been the perception that the KFTC's administrative actions have failed to curb collusive activity and are an insufficient deterrent for cartelists in Korea. At the same time, businesses have strenuously raised concerns that possible criminal investigations and punishment could have a chilling effect on legal activities and have objected to criminal authorities playing a larger role in competition law enforcement. The recent amendment had initially included a provision that abolished the KFTC's exclusive referral authority for criminal complaints in the case of cartels, but the proposal was dropped following strong resistance from the business community.

3. Bringing Korea's Competition Law into the Digital Era

(1) Recent Comprehensive Reform of the MRFTA

1) Expanding the Reach of Cartel Regulation

As noted above, a recent amendment to the MRFTA has specified information exchange as a possible act of collusion. This provision may also implicate information exchange facilitated by and between algorithms and other artificial intelligence systems, thereby positioning the KFTC to undertake actions against so-called robot cartels.

2) Fine-tuning Merger Analysis to Capture Data-relevant Deals

A major reform in the recent amendment is the adoption of "transaction value" as a threshold for merger notification. This follows in the steps of other major jurisdictions, especially Germany, that have adopted similar reforms. The reform allows the KFTC to capture acquisitions of valuable start-ups that do not have sales but are nonetheless important to competition in the market due to their collection and use of data.

3) Introducing Injunctive Relief for Competition Law Violations

As noted above, the amendment that came into effect at the end of 2022 allows private plaintiffs to seek injunctive relief in courts without waiting for the KFTC to initiate, let alone rule on, a particular case. The introduction of injunctive relief is expected to have wide-ranging impacts on competition law enforcement, and due to the fact that granting injunctive relief may well serve as final relief in some cases, it is expected that courts will have to grapple with what constitutes an "injury" that would warrant such relief under competition law.

4) Strengthening Due Process to Meet International Standards

❶ The Dawn of a New Era

The beginning of 2016 ushered in a new era for antitrust enforcement procedures in Korea. Months earlier, the KFTC had announced a package of procedural reforms dubbed "Case Handling 3.0,"[10] a move that was followed by updating its procedural rules to implement the reforms. These changes took effect on February 4, 2016.

The reforms have been characterized as the third phase in the evolution of the KFTC's antitrust enforcement process—hence the moniker "3.0."[11] During the first era, which ran from the KFTC's founding in 1981 to the early 2000s, the country witnessed the gradual development of an adversarial system in the KFTC's adjudication processes.[12] One of the hallmarks of this development was the creation of the General Counsel's Office (GCO) in 1997.[13] The establishment of the GCO was viewed as an effort to insulate the KFTC's adjudicative process from potential bias as

10 Press release, KFTC, *Reforms Dawn Raid Procedures and Strengthens Internal Controls!* (공정위 현장 절차 개혁하고 내부 통제 강화한다) (October 21, 2015), announcing planned reforms under Case Handling 3.0.

11 *Id.* at 3; Chang-Mo An, *Improvements of the Korea Fair Trade Commission Investigation and Enforcement Procedure* (공정거래위원회 사건처리절차의 주요 내용), 40 DANKOOK LAW REVIEW 1, 403, 405 (2016).

12 An, *supra* note 11, at 405.

13 KFTC, *A History of Three Decades at the Fair Trade Commission* (공정거래위원회의 30년사) 101 (2011) (KFTC, A History below).

a result of interaction between the commissioners and the investigative staff known as examiners.[14] The second era, which kicked off with major revisions to the KFTC's procedural rules in 2004,[15] was a period where due process and various procedural rights for respondents (i.e., businesses being investigated) were strengthened. Prominent examples include granting access, albeit limited, to evidentiary materials cited in examiners' reports and allowing for multiple hearings when necessary to ensure that the relevant arguments and evidence were properly considered.[16] The recent reforms, which launched the third and most recent era, is an attempt to remedy various perceived shortcomings in terms of due process and transparency in the KFTC's case procedures that have been subject to criticism both within Korea and abroad.[17] The jury is still out on the recent reforms, but there have been some positive responses.[18] At the same time, the KFTC has been subject to pointed criticism even in the new era.[19] Part

14 From an organizational perspective, the GCO is separate from the KFTC's examiners; among other things, it is tasked with independently processing cases brought by examiners and assisting commissioners in their adjudication of the relevant charges (*Id.*; Article 9(2) of Organization of KFTC and Its Organs (Presidential Decree, last amended September 19, 2017)).

15 An, *supra* note 11, at 405.

16 KFTC, *Improvements to the KFTC's Case Handling Procedures* (공정거래 사건처리의 개선) (Press release, October 21, 2004). The KFTC's investigation of Microsoft for allegedly tying media and messaging functionality with its operating systems coincided with such changes and was one of the first major cases where the changes in the rules were actually implemented.

17 KFTC, *supra* note 10, at 3.

18 In 2016, the Global Competition Review (GCR) conferred five stars (denoting elite status) to the KFTC for the first time in its annual enforcement ratings (GCR, Rating Enforcement 2016 (July 6, 2016) at http://globalcompetitionreview.com/edition/1000401/rating-enforcement-2016), citing "procedural improvements" as one reason for ranking the KFTC in the highest bracket (*Id.* at Introduction at http://globalcompetitionreview.com/benchmarking/rating-enforcement-2016/1068006/introduction). See also the GCR commentary on the KFTC in its rating (http://globalcompetitionreview.com/benchmarking/rating-enforcement-2016/1068050/koreas-fair-trade-commission), which notes that "... the KFTC ... also made moves to improve its procedural fairness." The four other elite status agencies in the same bracket were France's Competition Authority, Germany's Federal Cartel Office, and the U.S. Department of Justice and Federal Trade Commission. The KFTC maintained its elite status in GCR's ratings in 2017 (GCR, Rating Enforcement 2017 (July 21, 2017) at http://globalcompetitionreview.com/benchmarking/rating-enforcement-2017/1144939/star-ratings).

19 See, e.g., US Senate Committee on Finance Chairman's News, Hatch Questions Korea, Colombia on Implementation of Trade Agreements in Advance of Finance Committee Hearing (March 2, 2016) at http://www.finance.senate.gov/chairmans-news/hatch-questions-korea-colombia-on-implementation-of-

of that criticism may be a carryover from earlier times or the result of a discrepancy between the new procedures and the agency's actual practice in the field. But the problems raised also shed light on how due process issues are evolving in Korean competition law enforcement. Below, we will see how Korea is striving to achieve due process in antitrust enforcement with a focus on four aspects: (i) legal representation, (ii) access to information and evidence, (iii) access to investigators and decision makers, and (iv) judicial oversight of agency decisions, including the right to appeal. We will observe how due process issues in Korean antitrust enforcement have changed and attempt to discern the major factors driving that evolution, in an effort to identify important considerations for fledging antitrust agencies that wish to improve procedural fairness in their enforcement processes. To set the stage appropriately, we begin by taking a more detailed look at the recent reforms under Case Handling 3.0.

❷ Due Process in Competition Law Enforcement

Reforms under Case Handling 3.0 targeted four key areas: (i) on-site investigations (including dawn raids), (ii) case management and supervision, (iii) leniency programs, and (iv) case file and record keeping.

a) Promulgating rules for on-site investigations

As to on-site investigations, the KFTC issued a new set of rules that covered dawn raid procedures and the forensic collection of digital evidence: the KFTC Investigation Procedure Rules (KIPR).[20] A significant portion of previous criticism of KFTC practices concerned the insufficient guarantee of procedural rights for subjects of dawn raids and the disregard of due process and procedural safeguards exhibited from time to time by KFTC investigators on the ground.[21]

trade-agreements-in-advance-of-finance-committee-hearing; GCR, Ohlhausen criticizes "unsatisfactory" antitrust enforcement in Asia (December 9, 2016) at http://globalcompetitionreview.com/article/1078535/ohlhausen-criticises-%E2%80%9Cunsatisfactory%E2%80%9D-antitrust-enforcement-in-asia.

20 KFTC Goshi No. 2016-1, February 4, 2016. The KIPR calls for triennial re-assessments for the purpose of continued improvement, with the first reassessment process to be completed by June 30, 2019 (Article 25). The rules took effect on February 5, 2016.

21 *Will the KFTC's Innovation Enable it to Escape from Concerns of "Excessive Unreasonable" Investigations?* (혁신 나선 공정위 '과잉·불합리' 조사 논란 벗어날까),

The KIPR first restates the principle set out in the MRFTA with regard to the legal parameters for investigations under that act (Article 50-2). Article 3 of the KIPR stipulates that investigators must conduct their investigations within the "minimum scope necessary for enforcing laws under the purview of the KFTC" and must not "abuse their investigative authority for other purposes."

For on-site investigations, the KIPR requires investigators to notify the subject of the allegations under investigation and inform the subject of its right to refuse cooperation in the event that investigative actions exceed the expressed scope and purpose specified in the notification (Article 6).[22] It also allows for the participation of counsel throughout dawn raid procedures, including sitting in on investigators' interviews of company employees (Article 13). The KIPR explicitly provides for the subject's right to request copies of any documents and materials seized during the raid (Article 11(3)) and requires investigators to provide a written list of such materials within seven days of the raid (Article 14). The KIPR also stipulates that the forensic collection of digital evidence shall be limited to the minimum necessary to carry out the investigation (Article 18) and that the subject may request the protection of privacy and business secrets therein (Article 23(3)).

The promulgation of the KIPR marks the first time that the KFTC has provided comprehensive written guidance on procedures for on-site investigations.[23] The issuance of these rules was notable in several aspects. The KIPR provided much-needed clarity regarding the basic rules of engagement for on-site investigations, thereby avoiding the unnecessary friction between investigators and subject (and their counsel) that was increasingly becoming an impediment to both investigative effectiveness and due process. The KIPR also made it easier for subjects under investigation to

YONHAP NEWS (October 21, 2015) at http://www.yonhapnews.co.kr/bulletin/2015/10/21/0200000000AKR20151021063700002.HTML?input=1195m; KFTC, *supra* note 10, at 5.

22 According to the rules, such notification shall be provided in writing, and the investigators must also provide a detailed explanation of the content of the notification and the rights of the subject under investigation (Article 6(1)).

23 The KFTC had previously issued guidelines covering the collection and handling of digital evidence, which is often an integral part of on-site investigations. But these guidelines did not cover other but no less important procedural aspects of such investigations. The KFTC withdrew these limited guidelines with the promulgation of the KIPR, as the new guidance was viewed as subsuming all previous guidelines on the collection of digital evidence.

challenge or resist conduct by investigators that appeared to impinge on the subjects' rights, since subjects could now cite and rely on specific provisions set out in the KIPR.[24]

b) Strengthening internal control systems regarding case management

Regarding case management, the amended KFTC Commission Hearing Management and Case Procedure Rules (KCPR)[25] require the KFTC to register all cases in its internal system prior to commencing an investigation by, for example, making information requests or conducting a dawn raid (Article 10-3). This would leave an official record in the KFTC's case database even when an investigation was terminated based on a finding of non-liability or other reasons. There had been concerns that the lack of such case management could lead to unnecessary and repetitive future investigations (including dawn raids) due to a lack of proper records showing that a previous investigation had yielded little evidence of a violation.[26] The amended KCPR also stipulates time limits within which investigators must wrap up their inquiries either by issuing an examiners' report[27] or recommending other outcomes (e.g., terminating an investigation). The time limits are nine months for abuse of dominance cases, 13 months for cartels, and six months for all other cases. Extensions are possible but only if necessary, and they require the approval of the KFTC's Secretary General (Article 10-4). Another notable amendment to the KCPR is the inclusion of GCO staff as subjects of exclusions, challenges, and recusals in the event of

24 The KIPR also requires investigators to prepare an Investigation Procedure Confirmation Document at the end of the on-site investigation, which must be signed by a representative of the subject (Article 14(1)). The document's form is set out in Appendix No. 3 of the KIPR and includes an item regarding any objections and/or opinions raised by the subject concerning the description of the investigative process in the document. The KIPR further obliges the head of the division in charge of the investigation to listen to any difficulties or problems voiced by the subject following the on-site investigation (Article 16(3)) and allows the subject to voice such complaints to the KFTC's internal audit office if it is not feasible to do so to the division head (Article 16(4)).

25 KFTC Go-shi No. 2016-2, February 4, 2016.

26 KFTC, *supra* note 10, at 7.

27 Examiners' reports include the factual findings of the investigative staff, their assessment with regard to the respondent's liability, and their recommendation to the commissioners regarding appropriate measures to be taken. They can be understood as akin to the "statement of objections" issued by the Department for Competition staff at the European Commission.

possible conflicts of interest, including prior involvement in a relevant case as an investigator (Article 30-12).

c) Improving the factual scrutiny of leniency applications

In recent years, the KFTC has experienced several high-profile setbacks in the courts involving cartel cases, where evidence collected through the KFTC's leniency program was rejected or overturned.[28] These setbacks exposed deficiencies in the KFTC's process for examining and vetting evidence submitted by leniency applicants and appeared to confirm suspicions that applicants were in some instances exaggerating or distorting the facts to gain leniency benefits that they did not merit.[29] One of the main responses by the KFTC under Case Handling 3.0 was to amend its leniency guidelines to require leniency applicants to make their officers and/or employees available for direct examination by the commissioners during hearings.[30]

d) Improving case file management and record keeping

In the past, the KFTC has also been criticized for being relatively lax in maintaining orderly case files and keeping its records up to date. Much to the ire of respondents, this sometimes resulted in repetitive information requests by the KFTC, particularly when there was a reshuffling of personnel within the agency and new staff were assigned to a case.[31] In response, the KFTC established new internal rules regarding record keeping: the KFTC Case Record Management Rules (KCRMR).[32] The KCRMR requires the staff to maintain and update case files throughout a case's entire adjudication

28 See, e.g., Korean Supreme Court Decision 2013Du18759, January 29, 2015, refusing to infer an agreement between oil refiners from statements provided by an officer of the leniency party due to, among other things, inconsistencies and a lack of supporting evidence.

29 KFTC, *supra* note 10, at 7. This is a critical issue for the KFTC's cartel enforcement, as approximately 80% of cartel cases handled by the KFTC are based on leniency applications (KFTC General Counsel Sun-Ju Yoo, *Understanding KFTC Case Handling 3.0* (공정위 사건 처리 3.0의 이해), 6 JOURNAL OF COMPETITION LAW AND POLICY (Seoul National University Center for Competition Law) 12, 15 (2016)

30 KFTC Cartel Leniency Guidelines, KFTC Goshi No. 2016-3, April 15, 2016; the most recent guidelines include the same requirement (KFTC Goshi No. 2016-11, September 30, 2016).

31 An, *supra* note 11, at 414.

32 KFTC Ye-gyu No. 244, January 27, 2016.

process, including the litigation stage, following a decision by the KFTC (Articles 4 and 7). Records that must be kept include documents and materials not cited in examiners' reports (Article 3(i)).[33]

❸ Initial Takeaways from the Reforms

In its announcement of Case Handling 3.0, the KFTC acknowledged shortcomings in terms of its procedures and rather candidly admitted that in the past it had not focused strongly enough on ensuring due process.[34] Responding to the criticism of such shortcomings and ensuring that the KFTC's procedures meet global standards were undoubtedly a major driving force behind the reforms,[35] but those reforms were also propelled by the KFTC's recognition that such procedural shortcomings led to critical setbacks in the courts hearing appeals of its decisions and an erosion of trust in its enforcement.[36] This recognition signals a departure from the traditional view that due process entails a tradeoff between effective enforcement and the preservation of justice[37] and indicates that the KFTC has become more open to the view that due process can and does lead to more robust decisions and better enforcement.[38]

The specific reforms reflect a similar shift in the KFTC's approach to due process. One of the most striking departures from the past is the

33 Prior to the reforms, the KFTC's internal practice had been to maintain only records of materials referenced in an examiners' report, making it impossible to properly review an entire case file at a later date and sometimes resulting in the loss of important case materials.

34 KFTC, *supra* note 10, at 3.

35 *Id.* Meeting best practice standards on a global level is not merely a competition policy matter for Korea. The Korea–US Free Trade Agreement includes various provisions on due process involving competition law proceedings (e.g., Articles 16.1 and 16.5), thus adding a trade law and policy element to these issues.

36 KFTC, *supra* note 10, at 13.

37 Pieter Van Cleynenbreugel, *Effectiveness through Fairness? Due Process as an Institutional Precondition for Effective Decentralised EU Competition Law Enforcement*, in PROCEDURAL FAIRNESS IN COMPETITION PROCEEDINGS (Paul Nihoul ed.) 44, 69-71 (2015), which describes such a view in the context of EU competition law.

38 For a succinct description of this viewpoint, see D. Daniel Sokol, Due Process, Transparency And Procedural Fairness in Asian Antitrust, Competition Pol'y Int'l Asia Column 5 (January 2015) at https://www.competitionpolicyinternational.com/due-process-transparency-and-procedural-fairness-in-asian-antitrust/: "At its core, transparency and due process are inputs that lead to better outputs.... Having better processes through transparency and due process improves performance outcomes."

KFTC's embrace of transparency and its increased willingness to expose itself to outside scrutiny as a means of improving its procedures and strengthening enforcement.[39] This has primarily taken the form of the promulgation of formal rules regulating the KFTC's investigative practices, which were previously subject to undisclosed and therefore non-transparent internal rules and guidelines. Examples from the discussion above include enshrining formerly undisclosed time limits for investigative periods concerning the KCPR and stipulating counsel's ability to observe and participate throughout the KIPR's on-site investigative procedures.

The reforms also improve KFTC procedures with regard to other core aspects of procedural fairness that had been identified by commentators.[40] From an organizational perspective, the inclusion of GCO staff as subjects of the recusal system strengthens the separation and independence of the KFTC's decision makers and staff from the investigation teams. The strengthening of procedural safeguards during dawn raids, such as notification of the alleged violation and access to copies of the seized materials, improves the ability of the respondent to examine potential evidence and defend itself. As previously noted, a significant part of the criticism surrounding KFTC procedures was related to dawn raids, and that was one of the primary areas of focus for Case Handling 3.0. The KIPR not only improves overall due process related to dawn raids but also provides a minimum and uniform standard upon which all parties can base their expectations. This can reduce friction and concerns about unpredictable and sometimes uneven enforcement by individual investigators. If effectively implemented, the reforms do seem to provide the KFTC with a real

39 KFTC, *supra* note 10, at 13, mentioning, among other things, the reduction of "unnecessary arguments and disputes during investigative procedures" and "litigation defeats due to procedural flaws" as expected benefits of Case Handling 3.0.

40 Stanley Wong, *Thinking About Procedural Fairness of Competition Law Enforcement Across Jurisdictions: A Suggested Principled Approach*, COMPETITION POLICY INTERNATIONAL COLUMN 3 (2014) at https://www.competitionpolicyinternational.com/assets/Uploads/ICNApril142.pdf, suggesting "disclosure," "right of defense," and "independence of decision maker" as core principles of procedural fairness; Douglas H. Ginsburg and Taylor M. Owings, *Due Process in Competition Proceedings*, 11(1) COMPETITION POLICY INTERNATIONAL 39, 42-48 (2015), which lists the following five requirements for due process in administrative enforcement: "right to confront evidence and arguments," "hearing before the actual decision maker," "neutral decision maker," preventing "delay," and "review by an independent tribunal."

opportunity to increase trust in its enforcement decisions and could lead to improved competition law enforcement both procedurally and substantively.

❹ Current State of Due Process in Korean Competition Law Enforcement

Despite the reforms, the KFTC has continued to be the target of pointed criticism regarding due process in the new era.[41] Part of the criticism may be carryovers from the previous era or reflect the fact that implementing Case Handling 3.0 in the field will take some time, as is normally the case for any major reform. But the criticisms also shed light on how due process issues for the KFTC may evolve in the years ahead. One hitherto overlooked but increasingly likely challenge for the KFTC concerns its evidentiary rules and process during hearings and deliberations. The KFTC has been accused of unduly limiting access to evidence and failing to provide the opportunity for cross examination at hearings.[42] Whether to adopt a complete open-file policy and how to best ensure the right to cross examination are undoubtedly important issues. However, another related but separate question that may confront the KFTC as these issues are debated is whether and to what extent the KFTC commissioners should consider evidence collected or presented in a manner that fails to meet due process standards. Yet another issue centers on the appropriate standard of proof for the KFTC when it decides cases. There are two main reasons why these questions may become increasingly important going forward. First, despite being an agency within the government's administrative branch, the KFTC enjoys the status of a quasi-court of first instance under Korean law, as appeals to KFTC decisions are heard not by district courts but by appellate courts such as the Seoul High Court.[43] This aspect of the KFTC's adjudication process

41 See, e.g., US Senate Committee on Finance Chairman's News, Hatch Questions Korea, Colombia on Implementation of Trade Agreements in Advance of Finance Committee Hearing (March 2, 2016) at http://www.finance.senate.gov/chairmans-news/hatch-questions-korea-colombia-on-implementation-of-trade-agreements-in-advance-of-finance-committee-hearing; GCR, Ohlhausen Criticizes "Unsatisfactory" Antitrust Enforcement in Asia (December 9, 2016) at http://globalcompetitionreview.com/article/1078535/ohlhausen-criticises-%E2%80%9Cunsatisfactory%E2%80%9D-antitrust-enforcement-in-asia.

42 Qualcomm press release, Qualcomm Responds to Announcement by Korea Fair Trade Commission (December 28, 2016) at https://www.qualcomm.com/news/releases/2016/12/27/qualcomm-responds-announcement-korea-fair-trade-commission. Note that the specific merits or factual basis of Qualcomm's statements in its press release are not a subject of discussion in this paper.

has served as a persistent target for demands that the KFTC justify its status by modeling its rules and procedures to match those of the courts.[44] Second, many of Korea's competition statutes (including the MRFTA) provide for criminal sanctions, and the KFTC has shown an increasing willingness to refer cases to the criminal authorities for possible criminal sanctions.[45] The real possibility of a KFTC decision leading to criminal sanctions in addition to administrative penalties appears to have influenced the courts to take an increasingly strict approach in analyzing the KFTC's findings and requiring proof for such findings in KFTC decisions. In some cases, this has resulted in the courts overturning a KFTC decision for failure to meet the evidentiary burden of proof.[46] While some have criticized the courts for applying an overly exacting evidentiary standard to KFTC decisions, the quasi-judicial status of KFTC decisions and the possibility of additional penal sanctions will likely fuel debates on whether and what adjustments to the evidentiary rules and procedures for KFTC hearings are necessary to further improve due process and ensure that Case Handling 3.0 is a success.

Case Handling 3.0 made important strides by resolving numerous points of contention related to KFTC investigation procedures. While conflicts remain and are bound to be part of any investigation, it appears likely that the next main battlefield for due process in antitrust enforcement in Korea will be the KFTC's hearing and deliberation process.

43 MRFTA Article 55. Ohseung Kwon and Jeong Seo, MONOPOLY REGULATION ACT: THEORY AND PRACTICE (독점규제법-이론과 실무) (3rd ed.), Bubmoonsa 652 (2018).

44 Some have even argued that the KFTC should be stripped of its quasi-judicial status based on its failure to meet the evidentiary and procedural standards used in courts *"Two-Tier system for Fair Trade Cases Unreasonable"...Law Firm Throws down 'Challenge' to the KFTC* ("공정거래 사건서 2심제는 부당"...로펌, 공정위에 '도전장'), HANKUK ILBO (December 14, 2016) at http://www.hankookilbo.com/v/bfe9231bec24413fb209ce3405890a5a). Perhaps unsurprisingly, the KFTC stressed that the reforms rolled out under Case Handling 3.0 solidified the KFTC's status as a quasi-judicial body (KFTC, *supra* note 10, at 13).

45 Eun-Jae Park, CRIMINAL ENFORCEMENT OF ANTITRUST LAW IN KOREA (공정거래와 형사법) 4, Bakyoungsa (2014).

46 See, e.g., Supreme Court Decision 2013Du25924, December 24, 2015, overturning the KFTC's finding of an agreement between ramen noodle manufacturers. The reforms described above that attempt to strengthen the vetting of evidence provided by leniency applicants are also related to this issue.

(2) KFTC's Push to Regulate the Digital Economy

The KFTC has recently pushed for the adoption of its proposed Fairness in Intermediated Transactions by Online Platforms; it has also urged amendments to the Consumer Protection in Electronic Commerce Act as part of revamping both platform-to-business and platform-to-consumer regulation of the digital economy. Both initiatives have floundered in the National Assembly, due in part to differences of opinion on which agency or government branch should have primary regulatory powers over platforms and commercial activity in the digital economy. In January 2023, The KFTC also announced new guidelines for Assessing Abuses of Dominance and Unfair Trade Practice by Online Platforms.

4. Conclusion

Korean competition law has recently undertaken a major reform that has catapulted the nation's competition policy into the new digital era. The road to reform was not easy. However, what may prove to be even more daunting is the challenge the KFTC, the courts, and other central and local government agencies that wield regulatory power over market competition face in terms of building the requisite expertise and technological capacity to tackle the complex issues arising in digital markets and the broader economy.

Chapter 13

Labor and Employment Law*

Sukhwan Choi**

1. Introduction

(1) Labor in Korea: Cultural Background

1) *Hoesik*: A Survival Test for Working People

Have you ever heard of the word *Hoesik*? It can refer to an after-work party or company dinner, but neither term fully captures the unique phenomenon of *Hoesik* in the Korean workplace.[1] The coronavirus pandemic and social distancing requirements caused dramatic changes, among which the absence of *Hoesik* was of great impact. Though *Hoesik* is not as common as it once was in the working lives of ordinary Koreans, components like virtually compulsory participation, heavy use of alcohol late into the evening, sometimes karaoke and other forms of singing all contribute to the unique role of *Hoesik* in working life in Korea. Is it relevant to labor law? The answer is affirmative; in many cases,[2] the Supreme Court of Korea has held

* This Chapter is partly based on the author's articles, Sukhwan CHOI, *A Step against All or Nothing Policy: The Scope of Industrial Accident Compensation Insurance for Independent Contractors in Korea*, 1 JAPAN LABOR ISSUES 3, JILPT, November-December 2017; Sukhwan CHOI, *Narrowing the Gaps among Workers: Changes in Korea*, 2 JAPAN LABOR ISSUES 8, JILPT, August-September 2018.

** Associate Professor, Seoul National University School of Law.

1 For a vivid description of *Hoesik*, see Chang Kang Myoung, Fired, ASIA Publishers (2015).

2 Supreme Court Decisions 97Nu7271, August 29, 1997; 2007Du6717, November

that accidents during or after *Hoesik* are industrial accidents that are covered by the Industrial Accident Compensation Insurance Act. This means that having a group get-together is an official aspect of working life in Korea.

2) Hired at the Same Time: My Friend or My Enemy?

Another tradition one encounters at Korean workplaces, especially in large enterprises like Samsung and Hyundai, is hired-at-the-same-time mates. At those companies, people take the same exam and have a group interview on the same day as many other applicants, almost all of whom are that year's new graduates. Those companies train and educate those who are hired for that year, seeking to provide them with all the abilities they will need to perform their jobs. Certainly, occasional recruiting is increasing, but large companies and some other sectors use this traditional, group-based recruiting system. Same-day-hired mates are theoretically friends but at the same time can be enemies, because of the pyramid structure. After all, there is only one president, and no two friends can be president at the same time. Each new cohort shares experiences and cooperates in myriad ways, but in the end, they are continually compared to and thus compete with one another. This is rarely found in Western countries; it is largely observed in Japan and Korea among Organisation for Economic Co-operation and Development (OECD) countries.

These two examples may be extreme aspects of Korean companies, and recent developments suggest that these distinctive aspects of Korean corporate culture are changing. However, the background formed by that culture still affects the field of law. People have been working to survive since prehistoric times. This universality of labor is one good feature of labor and labor law, but at the same time, working conditions can and do differ from country to country. People in Korea perform their daily work like people in other countries, but they do so in the context of long-standing customs that have shaped the country's work culture and are reflected in the law. This chapter addresses the general framework of labor and employment law in Korea and aims not only to provide knowledge of the key regulations but also to understand the Korean way of working and how it is changing.

15, 2007.

(2) Brief Overview of Regulations on Labor

1) The Making of the Working Class and Efforts to Protect Them

Labor law shares certain characteristics with any other field of law, but it has its own distinguishing aspects. The three basic principles of modern law established after the French Revolution are as follows: 1) freedom of contract (private autonomy), 2) absolute ownership, and 3) negligence-based responsibility (fault, intent). However, labor law is fundamentally based on revisions of them. First, mandatory regulations for employee protection and support for collective action and collective power are the essence of labor law. Furthermore, Article 23(1) of the Korean Constitution states that the property rights of all citizens shall be guaranteed, but it also notes that "the contents and limitations thereof shall be determined by Act" and that "the exercise of property rights shall conform to the public welfare." Finally, changes in liability (product liability, environmental pollution, industrial accidents) have weakened the notion of strictly negligence-based responsibility.

Labor law has also experienced changes in the concept of the collective. In its early days, modern law did not recognize the concept of the collective. It excluded all the privileged classes, which largely meant the royal and noble classes. Consequently, it was opposed to any kind of group that could oppress free individuals. So, at first, republics strictly banned collective actions, with such effort punished as criminal conspiracies. As time passed, the age of collective laissez-faire emerged, and forming groups was no longer regarded as criminal. After that, affirmative recognition of the collective was introduced. This was partly due to the decline of community- and family-level labor. Once the Industrial Revolution had taken full effect, a new legal system was required, and the collective thus arose in the form of trade unions. This was followed by the age of development of the collective. Frederick Winslow Taylor introduced scientific management in his pioneering book, *The Principles of Scientific Management* (1911), and Fordism—characterized by the distribution of profits and sustainability—was another factor that made the collective a partner in industrial democracies. In the United States, the National Labor Relations Act (also known as the Wagner Act) was passed in 1935, giving trade unions support from an increasingly powerful federal government.

2) The Two Sides of Labor and Regulation[3]

As in many other countries, labor is universal in Korea too. There are two sides of labor reflected in the country's labor law system. First, it is characterized by subordination, which simply means that people work under someone else's control. By the nature of employment contracts, other people have the right to decide what workers do and how they do it. This is not common in the world of civil law, which presumes equal parties coming to an agreement. While workers can theoretically negotiate the conditions of their employment, they have no control over the means of production and nothing but their labor to sell in the market. Naturally, then, workers cannot be fully equal in an employment contract. Even if they disagree wholly or partially with the conditions set by an employer, they are required in most cases to accept those conditions. This is also closely connected to the fact that labor cannot be saved or stored like an aluminum can or another material good. Fundamentally, labor is inseparable from the person who performs it, so if an individual chooses not to accept the terms of a given employment contract, that person's present labor cannot be saved for a future date when a more appealing contract might be available.

People are paid in exchange for their labor, which is inseparable from their personhood. Once employed, they can be ordered to do something, are not free to do what they want, and provide their labor in a process that is controlled by the employer, although there can be differences in degree; this is an essential feature of labor law and how it views people.

At the same time, there are other features of labor law that are important to those it covers. In most instances, people do not work alone but with others. Working at a given position can confirm an individual's role in the community. We shall call this the active role of working people. In our societies, working means self-actualization and self-realization, at least much of the time. Work means something more than simply doing something one is ordered to do and getting paid for that effort. An interesting theory in recent research[4] shows that the long-standing tradition of rice planting in Korea is closely connected with its seniority-based wage system. This kind

3 See also, Yuichiro Mizumachi, LABOR AND EMPLOYMENT LAW (労働法) 9th ed, Yuhikaku (2022) (in Japanese).

4 Cheol-sung Lee, RICE, DISASTER, AND THE STATE (쌀, 재난, 국가), Moonji (2021) (in Korean).

of approach is also applicable to the perspective on labor. Rice planting was the main agricultural endeavor during the Chosun dynasty and demanded a great deal of water. For this, irrigation systems were important, and managing a reservoir required more effort than any one individual could deliver, resulting in the formation of a community. Finding one's role in a given community centered on a reservoir was a traditional feature of Korean working life, and older people whose performance had declined could find roles like teaching their skills to others.

The Korean tradition of working as a group and finding one's own position in the community is one explanation for the working system and its background in Korea; it is also key to understanding the formation and present status of labor and employment law in Korea. In addition, this kind of tradition suggests that changes for working people and their surroundings can be implemented through efforts to amend laws and at the same time guide the objectives of those revisions.

3) Basic System of Regulating Working Conditions and Industrial Relations

The Constitution of the Republic of Korea guarantees basic labor and social rights that involve individual labor relations, collective labor relations, and the labor market. First, all citizens have the right to work (Article 32), although this is not the same as guaranteeing everyone employment. Instead, it refers to state efforts to help people obtain jobs through a public job matching service and offering support to those unable to find a job in the form of unemployment insurance through the social security system. With this duty of the state to endeavor to promote employment, it also prescribes the duty to guarantee optimum wages through social and economic means and to enforce a minimum wage system under the conditions prescribed by legislation (Article 32).

To protect individual employees, the constitution of Korea adopts the principle that the standards of the terms and conditions of work should be determined by legislation in a way that ensures human dignity (Article 32, para. 3). This means that the minimum standards for working conditions should be regulated by law powered by congress rather than order or decree made by administrative power, and that those standards should be high enough to ensure decent work and human dignity. Enacting compulsory laws to achieve these objectives are practical ways of refining the modern principles of civil law. Special protections for working women and child labor also appear in the constitution (Article 32, paras. 3 and 4), and laws like the Equal Employment Opportunity and Work-Family Balance Assistance Act have been enacted to help meet the standards set out in the constitution.

Under these general constitutional provisions, labor relations are regulated through various layers of norms: first, there are binding laws that regulate working relations for individuals. The employment contract is the basic mode of regulating working conditions. An employment contract is a contract that is entered into so that an employee offers labor for which the employer pays wages (Labor Standards Act [LSA], Article 2, para. 1, number 4). As a general principle, the terms and conditions of employment shall be freely established on the basis of equality, as agreed upon between an employee and his or her employer (Article 4), as with any other civil law contract. But as we have seen above, employment contract typically involves unequal negotiating power between an employer and an employee, so binding regulations like the LSA and Minimum Wage Act set limits on what can be agreed to in an employment contract, and any such contract shall be null and void to the extent that its conditions are not in compliance with the standards prescribed by the LSA (Article 15, para. 1). In such cases, those parts made null and void shall be governed by the standards prescribed by the LSA (Article 15, para. 2). The terms and conditions of employment prescribed by the act are the minimum standards for employment, and no parties to labor relations can operate below the terms and conditions of employment under the pretext of compliance with the LSA (Article 3). This is a unique and original part of labor law. Usually when part of a juristic act is null, the entire part of the juristic act shall be made null (Civil Act, Article 137). However, the LSA is a striking exception to this principle, as the law itself intervenes in private contracts for the purpose of establishing the standards for terms and conditions of employment in conformity with the constitution, thereby securing and improving the fundamental living standards of employees and achieving a well-balanced development of the national economy (Article 1).

When an employment contract is made, renewed, or altered, the LSA prescribes that the employer should state certain matters clearly; the aim is protection of the employees. Without those regulations, employees would not be able to request detailed and clear working conditions, because of their inferior status in terms of power. Regulations also help prevent disputes over ambiguous contracts. The matters that should be made clear to employees are wages, contractual work hours, holidays, annual paid leaves, workplaces, specific tasks, and other matters that are required to be incorporated into work rules (Article 17, para. 1); furthermore, they are to be provided in writing (Article 17, para. 2). The recent Framework Act on Electronic Documents and Transactions stipulates that electronic documents qualify as written material.

Most working conditions in Korea are covered by work rules. There are compulsory matters that any employer hiring 10 or more employees must include in a written document: matters pertaining to the beginning and ending time of work, break hours, holidays, leaves, and shifts; matters pertaining to the determination, calculation, and payment method of wages; the period for which wages are calculated; the period for paying wages; pay raises; matters pertaining to the methods of calculation and payment of family allowances; matters pertaining to retirement; matters pertaining to retirement benefits under Article 4 of the Act on the Guarantee of Employees' Retirement Benefits, bonuses, and minimum wages; matters pertaining to the burden of employees' meal allowances, expenses of operational tools or necessities, and so forth; matters pertaining to educational facilities for employees; matters pertaining to the protection of employees' maternity and work family balance assistance, such as leaves before and after childbirth and child care leaves; matters pertaining to safety and health; matters pertaining to the improvement of a workplace environment according to employee characteristics like sex, age, or physical condition; matters pertaining to assistance with respect to occupational and non-occupational accidents; matters pertaining to the prevention of workplace harassment and the measures to be taken in cases of workplace harassment; matters pertaining to reward and punishment; and other matters applicable to all employees within the business or workplace (Article 93, numbers 1 to 13). Thus, the compulsory components of work rules are quite wide-ranging and regulate almost all working conditions for employees.

However, there are two issues that have raised criticism. First, an employer can establish additional rules without the agreement of every employee whose working conditions are regulated by those rules. The LSA does state that an employer shall, with regard to the preparation or alteration of the rules of employment, solicit the opinion of a trade union if there is such a trade union composed of a majority of employees in the business or workplace concerned or otherwise obtain the opinion of the majority of said employees if there is no trade union composed of a majority of employees (Article 94). However, as long as the changes do not violate Korea's minimum working conditions, they are entirely at the employer's discretion. When amending the rules of employment in a way that is unfavorable to employees, the employer is required to obtain the consent of the majority of its employees (Article 94, Proviso). But these rules are in many cases better for some employees and worse for others than the previous rules, so while there may be employees who do not agree with certain changes, they are still obliged to work under the new rules. What is more, the Supreme Court of Korea has sometimes upheld the validity of amended work rules that are unfavorable to workers and do not have the consent of the majority, as long as they are considered reasonable modifications,[5] despite the content of the LSA. The relation between Like binding laws and an employment contract, if an employment contract includes any term or condition of employment that falls short of the labor standards as provided for in the rules of employment, such part shall be null and void. In this case, the invalidated part shall be governed by the standards provided for in the work rules (Article 97).

In terms of industrial relations under the Constitution of Korea, workers have the right to independent association, collective bargaining, and collective action (Article 33, para. 1). However, public officials and workers employed by important defense industries are limited in their collective labor law rights, as are teachers (Article 33, paras. 2 and 3). The main relevant regulations are derived from the Trade Union and Labor Relations Adjustment Act (TULRAA). A collective agreement made by an employer and labor union overrules individual employment contracts and work rules (LSA, Article 33). When conditions determined by individual contracts and work rules are better than the conditions in a collective agreement, which should be applied? There is no clear answer; two conflicting interpretations are possible, unlike the relations between employment contracts and work rules.

For people who cannot work, the constitution guarantees basic social rights that support Korea's social security system. These are the right to a dignity, life worthy of human beings (Article 34, para. 1) and the duty of the

5 Supreme Court decision 2012Da43522, August 13, 2015.

state to endeavor to promote social security and welfare and to implement policies for enhancing the welfare of senior citizens, the young, women, and the disabled (Article 34, paras. 2 to 5).

2. Who Is Covered under Labor and Employment Law?

The sphere of labor law in Korea has a strict gatekeeping system. If an individual is inside the boundary line of "employee," that person is entitled to the full package of protections: working hours, minimum wage, and so on. Because of this all-or-nothing rule, it is extremely important whether one is or is not an employee, because simply working for another person or a firm does not always mean that one is an employee in the legal sense.

(1) The Concept of an Employee

1) Persons Protected by Employment and Labor Law

The LSA states that "employee" means a person, regardless of type of occupation, who offers labor to business or a workplace for the purpose of earning wages (Article 2, para. 1, number 1), but that alone is not enough to determine whether a person is an employee. A criterion like "regardless of the kind of occupation" does not set a boundary or perform a categorizing function, so the Supreme Court of Korea has laid out detailed criteria to determine whether a given individual is an employee. It considers whether the work rules or regulations inside the company apply to an individual, whether that person is supervised or directed during his or her work by the employer, whether his or her working hours and workplaces are designated and restricted by the employer, who owns the equipment, materials, or tools needed to carry out the work, whether an individual's duties could be performed by a third party hired by the person who is working, whether an individual's service is related to directly creating business profits or causing losses as in one's own business, whether payment is remuneration for work, whether the working relationship is continuous and exclusive to the employer, whether a basic (fixed) wage is determined in advance, whether income tax is deducted for withholding, and whether the person is registered as an employee by the social security insurance acts and other laws.[6] The most important criterion is where subordination (i.e., control over the employee's actions) lies in the context of the relation; in addition, a designated workplace and working hours, considerable control and directions by the employer, fixed wages, character as an independent business owner, and status in the social security system are all comprehensively considered when determining employee status.

At the same time, the Supreme Court also states that these criteria can be divided into two strata. Some conditions can only be considered to confirm a person as an employee when those conditions are met and should not be used to deny a person employee status when they are not met. Conditions of this type are whether a basic (fixed) wage is determined in advance, whether income tax is withheld, and whether the person is registered as an employee by the social security insurance acts and other laws. The Supreme Court has stated that these are conditions that can easily be determined by the employer because of its superior status, which means the employer side would be likely to design the contract not to meet these conditions.

With this, we also have the definition of employer (a business owner, a person responsible for the management of a business, or a person who acts on behalf of a business owner with respect to matters relating to employees [Article 2, para. 1, number 2]), and "work" here means both mental and physical work (Article 2, para. 1, number 3).

For trade unions, the notion of the worker is a little wider. We return to this issue below, but the working persons who are more inclined to the independent contractor side, persons who are unemployed and do not have active working relations for the present can also be included in the concept of worker in the context of the Trade Union and Labor Relations Adjustment Act [TULRAA].[7]

2) The Gray Zone Problem

These criteria are quite wide ranging, and there is no clear line to be drawn. The way to apply these criteria is by carrying out a comprehensive consideration that is based on actual working conditions, regardless of the term used for a contract. This somewhat murky way of determining the status of an employee is regularly the source of problems; in hard cases,

6 Supreme Court Decision 2004Da29736, December 7, 2006.
7 Supreme Court Decision 2001Du8568, February 27, 2004.

people have to wait for a court's judgement. When a highly specific issue is involved, it is very difficult to anticipate how a court will rule, and this waiting period can be unstable for both employers and employees.

Here, questions like "Are platform riders covered by the LSA?" or "Is that-part time salesperson outside the workplace an employee from the perspective of the LSA?" are basically meaningless. Instead, whether a working person is an employee depends on the substantive aspects of his or her actual working status and the subordinate nature thereof. Is this type of regulation system, which is often called an all-or-nothing policy, good for today's reality?

That policy means that someone deemed an employee under the LSA enjoys the full range of protections of employment law—regulations for working time, annual paid leave, and so on—while those who are not so deemed enjoy none of those protections. So, for employers, one easy way to achieve efficiency is by subcontracting or otherwise outsourcing peripheral (and sometimes core) posts, along with employing atypical workers. Another important aspect of Korean labor law is the strict regulation of terminating employment relations. The "just cause" clauses (LSA Articles 23 and 24) prohibit not only discriminatory dismissal but also require reasons that are sufficient for ending the employment relationship.

With this all-or-nothing policy, every facet of labor relations—working hours, severance allowances, industrial accidents, health and safety, layoffs, and so on—needs the "entrance ticket" of being an employee under the LSA. As noted above, the tendency of companies to limit employment contracts has inevitably broadened the pool of people who are not considered employees under the LSA. Environmental changes, advances in telecommunications, and the internet have made it increasingly difficult to determine whether people are employees in the LSA sense. One possible solution is to change the criteria of "employee" to better reflect current realities. In fact, there have been many cases concerning independent contractors, such as caddies in golf clubs, debt collectors, insurance solicitors, outsourced broadcasting producers, delivery people, and drivers. The conflicts are not only about the LSA but also touch on problems around the concept of worker in the TULRAA. However, an answer was crafted for this situation. There were debates about protection for industrial accidents in Korea, and special exceptions were made to overcome the traditional approach of an all-or-nothing policy.[8]

3) A New Approach: Law for Working People as a Whole

Recently, a new type of worker has emerged; these people run their own businesses but are completely dependent economically on another party to the contract. While most delivery drivers and riders are theoretically self-employed, their working conditions are actually determined by the platform that hires them. They are often monitored by GPS and evaluated according to the rate at which they accept delivery requests. The platforms may appear not to directly control or order these workers, but in reality, workers are forced to accept orders, often with very detailed instructions. For example, if they refuse to take an order, the platform service's algorithm will note that as a negative in terms of loyalty to the system, which will result in lower remuneration.[9] For these reasons, basic protections like fair contracts, access to information, and safety have become regarded as guaranteed as universal protections, even for those who are not employees in the traditional sense laid out in the LSA.

(2) The Various Types of Working People

The basic principle is direct employment by an employer, and an employment contract without a fixed term. But various types of atypical workers have emerged; they lack more than one characteristic of regular, full-time, and directly employed workers. There are three types of legal policies for atypical workers: entrance regulation, regulation, and working conditions regulation. These policies and the laws on which they are based can be mixed, of course. The strongest stance would be entrance regulation, which does not permit atypical types of employment in principle; it is only permitted for exceptional reasons, such as employment as a temporary substitute or for a fixed-term project. As we have seen, if regulations are too tight for atypical employment, employers will craft alternatives like developing a subcontract structure or using independent contractors. So, from the perspective of the labor market and worker protection,

8 Sukhwan Choi, *A Step against All or Nothing Policy: The Scope of Industrial Accident Compensation Insurance for Independent Contractors in Korea*, 1 JAPAN LABOR ISSUES 3, JILPT 6-8 (2017).

9 The German Supreme Court of Labor (BAG) has decided that delivery drivers are employees in light of these facts. BAG December 1, 2020-9 AZR 102/20.

these policies need to be carefully deliberated before being enacted into legislation.

1) Fixed-term Employee

The Act on the Protection of Fixed-Term and Part-Time Employees prescribes that "fixed-term employee" means an employee who has signed an employment contract for a specific period (Article 2, number 1). A fixed-term employee can be engaged for any reason or no reason in Korea, which means that the country does not have an entrance regulation regime. However, no employer may engage in discriminatory treatment regarding any fixed-term employee on the grounds of his or her employment status compared with other employees engaged in the same or similar kinds of work on a non-fixed term employment contract at the business or workplace concerned. What is more, any employer may hire a fixed-term employee for a period not exceeding two years, and where a fixed-term employment contract is repeatedly renewed, the total period of continuous employment shall not exceed two years. Anyone employed for more than two continuous years on a fixed-term contract shall be deemed an employee subject to a non-fixed-term employment contract (Article 4, paras. 1 and 2), with the following exceptions: 1) where the period required to complete a project or particular task is specified, 2) where a fixed-term employee is needed to fill a vacancy arising from an employee's temporary suspension from duty or dispatch until the employee returns to work, 3) where the period required for an employee to complete his or her schoolwork or vocational training is specified, 4) where an employer enters into an employment contract with a senior citizen as defined in subparagraph 1 of Article 2 of the Employment Promotion for the Aged Act, 5) where the job requires professional knowledge and skills or is offered as part of a government welfare or unemployment measure, and 6) where any reasonable ground exists equivalent to those mentioned in subparagraphs 1 through 5, as prescribed by presidential decree.

2) Temporary Agency Workers[10]

Temporary agency workers or dispatched workers are regulated by the Act

10 Sukhwan Choi, *Narrowing the Gaps among Workers: Changes in Korea*, 2 JAPAN LABOR ISSUES 8, JILPT 88-89 (2018).

on the Protection of Temporary Agency Workers in Korea. In principle, there are certain jobs in which the temporary placement of workers is permitted by presidential decree (Article 5, para. 1). However, if a vacancy occurs due to childbirth, illness, injury, or the like, or there is a need for temporarily or intermittently securing labor, temporary work agency business may be conducted (Article 5, para. 2). In principle, the employment period of a temporary agency worker shall not exceed one year, with another year permitted with the agreement of the temporary work agency, the client firm, and the temporary agency worker (Article 6).

The client company owes a duty to employ the temporary agency worker directly when the temporary agency worker works on jobs that are not open to temporary workers, when the designated period is exceeded, or when the worker comes from a temporary work agency that did not obtain the appropriate business permission. This duty to directly employ a temporary agency worker does not apply where the relevant temporary agency worker clearly expresses his or her dissenting opinion, or a justifiable ground prescribed by Presidential Decree exists (Article 6-2).

Concerning working conditions for the temporary agency worker, neither the temporary work agency nor the client firm is to engage in discriminatory treatment on the grounds of employment status compared with other workers engaged in the same or similar kind of duties at the business of the client company (Article 21).

3. Individual Relations and Basic Working Conditions

(1) Basic Rights of Working People

1) Equal Treatment: Gender, Nationality, and Social Status

Employers are not to discriminate against employees on the basis of gender, nationality, religion, or social status (Article 6). A prohibition against violence (Article 8) and a guarantee of exercising of civil rights (e.g., public services and voting, Article 10) are also provisions for the basic principles of employment relations. An employer shall not force an employee to work against his or her own will through the use of violence, intimidation, confinement, or any other means by which the mental or physical freedom of the employee might be unduly restricted (Article 7). This is significant when looking at other regulations like the prohibition against the predetermination of a penalty for breach of contract (Article 20), the prohibition of offsetting wages with advances (Article 21), and the prohibition of compulsory savings (Article 22). All these regulations enable employees to leave an employer when working conditions have become intolerable.

2) Prevention of Harassment

The 2019 amendment of the LSA inserted provisions against harassment. Employers are not to cause physical or mental suffering to other employees or harm the work environment beyond the appropriate scope of work by taking advantage of superiority in rank, relationship, and the like in the workplace (Article 76-2). Anyone who has noticed the occurrence of workplace harassment may report that fact to the employer, and where an employer receives a report that there is workplace harassment or is aware of the occurrence of workplace harassment, it shall, without delay, investigate the case to ascertain the fact (Article 76-3, paras. 1 to 2). In addition, when necessary to protect victimized employees while an investigation is underway, the employer shall take appropriate measures for the victimized employees, such as transferring their place of work or arranging for them to go on a paid leave of absence. In such cases, the employer should not take measures contrary to the will of victimized employees. Indeed, the employer should take all appropriate measures for such individuals, such as transferring their place of work, providing a lateral transfer, or providing a paid leave of absence if a victimized employee makes such a request. If the investigation shows that there was workplace harassment, the employer should, without delay, take all necessary measures, such as taking disciplinary action against the perpetrator of workplace harassment or changing his or her place of work. In such cases, before taking disciplinary measures, the employer shall hear the opinions of the victimized employees on such measures (Article 76-3, paras. 3 to 5).

(2) Regulating Working Conditions

1) Working Hours

Koreans have traditionally been regarded as working more hours than most other peoples, and this is confirmed in the most recent statistics. The national average is still above the OECD average, and when it comes to IT companies where intensive work before deadline is crucial, working hours are far longer. Recent amendments to the LSA also take this issue into serious consideration. On the employee side, long working hours disturb the work-life balance.

On the employer side, a 50% premium for overtime work is of course substantial, but it has long been used because employers have wanted to minimize the size of whole employees, sometimes to cope with layoffs by rapid changes production by depression. For employers, it is better to pay the 50% premium than to hire new employees, which involves training and education costs. For employees, long working hours can be difficult, but they do receive additional remuneration for the extra hours.

The new rules are widely referred to as a 52-hour-a-week system, but that is not accurate. Working hour regulations in Korea set a limit of 40 hours a week, with criminal sanctions for violators. Usually, however, employees agree to work a maximum of 12 extra hours a week, and that agreement means that exceeding the 40-hour limit is not a violation. Work hours shall not exceed eight hours a day, 40 hours a week, excluding break periods (Article 50, paras. 1 and 2). In calculating working hours under paragraphs (1) and (2), any waiting time and the like spent by employees under the direction and supervision of their employers that is necessary for the relevant work are deemed work hours (Article 50, para. 3). This is a very basic account of the Korean system of working hours. Any work that

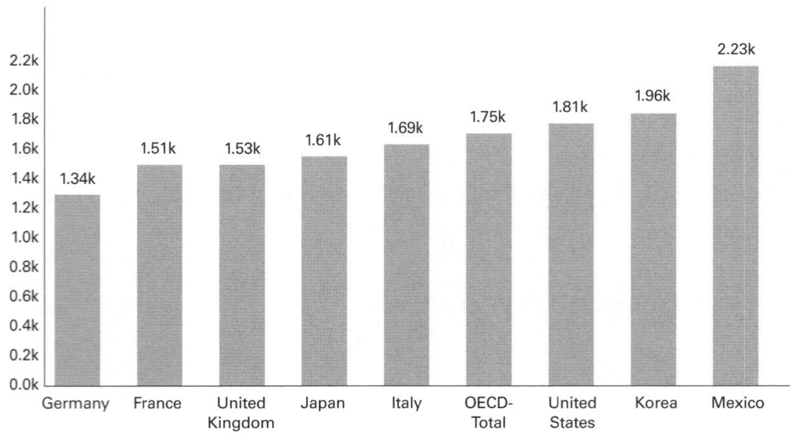

Figure 2 OECD (2022), Hours worked (indicator). doi: 10.1787/47be1c78-en (Accessed on 15 February 2023)

exceeds eight hours a day or 40 hours a week must be paid at time and a half; this is also true for overnight work (i.e., from 10:00 pm to 6:00 am; Article 56, paras. 1 and 3). Holiday work has special regulations: the first eight hours are paid at a time and a half, and any work past eight hours is paid at the double-time rate (Article 56, para. 2).

This approach is sometimes criticized as too rigid, so the LSA allows for a system that is more flexible in terms of both calculating work hours and assigning how the hours worked are assigned. For the former, Article 58 of the LSA deals with special cases. When it is difficult to calculate work hours provided by an employee because he or she carries out all or part of his or her duty outside the workplace owing to business trips or other reasons, it shall be deemed that he or she has worked for contractual work hours. But when it is ordinarily necessary for the employee to work in excess of contractual work hours in order to carry out said duty, it shall be deemed that he or she has worked for the hours ordinarily required to carry out that duty (Article 58, para. 1), and in cases where there is a written agreement between an employer and the labor representative in regard to the work concerned, the hours as determined by such written agreement shall be regarded as those ordinarily required to carry out the relevant duty (Article 58, para. 1). Additionally, in light of the characteristics of work designated by presidential decree, if it requires leaving the methods of performance to an employee's discretion, it shall be deemed that the work has been provided for such work hours as determined by a written agreement between the employer and the labor representative that specifies 1) the work to be provided subject to such written agreement, 2) that the employer will not give specific directions to the employee regarding how to perform the work, allocate work hours, and the like, 3) and that the calculation of work hours shall be governed by the written agreement concerned.

As to assigning hours, the flexible work hours system (Article 51) and selective work hours system (Article 52) both permit working longer than the daily and weekly thresholds of eight and 40 hours, respectively. Employees who want to concentrate their work into a narrower time span or employees who want to work on holidays or weekends based on their personal situations can use this type of working hour system.

2) Breaks, Weekly Holiday Pay, and Annual Paid Leave

On any given working day, an employer is to allow employees a break during work hours of not less than 30 minutes for shifts of four hours and a break of not less than one hour for shifts of eight hours (Article 54, para. 1). Employees are free to use these break periods as they wish (Article 54, para. 2). There have been debates over whether waiting time for drivers counts as working hours or break time, but any time that an individual is under the control of the employer counts as working time, even if that individual is simply waiting.

As to holidays, an employer shall guarantee employees at least one paid holiday per week on average. This does not apply when a company usually has fewer than five employees. In terms of annual paid leave, every employer shall grant any employee who has worked at least 80% of a year a paid leave of 15 days. First-year employees receive one day of paid leave for each month of continuous work. Every employer shall grant any employee who has worked uninterrupted for not less than three years paid-leave days that are calculated by adding one day for every two consecutive working years, not including the first year, to the 15 paid-leave days referred to in paragraph (1). In this case, the total number of paid-leave days, including any additional paid-leave days, shall not exceed 25. And every employer shall grant the paid leave at the time when an employee files a claim therefore and pay the employee an ordinary or an average wage during the period of paid leave as prescribed by the rules of employment, provided that in the event that granting the employee the paid leave at a time when such employee wants to take it greatly impedes business operations, the employer may change the time of the paid leave (Article 60).

3) Exemptions from Regulations of Working Time and Rest

The provisions pertaining to work hours, breaks, and holidays referred to in Chapters 4 and 5 of the LSA shall not apply to certain kinds of employees: an employee engaged in cultivation or reclamation of land, seeding, cultivation, or collection of plants, or other agricultural and forestry work; an employee engaged in breeding of animals, collection or catching of marine animals and plants, cultivation of marine products, or other cattle breeding, sericulture, and fishery business; an employee engaged in surveillance or intermittent work, whose employer has obtained the approval of the Minister of Employment and Labor; or an employee in a managerial or supervisory position(Article 63). These people are exempt either because the application of the standard rules is not appropriate, as with overnight security guards, or because managerial persons are generally not regarded as needing the protections of these clauses because they can set their own schedule.

4) Wages

The umbrella term "wages" refers to hourly wages, salary, and any other kinds of money or valuables, regardless of their names, that an employer pays to an employee as remuneration for work (Article 2, para. 1, number 5). Wages are the main purpose of the employment contract and thus have specific protection. A wage differs from other kinds of money to which people may have a right, because it is typically all that an employee can receive in exchange for his or her labor. There are four principles around wages: they should be paid directly, paid in full, paid in currency, and paid at least once per month on a fixed day (Article 43. paras. 1 and 2).

Yearly trends in minimum wage (in won, %)

Year	Houly minimum wage rate	Daily minimum wage rate (based on 8 hours)	Monthly minimum wage rate (based on 209 hours, based on Public notice)	Increase (an increase in the amount)
22.01.01 -22.12.31	9,160	73,280	1,914,440	5.05 (440)
21.01.01 -21.12.31	8,720	69,760	1,822,480	15 (130)
20.01.01 -20.12.31	8,590	68,720	1,795,310	2.87 (240)
19.01.01 -19.12.31	8,350	66,800	1,745,150	10.9 (820)
18.01.01 -18.12.31	7,530	60,240	1,573,770	16.4 (1,060)
17.01.01 -17.12.31	6,470	51,760	1,352,230	7.3 (440)
16.01.01 -16.12.31	6,030	48,240	1,260,270	8.1 (450)

Figure 3 Annual minimum wage in Korea (2016-2022). Republic of Korea Minimum Wage Commission

An important exception to the free contract between two parties is Korea's Minimum Wage Act. Every summer, representatives of labor, management, and the public sector gather to determine the minimum wage for the upcoming year. This is a powerful tool because it means that even if someone wants to work under minimum wage level for whatever reason, such as desperation to be hired or underrating the value of one's own labor, any such agreement is against the law, and the wage in such a contract is automatically upgraded to the minimum wage level. There are exceptions, such as an employee who has a very limited working capacity due to a mental or physical disability and is authorized by the minister of employment and labor and other employees to whom it has been deemed inappropriate to apply the minimum wage as authorized by the minister of employment and labor (Minimum Wage Act, Article 7).

5) Termination of Employment Contracts

The LSA has had a clause restricting the termination of employment by the employer since the legislation was first enacted in 1953. Under the current statute, dismissal requires "justifiable cause." Without it, dismissal, layoff, the suspension or transfer of an employee, a reduction in wages, or any other punitive measures cannot be justified (Article 23, para. 1). At the same time, for the protection of the employees in vulnerable situations, an employee may not be dismissed during a period of suspension from work and for 30 days immediately thereafter 1) due to a suspension of work for medical treatment of an occupational injury or disease or 2) in respect of any woman before and after childbirth. However, this does not apply case when the employer has paid lump sum compensation as provided under Article 84 or where the employer ceases conducting business (Article 23, para. 3). As to justifiable cause, the Supreme Court has stated this involves reasons for which the employee is responsible and that make the continuation of the employment impossible that under socially accepted principles.[11]

Even when there is justifiable causes for termination by the employer, two more hurdles must be overcome for a termination to be valid. First, the termination must follow all the procedures prescribed in the LSA, the most important of which are 30 days' advance notice of dismissal or payment 30

11 Supreme Court Decision 2001Du10455, May 28, 2002.

days' ordinary wage (Article 26), though there are exceptions like intentional damage by employee. Thus, the employer must provide a written notice that states the reasons and the accurate time of termination. Without these procedural measures, a dismissal is not effective (Article 27).

Then, there must be a balance between the reason for any punitive measures taken by the employer (including termination) and the nature of those measures. Termination of employment for a minor fault like being late for the work on one occasion would generally be difficult to justify as a balanced measure.

If the employer fails to adhere to any of the three components noted above, then the termination is void, and employer is obliged not only to pay all wages lost during the period of dismissal but also to reinstate the dismissed employee. If the dispute continues as the case moves up higher-level courts, then the amount of wage can become very large, and it becomes more and more difficult to reinstate the dismissed employee; for example, a period of three or four years will have significant effects on the dismissed employee(s) and any new employees hired to perform that work. Thus, the LSA has a financial remedy clause. If an employee does not desire to be reinstated, the Labor Relations Commission may, in issuing an order for remedy, instead order the employer to pay such employee the amount of money or other valuables equivalent to or greater than the amount of wages that he or she would have been paid if he or she had offered to work during the period of dismissal (Article 30, para. 3).

The LSA also has rule for termination for economic reasons, generally known as layoff. This differs from disciplinary dismissals in the sense that the affected employees are not at fault. Even though all employees are performing their work according to their employment contracts, there can be ups and downs in the business cycle, which may cause a firm to lay off some employees or otherwise restructure to avoid a total collapse of the business. Layoffs are justified because the survival of the company is at stake, and the loss of employment for some workers is regarded as preferable to the total failure of a firm. Because termination for economic reasons is initiated by the employer, there are four conditions to meet for a layoff to be deemed justifiable. First, there must be an urgent managerial necessity for the transfer, merger, or acquisition of the business in order to prevent managerial deterioration. Second, an employer must make every effort to avoid dismissal. Third, employers shall establish and follow reasonable and fair criteria for selecting those persons who will be subject to dismissal, and there can be no discrimination on the basis of gender. Fourth, where there is a union that represents more than half the employees at the business or workplace, the employer shall inform the union at least 50 days before the intended date of layoff and consult in good faith with the union regarding possible methods for avoiding dismissals, criteria for dismissal, and so on. When there is no union, this requirement shall be met by informing and consulting with a person who represents more than half of the employees. When an employer dismisses employees in accordance with these conditions, it shall be deemed a dismissal with justifiable cause under Article 23(1) of the LSA. When an employer who has dismissed an employee for managerial reasons and intends to engage in new hiring within three years of the date of the dismissal, any employee who will perform the same duty as the dismissed employee did at the time of dismissal, shall have the opportunity to be rehired if he or she wishes (Article 25).

Beyond employer-initiated termination, employment also ends when the period of the contract ends or the employee reaches retirement age.

After the end of the employment contract, whenever an employer is requested by an employee to issue a certificate specifying the term of employment, the kind of work performed, the positions held, the wages received, and other necessary information, it shall immediately prepare and deliver that certificate based on the relevant facts, even if the employee in question has retired (Article 39).

4. Collective Labor Law

(1) The Three Basic Rights of Working People

The Constitution of Korea prescribes three basic rights for workers. To enhance working conditions, workers shall have the right to independent association engage in collective bargaining, and take collective action (Constitution of the Republic of Korea, Article 33). Since the enactment of the constitution in 1948, these rights protecting workers have remained unchanged. Working rights are also prescribed by the constitution: all citizens shall have the right to work, and the state shall endeavor to promote the employment of workers, guarantee optimum wages through social and economic means, and enforce a minimum wage system under the conditions prescribed by act (Article 32, number 1), which is accompanied by the duty to work (Article 32, number 2). Standards of working conditions shall be determined by legislation in such a way as to guarantee human dignity (Article 32, number 1), and special protection shall be accorded to working women and working children. In particular, working women shall not be subject to unjust discrimination in terms of employment, wages, and working conditions and (Article 32, numbers 4 and 5).

The fact that these three basic rights are prescribed in the constitution is an essential aspect of Korean labor relations. These rights are specifically given to "workers," unlike the other basic rights in the Constitution, almost of which are refer to either "any person" or to "all citizens."

(2) Workers of the World, Unite! Creating a Union

While the LSA is the law that governs individual work relations, the TULRAA is the main act covering industrial relations. It is different from the regulations for individual employment relationships in that it basically tries not to interfere with labor-management relations (collective autonomy). On the contrary, it supports both parties so that they can conduct negotiations and come to an agreement to enhance working conditions and maintain industrial peace. Unlike individuals under the LSA, trade unions are regarded as equal partners that can fully handle their own issues. The rate of union organization rate is falling, and many companies do not have a union, but employees in Korea are basically free to organize or participate in unions. Trade unions offer a good way for employees to obtain protections in their relations with employers.

The range of workers protected by the TULRAA is wider than employees in the context of the LSA. The term "worker" means any person who earns his or her livelihood on wages, a salary, or any other income equivalent thereto, regardless of the person's occupation (TULRAA Article 2, number 1). On this issue, the Supreme Court of Korea has ruled that that "... the Labor Standards Act was enacted for the purpose of regulating individual labor-management relations in terms of the need for direct protection by state management and supervision of those who provide labor. However, TULRAA was enacted to define labor-management relations, in the perspective that whether there is a need to guarantee the right to independently associate among labor suppliers ... the two laws define the concept of workers differently according to their legislative purposes..."[12] As a result, courts have interpreted the TULRAA's concept of workers rather widely. In other Supreme Court case that dealt with a trade union consisting of foreigners without proper employment qualifications, the court said that, under the TULRAA, a worker refers to a person who provides work and receives wages in return and is employed by a specific employer; the three basic labor rights must be guaranteed, including those who are temporarily unemployed or are job seekers. In addition, the Immigration Act only prohibits the actual employment of foreigners without the right to stay and does not expect legal effects such denying the rights of work provided by foreigners without employment qualifications or infringing on their status as workers.[13]

(3) Collective Bargaining and Collective Agreements

It is natural for any party to a contract to want the counterparty to take its wishes seriously. The Constitution of Korea guarantees the basic rights to bargaining collectively (Article 33). Under this structure, the TULRAA has a clause requiring bargaining in good faith (Article 29-4) by both employers and unions. When an employer refuses to bargain without good reason, it will be charged with an unfair labor practice (Article 81), which can lead to criminal penalties. Whether there is a good reason for the employer's refusal to engage in collective bargaining is determined based on whether it is deemed difficult to expect the employer to fulfill the collective bargaining obligation by combining bargaining authority, bargaining location, bargaining attitude, and so on.[14] When there are more than two unions, a bargaining representative trade union shall be selected, and an employer as well as the representative union shall not discriminate other trade unions participating in procedures for the simplification of bargaining windows without reasonable grounds (TULRAA, Article 29-4).

At the conclusion of a given round of collective bargaining, a collective agreement shall be prepared in writing, and both parties shall affix their

12 Supreme Court Decision 2001Du8568, February 27, 2004.
13 Supreme Court Decision 2007Du4995, June 24, 2015.
14 Supreme Court Decision 2005Do8606, February 24, 2006.

signatures or seals thereto (TULRAA, Article 30, para. 1). The parties to a collective agreement shall make a report on the agreement to the relevant administrative agencies within 15 days of the date of its conclusion (TULRAA, Article 30, para. 2). Collective agreements have a special purpose. First, any part of the work rules or a employment contract that violate standards concerning working conditions and other treatment of workers as prescribed in a collective agreement shall be null and void (TULRAA, Article 33, para. 1). In addition, matters not covered in an employment contract and the part which is null and void under para. 1 shall be governed by those standards of a collective agreement (TULRAA, Article 33, para. 2).

(4) Collective Action

When a union and employer cannot come to a collective agreement through collective bargaining, there can be collective action. First, a trade union can begin a strike. Even if an employer has suffered damages due to collective bargaining or industrial action under the TULRAA, it cannot claim damages against a trade union or the workers who are members of it (Article 3.). What is important is the phrase "industrial action under this Act"; the Supreme Court has set out highly detailed rules, with standards such as who can be on strike, their purpose for striking, the processes they undertake, and how they perform it.[15] Second, the employer side can close the company, refuse to take the employers' work. This is possible only defensively, and not possible prior to union's strike.

(5) Unfair Labor Practices

Unfair labor practices are actions designed to interfere with the performance of proper basic labor rights and are strictly prohibited under TULRAA. They fall into four categories. The first is dominating or intervening in organizing or operating a trade union by workers, providing wages in excess of the time-off limit, or subsidizing a trade union's operating expenses, including dismissal or unfavorable treatment of a worker on the grounds that he or she has joined or intends to join a trade union, has attempted to

15 Supreme Court Decisions 91Nu5204, January 21, 1992; 99Do4837, October 25, 2001; 2002Do3450, May 12, 2006.

organize a trade union, or has performed any other lawful act connected to the operation of a trade union. The second is employment of a worker on condition that he or she cannot join or must withdraw from a trade union or on condition that he or she should join a particular trade union. The third is a refusal to execute or a delay in executing a collective agreement or other collective bargaining with the representative of a trade union or with a person authorized by the trade union without any justifiable reason. The fourth is dismissal of workers or acts against their interests on the grounds that they have participated in justifiable collective activities, that they reported to or testified before the Labor Relations Commission the fact that the employer has violated the provisions of this article, that they have presented other evidence to the relevant administrative agencies (Article 8).

5. Remedies

Korea has a distinctive system for remedies in labor disputes: the labor relations committee (LRC). Originally designed for collective labor disputes and unfair labor practices by employers, the LRC was authorized by a 1989 amendment to the LSA to handle individual employment disputes, including unfair dismissal cases. The majority of such cases are individual employment disputes. Compared with civil or criminal procedure, LRC's process of remedy is a fast, easily accessable, and reasonable way of addressing employee grievances.

There should be justifiable cause for any employee who is fired or been subjected to punitive measures. An employee who suspects wrongdoing can go to their Regional LRC (RLRC) within 90 days. There are two tiers of LRC, and a complainant must start at the RLRC level first before moving on to the National LRC if he or she is not satisfied with the RLRC's decision. Fundamentally, this is an administrative appeal, and a complainant who remains unsatisfied with the adjudication can file a lawsuit with the administrative court concerning the LRC's judgement. There are five members who hear these cases: three are neutral public representatives, and the labor and employer side each have one representative. Free legal support is available from a state-appointed certified public labor attorney for those whose salaries are below a certain level. Of course, ordinary civil procedure and LRC procedure can be used respectively, whether at the same time or

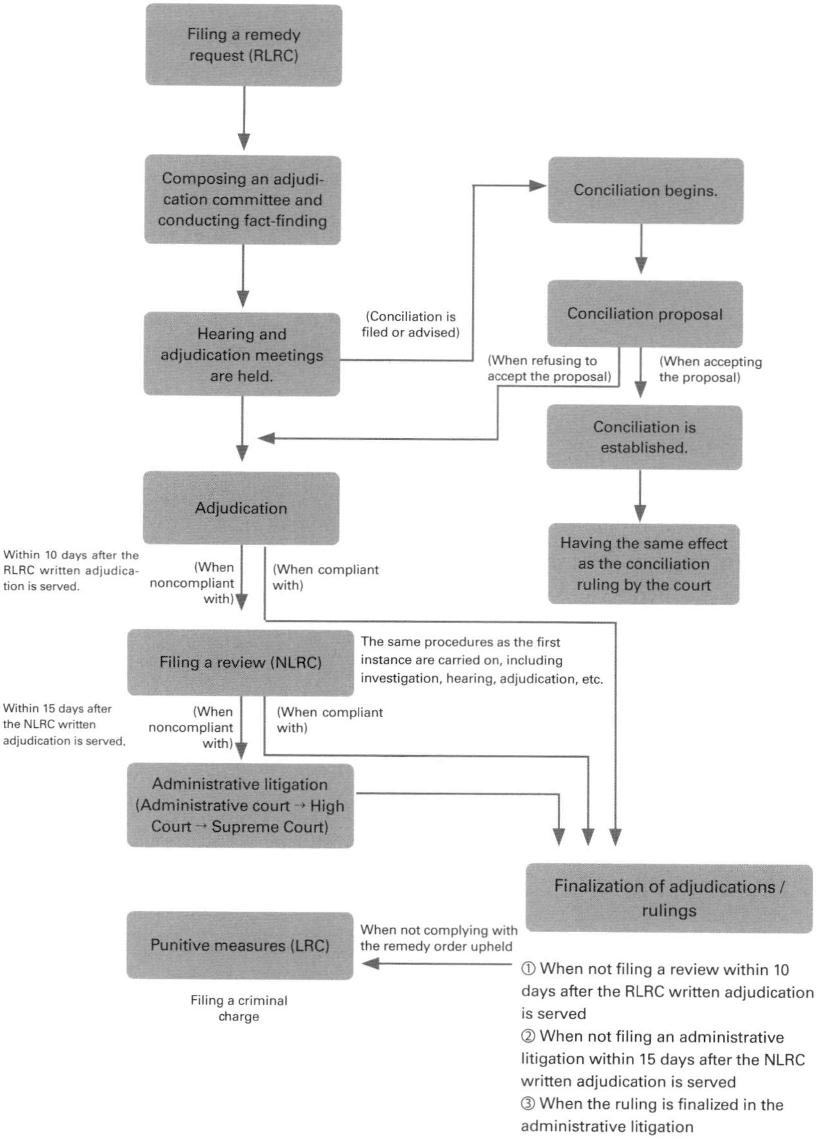

Figure 4 Adjudication procedures for unfair dismissal and the like[16]

16 Yu Seoung-jae, et al, *Labor Relations Commission in Korea*, NLRC 157 (2018).

consecutively.

6. Conclusion

The increase in employees working for multiple employers, in different types of workers and the various reasons for their emergence including technological developments are causing widespread changes in the working environment. These are recent changes in the environment surrounding labor relations. Thus, we can again consider the employee test: who should be covered under labor law?

Recent developments definitely foreshadow controversial issues that involve a distinction between traditional labor law and the need for advanced regulation of a new type of worker; these are closely connected with the ideal image of an employee. Self-determination for workers and protecting them by binding law can be in conflict in many situations. Do workers need to be protected, even if sometimes against their will? If not, should they be permitted to work under whatever terms they want? Are workers receiving enough information to make informed decisions? Do we obtain a different answer when they operate together, in solidarity? What about the role of collective autonomy? Can a platform be a new opportunity for an innovating approach to forming a union? Many of the old issues remain to be debated and explored in various ways, but we need to think more seriously about the very nature of working people and the role of regulations for them, especially in the age of digitalization.[17]

17 Sukhwan Choi, *Better Opportunity or Extended Sweatshop? - Labor Law and Policy in the Age of Digitalization in Korea*, 5 JAPAN LABOR ISSUES 32, JILPT 123 (July 2021).

Index

Authors

Ch 1. Constitutional Law and Adjudication

Woo-Young Rhee
LL.B. & LL.M. (SNU)
LL.M. (Harvard Law School)
J.S.D. (Stanford Law School)
Professor in Public Law, Seoul National University School of Law

Ch 2. Contract Law

Youngjoon Kwon
LL.B., LL.M. & Ph.D. in Law (SNU)
LL.M. (Harvard Law School)
Justice, Supreme Court of Korea (Former Professor in Civil Law, Seoul National University School of Law)

Ch 3. The Law of Real Rights

Ying-Chieh Wu
LL.B. & LL.M. (Korea University)
MSt. & D.Phil. (University of Oxford)
Associate Professor in Civil Law and Trust Law, Seoul National University School of Law

Ch 4. Tort Law

Kye Joung Lee
B.A. in Sociology, LL.M. & Ph.D. in Law (SNU)
LL.M. (U. C. Berkeley Law School)
Professor in Civil Law, Seoul National University School of Law

Ch 5. Civil Procedure Law

Wonyol Jon
LL.B., LL.M. & Ph.D. in Law (SNU)
LL.M. (Harvard Law School)
Professor in Civil Procedure Law, Seoul National University School of Law

Ch 6. Criminal Law

Jinyoung Hong

LL.B., LL.M & Ph.D. in Law (SNU)

LL.M. (Harvard Law School)

Associate Professor in Criminal Law & Procedure, Seoul National University School of Law

Ch 7. Criminal Procedure Law

Sang Won Lee

LL.B., LL.M. & Ph.D. in Law (SNU)

LL.M. (U.C. Berkeley)

Professor in Criminal Law & Procedure, Seoul National University School of Law

Ch 8. Administrative Law

Seongwook Heo

B.A. in Economics (SNU)

LL.M. & Ph.D. in Law (SNU)

Professor in Administrative Law & Environmental Law, Seoul National University School of Law

Ch 9. Intellectual Property Law

Sang Jo Jong

LL.B. & LL.M. (SNU)

LL.M. & Ph.D. (London School of Economics)

Professor in Intellectual Property Law, Seoul National University School of Law

Ch 10. Private International Law and International Civil Procedure Law

Kwang Hyun Suk

LL.B. (SNU)

LL.M. (Freiburg Albert-Ludwigs Universität)

Ph.D. (SNU)

Former Professor in Private International Law and International Business Transactions Law, Seoul National University School of Law

Ch 11. Corporate Law and Governance

Kyung-Hoon Chun

LL.B., LL.M. & Ph.D. in Law (SNU)

LL.M. (Duke Law School)

Professor in Commercial Law, Seoul National University School of Law

Ch 12. Competition Law

Yong Lim

LL.B. (SNU)

LL.M. & Ph.D. (Harvard Law School)

Associate Professor in Economic Law, Seoul National University School of Law

Ch 13. Labor and Employment Law

Sukhwan Choi

LL.B. & LL.M. in Law (SNU)

Ph.D. in Law (The University of Tokyo)

Associate Professor in Labor Law, Seoul National University School of Law